ALSO BY NEIL MILLER:

In Search of Gay America

Out in the World

▲

OUT in the WORLD:

Gay and Lesbian Life from Buenos Aires to Bangkok

NEIL MILLER

Random House New York

For my parents,

for Morgan Mead,

and for Jonathan Strong

Library of Congress Cataloging-in-Publication Data
Miller, Neil (Neil I.)
Out in the world: gay and lesbian life from Buenos Aires to
Bangkok/Neil Miller
p. cm.
ISBN 0-679-40241-1
1. Homosexuality. 2. Gays. 3. Lesbians.
HQ76.25.M55 1992
305.9′0664—dc20   92-6309

Manufactured in the United States of America
24689753

Book design by Lilly Langotsky

Acknowledgments

▲

I am grateful to many people around the world whose goodwill and generosity made this book possible. Although I cannot name everyone who was of help to me (and in some cases am unable to do so, out of respect for privacy), I would like to express my particular thanks to:

Argentina: Eileen Ahearn, Rafael Freda, Christopher Leland, Osvaldo Sabino;

Australia: Dennis Altman, Sue Brooks, Michael Browne, Rodney Croome, Ken Davis, Chris Dobney, Scott Fraser, Robert French, Chris Gill, Martyn Goddard, Ian Grubb, Scott Grundy, Keava and Vienna Leahry, Kimberly O'Sullivan, Cath Phillips, Yvette Sneddon and Louise Titcombe, Nick Toonen, Danny Vadesz, Nick Wade;

Czechoslovakia: Jan Lány, Andrzej Selerowicz;

Denmark: Ove Carlsen, Ivan Larsen, Mie Nielsen;

Egypt: Zachy Sherif;

Germany: Burt Falkenstein, Kersten Handau and Liszie Libera, Michael Haney, Jürgen Lemke, Camille Mandler, Jörg Ossowski, Colin Sherman;

Hong Kong: Julian Chan;

Japan: Minako Hara, Atsuko Ito, Masanori Kanda, Gary Leupp, Teishiro Minami, Hiroshi Niimi, Gregory Pflugfelder, Yasushi Sawasaki;

New Zealand: Terry Fairchild, Paul Kinder, Tony James, Bill Logan, New Zealand AIDS Foundation, Albert Sword, Gays and Lesbians of Timaru, Tony Walker and Tony Hughes, Fran Wilde;

South Africa: Peter Busse, Kim Berman, Cindy Berman, Edmund Cameron, Gays of the Gold Fields (GOGS), Mark Gevisser, Gordon Isaacs, Matthew Krouse, Sheila Lapinsky, Simon Lewin, Ron Nerio, Simon Nkoli, John Pegge, Lee Randall, Kevin Ruthuen, Barbara Speyer;

Thailand: Eric Allyn, Nukul Benchamant, Mayuree Rattanawannathip, Natee Teerarojjanapongs;

Uruguay: Clever Velázquez;

U.S.A.: Hassan Abouseda, Don Austin, Mike Blim, Michael Bronski, Chris Bull, Richard Burns, Siong-Huat Chua, Elyssa Faisson, Lesli Gordon, Kathleen Hirsch and Mark Morrow, Sue Hornik, Ken Mayer, Jane Miller and Robert Mackler, Jim Marko, David O'Brien, Eric Rofes, Jason Schneider, Steve Schwartzberg, Philip Shehadi, Ross Terrill, Michael Watson, Daniel Wolfe.

I am especially grateful to my friends who read portions of this manuscript: Ken Rabb helped me to formulate ideas and offered valuable critical suggestions at key points; Jonathan Strong waded through innumerable drafts, always offering ways to improve them (he also provided the book's title); Katie Garate was a generous and insightful reader; Morgan Mead provided his usual keen eye for character and detail; and Stephen McCauley offered astute advice and affectionate remonstrance. Scott Elledge and Jonathan Strong looked after my house during my frequent absences. I would also like to single out a number of people who were particularly kind to me on my travels: Kim Berman and Lee Randall paved the way for me in South Africa; Camille Mandler was an invaluable guide and translator in Berlin; Chris Gill and Ian Grubb were terrific hosts in Melbourne; Chris Leland and Osvaldo Sabino put up with me for far longer than was necessary in Buenos Aires. My agent, Arlene Donovan, was extremely helpful and encouraging, as always. Above all, I am indebted to my editor, Ann Godoff, for her confidence in me and for her smart, no-nonsense approach to . . . everything.

Contents

▲

Introduction

▲

During the two years I spent in Jerusalem, teaching English, in the early 1970s, I made the acquaintance of only one other gay man. We met on a bus from Tel Aviv. The bus was crowded and we both stood in the back, gripping the same railing and trying to avoid being swept down the aisle. As the bus climbed the Judaean hills, I felt the slightest pressure of his fingers against mine. I didn't pay any attention. Then I felt the pressure again. We didn't look at each other or speak. We were both in the closet in a closeted society.

When the bus arrived in Jerusalem, we drifted into the same cafeteria and began to talk. The young man was studying psychology. He lived with his parents and had been in the elite navy commandos. After some initial hesitation, he told me he was gay. All his gay friends had left the country. He planned to do the same. Israel was no place to be homosexual, he said. The pressure to marry was intense. There weren't any bars or gay and lesbian organizations, just a few spots, known only to the initiated, where men met for a hurried, furtive sexual encounter. He promised to call the following day. But he never did.

In Jerusalem, I spent a good deal of time with Dahlia, a dark-eyed nursing student who was the daughter of poor Moroccan immigrants. Her mother would make couscous in large bowls, and sweet mint tea. Once when I was having stomach problems, she made me a garlic sandwich, a folk remedy. I reeked of it for days. Dahlia and I would go to the movies, usually to Turkish tearjerkers.

By the last scene, everyone in the audience would be weeping. Dahlia and I wept too, perhaps for different reasons.

Dahlia took me to a fortune-teller, an old Moroccan rabbi. The waiting room was crowded with women with scarves on their heads, squawling babies on their laps. The rabbi wore a black robe and black skullcap. "You will leave Israel," he told me somberly, "but you will return after many years, with your wife and children."

I did leave Israel soon after, but a wife and children weren't in my future. That meeting on the bus was more vivid in my imagination than anything else. I began to come to terms with being gay, eventually settling into the cozy and (relatively) liberal-minded world of Boston and Cambridge. Within a couple of years, I was the editor of the national weekly the *Gay Community News.* Later, I worked as a staff feature writer at the *Boston Phoenix.* In the late 1980s, I wrote a book called *In Search of Gay America,* in which I examined changes in the lives of lesbians and gay men in the United States, particularly in small towns and rural areas. Places like Bunceton, Missouri, and Bismarck, North Dakota, became my idea of exotic. I rarely looked back or thought very much about my years in Israel. It was all ancient, tortured history.

Years later, I attended a talk by an Israeli lesbian at the Boston Center for Lesbians and Gay Men. She strode to the front of the room, picked up a piece of chalk, and wrote the name, address, and telephone number of the Israeli lesbian and gay organization on the blackboard. The country's sodomy laws had recently been abolished, she told the audience; a delegation from her organization had met with liberal and left-wing members of the Knesset; a gay disco had opened in Tel Aviv. She was sure of herself, idealistic yet practical, in the sabra manner.

I was somewhat astonished by all this. In my mind, Israel—gay Israel, if one could use so contradictory a term—had remained frozen in the repressed and repressive 1970s. Suddenly it was alive, fluid—dynamic, even. It was shortly after the Israeli lesbian gave her talk that I decided to go out in the world. I would go in search of gays and lesbians, to see what their lives were like. I had changed; gay life in America had changed, even in obscure places like Bunceton and Bismarck; I was suddenly intensely curious about the rest of the world.

I didn't start out with any particular preconceptions, any grand theory I wanted to prove. My intention was to paint up-close portraits of people and communities, letting my subjects tell their own stories. This book makes no claims to being definitive or encyclopedic—it was obviously impossible for me to go to all the places I would have liked or to provide some all-inclusive overview.

By profession and inclination I am a journalist—not an anthropologist, sociologist, gay theorist, or gay travel writer, although *Out in the World* owes something to all these approaches. Readers interested in where to stay in Cairo or what bars to go to in Copenhagen are warned to look elsewhere. This is a volume of reportage, an examination of lives of gays and lesbians and the societies that formed them, reflected them—and were often (but not always) at odds with them.

I have looked at many of the same topics as I did in my previous book—sexuality and relationships, social patterns and community-building, politics and culture, and the impact of AIDS. Because of the cross-cultural nature of the project, I asked broader questions, too: What are the preconditions that make it possible for individuals to live an open gay or lesbian life? What roles do economic, cultural, social, and religious factors play? What has been the impact of social movements like gay liberation and feminism?

In the process, other, more fundamental questions began to preoccupy me. Just what did "gay" or "lesbian" or even "homosexual" mean? Was a gay or lesbian identity (as distinguished from behavior) merely a Western cultural notion? How relevant was the dichotomy we in the West set up between "homosexual" and "heterosexual," between "gay" and "straight," to a non-Western society, say Egypt or Thailand? Was it a mistake to hold up Western-style openly gay or lesbian models for such countries?

I observed gays and lesbians in non-Western societies as they put together their own concepts of gay identity and relationships. Sometimes, as in the case of Egypt, where the lines between gay and straight were more blurred than elsewhere, I wound up writing about the relationship between sexuality and society in a way that went beyond the subject of sexual orientation.

I spent two and a half years working on *Out in the World*. At the outset, a major question was what places to choose for my research.

I wanted to achieve a mix of East and West, of developed and developing countries, of culture, race, religion, social and political systems. In a world where authoritarian structures are breaking down, I was particularly interested in examining the impact of this process on the emergence of lesbian and gay communities. For those reasons, I looked at South Africa, as the institutional fabric of apartheid unraveled; at Argentina and Uruguay, following the collapse of the right-wing military governments that had ruled those countries throughout much of the 1970s and 1980s; and at Czechoslovakia and the former East Germany, after the fall of hard-line Communist regimes.

My interest in the interplay between culture and sexuality caused me to spend much time in the non-Western world. I was curious about societies where homosexual relations (between men, at least) have traditionally been acceptable, but where gay identity has not. So I decided to go to Egypt, Thailand, and Japan. In Hong Kong, I examined how the particular political situation of the colony—the looming Communist Chinese takeover—was affecting the gay community and attempts to improve the legal status of homosexuals. Hong Kong was also my window on mainland China. And the dilemma of trying to combine gay identity with cultural and racial identities was a subject I explored among black and mixed-race South Africans and among the Aboriginals in Australia and Maori in New Zealand.

I decided to look closely at Australia because in many respects it is the country that most resembles the United States—a frontier society comprising sophisticated cities with vibrant gay communities, and more rural and traditional-minded areas where homosexuals are fighting for the most basic civil rights. It is also a nation with some of the most enlightened AIDS policies and AIDS education programs on the planet.

Although I made a deliberate decision not to emphasize Western Europe, I thought it was important to look at a society where, in political and legal terms, lesbian and gay progress was at its most advanced. I chose Denmark, the only country in the world where, at this writing, gay and lesbian partnerships are recognized by law and enjoy virtually the same legal status as heterosexual marriages.

As I knew from the United States, an openly gay and lesbian life tends to emerge in small towns and rural areas only after it develops in urban centers. Since in many of the countries I visited the emergence of gay communities is a recent phenomenon, I spent most of my time in cities. On some occasions, I did get an opportunity to explore gay life in smaller places: an Afrikaner gold-mining town in South Africa; a desert oasis in Egypt; country towns on the northwest coast of the Australian island of Tasmania. But *Out in the World* remains largely an urban-oriented book.

In each country I report on, I write about the situation of lesbians and gays at a particular moment in time. Governments rise and fall; economies go from boom to bust and back again; social changes have transformed many Third World societies, in particular. By focusing on the personal and the cultural as much as the political, I have attempted to give the book a greater resonance. On the other hand, I also wanted to capture people and places in the midst of specific historical changes: South Africa at a time of optimism, when a nonracial future seemed a tantalizing possibility; the former East Germany at the moment when the euphoria over the fall of the Wall gave way to the economic distress and personal disorientations of unification; Hong Kong during the period of fear and uncertainty in anticipation of the projected takeover by the Chinese Communists.

It is my hope that this book uses the particular vantage point of gay men and women to shed light on subjects such as race in South Africa, political repression in Argentina, the transition to the market economy in Eastern Europe, and marriage and social relations in Japan.

In researching *Out in the World,* I encountered many difficulties. The scope of the book was daunting, to say the least. In some countries, I had the advantage of introductions to gay and lesbian organizations and a list of gay bars and meeting places (often culled from the *Spartacus Guide for Gay Men*); in others, I arrived with a name and address scribbled on a scrap of paper, and hoped for the best.

One of the major difficulties was in writing about the lives of both gay men and women. This was particularly so in the non-Western world, where the social status of women is low and there are few open lesbians. In Hong Kong, I was unable to meet any lesbians at all; in Egypt I met one. The only Thai lesbian whom I talked to at any length was a woman I was introduced to in Tokyo. In other countries I visited, such as Australia and New Zealand, lesbian separatism has persisted far longer than in the United States; in Melbourne, I found that it was almost as difficult as a gay man to meet lesbians as it was in Cairo. Overall, I have tried to achieve a balance between gay men and lesbians in the book, but I have not been as successful as I would have liked. The closeness and cooperation that one increasingly encounters in the United States between gay men and lesbians—and the growing lesbian visibility—was absent in many of the places I visited, making my task harder.

In virtually all the countries I covered, I looked at the impact of AIDS on the gay population. I went to countries where AIDS was a significant factor—Australia and Thailand, for example—and to others—Japan and Egypt—where it was not, thus far. Whether or not AIDS appeared an immediate threat, I was interested in exploring the role of the epidemic in shaping gay identity and community. *Out in the World* is not primarily a book about AIDS. Nonetheless, I have tried to to elucidate attitudes toward AIDS in various societies and to record its toll and its political and social consequences.

I should note that many of the people I interviewed for the book did not want their names and identities made public. In such cases, I have used a pseudonymous first name only, and changed small details to protect privacy.

In the end, ironically perhaps, I never did return to Israel. The old rabbi was wrong. I had wanted to go, had planned to go. When I was in Cairo, I peered into the windows of travel agencies advertising buses to Tel Aviv; I pored over timetables. But something held me back. Perhaps it was an instinct of self-protection, a feeling that one shouldn't try to remake the past, that one should look forward, not back. Maybe I just couldn't bear the prospect of twenty-four hours on a bus from Cairo to Tel Aviv. In any event, for me *Out in the World* represents a journey very different from any I've taken before.

—Somerville, Massachusetts
February 1992

Out in the World

▲

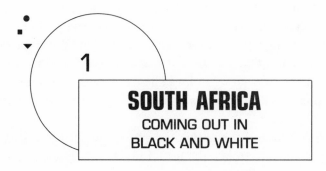

SOUTH AFRICA
COMING OUT IN
BLACK AND WHITE

Johannesburg

We were driving to a party in kwaThema, a township east of Johannesburg, and we were lost. It is easy to get lost while trying to find a black township in South Africa. The maps don't list the townships and until a couple of years ago there were no road signs indicating them at all. We took a couple of wrong turns and a long loop through flat and depressing country. Out the window, you could see the grand design of apartheid—townships that were little islands cut off from the rest of the world, dumped out of sight behind a rise, on the other side of the tracks, off poorly marked highways. It began to rain, as it often did in late afternoon in the Transvaal in midsummer.

Besides myself, there were four of us in the car: Liz, my host, a white South African woman who had lived in Boston for seven years and had recently returned home; Ron, a young American who was doing his undergraduate thesis on the lesbian and gay movement in South Africa; and two nineteen-year-old black South African lesbians—Phybia, a drama student who everyone said looked like the singer Tracy Chapman; and Bev, a teacher of Afrikaans and English, who had grown up trying to look like Boy George.

KwaThema is a bleak place, a dusty sprawl of tiny matchbox houses set down amid the red earth and ash-gray mine dumps of the East Rand. The streets are unpaved and rutted and there are no sidewalks; there isn't a car or even a tree in sight. But on a Saturday night the streets are full of people. They cluster in groups on street corners, gossip on front stoops, promenade in their weekend best. Children are everywhere. A band passes by, with a group of people following enthusiastically. Everyone seems to be going to a party. The party we were heading for, though, was different from the other ones taking place that evening in kwaThema: It was sponsored by the local chapter of GLOW, Gays and Lesbians of the Witwatersrand.

When we finally found the appointed spot—the yard of a small brick house just off the street—the festivities were well under way. A boom box was pounding out a disco version of "Hava Nagila," of all things, and steak and sausage were simmering on the *braai.* KwaThema is said to be one of the more prosperous townships, and it boasts a number of attractive brick and stucco houses with well-tended lawns and flower beds. The house where the party was being held was of the basic matchbox variety, however: two small rooms and a kitchen, modestly furnished, with peeling, yellowish walls and a concrete floor.

The forty or so guests were mostly men, all quite young and very campy. They referred to their boyfriends as their wives, and barked orders at them. The boyfriends were deferential and kept their distance. Everyone was drinking a lot. Liz, Ron, and I were the only whites present. A dashing man in a flowered shirt and jeans gave Ron the black solidarity handshake and asked boldly, "Are you king or queen?" Ron didn't know what to say. No one asked questions like that in Flint, Michigan, where Ron hails from.

We stood in the yard, in the midst of the crowd, and drank beer and devoured bowls of cornmeal mush, called pap. The rain had stopped, and it had turned into a cool, pleasant evening. Bev, the teacher, was in romantic conflict: She had a mad crush on a woman at the party who was dressed in a funny cap and jumpsuit and was said to be involved with a female pop singer. The problem was that Bev had a lover at home. Meanwhile, Phybia, who didn't share Bev's melodramatic temperament, was offering a critique of the music. She rattled off the names of her favorite performers: Edie Brickell, Sinèad O'Connor, Suzanne Vega, and, of course, Tracy Chapman. These artists were not featured on the boom box at kwaThema, which leaned more in the direction of Gloria Gaynor and Donna Summer when it wasn't offering earsplitting kibbutz melodies.

The man in the flowered shirt, who had been putting the moves on Ron, worked for an air-freight company. "I steal," he said. "Everyone there steals, even the boss." He could get us a TV, a VCR, anything we wanted. A major portion of the air-freight company's customers these days were Greeks who were moving to Zaire. "They come to South Africa, they make a lot of money, then they leave," he said. "They're taking our money!" He had been at the nearby township of Thokoza the previous week during a night of terror in which Zulu migrant workers slaughtered seventy people, part of the endemic township violence that many believed was fomented by government security forces. When I asked him what it had been like, he said only, "I was trying to stay alive."

Inside the cramped kitchen, I was introduced to a rather large woman in a polka-dot dress, who sat on a metal chair as if it were a throne. She was called Ma Thoko, and the yard where the party was taking place was hers. She wasn't gay herself but regularly made her home available to the gays and lesbians of kwaThema and the surrounding townships as a kind of "drop-in" center. "They are good people," she said. "No, my neighbors don't seem to mind. Everyone should be able to have fun."

We had a difficult time leaving. The other guests crowded around the car. The man in the flowered shirt, quite drunk by this time, sat in the front seat and wouldn't budge until Ron gave him his telephone number. A woman was engaging Liz in intense conversation; the woman's lover was alcoholic and apparently abused her. Liz was always getting into conversations of this sort; she was the kind of person whom everyone—particularly young black lesbians—bared their soul to. As for Bev, she was undecided whether to stay or go. She just couldn't get the woman in the jumpsuit out of her mind. "I'm staying," she announced. And then a minute later: "I was just joking." By midnight, we were all back in Johannesburg in our respective beds, Bev included. I later heard the party continued until Monday morning.

The kwaThema party would never have taken place a year or two before; at that time, there wasn't any organized lesbian and gay life in the townships around Johannesburg. A new South Africa was being forged, and the evening at kwaThema was part of that process. Apartheid, the system of political dominance and enforced social separation by which five million whites ruled over thirty-five million blacks, Indians, and mixed-race "Coloureds," was fading. Nelson Mandela had been released from prison eight months before, and the long-banned African National Congress, the ANC, was in the midst of the painful transition from revolutionary organization to political party. All remaining race laws were in the process of being repealed; local governments were desegregating swimming pools, libraries, and some schools. The white minority government and the ANC still hadn't agreed on a formula that would transfer political power to the nonwhite majority. And even with the dismantling of the legal basis of apartheid, economic disparities between the races remained vast, and white control of the economy almost complete. It was sometimes hard to conceive how a fair and just society could ever emerge in South Africa. But the country was changing. It was a moment of hope—and fear—in which the cruelest injustices of the past seemed to be dying, and the injustices of the future had not quite manifested themselves.

Even as the institutions of apartheid were being dismantled, Johannesburg, the former mining camp that is now the nation's largest city and its business and cultural hub, remains largely segregated. Whites live in Bel Air–like suburbs behind high walls and barbed wire, protected by attack dogs and waited on by black servants, who are said to number a hundred and twenty thousand in Johannesburg alone. The aging downtown commercial center, except for a few glass-and-steel corporate headquarters (and imposing buildings housing the law courts and the security police), has been largely ceded to blacks. Just eleven miles away lies Soweto, the biggest black township in South Africa, with a population of more than two and a half million. Increasingly, however, the patterns of segregation in Johannesburg were beginning to resemble the more informal ones of an American city, not the obsessively rigid demarcations of apartheid.

I was staying in Yeoville, the inner suburb that is a "gray area," meaning mixed black and white. Yeoville is a mixture of ugly brick apartment buildings and colonial-style bungalows with red tin roofs, front porches, and back gardens. It has a reputation as a haven for left-wing, antigovernment whites; it also is home to Portuguese, Hasidic Jews, and blue-collar Afrikaners. (The Afrikaners, of Dutch and French Huguenot descent, make up about sixty percent of South Africa's white population.) On Rocky Street, the neighborhood's main drag, there are used-clothing stores, a health-food shop, and a club called Dylan's, after Bob. At night, they sell *dagga*—marijuana—on street corners and you fall asleep to the sound of car alarms and barking dogs.

My hosts, Liz and Jennie, were two white South African lesbians who had recently returned home from long stays in the United States. Both were in their late twenties and involved in relationships with women in Boston who were fifteen or twenty years older. At midnight, when the rates went down, the phone would begin to ring; it was Boston calling.

Liz and Jennie were on the left of the political spectrum. The walls of the house were covered with political posters and quotes from Gandhi and Thoreau. The women ate fresh fruit salads for breakfast, and vegetables and rice for dinner. Before I had left the States, I had called Liz on the phone and asked what I could bring her. "A tube of Tom's Natural Toothpaste," she replied. Liz was an artist; she had done a drawing of Nelson Mandela that a U.S. anti-apartheid group had turned into a poster. Jennie was a social worker at a local mental-health clinic; in her spare time, she was bringing recycling to Johannesburg. Both were ambivalent about whether to stay in South Africa or to return to Boston, to their girlfriends and to the women's community there.

At least some of the perceived advantages of Boston were coming to Johannesburg, however. As a result of the racial and political opening of the new South Africa, a lesbian and gay community was emerging. In October 1990, scarcely eight months after the government had ended its long-standing ban on marches and demonstrations, eight hundred people—black and white—showed up in downtown Johannesburg on a rainy Saturday morning for the country's (and the African continent's) first lesbian and gay pride march. At a picnic after the march, organizer Simon Nkoli, dubbed the "gay Mandela" for having spent four years in prison as an anti-apartheid activist, told the crowd, "I feel like crying. I feel like just tearing my clothes off."

For many years, there had been gay communities in cities like Johannesburg and Cape Town, but they had been quite closeted—and totally white. White gays could enjoy the advantages of bars, bathhouses, a monthly newspaper, even a pivotal role in a race for a Johannesburg parliamentary seat. But for blacks, there had been virtually nothing. Until a few years before, blacks hadn't been allowed into gay bars or clubs—or *any* white bars or clubs, for that matter—and whites weren't allowed to visit black townships without a permit. Apartheid had kept white and black homosexuals from the most basic social interactions, let alone the formation of a unified sense of community.

Today, however, the emerging lesbian and gay movement was nonracial. GLOW, the greater Johannesburg–Soweto group, founded in 1988, had nearly four hundred members, sixty percent of whom were black. This was particularly noteworthy because many black Africans, especially those on the left, tended to dismiss homosexuality—and gay identity—as Western cultural imports. GLOW had ambitious ideas: purchasing a block of flats to enable black gays to move out of overcrowded townships; setting up a community center; starting a job bank.

Increasingly, gay rights was being viewed as part of the broader South African struggle, by both gays and heterosexuals. The African National Congress had drafted a model bill of rights for South Africa that included a provision barring discrimination on the grounds of sexual orientation.

As white Johannesburg activist Alan Velcich noted, "Five or six years ago, the only black gays you ever saw were prostitutes or transvestites. You rarely saw mixed couples. I knew a white man who worked for a broadcast studio and had his black lover living with him as his gardener. That was the only way you could do it. But today, you have GLOW bringing whites and blacks together socially for the first time." Within GLOW, white and black men sometimes had different expectations, Velcich added. The whites tended to be more politically minded; they wanted to discuss things. With many activist blacks involved in the African National Congress, GLOW attracted younger black men who, traditionally deprived of many social outlets, saw the organization as a place to have fun. Black lesbians remained virtually invisible. "Still, it's a different world than it was just a few years ago," Velcich said.

For lesbians and gays, the new South Africa was full of contrasts and contradictions. Consenting sexual activity between adult males remained illegal, although the law was rarely, if ever, enforced. (The law did not apply to women.) Censorship had been relaxed, but pornography, gay or straight, was still outlawed. During my visit, three issues of the gay newspaper the *New York Native* turned up on the "banned" list, along with *Devil Love, the Newsletter of the Sons of Satan* and something called *Diana's Paradise.* A Cape Town AIDS activist reported that on three separate occasions when he had returned from international AIDS conferences, his house had been raided by the police, presumably searching for sexually explicit material.

Nonetheless, there was a sense of excitement among gays and lesbians in South Africa, and a visitor couldn't help but feel it. The world was opening up. Phybia, the drama student who had driven out to kwaThema with me, had had her picture on the cover of a Norwegian gay magazine. She had participated in the gay and lesbian march and was involved in the newly formed gay student group at her university. Only a few months before, she had been closeted and traumatized about her attraction to other women. "Because you're black, you're not expected to be gay," she told me. "People say, 'It's white people who are gay. You're not gay. You're African. It's not part of your culture.' But look at me. I'm here!"

I met Simon Nkoli for dinner at Garbo's, a predominantly gay restaurant in Hillbrow, Johannesburg's version of Greenwich Village. Framed photographs of the actress stared down from every wall, indication that the international gay iconography extended to the farthest reaches of the Southern Hemisphere. Garbo's was crowded with white gay yuppies, showing off their suntans and comparing the merits of this beach in Cape Town with that beach in Durban. Simon was the only black in the restaurant. If he felt at all out of place, he didn't let on.

Simon made an unlikely "gay Mandela." On first acquaintance, you had no sense that the thirty-three-year-old founder of GLOW had spent four years in apartheid's prisons. He was cheerful and good-humored, displaying little animosity toward white South Africans. He betrayed no hint of the political ideologue, either. Trim, bearded, dressed in jeans and a black T-shirt, Simon told me he ran marathons in his spare time and was just "getting into" leather. He had the jacket, the vest, and the cap. What he didn't have was a pair of leather pants: They were hard to find in South Africa. Simon was charming and appealing, often going on like a teenager about men he found attractive. That side of him—often the only side he displayed—made Simon easy to underestimate. The South African police hadn't underestimated him; I was prepared to take their word for it.

When Simon was twenty-one and first came out after falling in love with a white man, his parents had taken him to a *sangoma,* a witch doctor. The *sangoma* pronounced him possessed but was unable to cure him. Meanwhile, the mother of Simon's would-be lover wrote a letter to Simon's mother accusing Simon of corrupting her son, even though the two hadn't had sex yet. Simon's mother wrote back suggesting that it was the woman's son who had done the corrupting. The white woman proposed that the two young men go to a psychiatrist; she would foot the bill. Simon described the scene in the waiting room that first day: Simon and his mother, and next to them, the lover and *his* mother. After that first session, Simon and his friend continued seeing the same psychiatrist within an hour of each other for months, usually meeting before for coffee. On the therapist's advice, they had sex for the first time—in an attempt to wean themselves from their predilections. That "cure" failed, as well.

Later, Simon became involved with another white man and lived with him in an apartment building in Johannesburg. The only way Simon could live there legally was to register as the man's servant.

Eventually, Simon joined what was then the country's leading gay organization, GASA (the Gay Association of South Africa), a group, founded in 1982, that was almost entirely white and male. In 1984, he started the Saturday Group, a GASA adjunct for black men. At that time, gay bars and clubs remained off-limits to blacks. Sometimes, GASA would hold functions at those establishments, resulting in the exclusion of members of the Saturday Group. "Blacks were uncomfortable with GASA from the word go," Simon recalled. "Lots of people resigned. I didn't resign. I was hoping things would improve."

Simon was active in other organizations, as well, particularly the

United Democratic Front, the internal political arm of the then-illegal ANC. Some months after he founded the Saturday Group, Simon's anti-apartheid activism led to his arrest on charges of high treason, subversion, murder, and terrorism. He was among twenty-two defendants in the Delmas Treason Trial, one of the most highly publicized political trials of the 1980s. Eventually he was acquitted, but not before he served four years in prison, including one year in solitary confinement with only the Bible to read.

At the time of Simon's arrest, rumors circulated among black gays that the police had nabbed him because of his involvement in the Saturday Group, and that the organization's membership list had been seized. There was panic. The Saturday Group dissolved, bringing a halt to the first attempt at organizing black gays anywhere in South Africa. Simon suspected the rumors were spread by some GASA members who didn't want the black gay group to continue functioning. As it turned out, the police never did get the Saturday Group list.

Before and during the trial, Simon was open with the other defendants about his sexuality, even though at the time the ANC did not officially support gay rights. "Some of the other trialists were fine about my being gay," he said. "Others weren't. They'd make antigay jokes. But the fact was that, while the other people were separated from their wives and girlfriends, I was also separated from my lover. Sure, I was gay. But the feelings towards the community and society and families were the same for all of us: We all missed them. We learned to cope."

In prison, Simon became a hero to gays and lesbians around the world. The European gay press—particularly in Britain and Scandinavia—took up his cause. But in his own country, his fellow GASA members made no attempt to help him. "I survived those four years; GASA did nothing" was the way Simon put it. The organization declined to take any position against apartheid or in support of Simon. One GASA leader during this period told me there was simply nothing GASA could have done, especially in the repressive climate of the then-existing state of emergency. "In Russia, you don't drive to Siberia and say, 'We're here to see a queen,' " he said. "It wasn't much different in South Africa at that time." Besides, Simon, "a minor player in the gay movement," as the man characterized him, wasn't in prison on a gay issue. GASA, which was having organizational and financial problems at the time, paid the price for its inaction. It was suspended from the International Lesbian and Gay Organization. Soon after, primarily as a result of internal problems, it faded from the South African scene.

When Simon was released from prison in 1988, he was determined to start a gay organization that was nonracial. That same year, GLOW was launched. Three years later its original thirty-six-person membership had grown tenfold, its success in organizing capped by the October 1990 lesbian and gay pride march.

One evening Simon invited me to his house to see a video of the march. He lived in a little cottage in Mayfair, a Johannesburg neighborhood that had been entirely white until a few years before and was now largely Indian. You could hear the muezzin call the faithful to prayer from a nearby mosque. The cottage was in the yard of a house owned by the lawyer, also black, who had defended Simon during his trial. "When we first moved in, whites in the neighborhood would throw dead cats into the garden," Simon told me. On the wall of Simon's cottage were safe-sex posters depicting muscular men ("No glove, no love," went one slogan), as well as a calendar called "Treason Trialists of 1956," featuring black-and-white photographs of Nelson Mandela, Walter Sisulu, and other ANC leaders in their younger days.

Simon put the cassette into the VCR and was glued to the screen. Like most gay parades anywhere in the world, the Jo'burg march featured balloons, chants, and high spirits. The signs ranged from BLACK GAYS ARE BEAUTIFUL to GOD HET ALMAL LIEF (Afrikaans for "God Loves Everyone"). A Dutch Reformed Church minister, so boyish-looking that he appeared barely out of high school, announced to the cheering crowd that he was resigning as a member of the church. A couple of bystanders were asked what they thought of the march. "What can we do? They must be given their rights!" said one. "Everything has changed!" said another. And then there was Simon, dressed in black shorts and black T-shirt, overwhelmed by it all and telling the crowd that he wanted to cry and tear his clothes off.

"How many times have you seen that video?" I asked him.

"I've stopped counting," he said, laughing. "Do you want to see it again?"

Simon took me on a tour of Hillbrow. While most of downtown Johannesburg is deserted by six or seven in the evening, Hillbrow stays open all night. There are sidewalk cafés, book and record shops, movie theaters, and Indian and Near Eastern restaurants. Vendors hawking sandstone hippos and wooden sculpture set up shop on sidewalks. Most of Johannesburg's gay bars are located in Hillbrow, and the area's unsightly high-rise apartment buildings are the closest Johannesburg comes to a gay neighborhood.

"Five years ago, you wouldn't have seen black people on the street at night in Hillbrow," Simon told me, as we waded through the crowds of black strollers and white kids lining up in front of a popular disco. Gone, too, were the days when blacks were refused admittance to Hillbrow's gay bars and restaurants. Today, Jo'burg's gay clubs remained largely white, but the reason had less to do with official discrimination and more to do with the fact that most black gays still lived in the townships, usually without transport of their own.

We stopped by Simon's favorite watering hole, Skyline, which was the most integrated of Johannesburg gay bars, with a clientele that was about half black. Located up a flight of stairs on Pretoria Street, Hillbrow's main thoroughfare, it was painted a garish red, and tended to attract a fair percentage of hustlers ("rent boys," as they are called in South Africa). But the drinks were cheap, the crowd varied, and the bartenders friendly, especially friendly to Simon and anyone who was with him.

At Skyline, Simon was an important figure, a cross between a Chicago ward boss and an African tribal chieftain. If you wanted to get anything done in the gay community, you talked to Simon. An older white man came up to us. He was opening a new gay bar and wanted Simon's stamp of approval. When he indicated the bar would be for men only, Simon balked. "What about at least having one night for women?" Simon suggested.

"Why not come and see it, anyway?" asked the bar owner.

"If you consider having a women's night, I will," said Simon.

Skyline was where the First and the Third Worlds met. There

was, for example, a twenty-year-old black man who worked in "quality control," had a wife and baby as a result of a tribal marriage, and showed me a scar on his chest he had gained in township violence. He was there with his white boyfriend, an industrial chemist, who informed me he wanted to be "president of the blacks of South Africa." South African blacks, the future president told me, "are so uncomplicated, so instinctive, so real. With them, there is no bullshit!"

At Skyline, I also met a friend of Simon's named Linda Ngcobo. (Linda is a commonly found man's name in South Africa.) Linda was twenty-eight and lived with his family in Soweto. One afternoon, over glasses of watery beer, Linda expounded on the complicated interworkings of issues of identity, culture, and lack of education and opportunity that defined gay life in South Africa's black townships.

Township gay male culture, as Linda described it, revolved around cross-dressing and sexual role-playing and the general idea that if gay men weren't exactly women, they were some variation thereof, a third sex. No one, including gay men, seemed to be quite sure what "gay" meant—were gay men really women? men? or something in between? This confusion was compounded by the fact that sex education was extremely limited in the townships; moreover, among some tribes, talking about sex at all was taboo. "Moffie," the derogatory Afrikaans expression for male homosexual, widely used in South Africa, literally means "hermaphrodite."

When Linda was in high school, word went out among his schoolmates that he had both male and female sex organs. Everyone wanted to have sex with him, he claimed, if only to see if the rumors were true. When he didn't turn out to be the anatomical freak they had been promised, his sexual partners were disappointed.

Then, there was the male lover who wanted to "marry" Linda when they were teenagers. "Can you have children?" the boy's mother asked Linda. The mother went to several doctors to ask if a gay man could bear a child. The doctors said no, but the mother didn't believe them. She urged the two boys to have sex as frequently as possible so Linda could become pregnant. Linda went along with the idea. On the mother's orders, the boys would stay in bed most of the weekend. "We'd get up on a Saturday morning, she'd give us a glass of milk, and she'd send us back to bed," Linda told me. After three months of this experiment, the mother grew impatient. She went to yet another doctor who managed to convince her that it was quite impossible for a man, even a gay man, to bear a child. Linda's relationship with his friend continued for a time until finally the young man acceded to his mother's wishes and married a woman, who eventually bore the child Linda could never give him.

I wouldn't have lent much credence to this story except for an article about township gay life I had read in the *Weekly Mail* newspaper. In the article, the reporter asked a member of a gay male couple if he practiced safe sex. The man said he was "scared" of condoms because, "if I used them I won't be able to have a baby. I am throwing my sperm away." The reporter pressed him: By sleeping with a man, wasn't he throwing his sperm away as it was? "No," the man replied. "One day my 'wife' and I hope to have children like any normal couple."

Linda didn't strike one as particularly effeminate. He was lanky and graceful, with the body of a dancer. The day we met he was wearing white pants and a white cotton sweater with big, clear-framed glasses and a string of red African beads around his neck. But even as an adult, he was treated like a girl at home by his parents. They expected him to do women's jobs—to be in the kitchen, do the washing and ironing and baking. "You can get me at home almost any morning," he told me. "I'll be cleaning the house." There were "girls' shopping days" when he, his mother, and his sister would go off to buy underclothes and nighties. Each day, he would plan his mother's and father's wardrobes.

As a teenager, Linda began undergoing female-hormone treatments, on the recommendation of a doctor. When he finally decided to halt treatments, his father, a minister of the Twelfth Apostle Church, was disappointed. It seemed he would rather have a son who grew breasts and outwardly appeared to be a girl than a son who was gay. Even today, Linda sang in the choir at his father's church—in a girl's uniform.

What part do you sing? I asked him.

"Soprano, of course," he replied. "What did you think?"

Linda had worked as a teacher and an office clerk but had been out of a job for a year and a half. He was spending his time teaching dance and drama and being general mentor to members of the Soweto chapter of GLOW. "They call me Mama GLOW," he said. "I help them with their problems and offer them a shoulder to cry on. I talk to their parents. I tell the parents that the boys are discovering the woman inside. Sometimes, I tell the families it is a passing feeling. Then, instead of rejecting the boys, they start doing everything for them."

In Soweto, he said, because of GLOW, young gay men were able to act more freely at home. Families were allowing their sons to bring boyfriends to the house. When parents were away, Linda and his young protégés organized pajama parties, at which they wore women's clothing. (There had been a predominantly gay shebeen in Soweto, but it had closed down, so the men were limited to socializing at private parties.) Still, according to Linda, a majority of people in Soweto were quite antigay. "Most people think it is a curse and they don't want gays anywhere near them," he said. "They think it is a curse against both gay people and their parents. There are others, more highly educated, who feel pity. So maybe sixty percent are against and forty percent are in favor."

I asked Linda about safe sex in the townships. AIDS was making its way down the African continent, primarily by means of heterosexual transmission; in 1991, it was estimated that 100,000 to 475,000 South Africans were infected with the human immunodeficiency virus (HIV), which causes AIDS. A Soweto-based organization called the Township AIDS Project, with money from the Norwegian and the U.S. governments, was trying to promote safe-sex education. The group had just hired Simon Nkoli for this purpose. But AIDS seemed to have made little impression on black South Africans, gay or straight. The vast majority were unaware of knowing anyone infected with the disease. Condoms were widely viewed as a government plot to stop blacks from procreating, and government health officials were viewed with suspicion. "Most people want flesh-to-flesh sexual contact," said Linda. "They think that having a checkup after sex is enough. I too am against this condom. I love it straight, flesh to flesh." Linda noted that most gay men in Soweto were in couple relationships and knew their partners well, so he doubted that safe sex was very important in any event.

Among black South African gays, heterosexually based roles dominated relationships. Ideas about relationships were based on what township gays saw around them: the traditional patriarchal norms of African tribal societies that had only been recently urbanized. These roles were extremely rigid. Add to this the fact that some gay men, like Linda, were treated as women by their families and seemed to believe that deep down they actually *were* female. So it wasn't surprising that in gay male relationships, one man was considered the "husband" and the other the "wife," and that role-playing was strong among black lesbians as well.

Not surprisingly, there was a good deal of interest in gay marriages. Linda reported that five gay couples in the kwaThema GLOW chapter were planning to get married. In Soweto, the group was considering instituting group weddings, perhaps eight couples at a time. "We have a minister and a lawyer who can countersign," he said. "GLOW offers a wedding certificate and a ceremony." Such marriages have no legal significance.

Linda told me about his own near "marriage" a few years before. He and his fiancé had chosen rings and wedding apparel, including a white gown for Linda. But the wedding never took place; Linda's intended had accidentally killed a man and had to stand trial a few weeks before the wedding. Linda and the man's mother appeared in court as character witnesses. It was decided that Linda would pretend to be the man's wife to prove the defendant was a "good family man." Linda's hair was long at the time, and he entered the courtroom in a straw hat and a maroon-and-white pants suit. In the witness box, he informed the judge that he and the accused had been married for five years and had two children. No one doubted that he was the man's wife, at least according to Linda's account. But his testimony didn't have much effect. The judge sentenced Linda's fiancé to four years in prison. When the sentence was announced, Linda began wailing uncontrollably in the courtroom. "I was crying for that wedding," he said. By the time his fiancé emerged from prison four years later, Linda had lost interest. He was convinced something bad would happen if they again attempted to marry.

"I still have the wedding dress," he said. "I am going to lend it to the kwaThema boys."

• • •

If the emergence of organized gay life in the townships was one sign of changing times, so was the fact of black gay and lesbian couples living in Johannesburg itself. Some days after the kwaThema party, I went to visit Bev, the teacher who had driven to kwaThema with me, and her lover Mary Anne at their Hillbrow apartment. When I knocked on their door at one o'clock on a weekday afternoon (it was Southern Hemisphere summer, and Bev wasn't teaching), Bev appeared in a nightdress, obviously not yet quite awake, and apologizing profusely. "I forgot completely that you were coming," she murmured, her voice husky with sleep. "Would you mind coming back in an hour?"

Less than a month before, Bev and Mary Anne had moved out of their respective family homes in Soweto and had gotten their own apartment for the first time. Suddenly, at age nineteen, they were free. And for them, the greatest sign of freedom was not sex or booze or drugs but simply the opportunity to sleep till noon—or even later.

I went to kill some time at a sidewalk café near their flat. Hillbrow, traditionally the center of Johannesburg's white bohemia, was rapidly turning black. With the impending repeal—and increasing nonenforcement—of the Group Areas Act, owners of large Hillbrow apartment houses were capitalizing on the acute black housing shortage and discovering that they could actually get higher rents from black tenants than from whites. Hillbrow had long been the place where white gays from all over the country migrated to come out. Now, with the easing of apartheid, it was starting to be the place where young black gays and lesbians could do the same—assuming they could afford it. Bev and Mary Anne were among this first generation of black gay urban pioneers.

By two o'clock, Bev and Mary Anne were wide awake and positively jaunty. Their apartment, down an outside corridor on the second floor of a ramshackle building, included a sitting room, two small bedrooms, and a kitchen. French doors led out to a balcony that offered a view of the office towers of downtown Jo'burg. The living room was relatively bare—a few chairs, some Christmas cards on the mantelpiece, a black-and-white drawing of a woman's torso on the wall. "It'll take a while before we get more furniture," Bev said. You could still smell fresh paint.

Mary Anne, who worked as a secretary for a company that sold dustbins and portable toilets, was getting ready to return to her family in Soweto for the Christmas holidays. Mary Anne was beautiful. It was her eyes, dark and serene, that did it. She was born in Zimbabwe, where all women were said to be beautiful. She had briefly been a model but had quit because she couldn't stand people staring at her. The fact that, at the kwaThema party, Bev had even considered risking her relationship with Mary Anne for a fling with someone else seemed foolish indeed.

In preparation for the journey back to Soweto, Mary Anne was dressed in a polo shirt, jeans, and men's oxfords. She had short, spiked hair. "No one could ever tell that you're a girl!" Bev told her proudly. Bev was dressed more casually: a long striped dress shirt over a pair of baggy shorts. Her hair was spiked, as well.

If there was a calm, almost a diffidence about Mary Anne, Bev was tense, talkative, always eager to make an impression.

Bev had grown up convinced that she was a boy. Then, at thirteen, she found herself menstruating and growing breasts; her image of herself was turned upside down. She was attracted to girls, which made things even more confusing. She tried to commit suicide. She took thirty-two tablets, that turned out to be pills for high blood pressure.

She had been abused as a child. On three occasions, trusted family friends—men in their forties—had tried to rape her. Her father didn't live at home, and Bev's mother would go on drinking sprees and turn the house into a shebeen. There would always be a lot of men around. One night, Bev recalled, she and her sister went and slept in a broken-down truck near the neighborhood shops to get away from one of her mother's drunken parties.

Mary Anne had had a difficult childhood, as well. Her parents were divorced; her father owned a supermarket in Zimbabwe, while Mary Anne grew up with her mother (and later with her brother and sister-in-law) in Soweto. When she was fourteen, her father took her on a trip to Atlanta, Georgia. There she had a romance with another girl, her first. "I'm just like you," Mary Anne told her. When Mary Anne went back to South Africa, the girl was hysterical. Though Mary Anne didn't quite view herself as a boy, she always wanted to do what boys did. When she went shopping with her mother, she immediately headed to the boys' department. Her mother had to force her to buy female clothes. She also made her join a ballroom-dancing class. "I hated it," Mary Anne said. "The boy would lead me everywhere."

In high school, Mary Anne had a nervous breakdown. Being a lesbian in a township high school was "terrible," she said. "On Mondays, everyone would come in talking about their boyfriends," she recalled. "I was lonely and miserable."

There was a bright spot during her adolescence: Bev. Mary Anne was in love with her from afar. "Bev was the center of attraction in Soweto," said Mary Anne. "People would ask, 'Is she a boy? Is she a girl? Could she be white?' Bev was always in crazy clothes. She was the crazy kid in Soweto. Everyone in Soweto knew Bev was gay!" But it wasn't until they both finished high school that they were actually introduced.

It wasn't too long after her suicide attempt that Bev discovered the androgynous British pop singer Boy George. "He saved me from myself," she said. "He made me proud of being gay." When she first read about him in a magazine, she thought, "This is a girl!" She was convinced she had found someone with the same gender problem she believed she had. She read on and found the word "gay" in reference to Boy George; it was her younger sister, reading over her shoulder, who said, "You're gay." Bev realized her sister was right.

Bev began to dress like Boy George. She cut her hair exactly like his. "I would wear a skirt this long!" she said, pointing toward her ankles. "With jeans and sneakers. Did you ever see my jacket with the safety pins all over it?"

She found a kindred spirit, a girl named Happy, who tried to convince Bev that she was a boy. They briefly became lovers. "We would wear big jackets and big sweaters and look at girls at the bus station," Bev recalled. "We'd go up to them and say, 'Hey baby, howzit?' " They found still another partner in androgyny, a clothes designer who wore long trench coats and baggy pants and hung up pictures of Boy George in every room of his house. The three formed a group called Culture Club, after Boy George's band. "We got everything from Boy George," said Bev. "He makes you realize your identity!" It was the designer who eventually took Bev to her first GLOW meeting.

Today Bev said that she didn't feel any longer that she was a boy. She was proud of her body and her femininity. Her family knew she was gay and she assured me they were pleased about it. "Because I'm a lesbian, I'm more ambitious," she insisted. "I need to prove myself. You've got to understand the whole procedure in Soweto. Everybody I grew up with is trying to find a rich guy, have a baby, and trap him into marriage. If they don't marry, they stay at home and take money from their boyfriends. The boyfriends get into guns and stealing cars. I'm the only one who started teaching. The other girls in school were all above me. Now I'm above them!" She wasn't content to remain a teacher, though: She was was applying for a scholarship to study hotel management.

Mary Anne had her ambitions, too. She wanted to open a gay pub-hotel in Johannesburg. The year before, she had even discussed the idea with a loan officer at a bank. She was told she would need to invest sixteen thousand rand (about sixty-five hundred dollars). Mary Anne didn't have that kind of money, but she was determined.

Her father was very unhappy with her. He wanted her to return to Zimbabwe to live with him and go to university. She refused, in part because she wanted to remain with Bev, in part because she wanted to start earning money. In their most recent phone conversation, her father had announced he was disinheriting her.

Bev was active in GLOW and had been suspended from her teaching job for a week after speaking at the lesbian and gay pride march. She noted that few black lesbians in Johannesburg and Soweto were open about their sexual orientation, especially in comparison to the numbers of black gay men. While the majority of men in GLOW were black, most of the women were white. You could count the number of black lesbians on one hand. "Women just can't come out," she said. "Even the ones that know they're gay have boyfriends. They are depressed, pregnant, alcoholic. They would be so much better off if they joined GLOW. It is easier for guys. Wherever you walk in Soweto, you see gay guys camping in the street. But black women, never."

Mary Anne agreed. "There are black lesbians in Soweto," she said. "But they are afraid of being thrown out by their family. They are afraid of the community. You can always see among the guys who is gay and who isn't. But not among the girls." She was convinced there was another factor, too. "Parents are unwilling to accept that their daughters could be gay because they want a *lobola* [bride-price] when they marry," she said. "That's why they believe that only boys can be gay, not girls. It's convenient for them to believe that. They want the *lobola*."

Moving into the city had been a major step for Bev and Mary Anne. At Bev's family's house in Soweto, seven people were crammed into a few rooms. It was difficult to have a moment's privacy. Mary Anne's sister-in-law, with whom she had been living, disapproved of her relationship with Bev. "Getting our own flat has really been an experience," Mary Anne told me. "All the responsibility is ours. We have to be sure and have the money to pay the rent at the end of the month." In Soweto, she said, her neighbors were "shocked" at the idea of two nineteen-year-old women living by themselves in Johannesburg. "They think we must be prostitutes," she said.

If having their own apartment was something new for them, so was being in a relationship. They had been together for eight months now but really didn't have any models as to how two women in a couple should relate to each other. Like the gay men in the townships with their "husbands" and "wives," Bev and Mary Anne tended to fall back on the only kinds of relationships they had ever been exposed to: traditional heterosexual ones.

While Mary Anne said she was Bev's "girlfriend," she described Bev as her "boyfriend."

"What do you mean by 'boyfriend'?" I asked.

"Bev is more of a man," she said. "She protects me if there is trouble. She fights like nothing! She is brave!"

Mary Anne, it turned out, did the cleaning, washing, and ironing. When they moved into their apartment, it was Bev who insisted on doing the painting; that was a "man's" job. Bev broke gender stereotypes to do the cooking, however.

"Bev gets proud if you call her my 'boyfriend,'" Mary Anne said. "She'd give you a million bucks."

Mary Anne related a recent incident in which Bev had earned her stripes for bravery. The two were having dinner with three other young women at a Jo'burg restaurant frequented by teenagers from Soweto. A young man approached the table and asked Mary Anne if he could talk to her privately. They walked to the back of the restaurant. In a low and menacing voice, he told her that if she didn't agree to go to bed with him, he and his friends would rape her. He knew she was gay, he added, and he was going to "change" her. Mary Anne was terrified. She returned to the table and told Bev and the other girls what had happened. All five rushed for the door.

The young man and his friends tried to bar Mary Anne's way. "Do you love me or not?" demanded her tormentor.

"She hates boys!" Bev broke in defiantly.

Bev then grabbed Mary Anne's hand and led her running down the street until they found a taxi. The other three girls just stood at the front of the restaurant in a state of shock and were "very nearly raped," said Mary Anne. "They were hysterical. One of them lost a shoe."

It was this kind of incident that made Mary Anne grateful to have a "boyfriend" like Bev. In a society where rape, gay-bashing, and other acts of violence were commonplace, it didn't hurt to have at least one "butch" in a lesbian couple. "Soweto boys are too wild," said Mary Anne. "They don't believe there is such a thing as lesbians. But Bev, Bev fights like nothing!"

Bev and Mary Anne were looking for someone to share their flat (and the rent), and Phybia, the Tracy Chapman look-alike, was considering the idea. She was in her first year at the University of the Witswatersrand, generally considered the best and most liberal English-language university in Johannesburg. She had been living with a gay male friend but their rent was going up and they had to leave their apartment. Still, Phybia had her doubts about moving in with Bev and Mary Anne, as much as she liked them.

"I really object to the roles Bev and Mary Anne are into," she told me one morning when she dropped by my host Liz's house for coffee and some advice. Liz wasn't home and Phybia was disappointed. Like the other young black lesbians I met in Johannesburg, Phybia viewed Liz as a role model and confidante.

"Bev is the husband and Mary Anne is the wife," Phybia went on disapprovingly. "I was over there the other day when Bev was yelling at Mary Anne for not ironing her shirts right. So I said,

'Why don't you do your own laundry, Bev?' Then she got mad at *me*. I think that they learned from their families that arguing and fighting are what relationships are all about." It was difficult to get mad at Phybia. She was witty and exuberant and had a penchant for self-parody. Whenever she came out with anything overly serious, she would stand back from herself and exclaim, "Oh, God, another cliché!"

Phybia was short and cute and had her hair in cornrows. She was said to be the descendant of Swazi nobility. She had a sixteen-year-old girlfriend, a Jewish high school student named Laura, whom she had met a year before. "She is a kugel," Phybia said, using the Yiddish word for "pudding," which is South African slang for "Jewish princess." "At least, she was a kugel until she met me. There aren't too many kugels who have black girlfriends!"

The two would meet every two weeks or so, when Laura supposedly went to play squash with an older cousin who was also a lesbian. Laura's mother had met Phybia and knew that she and her daughter were friends. To throw her mother off the track, Laura had concocted the story that Phybia had a boyfriend at the university. But perhaps the mother suspected that something was up. She told Phybia, "I don't want you teaching your township ways to a nice Jewish girl!"

Phybia knew all about township ways. Even though she was proud of who she was and where she came from, there were aspects of township life she found troubling. When she had first realized she was a lesbian, in a township not far from kwaThema, she felt "lost," she said. She said that gay men in the townships—and lesbians, too—had no one to talk with or look up to, nothing to do but drink.

I suggested that they play sports.

"I agree," said Phybia. "But where is the volleyball and where is the net?"

Part of the problem, she said, was the pervasive culture of alcohol in black South Africa; another was attitudes toward homosexuality. "It isn't so bad for me because I'm lucky enough to be at university," she said. "I'm never in the townships. The other girls there, it's very hard for them. Drinking. That's all they ever do. I'm in a better position. I'm more in control of my life than they are.

And the gay guys—the teachers really give them a hard time. Most of them don't finish high school.

"I just don't know how to raise consciousness," she went on. "Talking is so white. People say that we have to win the political fight first and then attend to community problems, like drinking. I don't agree. How can we have a strong community with everyone drunk and into these roles? No one is exposed to anything. They just go to bars and drink. There must be more to life than that.

"Oh, God." She laughed. "Another cliché!"

Constance had a crush on Liz. They had the same birthday, a fact that pleased Constance immensely. Constance was going to be seventeen. Unlike Bev and Mary Anne and Phybia, Constance hadn't escaped the townships yet. She was still in high school in Soweto. "Life will be more enjoyable when I grow up," she said. Constance was number one in her class in electrical engineering, a wizard at chess, and not too bad at tennis. When I asked her what she was reading, she replied, "A biography of Lincoln, a biography of Martin Luther King, and the encyclopedia." Constance was also depressed.

I had wanted to meet Constance at her home in Soweto, but she insisted on coming into town to Liz's house. Her mother didn't know she was gay.

The day we met, Constance was dressed in a green-and-red African print blouse, olive shorts, white socks, and canvas shoes. Her hair was spiked, like Bev's and Mary Anne's. The weather was mild, so Constance and I sat in the back garden while Liz prepared lunch.

If Bev had realized she was gay from reading about Boy George, Constance figured it out from an article about the tennis champion Martina Navratilova. Soon after, she fell in love with a girl in her class named Euphymia; Euphymia loved her back. They were both fifteen. Everyone in school referred to them as "the terrible twins." "She was my world, my everything," Constance told me. "We used to write books together. We did funny things together. We used to climb on the roof and sing and dance, and people would come and look at us. We always got punished. But we didn't stop. One time, Euphymia got a terrible haircut and everyone was laughing at her. So I took a scissors and did the same thing."

Then life began to conspire against Constance. At a certain point, Euphymia had a brief affair with another girl. Euphymia's mother found out about it. She told Euphymia she had sinned and gave her daughter an ultimatum: Either leave behind the "lesbian life" or leave home. Euphymia chose to go, eventually winding up with her grandmother in Transkei, the tribal "homeland" to the south, near the Indian Ocean.

With Euphymia's departure, Constance's world was shattered. "I blamed Christ," she said. "I hated my parents for making me gay. I was smoking dope. I didn't care about life." Later, Euphymia called her from Transkei to tell her she still loved her but had found somebody else.

Things went badly in other ways, too: One day on the way to mathematics class, three guys attacked Constance with sticks, shouting antigay epithets at her. Fortunately it was winter and she didn't have to worry about people noticing the bruises on her legs.

When Constance told her father that she was a lesbian, he responded by breaking ashtrays and rescinding his offer to pay her tuition to go to another, academically superior school. Her father, who no longer lived with the family, refused to talk to Constance for months, although he frequently chatted on the phone to Constance's sister. This made Constance feel even worse. "I was never very close to him," she said. "The reason I told him was because I thought it would make us closer." The morning of the day I met Constance, her father had finally broken his silence, offering her tuition money once again. But Constance was proud. "I won't take it," she said.

There were some bright spots, though. When the teacher who was the adviser to the chess team at her school found out that Constance was gay and threatened to oust her, her teammates rallied to her defense. The star player told the teacher that if Constance was forced out, the entire team would quit. The teacher relented and apologized to Constance. "He apologizes to me every day," she said.

More recently, the chess club had been forced to dissolve. All funds for school sports in Soweto, including chess, had been cut off after a brawl in which a member of a high school soccer team had been killed. So the chess teacher and many of the players on the chess team, including Constance, re-formed into something called the Talk Group, essentially a discussion and debate society. The students in the Talk Group were "brilliant," Constance said. "They don't have any time for jokes. They think jokes are just a waste of time. They spend all their time reading. Whatever they do, it's serious. They won't play at anything because they could have been finding out about something new instead. You've got to think before you even argue with them. They know everything, you know."

A month before the lesbian and gay march, Simon Nkoli had come to Constance's school and spoken to the Talk Group. "Simon was *so* cool," Constance said. After he spoke, the Talk Group members, none of whom were gay except for Constance, decided they would participate in the gay march. They informed the principal, who refused to permit it. The Talk Group demanded a meeting with him. After two hours of argument, one group member stood up and said, "I heard the ANC is supporting the gay march. I think we should take legal action if you won't let us go." At that point, according to Constance's account, the principal backed down.

The members of the Talk Group participated, all except Constance. She was late and, not knowing downtown Johannesburg very well, she was unable to locate the starting point of the march. By the time she found it, the crowd was breaking up, and she saw her Talk Group friends getting into a taxi. "Next year I'll be there at seven in the morning waiting for it to begin!" she assured me.

As much as Constance showed flashes of enthusiasm describing the Talk Group and the march, it wasn't long before she brought the conversation back to Euphymia. She blamed herself for Euphymia's departure. "Euphymia made me a human being when she came into my life," she said. "Before that I was always by myself. I used to be alone, talking alone, meditating in the rain. I loved her like hell and I still love her. It is so hard to forget someone like Euphymia."

The three of us ate Liz's fruit salad—litchi, mango, and pineapple. We chatted some more and drove Constance downtown to the place where group taxis leave for Soweto. If she didn't get back soon, her mother would worry.

What will you do tonight? I asked her, as we said our good-byes.

"Stay home and read the encyclopedia," she said, trying to sound cheerful. "I'm up to the C's already."

Welkom, Orange Free State

On a Saturday night in white Welkom, in the goldfields of the Orange Free State, not much goes on in terms of entertainment. So, like virtually everyone else in town, we went for a spin in the car. While the straight boys were cruising around the horseshoe-shaped downtown business area, we headed out toward the mines.

The night was warm and the car windows were open; we must have been going close to ninety miles an hour. The mines were bathed in a blue and green light. The driver put the score from Andrew Lloyd Webber's *The Phantom of the Opera* on the cassette player and turned it up full blast. The music, the illuminated mine shafts, storehouses, and mine dumps, all created an eerie, unworldly effect. It was Welkom, the music video.

Time stands still in Welkom. Once you cross the Vaal River, you enter the Orange Free State, the unvarnished heart of Afrikanerdom. In the nineteenth century, before the British defeated the Afrikaners in the Boer War, the Free State, like the Transvaal, had been an independent Afrikaner republic. The whites of Welkom (pronounced "VEL-kom") are still overwhelmingly Afrikaans-speaking, descendants of the Dutch and French Huguenot settlers who arrived in the Cape Colony thirty years after the Pilgrims landed at Plymouth Rock; in the 1830s, the Afrikaners began the Great Trek, which took them to the fertile flatlands between the Orange and Vaal rivers. Today in Welkom, you rarely hear English on the streets and even less often in people's homes.

The Free State remains farming country, but as you approach Welkom, the landscape changes. Mine dumps guard the approaches to the city—green, gold, and sand-colored slag heaps that tower above the highway and look like Aztec pyramids. In South Africa, where fluctuations in the price of gold are the barometer of the nation's economic health, the gold mines of Welkom are fabulously wealthy. They produce twenty percent of the Western world's gold. Welkom is a mining community, all right, but this is no impoverished Appalachia; it is a blue-collar city with a white-collar standard of living—the highest per capita income, in fact, of any city in South Africa.

Welkom is a planned city that was built in 1947, shortly after the Free State goldfields were discovered. In Welkom, there are no "robots"—South African parlance for traffic lights—only landscaped traffic circles, thirty-three of them altogether. Buildings are low because of the danger of earthquakes, so downtown looks like a series of suburban shopping malls. (Earth tremors, or "bumps," as they call them here, are commonplace.) The climate is hot and dry in summer and there are periodic dust storms, when the street lamps are turned on at two in the afternoon; earlier in the year I visited, a tornado had wreaked havoc on Welkom.

In Welkom, everything is in its place, including blacks. There are no racial "gray areas" in Welkom. The residential neighborhoods of the city, population sixty-four thousand, are entirely white; across a road lies Thabong, the black township, with a hundred thousand inhabitants. A few miles out of town, near the mines, are hostels that house some hundred and fifty thousand black miners, mostly from Lesotho and nearby "homelands" like the Transkei. On the street that leads from white Welkom to black Thabong is a house said to be the local headquarters of the Afrikaner Resistance Movement (AWB), an extreme right-wing paramilitary organization.

The previous year, shortly after the release of Nelson Mandela and the unbanning of the ANC, Welkom was the scene of racial strife, much of it provoked by the AWB. There were indiscriminate attacks on blacks, including murders, and acts of black retaliation against whites and alleged black informers; school and consumer boycotts by blacks; bombs found at the office of a mine union and at a taxi stand; an incident in a neighboring town in which police opened fire on black protesters. At one point, AWB members wearing swastika armbands patrolled the downtown streets. Johannesburg's *Weekly Mail* described the entire scene as "something out of [the film] *Mississippi Burning*." Although tensions had ebbed somewhat by the time I arrived, Welkom had become a symbol of Afrikaner "massive resistance" to the new South Africa.

I had come to the Free State in order to see a different side of gay

South Africa, specifically to attend a New Year's Eve party hosted by a lesbian and gay social group called GOGS (Gays of the Gold Fields). I had expected to find conservative racial and sexual attitudes in Welkom—and I did. What I hadn't expected to find was the charms of small-town life.

On a Sunday afternoon, my hosts drove their cars onto the front lawn and spent half the day washing and polishing them. There were innocent hours of miniature golf, known as putt-putt, in the town center, and an outing for what was reputedly the largest ice cream cone in the Free State. Except for the presence of a maid from Lesotho and the sounds of Afrikaans, I could easily have been in Kansas or North Dakota.

I was staying with two gay men and a lesbian, all active in GOGS, in a ranch-style house in a subdivision of Welkom. The subdivision was new, and there were no trees or sidewalks. Thorny vegetation poked through the red soil, and the sky seemed everywhere. From the front steps, you could see a mine shaft in one direction and a great slag heap in the other. My hosts were Afrikaans-speaking and in their twenties, and the place had the feel of a student "pad." There were crates of Coca-Cola and a stereo blasting disco music from morning to night; instead of doors, the house had accordion-like room dividers that hooked to the moldings.

"On Monday, we have arranged for you to go underground," one of my hosts announced. His name was Tom and he worked as a surveyor at one of the mines. When he spoke English, Tom's voice sounded uncannily like that of the actor David Niven.

To a large extent, I was already underground. Welkom gays and lesbians were very much in the closet, their existence virtually unknown to anyone in town who didn't share their sexual orientation. Tom related how, one weekend night, he had been standing at the door of a local hall at an event sponsored by GOGS. When a group of people tried to enter, he explained it was a private party for gays and lesbians. The would-be gate-crashers were mystified. After much discussion they finally understood. "Homosexuals in Welkom!" they said. "Homosexuals in the Free State! We thought they were all in Jo'burg."

In Welkom, you blended in. You worked at the mines or some mine-related business, like everyone else. Lesbian couples were into traditional butch-femme roles; gay men were often in heterosexual marriages. When Welkom lesbians and gays weren't married to someone of the opposite sex, they talked about marriage to someone of the same sex. Sometimes, you drove up to Johannesburg to the gay clubs for a *jol* (a good time) but usually you stayed home, polished the car, had friends over for a *braai,* and, late at night, drove around the *sitkamer.*

The *sitkamer* (Afrikaans for "lounge" or "sitting room") was a strip of tar road downtown across from the Pick 'n' Pay—the biggest supermarket in town—and the First National Bank. It was the center of gay male life in Welkom. Tom had met his current boyfriend there, only a few months before. In its heyday, I was told, you could see fifteen to twenty cars parked at the *sitkamer* on a Saturday night. These days, gay men mostly drove by for a glimpse and continued on.

The popularity of the *sitkamer* was due to the fact that there was no gay or lesbian bar in Welkom—or, for that matter, any public place where gay people could feel comfortable. (One bar had had a "gay night" for several months, but discontinued it; most local gays and lesbians were apparently reluctant to be seen there.) There were private parties, held every second week and alternating with similar parties in Bloemfontein, the Free State's capital and largest city. In Welkom, it wasn't always easy to find a place for social gatherings, however. A hall where parties used to be held had been heavily damaged by the tornado earlier in the year. While the hall was being repaired, the organizers had to look elsewhere for a site. More often than not, when the owners learned that it was a gay and lesbian group that proposed to lease the premises, they withdrew their offer.

In a closeted place like Welkom, AIDS was underground, too. When I visited, a total of three cases (there were twenty-two in the entire Free State) had been officially reported since the beginning of the epidemic. Petrus, another of my hosts and the head of GOGS, told me about a local gay man who had tested HIV-positive and was continuing to have unsafe sex with people without telling them his antibody status. Petrus and others had urged him to practice safe sex but he refused. Still, Petrus was reluctant to reveal the man's identity to other gays in Welkom. He would warn friends that there was "someone" who was likely to be infectious and that they should be sure to use condoms. But that didn't seem to have much impact. "People pay attention for a few days," he said, "and then they forget about it." Meanwhile, one of the man's sex partners was suing him for not revealing that he was HIV-positive; the infected man himself was threatening to sue anyone who spread information about his HIV status.

One of the major reasons why gays and lesbians in Welkom were so hidden was that the mines, the city's biggest employer, were not exactly an environment congenial to homosexuals. "In the mines, people work very closely," said Tom, the David Niven–voiced mine surveyor. "You change together in the changing room. People make gay jokes all the time. If they found out I was gay, the management wouldn't fire me because I do my work well. But the people you are working with will give you such a hard time that by the end of the day, you'll resign."

There were some workplaces where being gay was acceptable—a major department store called Dion's, for instance. The store had six gay and lesbian employees, including Emma, who also lived in the house where I was staying. At one point, Dion's had had thirteen gay people working there. "In those days, we had a ball," said Emma.

One afternoon, I stopped by Dion's in the company of Petrus. The store was virtually deserted; it was the post-Christmas doldrums. Emma was nowhere to be found; she was apparently on an extended smoking break. Petrus pointed out a woman, dressed in a man's shirt and jeans, keys jangling from her belt, who worked in the sporting goods department. "You won't know she's female," he said. "Most people don't." We chatted briefly and she introduced me to her "affair," who also worked at Dion's (gay people in Welkom always referred to their lovers as their "affairs"). They were off to Jo'burg that afternoon to visit friends over the New Year's holiday. We made plans to meet there on my return.

Another clerk took me aside. "The manager thinks gay people make the best workers," he said. He told me about a store-wide meeting that had taken place before Christmas, at which the manager had concluded by saying, "I want to wish a Happy Christmas to your husbands and wives." The clerk then called out, "What about our affairs?" The manager took it in stride. "And Happy Christmas to your affairs, too."

Emma had come back from her smoking break and joined us. Why was the boss so liberal? I asked her.

"He is from Johannesburg," she said, as if that explained everything.

The small-town gay style of Welkom was familiar, sometimes verging on the stereotypical. One evening I went to visit Andries, a man in his thirties who was employed at the public-works department. In his spare time, Andries collected Dutch pottery and did needlepoint in a style imitative of eighteenth-century British and French paintings. His works hung above the sofa. He had a white poodle named Lulu. Some friends of Andries had come by: Nigel, a burly and gregarious mine shift boss who collected antiques, and Nigel's lover, Rolf, a journalist with the gravity of demeanor of a Dutch Reformed Church dominie.

Andries described a vacation the three had taken together to the Cape Province earlier that year. Their original intention had been to sun themselves on the beaches of Cape Town but they ended up spending most of their time exploring little inland towns, instead. "We stopped at every antique shop," Andries said with delight. "We were gone for eleven days and saw the sea for only two."

He introduced me to a young woman, a colleague at the public-works department. Within minutes of my arrival, she fled. Andries apologized for her: She hadn't been out as a gay person for very long, he said, and her mother was giving her a difficult time. Later that evening, when Petrus came to give me a lift home, he discovered he had a flat tire. Andries immediately rang up this same woman. She fixed the flat within minutes.

Nigel, the shift boss, had his own particular view of being gay in the mines. "I always used to worry what people would say if they knew I was gay," he said. "Now, I've got to the stage where one of the mine captains knows. He and his wife have been to a few of our parties. As for the other guys, some of them think they know and some of them can't make up their minds, but I never tell them.

"They'll take a dig at you now and again and I just laugh at them. They look for people who get upset. So I just give them back what they give me. They tell gay jokes, and I can tell more jokes than they can tell me."

Nigel and Rolf had been together for eight years. Nigel's family was of English descent, and he and Rolf would go to his parents' house for dinner every Sunday. Even Nigel's father, an otherwise conservative and not very affectionate man, was supportive of their relationship, he maintained. "He doesn't like it when they tell gay jokes," Nigel said. "He looks at me. I laugh. Then it's okay. My uncle's little son made some comment about 'moffies.' And my father said to him, 'Remember what I told you about "moffies"!' And the kid totally switched off."

Rolf's family was less accepting. For years, his mother barely acknowledged Nigel, although she had softened in the past year or so. She was a member of the Dutch Reformed Church, and very devout. "In her view, we are going to hell," her son said.

Rolf worked as a reporter for an Afrikaans-language newspaper. "I am a flapping queen at work," he told me. But when he wrote an article about Free State gays and lesbians, the newspaper's head office, which had approval over everything Rolf's paper published, turned it down.

"English people are more open-minded than Afrikaners," said Rolf. "Afrikaans people don't even know what gay people are. I grew up on a farm. I never knew there was such a thing as gay people. I knew there was something wrong with me. But I didn't know what. When I was in matric [high school], I was with my parents on a trip to Cape Town. In the Cango Caves, a married man got hold of me. That is when I found out what's what!"

Nigel, who had never heard him speak anything but Afrikaans, was impressed by Rolf's English. "Even with my parents he doesn't speak English!" he said admiringly.

Andries served coffee and a coconut torte and told stories about the army that resembled accounts I had read of the experiences of gay American GIs during World War II. In South Africa, military service is compulsory for young white men. In Andries's time—he had served in the military starting in 1977—everyone had to go to the army for three years; now it was only for one. The South African Defence Force makes no attempt to exclude gays, perhaps because the pool of available recruits is so small. Overtly gay men, however, are channeled into certain occupations that are viewed as less than macho, becoming chefs, medics, and clerks.

For Andries, as for many other white gay men in South Africa, the army was the place he came out. He noted, "Your parents say, 'You must go to the army. When you're finished, you'll be a real man.' My God, when you're finished, you'll be a real queen, I promise you that!" When Andries entered the military, his hair was down to his shoulders and he had "the longest nails in town." Because of his flamboyant appearance, he was eventually sent to a psychologist and then to a military hospital in Pretoria.

"At this stage in my life I didn't know any other gay people," he said. "I just knew I was different. So I walked into the hospital and saw all these queens sitting there doing their nails and plucking their eyebrows and I went, 'No!' They put us in with drug addict people in the same ward. The drug addicts were upset. So we went and stole some pills. And when it came time to go to bed, we said to the drug addicts, 'We've got the pills. We want *you*!' Oh, we had a roaring time in the hospital."

After a few weeks, Andries returned to basic training and learned to be a chef. In basic, he said, they were "twelve queens in one tent"; they performed drag shows for general entertainment. Later, the gay men were separated and sent off to different companies, where there was less of a sense of gay camaraderie. But Andries's life had changed completely. "It was an interesting time," he said. "It was a mad time. It was a roaring and a good time. But I don't want it back again."

As in most conversations I had in Welkom, talk eventually turned to politics—and race. Welkom's gay community, like the town as a whole, was totally white. If there were any black gays and lesbians in the black township, Thabong—or at the mine hostels— no white gays had contact with them. "We wouldn't mind if they wanted to come to our parties," said Nigel, the shift boss. "But there are none of us who mix with them."

Nigel contended that the gay community tended to be more open on racial issues than the rest of the town. "Because, as gays, you are not accepted, you are inclined to accept a lot of other people's differences," he said. "I don't think you'll find a gay AWB guy." He went on, "This is a mining community. It is an uneducated community. People are afraid of black people, that black people are going to take their jobs and that they are going to have to work for blacks."

Despite their protestations of open-mindedness, talking politics with Nigel, Rolf, and Andries primarily consisted of listening to a litany of complaints about alleged favoritism toward blacks: blacks refusing to pay water and light bills; blacks receiving loans on easier terms than whites; black miners getting overalls and boots supplied free of charge while white miners had to pay. Sometimes, their complaints verged on the ludicrous. Andries, for example, felt it unfair that a black co-worker had bought a house in a black township for only 40,000 rand, while a similar house in white Welkom would have cost 250,000 rand. To Andries, that difference in real estate prices between a run-down township and a suburbanized white city was merely further evidence that in the new South Africa, whites weren't getting a fair shake.

Over at Tom and Petrus's house, as I talked with a group of their gay friends one afternoon, I heard a similar refrain. Of course, they said, blacks were welcome at GOGS's parties, and blacks did go to gay parties in Bloemfontein. It was true that these white gays really didn't know any nonwhites, except for a "Coloured" man who worked at a jewelry store downtown. But this was Welkom, they emphasized, a city where the races didn't mix.

There were other complicating factors. Just the other day, one man in the group informed me, four white people had gone to Thabong to buy liquor at a shebeen there, and had been murdered. It was difficult, he said, to go to a township and call on a black gay and say, "Hi, there's a party." "If he finds out, he is more than welcome to come," he went on. "But I'm not going in there to invite him."

Another man spoke up. "Some of the parties we have you couldn't invite blacks to even if we wanted," he said. "The owner of one hall is totally Conservative party. He is against the blacks. He won't let them in his place." GOGS, he said, had enough trouble finding a site for its parties without insisting on integrated facilities. "We are having to change the location every day," he said.

In the minds of Welkom's white gays, a number of sometimes

contradictory ideas coexisted: a grudging admission that blacks were "people" with rights like anyone else and that change was inevitable even in Welkom, alongside a fear of blacks and an association of blacks with violence and anarchy. This latter point had been exacerbated by the racial strife of the past year. Many white gays saw themselves caught in the middle between the white extremists of the AWB—who, they said, "rule this town"—and the confrontation-minded blacks in the townships, who were "burning their own homes and schools down" and harassing anyone who questioned their tactics.

The clerk whom I'd met earlier at Dion's was the most vocal of the group, and the most conservative on racial matters. He wouldn't dance with a black man, he said, and used the derogatory expression "kaffir" unapologetically. "They are much, much lower than us," he said. "There is no doubt about it." He delighted in describing an incident during the black consumer boycott in which a black employee at Dion's broke ranks and bought a plate of pap at a white-owned café. The man then returned to work, carrying his food. When a black co-worker demanded to know where he got the pap, he admitted the truth. "So you know what the other one did?" the clerk demanded. "He hit him with a fist. The next moment, he took a cup and broke it on his head. Can you believe it? On his head. They kill each other. There is one strange thing about the politics in this country. The blacks hate the whites but they kill each other. You can't believe it. Hundreds, hundreds, sometimes a hundred a day!"

Yet even he said, "I am accepting the changes here. Everything is open now, and Nelson Mandela still talks about sanctions against South Africa. He is crazy. There will be no stop to the changes. There can't be a stop."

Another friend of my hosts explained how the racial strife of the past year had begun: "There was a woman who lives in Welkom who went with her gardener to fetch some plants and things. And she was strangled with wire and her hands were tied together and she was raped and she was stabbed. I don't know how many times. They never found the bloke. But now the AWB says, 'Look at that bloody kaffir, what he just done to her.' After that incident, two white blokes caught a black and cut off his arms and stuck them in his pockets. Just to return what happened! This is why there was such a boycott by blacks of white businesses."

This man argued, once again, that gay people in Welkom tended to be more accepting of blacks than the town as a whole. "Because his skin is black, he is having the same difficulties we are," he said. "We are having the same difficulties because we're gay. Blacks are people; they've got rights like we have. But it is just that sometimes I feel things get so unfair. Like revenge on revenge. The AWB and, on the black side, the ANC. They are causing a lot of bad vibes in Welkom."

Those views passed for moderation in Welkom, but not everyone shared them, even in that mildly enlightened living room. As the conversation wound down, Emma handed me a book. "You should read this," she said. On the cover was a cross, a soldier with a gun, and a helicopter. The title was *God's Miracles Versus Marxist Terrorists.*

In Welkom, whites drove cars. Blacks walked. To the whites of Welkom, blacks were a shadowy, potentially insurrectionary force on the streets, always in their peripheral vision. "Why are the men from the neighbor states who work at the mines always walking through white neighborhoods?" Petrus demanded.

"Why?" I asked.

"That's what people want to know."

I had gone with Petrus on a drive to the nearby town of Odendaalsrus (known as Ody). A gay man in Ody had promised to donate five hundred rand (about two hundred dollars) to GOGS. Petrus had spent seven hundred rand of his own money to buy the latest in disco lights for GOGS's parties. Someone had convinced him that the investment was a good way to lure gays and lesbians from Bloemfontein, "the big city" in these parts, to Welkom's parties. The strategy didn't work, and GOGS's finances—and Petrus's—were deteriorating. The money was a potential godsend, but Petrus worried that the man would back out. He wanted to collect the money in person.

After a drive through stunted fields of corn (a drought was crippling the farmers of the Free State that summer), past more towering mine dumps, we arrived in Ody. Several months before, Ody police had opened fire on a crowd of protesting black students, killing three. Today, the town appeared peaceful. We stopped at the "angel's" shop—he was a florist—but there was no one around. As we got back into the car, the man we were looking for drove up, stopped, and shouted something out the window in Afrikaans. Petrus looked crestfallen. The man didn't have the money right then but would bring it to the New Year's Eve party. "I just don't think he'll do it," Petrus said. "Why did he tell me to come all the way out here?"

On our way home, Petrus took me on a side trip through the area where the mines were located. I hadn't been there in daylight. He pointed out the rows of two-story brick hostels where the miners contracted from the "neighbor states" lived, sixteen to a room. The way he described the facilities, they sounded like luxury spas, with soccer fields, TVs, bars; to me, they looked like prisons. (In November 1991, ninety black miners were killed in intertribal violence that erupted in these same hostels during and after a general strike.)

There were few cars around and, as we turned a corner, two black men standing at the side of the road tried to wave us down. We drove on, but they continued motioning in our direction and running after us. Petrus became panicky. He stopped the car suddenly in the middle of the highway. He wasn't sure if the men were trying to stop us—and perhaps rob or kill us—or merely wanted to warn of trouble up ahead. The intense midafternoon sun made it difficult to see; everything was a glary miasma of heat and dust. Petrus seemed paralyzed, unsure whether to continue on or go back. The men were getting closer and continued to wave their arms. After a very anxious moment, Petrus pressed the accelerator to the floor and sped off, without looking back. "I think I remember a turnoff ahead," he said. He was right.

The conversation returned to disco lights, GOGS's financial problems, and the upcoming party, as if nothing had happened. We returned home without further incident. But it was at that moment on the highway, and not in my conversations in people's living rooms over coffee and coconut tortes, that I realized how utterly terrified Welkom whites were of their black neighbors.

The next morning, the day before New Year's, I went underground. Petrus went with me. He used to work at the mines—he had run the steel cage, the elevator—but hadn't been back in a couple of years.

When we arrived, at seven A.M., we were each given a pair of blue overalls, boots, a mine helmet, and a lamp. Another gay shift boss, a friend of Petrus's, was supposed to take us underground, but at the last moment something came up. So a mine captain, gay but married, was our guide. "We know he's gay," Petrus said. "But he doesn't know that we know." As we were waiting for the cage, Petrus mentioned to the mine captain that I was writing something about Welkom. He didn't say what the subject was.

Within minutes, we were two kilometers below the surface of the earth. It was hot underground. We walked for a long way along locomotive tracks through a gray cavity about ten feet high and twenty feet wide. Water covered the ground. I noticed graffiti sprayed on the rock face along the tracks: ANC, PAC (for the militant Pan-Africanist Congress), and AFRICA FOR AFRICANS. The mine captain had fifty white miners and 550 black "mine assistants" working under him. (A mine captain was one rank above a shift boss, who in turn was one rank above an ordinary miner.) The captain was an Afrikaner and looked a bit like Nigel, the shift boss I had met the day before—fortyish and burly. He was intelligent and quite well informed about international affairs. He asked me questions about U.S. foreign policy. I asked him about President F. W. de Klerk's reforms. He was willing to go along with the new South Africa, but only up to a point. "We'll fight for what is ours," he said.

We turned off the "loco" tracks and headed down a steep and narrow incline shaft where walls of black "reef"—covering the gold within—gleamed on each side. This was where the mining operations took place. The way was hard going, and it was easy to lose one's footing. On our left, piles of wood shored up areas where reef had already been blasted out. On our right, some black miners were drilling into the reef, while others were going at it with pickaxes; they were preparing the area for blasting. Sweat was pouring down their faces. White miners supervised. In a few hours, explosives would be brought in and everyone would be evacuated prior to blasting.

The mine captain stopped and huddled in conversation with some of the black miners. He spoke in Fanagalo, the lingua franca of the mines, a combination of English, Afrikaans, Xhosa, and Zulu. There had been trouble over the weekend: Some shoring had come loose. The situation would have to remedied before blasting could take place; the mine captain was concerned that they might not be able to blast that day and he wouldn't be able to meet his production quotas.

Having descended from the incline shaft to the level below, we were on still another set of "loco" tracks. As the reef was blasted, the mine captain explained, chunks fell through openings from the incline shaft to the locomotives in the tunnel below, where we were now standing. The locomotives then transported the reef to another area, where the gold was removed.

"What are you writing about?" the mine captain asked as we walked along the tracks. I told him, but he didn't pursue the subject.

Afterward, in the mine captains' private changing room, we showered, drank strong tea, and chatted some more, mostly about politics and the price of gold. The mine captain made sure to talk about his children; he had five. "I wouldn't want my son to grow up to be a miner," he said. "It's too dangerous." A couple of his colleagues wandered in. "He came to Welkom to see another side of South Africa," the mine captain said, introducing me. "The right side!" The other captains chuckled appreciatively.

Back in town, Petrus and I stopped at a travel agency, so I could buy an advance bus ticket to Jo'burg. As we were waiting, the pictures on the wall suddenly began to shake. A coffee cup fell from a shelf and smashed; a customer screamed. In seconds, everything was back to normal. "Just an earth bump," said Petrus, reassuringly. "But we're lucky we weren't underground." Later, I read in the newspaper that, as a result of the tremor, two miners had been killed at a shaft near Welkom.

It was New Year's Eve. The GOGS party took place in an open-air pavilion in a park on the edge of Welkom. Tables and chairs were set up around a concrete dance floor; off to the side was a place to *braai*. The moon was full, almost obscuring the state-of-the-art disco lights in which Petrus had invested so much money.

There were about forty people in attendance, all of them white, although the park had been open to members of all races since the previous year. The crowd was divided equally between men and women. As in smaller cities in the United States, here there seemed to be more socializing between gay men and lesbians than one tended to find in the large urban centers. In a place like Welkom, gay men and lesbians had no recourse but to stick together.

When I arrived, "Rock Around the Clock" was playing. But the most popular music proved to be traditional Afrikaans fare that sounded like a polka. When it came on, everyone rushed to the dance floor, joining hands in a circle and kicking up their heels.

The disk jockey turned out to be the shift boss who was originally supposed to take me down into the mines. He asked me about my trip underground. "There are hundreds of gay miners, hundreds," he said. "Married but gay."

I chatted with a rather fashionably dressed woman who was a buyer for the corporation that owned the mine I had visited earlier in the day. Her job was to purchase equipment such as conveyor belts and electrical devices. She was at the party with her lover and already seemed a little tipsy. "I have a complicated story," she said.

"Let me guess," I said. "You used to be married and have three kids."

"Two kids," she said. "They are living with my mother in Welkom. But how did you know?"

The woman who had left Andries's house so abruptly the other night motioned to me. Her name was Marla. "I want to tell you about myself," she said in heavily Afrikaans-accented English.

Marla had had a two-year relationship, her first, with a woman almost twice her age. The woman had two grown sons—one a lawyer and one an accountant—who both lived in Welkom, and who had forced their mother to discontinue the relationship. Marla was still in love with her eight months after the breakup. "It is so difficult to find anyone in Welkom," she said. "Please, if you find someone for me, let me know."

At midnight, everybody cheered and kisses were dispensed all around. "Let's hope this year is a better one," I overheard one woman telling another.

"Was last year so bad?" I inquired, innocently.

"In Welkom, yes," they said.

The party went on for several hours. There was still more dancing and sausage to *braai*. Petrus took over as disk jockey and was completely absorbed by his new task. His "angel" from Ody had never shown up, but Petrus seemed to have put the promised five hundred rand out of his mind, at least for the duration of the evening. By four-thirty A.M., the remaining guests had sacked out on the dance floor, trying to snatch a few hours' sleep before partying all over again on New Year's Day.

In the minds of my liberal-minded friends at home, these were the villains even though they were gay: the oppressors of South Africa's nonwhite majority. And I couldn't help but wonder how the partygoers would have reacted had I shown up with my Johannesburg black friends—Bev and Mary Anne and Constance and Simon. But as the moon went down and a new and uncertain year beckoned, the lives of Welkom's white lesbians and gays seemed extremely precarious. The ground under their feet was shifting. They called it a bump and put it out of their minds. I wondered what would happen when the big one hit.

Welkom Postscript

Violet and Suzette taught me how to play pool. They were the Afrikaner lesbian couple I had met briefly at Dion's, the department store in Welkom, where they both worked. They had been in Johannesburg over the long New Year's stretch, visiting friends, and we overlapped there by a few hours on my return from Welkom.

It is embarrassing to confess that I had never played pool in my life. Then again, Violet and Suzette had only played once before. We were all three of us hoping to run into that elusive commodity, beginner's luck. We encountered it now and again—but it never stuck to any one of us for very long. Fortunately, we met in the middle of a weekday afternoon in a Jo'burg bar when there was no one else around to watch.

Violet and Suzette were a butch-femme couple of the old school. Violet, who was thirty, was the "man" of the two, and looked it. It wasn't just her compact and athletic build, her short haircut, or the masculine attire she preferred—the blue dress shirt, pleated khaki pants, man's shoes, and man's watch. It was also the way she moved and carried herself, her impish grin of satisfaction when she sank a ball. There was something sweet, almost innocent about Violet, in the way a teenage boy can be sweet and innocent, even as he tries his best to be as tough as his older brothers.

Violet had spent her entire life in Welkom. Before starting at Dion's, she had worked for nine years as secretary to an executive at one of the mines. In those days, she would ride her motorcycle to work, dressed in men's clothes, with her dress and heels neatly packed in her rucksack. Someone in Welkom told me that Violet shaved every morning. I was reluctant to ask her if that was true, but if I had, I doubt she would have been offended.

Suzette appeared her opposite. She was twenty-seven, pretty, big-boned, looking a little like a French chanteuse on the skids who had found herself playing the lounges of Holiday Inns in the suburbs of Paris. Her hair was long and blond. She was dressed in femme fashion—a black, red, and turquoise floral-print dress, a white pocketbook, and black heels. A former policewoman, she was now in charge of security at Dion's.

Violet and Suzette both appeared honest and absolutely straightforward. Suzette, the femme, was really the harder one of the two, I thought, the one you didn't want to cross.

Suzette loved to tell stories about Violet's successful impersonations of a man: Violet getting thrown out of women's toilets; customers saying, "Sorry, sir," when they brushed past her on a crowded sales floor; still another customer taking Violet aside and saying, quite seriously, "Can I ask you a personal question? Do you have problems with your voice? You have a *woman's* voice." One of Suzette's favorite Violet stories took place when the two were on holiday at a resort on the Indian Ocean, where they became friendly with a married couple in their seventies. The older couple invited them to a fish *braai*. Violet and Suzette were sitting outside having a beer with the men, when the wife called to Violet to help out in the kitchen. "Imagine Violet in the *kitchen*!" said Suzette, hilariously.

According to their prescribed roles, Suzette, not Violet, was the cook. Violet only knew how to prepare the "small stuff"—rice, eggs, and sausage. She did the gardening (always the man's job in South Africa), and was in charge of the cars and bikes.

Butch Femme

I asked Suzette if there weren't any so-called male tasks she enjoyed.

She rolled her big blue eyes. "I'd never want to do the garden!" she said.

As she spoke, Suzette, in heels, was killing us both at pool.

Violet and Suzette were extremely serious about the business of butch-femme. "In straight love," said Violet, "there must be someone stronger in the house. In gay love, that is true, too. I make Suzette feel like a woman. That's the man's role in a relationship." As for Suzette, the idea of "two women in makeup having sex with one another" struck her as simply ridiculous.

If people often mistook Violet for a man, it was hard for many to believe that Suzette was a lesbian. "Thirty percent of lesbians don't care how they look or what they wear," explained Violet, who was fond of quantifying everything. "That is why people can't believe a sophisticated-looking woman like Suzette is actually gay."

Most lesbians in Welkom were into roles, they said. They knew one couple whose roles depended on their mood, however. One day, one was the butch; the next day, she was the femme. Violet and Suzette strongly disapproved. In their view, you had to choose your role and stick by it. Those were the rules. They were also critical of gay men who went to parties dressed as "ordinary men." "At the parties in Welkom and Bloemfontein eighty percent of the gay men wear normal clothes," complained Violet. "The queens don't feel they belong there." There was a bar in Jo'burg, she said, where ninety percent of the men were in drag. In her estimation, that was how things ought to be.

Violet and Suzette had been each other's "affairs" for almost three years. When they first became involved, Suzette was in a relationship with a man and considered herself heterosexual. She and Violet had been players on the same women's soccer team before they got together. Then the team went off to a tournament in Durban. That week, the two became "drinking partners," largely to help Violet ward off the advances of yet another teammate. They also shared a hotel room. One night, they decided to shock people. Violet gave Suzette a love bite and, in exchange, Suzette presented her with a gold chain. When they appeared at breakfast the next morning, they created a stir. Neither remembered the sequence of events after that very clearly. Suzette recalled sitting in a bathtub at home one evening, saying to herself, "Suzette, you will never see that woman again." But she did.

Violet said proudly, "I never forced myself on Suzette."

Suzette said, "I was straight, straight as a lamppost, and then . . . There is an expression in Afrikaans—it means 'slapped by a windmill.' That is the best way I can explain it."

When she became involved with Violet, Suzette had been working as a policewoman for six years and was about to be transferred to Johannesburg. She told Violet that if Violet could get her another job within two weeks, she would stay in Welkom. The position of security manager at Dion's was open; Suzette took it. By the time I met her, she was thoroughly bored with the job. "You don't have any sense of satisfaction," she said. "You are supposed to cut down on pilferage, both inside and outside. You spend your time checking up on people."

Suzette wanted to return to police work but was sure that because she was gay she would never be rehired in Welkom. "I am too well known and Violet is too well known," she said.

They were planning to get married in October. The wedding would take place in Johannesburg, where there was a minister, they said, who performed gay and lesbian weddings. "In a place like Welkom, you can't exactly go up to a minister and ask him to marry two women," said Violet.

In fact, gay marriage was a subject of increasing interest in South Africa. An issue of the popular magazine *You*—the counterpart of *People* or *Us* in the United States—featured a splashy, full-color spread that included a photo of two blond women, one in a white man's suit and one in a white gown, posing in front of a crepe-paper-bedecked Ford Cortina. The headline was "What a wedding gay! SA's first lesbian bridegroom."

Violet and Suzette planned to invite both sets of parents to their wedding ceremony but not to the reception afterward. They were afraid their parents would be uncomfortable seeing male and female couples dancing together.

I asked Suzette why she wanted to marry.

"For security," she answered. "In gay life, you can never be sure that 'tomorrow she'll still be my butch.' "

Prefeminist

Eventually, they hoped to adopt a child. Although gay and lesbian adoption was not permitted in South Africa, they were optimistic. "In three years so much can happen," said Suzette. "More and more people are coming out each year. Things are changing."

Suzette's game was starting to go downhill, while Violet was playing better. My game remained atrocious, capped by hitting the eight ball into the pocket by mistake. At that point, I graciously volunteered to get another round of beer.

When I returned, I brought up the subject of butch-femme again. Role-playing was a pervasive aspect of South African gay and lesbian culture—from Linda and the drag pajama parties of Soweto to Violet riding her motorcycle to work with her dress folded in her rucksack. South Africa was, in many respects, still a prefeminist society, cut off from the social currents of Western Europe and North America by geographical distance, sanctions, and the censor's pen. Role-playing reflected the strong patriarchal strains of both Afrikaner and black tribal culture. (It seemed less evident among white South Africans of English descent, who traveled abroad more frequently than the other groups and tended to be less isolated.) One white gay activist, who had been around Johannesburg's gay scene for many years, told me: "South Africa is ten to fifteen years behind the U.S. And blacks are ten to fifteen years behind the whites. They think 'gay' means dressing up. In the mid-1970s, white gay South Africans were into all this husband-and-wife stuff, too. They still are, in small towns. It is a question of gay consciousness." That may have been true, but what was "gay consciousness" anyway? One of the lessons of a society with the cultural variety of South Africa was that there wasn't necessarily one absolute model of gay or lesbian relationships.

I stuck to my egalitarian position, though, partly out of conviction, partly out of habit, mentioning to Violet and Suzette the large number of lesbians in Europe and the United States who saw their relationships as equal and didn't feel they had to "choose" between butch and femme.

"In my opinion," Suzette replied politely, "the women you describe sound like they are too lazy to look after themselves. They are like married women who get so secure that they don't bother to take care of themselves anymore."

reactions to egalitarian relationships

To Violet, the idea was just incomprehensible. "If two women look the same, they are not serious about one another," she said.

That was as far as I could get. In Violet and Suzette's view, roles weren't something you needed to explain or defend. They just *were*.

By now, it was late in the afternoon, and Violet and Suzette wanted to start back to Welkom before sundown. Their holiday was over. Suzette had time for another Violet story, though. This one took place one afternoon at Dion's, when a man approached Suzette and asked her out on a date. "I'm engaged," she told him. He replied, "That doesn't matter." Violet, who was standing nearby, overheard the conversation. She approached the man and told him in no uncertain terms that she and Suzette were a couple and that he had better leave her alone or else. He apologized. Now, whenever the man came into Dion's, he was so scared of Violet that he wouldn't even say hello to Suzette.

"Bloody bastards!" Violet said. She looked at me, grinned, and sank the winning ball.

Cape Town

The police knocked on the door of the apartment of Leon Linz, the head of Cape Town's safe-sex campaign, at five-fifteen on the morning of October 17, 1990. Leon's mother answered. The officers—a man and a woman—identified themselves as members of the narcotics squad. They said they had received a complaint concerning *dagga* on the premises. Leon was just getting into his clothes when the police came into his bedroom.

"Do you smoke marijuana?" the policewoman asked Leon.

He said he didn't.

According to Leon's written statement of events (from which this account derives), no attempt was made to search for drugs. Instead, the officers turned their attention to a stack of videos on a table next to the bookshelf. Did any of the videos contain pornography? the policewoman demanded.

Leon answered in the negative and handed her a list of the contents of all his videos. In South Africa, it is legal for the police to enter someone's home without a search warrant to search for drugs; it is illegal to do so to look for pornographic materials.

The officers then went through his books and magazines. A volume called *Gayspeak*—a compendium of academic essays on homosexuality—caught their eye; so did back issues of the American gay news magazine *The Advocate*. Was *The Advocate* banned in South Africa? the policewoman inquired. Leon said that wasn't so, although he conceded that certain issues might have been declared "undesirable" by the Publications Control Board. The policewoman again asked whether he had any pornography; Leon again assured her he did not. The officers took down Leon's phone number and left.

Leon's statement concluded, "Having made absolutely no effort to search for what they were apparently looking for and had used as the pretext to gain entry into the flat, the police then left."

I didn't get a chance to meet Leon Linz when I was in Cape Town. He had already left the country, in an effort to avoid military service. But there were other angry young men in Cape Town.

Cape Town isn't exactly where you'd expect to find angry young men. Located almost at the continent's southernmost point, it features one of the most spectacular settings of any major metropolis in the world. The city climbs away from the sea and up the slopes of Table Mountain, the dramatic half-mile-high and two-mile-long wall that seems to block off Cape Town from the rest of Africa. Affluent beach communities stretch down the peninsula toward the Cape of Good Hope. Someone in Johannesburg complained that "people in Cape Town believe there is no civilization away from their mountain," and the city does appear to be a perfectly contained universe. Here, salaries are twenty-five percent lower than in Johannesburg, but who cares? In Cape Town the best things in life really are free: the beach, the mountains, the exhilarating lift of the salt air, a stroll along the promenade at Sea Point on a Sunday afternoon.

The Sea Point promenade is where the ethnic richness of Cape Town is most apparent: Muslim women with scarves covering their heads; elderly Jewish men in boater hats; pretty "Coloured" girls munching lime-green cotton candy. Afrikaner teenagers play rugby. A punky lesbian couple, arm in arm, linger, looking out at Robben Island, where ANC leaders were formerly imprisoned. White yuppies jog by; black kids selling ice cream go up and down the beach on two-wheelers. The sun will soon sink into the sea, and the shadows are long. An Indian woman, in a bright red-and-yellow sari, says to another, "He is big and fat! And he is spoiled! And if he doesn't get his way, he throws a tantrum."

Sea Point on a Sunday afternoon is the new South Africa, but it is also the old Cape Town, the racial and cultural mix that apartheid was never quite able to destroy. In his 1988 memoir-cum-reportage *White Boy Running,* the novelist Christopher Hope recalled, "Cape Town a quarter of a century ago was striking, not only in its natural beauty, but for the manner in which the inhabitants of the city, Whites and Coloureds (which is to say the mixed race descendants of earlier settlers), met and mingled. To a Transvaler reared in the Black and White stringencies of the Highveld, this dilution of the usual racial severities, the relaxed jumble of White and Coloured neighbourhoods, the integration one saw on the buses, the camaraderie of the streets, all came as a revelation."

Apartheid did try to destroy the racial harmony of Cape Town, as hard as it could. The racial planners bulldozed whole neighborhoods like District Six, from which the Afrikaans-speaking "Cape Coloureds"—who make up a majority of the population of greater Cape Town—were deported to the bleak townships on the Flats, to the southeast of city. Crossroads, the nearby black squatter settlement, was the scene of bloody conflicts between residents and police throughout much of the 1980s. But even if Cape Town has been unable to escape the troubles of the rest of the country, today it still has a relatively easygoing quality, and the racial tensions of Johannesburg seem far away.

Cape Town's relaxed atmosphere is manifested in yet another way: It is the gay mecca by the sea. One resident exuberantly put the city's population at twenty percent lesbian and gay; among the Cape Coloureds, there is reputed to be a long tradition of acceptance of homosexuality. But despite the city's liberal and laid-back reputation, it is still a closeted mecca. Middle- and upper-class white gays lead the good life in seaside communities like Bantry Bay and Clifton, but discreetly. The geographic sprawl of the city and the social divisions imposed by apartheid have made it difficult to forge a lesbian and gay community. There was no GLOW in Cape Town; a black gay organization failed a couple of years ago. Cape Town's leading gay group, the Organization of Lesbian and Gay

Activists (OLGA), was largely composed of white, university-educated professionals and had thus far made little effort to replicate the grass-roots organizing of the Witwatersrand.

In Cape Town, gay politics and AIDS politics were struggling to be born.

John Pegge was one of Cape Town's angry young men. He lived in Woodstock, a mixed-race, largely Portuguese-speaking neighborhood of pink, purple, and sea-green attached houses that meanders up the lower slopes of Table Mountain. Three weeks before I arrived, the Group Areas Act, mandating residential segregation by race, had been abolished in Woodstock. Housing prices had shot up forty percent. In reality, residential segregation hadn't been strictly enforced in Woodstock in recent years, primarily, according to John, because the neighborhood's polyglot character meant that "no one could figure it out." For example, John, who is white, lived on the officially "Coloured" side of the street.

John wasn't exactly the prototype of the angry young man. He was in his forties, for one thing, had been married, and had two children. He was now living with a young Afrikaner man who was active in Cape Town's gay Christian group. A social worker and the director of the local gay and lesbian mental-health clinic called GASA-6010, John was edgy, high-strung, always on the go.

John was angry because of AIDS and the South African government's abysmal response to it. He was angry because there had been no high-level contact between the government and any gay organization about AIDS until mid-1990, when the number of officially reported AIDS cases was closing in on six hundred and the total was doubling each year. He was angry because the state health-care system refused to give out the drug AZT to people with AIDS, on the grounds that it was too expensive. He was angry that government grants to disabled persons, including those with AIDS, were so minimal that they provided "barely enough to pay rent and electricity."

The targets of his wrath were endless. The University of Cape Town's medical school, the finest in the country, didn't have an HIV clinic or a machine to do T-cell counts, which meant its laboratory could only do four a week, often with inconsistent results.

State-owned corporations like South African Airways and the Electricity Supply Commission had been testing potential employees for AIDS, even though the Ministry of Health officially opposed such testing. The Entry to South Africa Act barred foreigners who were infected with HIV. As a result, AIDS activists—often with the help of sympathetic crews of foreign airlines—were forced to virtually smuggle in South Africans who had moved abroad, no longer held valid South African passports, and wanted to come home to visit family or to die.

"Perhaps I am being too harsh," John said. "The government tells me I am being too harsh when I say they have a deliberate campaign to get rid of persons with HIV disease as fast as possible. I don't agree. I think I am probably spot on."

What could explain, he demanded, the official harassment of Cape Town's safe-sex campaign? Long before the police had searched Leon Linz's bedroom, they had done the same to John—three times. Each time his home was raided, he had just returned from an international AIDS conference; and each time the police had clearly been looking for sexually explicit material, although they claimed they were searching for drugs. On the most recent occasion, the police hadn't actually searched his house, just come by to "talk" to him. "This was apparently to remind me that the Gestapo continues to exist and operate," he said.

He attributed these raids to the "underlying principles of Calvinism and the government's moralistic approach to HIV infection and AIDS. Homosexuality itself is seen as something undesirable that should be stamped out. The police see themselves as doing their moral duty by harassing gay leaders."

Nonetheless, the safe-sex campaign seemed to be having some success, at least among white gay men. In 1989, there had been eighty-one newly reported cases of full-blown AIDS among the gay population in South Africa; in 1990, the number dropped to fifty-nine. "We may have peaked in terms of homosexual spread, among the white population," John suggested.

When it came to the nonwhite population, however, a series of economic, educational, and political factors made the task of AIDS prevention more difficult. "If you look at just the issue of economic disadvantage, that makes the condom an expensive item on your shopping list," he said. "At one rand a condom, there are very few persons within these groups who can afford them." There were other problems, too. There was a disco downtown that catered mostly to Coloured gays, and it was relatively easy to reach its patrons with a safe-sex message. But the Coloured community who lived out on the Cape Flats, and who rarely came into town, was a different story. The homosexual, transsexual, and transvestite prostitutes on the Flats were extremely suspicious of any governmental or organizational intervention.

John told me that if I came around to the GASA-6010 clinic, he would introduce me to a Coloured client who had worked as a transvestite prostitute.

The clinic had a unique character: Its large waiting room, with a kitchen and a counter area off to one side, made it look like a restaurant. On the evening I visited, close to twenty people were sitting around chatting animatedly and drinking coffee. Clients waited to see therapists and physicians. The crowd all seemed to know one another—many of them were social workers, clinic volunteers, and AIDS "befrienders" (buddies). A young man was hawking tickets to a benefit premiere of *Longtime Companion,* the Hollywood feature film about a group of gay men living in New York City during the AIDS epidemic. The physician on duty—a woman in her forties—breezed in and out, dispensing pleasantries and general good cheer. A woman named Barbara, who ran the local AIDS residence, invited me to Shabbat dinner. Except for the faint smell of rubbing alcohol emanating from the medical consulting room, the place had the feel of a perpetual office party.

The clinic was the closest thing Cape Town had to a gay and lesbian center. But as warm and friendly as the place was, it had a strange dynamic. A client would come in, suffering from depression or worrying about HIV infection, and find himself in the middle of a noisy, festive crowd. When I mentioned this to John, he said that he tried to get particularly troubled clients into his office quickly, so they didn't have to confront all the coffee-drinking and general gaiety.

The coffee drinkers, without exception, were all white. Many of the people waiting to see therapists were black and Coloured. The Coloured transvestite prostitute was sitting off in a corner by himself. He was eighteen, slight, and dressed in a brightly colored sport shirt and a pair of baggy trousers. I went over and tried to make conversation. No one knew he was HIV-positive except for John, he told me; he complained of being constantly tired.

"I have had enough of my life," he said.

He was shy and uncommunicative and utterly out of his element.

Later, John introduced me to another client, a thirty-two-year-old black man named Robert. Robert had arrived in Cape Town just fifteen days before from Kimberley, the famous diamond-mining center far at the other end of the Cape Province. Geographically and spiritually, Kimberley was a lot closer to Welkom than it was to cosmopolitan Cape Town. Robert was gay and married, and that was a big part of the reason he had come south. Cape Town, after all, was the place you came to start life afresh, to put the past behind you. His other reason was to study psychiatric nursing.

Robert had left his wife and child in Kimberley. He also left behind a twenty-year-old male lover, who was scheduled to visit that week. They had been involved for three years. "I love him and he loves me," he said. "It is truly an intimate relationship."

Robert was thoughtful and well-spoken and radiated a sense of calm and intelligence. But he was also filled with guilt and remorse. "I keep imagining," he said, "what it will be like the day my wife starts telling people that I'm gay: They will look at me like an object sitting in a museum. To them, it is very negative, very abnormal. I can't take that! If I told my parents, I'm not sure if they would even know what I am talking about. In Kimberley, homosexuality is not understood or known. They will think that I'm bewitched and will take me to a witch doctor. My parents won't disown me. But they will bear a social stigma—they produced a gay child. Being gay is terrible in Kimberley."

We sat off to one side of the waiting room, under a German safe-sex poster that someone said was the closest thing to pornography you could find in South Africa. Robert was a handsome man, broad-shouldered, with curly hair and deep-set eyes. Before his marriage, Robert said proudly, women would do everything to "trap" him. He was a "playboy, a social butterfly, a virgin-breaker." In retrospect, he thought that his Don Juanism served the function of disguising to himself the fact he was gay. Just a month before he was to be married, he met his current lover; it was the first time either had had sex with another man. Still, he went through with the wedding. "I stood in front of the minister and my mind was on that boy," he told me. "To him, I am father, teacher, husband, everything. He is everything I have ever wanted. After meeting him, I lost interest in women. I wasn't the virgin-breaker anymore. My life completely changed. People wouldn't believe it!"

After the marriage, the young man came and lived in his house as Robert's "second wife." His legal wife, a nurse, would go on night duty, and he and his lover spent the evenings together. After two years of this arrangement, his wife became suspicious. She chucked the young man out of the house. But the two men's relationship continued. She found a love letter he had written to Robert. Since these events, Robert's sense of guilt toward his wife had intensified. "This is shameful in traditional culture," he said. "She hears rumors. She hates the boy and wishes him bad luck. She asks me about it, but I am denying everything to her."

So here he was in Cape Town at the counseling service—his first encounter with any kind of organized gay community—trying to find a way out of the situation. His lover was arriving for a visit that very week. And his wife was making noises about coming for a visit soon, as well. Cape Town might be land's end, walled off from the rest of the continent, but finally that didn't matter much. You had to face your problems.

Ric Howell was the man who was hawking tickets to *Longtime Companion* at the GASA-6010 clinic that evening. Was it a good film? the other coffee drinkers wanted to know. "Superb," said Ric, who had never seen it. Ric was a persuasive salesman. He also had credentials you couldn't exactly say no to—he was gay, hemophiliac, and HIV-positive.

"I'm an angry young man," Ric told me over drinks the following evening. "I'm aggressive. I fall for sob stories. I'm into anything—women's lib, men's lib, anti-apartheid. I'm Jesus Christ." We were sitting looking over the harbor from the terrace of an outdoor restaurant at one of those trendy waterfront shopping complexes found in port cities all over the world. Through an open window just behind our table, we could hear someone playing a piano. The breeze off the ocean was gentle and fresh. Table Mountain, floodlit at night, was a great gray smudge in the sky. "Another shitty day in paradise," Ric said, and ordered another beer.

Ric, who was twenty-five, was stubborn and contentious and proud of it. He was trim, attractive in stone-washed jeans, sneakers, and a black T-shirt that said BOY. He had had a hard life, full of disappointments, which gave his personality an abrasive edge.

The disappointments began early. As an adolescent growing up in a white upper-middle-class family in Pretoria, he had had so many conflicts with his parents that they asked him to move out of the house. He was kicked out of the Pretoria Technion, where he had gone to study drama, because he was hemophiliac, he said: Apparently school authorities were afraid that he would stumble into a chair in the middle of *Uncle Vanya* and start to bleed. During a routine medical examination when Ric was nineteen, the doctor performed an HIV test. He informed Ric it was positive (Ric had apparently been infected by contaminated clotting fluid), offering him no counseling save that it would be "fair" to tell his partner. Ric, who had no partner to tell, mumbled his thanks and left convinced he would be dead in six months. He didn't die, went on to study computers, and landed a job at a computer firm in Cape Town.

Ric's brother, also hemophiliac, committed suicide when he was told that he, too, was HIV-positive.

When Ric's parents asked when he was going to get a girlfriend, he used his HIV status as an excuse. At that time he was deeply closeted and ashamed of being gay. A gay man, in his estimation, was the sort who "gets a flat tire and calls the petrol station to get it fixed." Ric knew how to fix a flat.

In Cape Town, he was lonely, isolated, depressed. He knew no one else who was HIV-positive. This went on for a long time. Finally, about a year and a half before I met him, he summoned the courage to browse through the South African lesbian and gay monthly newspaper, *Exit,* at a local bookstore. There, he found a notice for Body Positive, a support group for HIV-positive men. He rang them up, and his isolation ended.

Ric took up being gay and HIV-positive as his cause. After being completely uninformed about AIDS for years, he learned "every-thing," he said. He became the head of Body Positive and tried to give the group an activist bent, stressing issues like treatment and AIDS education. But the other members didn't appreciate his ap-proach. "They just wanted it to be a queens' tea party," Ric said. "They wanted to discuss theater. They were totally in denial. Their view seemed to be, 'It'll only be two years and I can die and it will be tragic!' "

The apathy of Body Positive members, he thought, reflected that of white South African society in general. "In South Africa the population is disempowered," he said. "Strikes are unheard of. People don't complain in the shops. They get bad service in res-taurants and tip anyway. Gay people don't think they are op-pressed. They don't know things the overseas gay community have achieved. They don't see a problem. There is a wall of fear and intimidation. You discover this when you try to motivate them."

By now, Ric had given up on Body Positive. He was starting another organization, modeled on ACT UP. A South African ACT UP, he thought, could use street-protest tactics to pressure the government to mount a serious AIDS education campaign, make treatments more available, and decriminalize homosexual acts be-tween consenting adults. But he was increasingly pessimistic about this new group, too. At the first ACT UP meeting in Cape Town, people suggested ideas like puppet shows and theater, a far cry from what Ric had in mind. He admitted that taking to the streets could be dangerous—the police force wasn't under control of the govern-ment, he claimed. But the issue went further. "First people have to be empowered," he said. "When enough people are desperate enough, something will happen."

Ric was less than impressed by the gay community in Cape Town. The bars were "seedy and awful," he said; gay-oriented restaurants were "upmarket and pretentious." Basically, gay Cape Town was a series of dinner-party networks. He wanted a "real community," he said, with gay shops, cafés, and cinemas.

By now, we had moved inside to another nearby restaurant, where Ric's lover, Kerry, worked as a waiter. I asked Ric how comfortable he was about being gay these days. "I'm getting there," he said. "For me being HIV-positive has not been the problem.

Being gay has." He had gotten involved with Kerry just a month before. None of his previous tries at relationships had been successful; Ric's pattern had usually been to "rip the other person apart," as he put it.

He had met Kerry while participating in the Edge, a personal-growth seminar, on the est model, devised by a gay Cape Town therapist. At the first session, the lights were turned out and participants wandered about in the dark. The first person you encountered became your "buddy" for the rest of training. The person Ric collided with was Kerry. "There was a blatant honesty between the two of us right from the beginning," he said. "I exposed so much of myself to him during the training. It was a safe environment to do that." Now, Ric was thoroughly committed to the relationship.

Ric had not only found a lover, he had also found the sister he never had, a heterosexual woman whom he met at the Edge. The two were now best friends and did everything together.

Ric, who had been raised a Protestant, now considered himself Jewish. He was beginning to learn Hebrew and was considering official conversion. "I am disgusted with Christianity," he said. "Among Jews, there is a real sense of community." He spent Friday nights at Shabbat dinner with a group of people who had all met one another at the Edge.

One Friday, I went to synagogue with Ric and other Edge veterans. (Ric's boyfriend, Kerry, was at work.) The Gulf War was about to begin, and the newspapers reported that Cape Town synagogues would be praying for peace. At the service we attended, the rabbi, an American, was instead calling for Iraqi dictator Saddam Hussein's head. Barbara, the director of the AIDS residence whom I'd met at the counseling clinic, swayed back and forth as she prayed, in the Orthodox Jewish manner. Ric, in a sport jacket and jeans, was attentive and serious. The rabbi's hard-line stance was the kind of thing that cheered Ric immensely.

Back at Barbara's place after shul, we lit Shabbat candles and said prayers over challah and wine. Her apartment was upstairs from the AIDS residence; it was dominated by a massage table and a larger-than-life diagram of the human foot. Ric's newfound "sister" made stir-fried chicken and vegetables. Ric seemed relaxed. I wondered if he had finally found the sense of family and community he had been searching for. Over dinner, he and the others described how, at the Edge seminar, each person had been asked to write down a phrase that represented his or her deepest self. Barbara wrote, "I am a Jew." Ric's "sister" wrote, "I am everything." As for Ric, his description of himself was: "I am tough."

It was D day. U.S. and British bombs would start falling on Baghdad at two in the morning, South Africa time. I was sitting in a Muslim restaurant talking to a gay Coloured man named Nizham. With its large Muslim population—mostly the descendants of immigrants from Java and the Malay peninsula—Cape Town wasn't as far away from the Mideast struggle as one might assume. Members of an organization named the Call of Islam had burned U.S. and Israeli flags at an emotional rally a few days before; the head of the local branch of the ANC was denouncing the anti-Iraq coalition in language that made Radio Baghdad sound almost restrained. Nizham was a Muslim himself, but he wasn't particularly militant. For one thing, his lover, a Cape Town lawyer with whom he lived, was Jewish.

We ate lamb and potatoes on roti and drank ginger beer. On the wall behind us was a poster advertising the charms of Beirut. Nizham pointed in my direction. "He's American!" he mischievously told the woman behind the counter. I smiled wanly. The woman, apparently the owner of the place, wore a head scarf in the Islamic manner, and spoke English with an educated British accent. She was friendly enough; the bombs hadn't started dropping yet. When I came back a few days later for more lamb and potatoes, she acted as if we had never been introduced.

Nizham was a social-work student at the University of the Western Cape, a mostly Coloured university twenty-five miles from Cape Town. Black and Coloured universities in South Africa were referred to as "bush campuses." "Named after your president!" teased Nizham.

Nizham was short and wore his hair in a ponytail. He was one of twelve children. His grandparents on one side had come to the Cape from the island of Madagascar; on the other side, there had been a German grandmother who married a Cape Coloured man and was disinherited. One of Nizham's brothers was also gay; he lived at home. "The only time he can have sex with his lover is in the middle of the night when everyone is asleep," Nizham explained. Nizham went to the mosque frequently. He also professed to be an admirer of Fidel Castro.

After lunch Nizham took me to a Muslim neighborhood that commanded the heights overlooking the harbor. We could see the remains of District Six, the historic heart of the Coloured community in Cape Town until apartheid's bulldozers destroyed it; it was now a wasteland memorial of dirt and rubble. Nizham pointed to the courthouse building. "The South African flag shouldn't be flying there," he said. "The ANC flag should."

Nizham was trying to start a gay group at his university. He was the only openly gay student there. "Everyone knows that I'm different," he said. "I show that gay people are human beings." His situation was very different from that prevailing at the liberal and mostly white University of Cape Town, where a multiracial gay and lesbian student group attracted thirty to fifty students at each meeting. On the "bush campuses," by contrast, jobs and degrees were on everybody's mind, not politics. "At my university, gay people are just suppressing their feelings," Nizham said. Unlike white students, who often lived in dormitories or had their own apartments, many black and Coloured students were forced for economic reasons to live with their parents. That made it harder to come out. "We just can't be independent of our families the way the white students can," Nizham said. "For some of us, the issue of being gay is the fourteenth or fifteenth on our list of problems."

One could see the difference in white and black campus attitudes toward homosexuality in another context, as well. A conference of the National Union of South African Students (NUSAS), comprising the country's five liberal English-speaking campuses, had overwhelmingly passed a resolution promising to work toward "non-heterosexism." But at a recent meeting of the equivalent grouping of black and Coloured campuses, the South African National Students Congress (SANSCO), no such resolution was offered and there was next to no awareness of or support for lesbian and gay issues. With the two organizations slated to merge later that year, lesbian and gay students were apprehensive that their concerns might vanish totally. "On the 'bush campuses,' just making contact among gay students is difficult," said Nizham. "There is zilch understanding of homosexuality. It is seen as a white man's ideology."

The campus organizations were a microcosm of the rest of the country. While white liberals were beginning to view lesbian and gay issues with some seriousness, black groups were more resistant.

So OLGA, the Cape Town–based Organization of Lesbian and Gay Activists, of which Nizham was an active member, had been working to convince the African National Congress and the other anti-apartheid groups to take up the issue of lesbian and gay rights. While AIDS activists like John Pegge and Ric Howell had few ties to the organized black and Coloured communities, OLGA had become an affiliate of the ANC-allied United Democratic Front (UDF), a coalition of several hundred groups nationwide. And while John and Ric didn't have a moment's conflict about pressing the government on funding for AZT, for instance, OLGA did. What was more important, OLGA activist Sheila Lapinsky wondered aloud—money for AZT for white gay men or money for a clinic in a black or Coloured township?

At least in terms of its public positions, the ANC had come a long way in its attitudes toward lesbians and gays. Like many other Third World liberation movements, the organization had been strongly influenced by orthodox Communist views on morality and the family. Only a few years before, Ruth Mompati, a member of the ANC executive committee in London, had stated publicly that "In a normal society, there will be no gays because everyone will be normal." That comment caused an uproar among gays and lesbians involved in the anti-apartheid movement in Britain. When Mompati got up to speak at women's meetings, lesbians in the audience would walk out in unison. In an attempt at damage control, ANC international affairs secretary Thabo Mbeki stated in a December 1987 letter to a London gay newspaper that the ANC was "very firmly committed to removing all forms of discrimination and oppression in a liberated South Africa" and that "as a movement, we are of the view that the sexual preferences of an individual are a private matter."

The episode led the ANC to rethink its official line on gay and lesbian rights. In 1990, largely as a result of lobbying by OLGA, the

ANC included opposition to antigay discrimination in a model bill of rights it hoped would eventually become law. In its section on gender rights (Article 7.2), the ANC bill of rights states: "Discrimination on the grounds of gender, single parenthood, legitimacy of birth or sexual orientation shall be unlawful."

Many white gays and lesbians remained distrustful of the ANC's change in policy. They felt it smacked of opportunism. These suspicions were heightened in the spring of 1991 when Winnie Mandela was tried on charges of kidnapping and assault growing out of the murder of a fourteen-year-old boy and the beatings of three others. In her defense statement, Mrs. Mandela claimed that she had been told that the youths in question were being sexually abused by a white Methodist minister and were following his example by engaging in homosexual acts. Mrs. Mandela's defense lawyers implied that the boys' supposed involvement in homosexual activity justified the beatings. The lawyers also used allegations of gay sexual activity to discredit witnesses. Meanwhile, outside the courtroom, supporters of Mrs. Mandela picketed, carrying placards that read HOMOSEX IS NOT IN BLACK CULTURE. Eventually, Winnie Mandela was found guilty.

Although a number of ANC branches passed resolutions criticizing Mrs. Mandela's tactics, the atmosphere of homophobia surrounding the trial did not bode well for the organization's commitment to lesbian and gay issues and to the sexual-orientation clause contained in the bill of rights. Even before the trial, one prominent Johannesburg civil-rights attorney told me that he suspected the clause might eventually be dropped, especially if the ANC and the government, which was proposing its own bill of rights, tried to forge a compromise between the two documents. Nonetheless, the clause remained. It had been published in an ANC booklet in nine different tribal languages, some of which didn't even have a word to describe homosexuality, and was debated by ANC branches all over the country.

OLGA activist Dr. Ivan Toms put it this way: "The sexual orientation clause is probably is mainly lip service. But the fact we got even that far is significant."

Ivan Toms was one of of South Africa's best-known anti-apartheid military resisters. A thirty-eight-year-old white physician, he had worked for ten and a half years in squatter communities outside of Cape Town, where he pioneered a training program for black health-care workers. An OLGA member, an ANC supporter, a veteran of apartheid's prisons, and a committed Christian who was on friendly terms with Cape Town's Anglican archbishop Desmond Tutu, he exemplified the merging of gay and other human-rights issues that OLGA was attempting to achieve in South Africa. To many people in South Africa, Ivan Toms was a hero, if not a saint.

Ivan didn't appear particularly saintly, though. On the surface, his life-style wasn't that much different from that of the bourgeois white gay men he enjoyed railing against. The evening I visited him and his housemate, Peter, for dinner at their bungalow in the shadow of Table Mountain, Ivan had just returned from the gym. He was fretting about his weight and worrying that his new job, with a nongovernmental health-care agency, would take him on the road so often he wouldn't be able to find a lover. A short and stocky man with straw-colored hair, he positively brimmed with self-confidence. All this came somewhat as a relief—I had feared he would be too perfect.

Peter, who was cooking dinner, designed architectural models and had moved down from Durban after being expelled from a Pentecostal church for being gay. He was wearing an "I refuse to serve in the SADF [South African Defence Force]" T-shirt, with pictures of four draft resisters, including Ivan, on the back.

"At nine-thirty, we'll have to stop talking," Ivan announced. "*Golden Girls* is on TV."

Ivan became a public figure in 1983 when he refused to do his once-a-year, thirty-day military stint at a time when the South African army was fighting guerrilla wars in Namibia and Angola. At the time, he was working in the Crossroads squatter community, where large numbers of people were arriving daily from drought-stricken "homelands" and building shelters of branches and black plastic. At the end of each day, the police would show up, tear down the structures, and burn the branches and plastic in front of the inhabitants.

As Ivan recalled, "At the clinic, we were seeing the results of it all: bronchitis, women having babies and being sent out of the hospital after twenty-four hours into that sort of situation, left in the rain in the Cape winter. One Friday, after three weeks, some women were holding on to the branches and the police said it constituted a riot. They used tear gas, rubber bullets, police dogs. At the clinic, we treated all the injuries. A week later I was interviewed by a reporter who asked if this made any difference to me. I realized that I couldn't be part of that system. So I refused my call-up." (In 1985, eighteen people died at Crossroads in one day after police opened fire; some of the victims bled to death at Ivan's clinic.)

It was the period of the Reagan administration's policy of "constructive engagement" with the government of P. W. Botha. The U.S. ambassador intervened on Ivan's behalf, and his call-up was withdrawn. The government left him alone until November 1987, when he was called up again. He refused to serve and went on trial. He was sentenced to twenty-one months in prison, eventually serving nine.

At the time of his trial, Ivan had wanted to raise the gay issue in his public statements, but leaders of the End Conscription Campaign saw this as unwise. Still, the issue was used against him. According to Ivan, the dirty-tricks department of the SADF scrawled graffiti on Cape Town bus shelters: IVAN TOMS FUCKS LITTLE BOYS and TOMS DOES IT REGULARLY. HOMO PIG and MOFFIE PIG were sprayed on his car. At the trial he was asked if he was a member of the gay organization that preceded OLGA. He admitted that he was. The prosecutors also brought up his attendance at an ANC conference in Zimbabwe, during which Ivan had had a spat with Ruth Mompati. "They didn't ask me directly if I was a gay person, but the implications were that I was gay," said Ivan. "It was so obviously a smear tactic. But the credibility of being a Christian, working in a township for years at a ridiculously low salary, putting my life in danger day to day . . . That just made the issue of my sexuality rather a joke, even to the Afrikaans press."

Did he now regret not having been more open about being gay at the time? There had been some criticism from other gays, he admitted. But in South Africa, you had to work "strategically." Today, he said, he was well known and respected in church and liberal circles and widely known as a gay activist. "Archbishop Tutu knows I am gay," he said. "When OLGA recently had a press conference on our submission to the ANC constitutional committee, I chaired it. And the only name quoted in the newspapers was mine."

Ivan attributed his commitment to resisting military service not just to working in the townships but to being gay, as well. His work at Crossroads, where "blacks were treated like animals," had helped him to see links between gay and black oppression. "Being gay helps you to understand oppression in a way that I think straight people often don't," he said. "Because as a gay person you are also oppressed. It's true that most gay people can determine when they are going to state they are gay. A black person can never *not* be black. But being gay gives you a kind of inner feeling about oppression because you're treated that way yourself. It isn't because of anything you *do* as a gay person. It is because you're gay. That is the thing about racism—it isn't that you're a nice black or a horrible black. It is because you're black that people mistrust you."

Needless to say, many gays and lesbians didn't make those connections. In Ivan's view, South African white gays tended to be "bourgeois and middle-class yuppies and quite racist, actually." He could understand why the ANC might be distrustful of gays, "when you look at white gay men, totally uninvolved in politics, raving capitalists, who exploit their domestic workers and so forth. They don't give much credibility to lesbian and gay causes, do they?" That is why organizations like GLOW and OLGA were needed. "One of our aims," Ivan said of OLGA, "is to create an environment in Cape Town where lesbian and gay people involved in anti-apartheid organizations—and there are many of them—can come out. That starts to break down the stereotype of the bourgeois, nonpolitical gay."

Ivan was optimistic about the ANC and about South Africa in general. If the antidiscrimination clause remained in the ANC bill of rights, it would make the ANC the first national-liberation organization anywhere in the world to endorse lesbian and gay rights. "The possibilities are very great," he said. "Whites are being challenged on their racism and this is permeating the gay and lesbian community, as well. You are starting to see change. Gay people are waking up to the fact that we are a minority and there are a lot of other people around, too." There was still much to be done. White gays were too complacent and comfortable. OLGA was still predominantly an organization of white intellectuals. It needed to follow GLOW's example and work to help create social settings for Coloured and black gays to meet in the townships. "That is GLOW's strong point," he said. "They are very good at it. And we are very bad at it, at this stage."

But there were moments when Ivan and others in OLGA knew that they were on the right track. One of these moments was the Cape Town rally to welcome Nelson Mandela on the day he was released from jail. It turned out that OLGA members were the first to arrive at the event. For quite a while, in fact, the only banner being held aloft was that of OLGA. Meanwhile, young blacks were beginning to stream in, ecstatic that their leader was being released after so many years in prison. "So there they were," Peter recalled, "hundreds of ANC comrades dancing, and singing, under a banner that said ORGANIZATION OF LESBIAN AND GAY ACTIVISTS. It was just amazing!" If there was an image of the new South Africa that gay people like Ivan and Peter were working for, that was it.

Ivan nodded. He had heard the story a number of times before and was starting to become impatient. He looked at his watch. It was nine-thirty: time for *Golden Girls*.

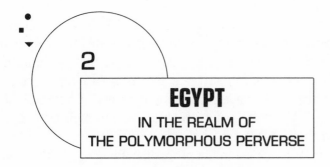

2

EGYPT
IN THE REALM OF
THE POLYMORPHOUS PERVERSE

Cairo

I met Ali on my first day in Egypt while trying to cross Tahrir Square. "Trust in God and keep one step ahead of the cars" is what they say about Cairo traffic. That day, I was contemplating whether I would be killed or just maimed when I heard a voice behind me say over the din, "Welcome to Libya." It was Ali. The touts in downtown Cairo were always trying to get your attention with "Welcome to Egypt" or "Come into my shop" or "Where are you from? Boston! I have a fiancée in West Canton, Massachusetts." Here was someone, at least, with a refreshing sense of the absurd.

I followed Ali across the chaos of smoke-belching buses, horn-honking taxis, status-seeking Mercedes, and choking pedestrians. Ali was trying to persuade me to buy papyrus painted to look like ancient Egyptian tomb art. I resisted. He was twenty-two and a student at Cairo University. He came from a family of musicians and had grown up in El Mansûra, a city in the Nile Delta, about sixty-five miles north of Cairo. With a shock of black hair, protruding ears, and a scraggly goatee, Ali looked like an anarchist, circa 1905. He had been married for six months to a young American teacher, whose mother was arriving the following week for a visit. The only trouble was that the young woman (her name was Caroline)—a tall, blond dream of an American wife who had been on the women's squash team at the University of Pennsylvania—had neglected to tell her mother that she had married a penniless Egyptian student who was as interested in the green card she could provide as anything else.

Ali was always concocting schemes—how else could one survive in this desperately poor and overcrowded city of fifteen million, after all?—and marrying Caroline seemed, partly, just another scheme. But if marriage might gain him entry to the States, it wouldn't get him out of his Egyptian military service. "I am thinking of taking on the identity of a dead man," Ali confided. "Tell me what you think of that!"

I soon became immersed in the problems of young—in this case, heterosexual—love. I typed letters from Ali to Caroline (even though they lived together), gave him advice on how to address his mother-in-law (should it be "Mrs. Sally" or "Mrs. Morrow"? he wondered), and spent endless hours discussing whether Caroline was doing the right thing by keeping the marriage secret from her mother or whether she was insulting Ali—and Egypt as well. Should Ali insist on going to the airport to meet Caroline's mother? Should he move out of their apartment for the week of Mrs. Morrow's visit? Should he and Caroline say they were just boyfriend and girlfriend? And, if Ali did go to the airport, could he please borrow my sport coat?

All this seemed to me a reasonable way to pass the time, at least temporarily. For making contact with a gay or lesbian community in Egypt was difficult. There was essentially no such thing. Egypt was the place I visited where there was the strongest social sanction against an openly gay or lesbian life, where a sense of homosexual identity was weakest, where there was the least degree of AIDS awareness.

Paradoxically, in a society where the sexes remain strictly segregated, same-sex relations were commonplace, at least among men. But you didn't talk about the subject, except to your very closest friends, and perhaps not even then. In Egypt, sex had to be kept secret, and homosexual sex in particular was *haram*—taboo. Categories of sexual identity and orientation were slippery, elusive in Egypt and in the Arab world in general. Once you crossed the Mediterranean, the terms "gay" and "straight" revealed themselves to be Western cultural concepts that confused more than they

definitions

elucidated. In modern-day Cairo, male homosexual sex was every-where and nowhere.

And lesbians? One Egyptian acquaintance bet me ten U.S. dol-lars I wouldn't meet any lesbians in this city of dutiful daughters, where most women wore scarves on their heads as a sign of religious piety, and social mores were so conservative that even dating be-tween the sexes was strongly frowned upon. How about ten Egyp-tian pounds (three dollars) instead? I asked. Ten dollars, he insisted. In Egypt, you had to bargain over everything.

On Ali's suggestion, I took a flat in Dhokki, across two Nile bridges from downtown. Dhokki is a middle-class Cairo neighborhood, residential and pious. Men play chess and dominoes and drink sweet tea in coffeehouses and smoke tobacco out of hubbly-bub-blies; vending carts overflow with melons, peaches, oranges, and strawberries; shops sell goat cheese and yogurt and fresh milk out of huge vats. Every afternoon when I was there, a religious person-age in a white skullcap, long, flowing galabiya, and brown plastic shoulder bag labeled ADIDAS wandered from shop to shop dispens-ing incense from an incense burner. Merchants rewarded him with a few piasters. Amplified calls to prayer wafted through the air like the breeze off the desert or migrating birds. God was everywhere, but so was the honking of horns.

My apartment was on the top floor of a decaying but still solid concrete building, vaguely French in architecture, that had green shutters and balconies with washing hanging off them. Women beat rugs on the roof; cocks crowed at bizarre hours throughout the night. Many of the people in the building were short-term renters, mostly Saudis and Kuwaitis who came to Cairo on holiday for a week or so. Cairo was their idea of Sin City; they were visited by prostitutes and had noisy parties. My apartment featured brocaded couches, a quote from the Koran in a gilt frame on the living room wall, an ancient washing machine, and fluorescent lights that mys-teriously continued flickering for hours after you shut them off. It was getting hot—uncomfortably hot, even for Cairo in May—and the only relief came from evening winds that blew in from the desert and covered the apartment with a layer of dust.

As soon as I moved in, I was immediately assailed by all variety of people demanding money—the *bawab* (doorman), the rubbish collector, the man who came to change the light bulb. At first, I blamed the Saudis and Kuwaitis, whom I suspected of dispensing excessive baksheesh. More likely, all this was just the reality of life in a poor country. Meanwhile, the building "servant," a plump woman in her early thirties, marched into my apartment one afternoon, plopped herself down on the couch, and sighed languidly and suggestively. Clearly, she had other things on her mind than doing the washing-up. The only English expression she knew was "tomorrow." I repeated the word like an incantation and she departed, sulkily, never to return.

Ali watched out for me at all times with an often smothering attentiveness. He seemed to think there was no reason for me to speak to anyone else in Cairo about the subject of homosexuality. It was enough to talk to *him*. He had had a relationship with a male schoolmate when he was fifteen and sixteen. Beyond that, he indicated that he no longer had any sexual involvements with men. "It is *haram*," he would say, shake his head, and return to the subject of his wife, his mother-in-law, and the U.S. Immigration and Naturalization Service.

He took to carrying around a paperback copy of my book *In Search of Gay America*. He kept it in a clear plastic bag and would show it to people without removing it from the bag. The idea was to point to my picture on the back (and thus prove what an allegedly important person he was shepherding around Cairo) without calling attention to the title on the front. One of his friends demanded to inspect the book more closely, however, and was highly disapproving. "You cannot bring such books to Egypt," he informed me. "They are dirty, not normal." Then, he looked at the acknowledgments page and saw the name "National Gay and Lesbian Task Force." He was convulsed with laughter. "This is extremely strange," he said. "I cannot believe this. We do not have such things in Egypt."

Indeed they didn't. In this, the most cosmopolitan city in the Arab world, there were no gay organizations or gay bars—although the Taverna bar at the Nile Hilton Hotel in Tahrir Square was reputed to be "mixed." In Islamic Cairo, there was a *hammam*, a Turkish bath, where men had sex with other men, but it was a decrepit place. It was unusual for someone to refer to himself as "gay" or even "homosexual," and generally indicated the speaker had lived for many years in the West. Cases of AIDS were rare, too, or hushed up, so that AIDS activism did not provide a basis for gay identity or organizing, as it did in some other Third World countries. There was no women's movement to speak of in Cairo, either, and works by Egypt's most noted feminist writer, Nawal El Saadawi, had been banned for many years.

Within the six months prior to my arrival, there had been a police crackdown on what passed for a gay scene in Cairo. A man had been murdered, and the ensuing police investigation had revealed that on the night of his death the victim had been drinking at the Taverna. Cairo police then began interrogating men known to have sex with other men, keeping them at the police station overnight or longer, in generally humiliating circumstances. The sweep was a time-honored Cairo police practice that was not restricted to crimes believed linked to homosexuality. Since the assassination of President Anwar Sadat almost ten years before, a state of emergency had been in force in Cairo; it gave the police the power to detain people without charges.

I received much of this information from a fashion designer named Zachy, who was the closest thing to a Western-style gay man that I found in Cairo. (Zachy had previously lived for some time in New York.) He related how a friend had been brought in by the police for questioning, held for a few nights, and then forced to sign a statement that he took the receptive position in anal sex. In the mind of the police, said Zachy, the killer they were looking for probably wasn't "really" homosexual but was preying on gays. Therefore, it was self-evident that he took the "active" position in anal sex. According to the stereotypical police view, a man who had sex with men and took the "passive" role was too weak and too degraded to murder anyone.

Zachy was outraged by all this. In the course of the investigation, as many as three-quarters of his friends had been detained and treated rather badly. "I want to get in touch with Amnesty International," he said, although he hadn't done so. "I'm probably the only gay man here who has even thought about doing something," he added. He didn't believe the intention of the police was solely to harass men who engaged in same-sex relations. "The police do want to solve crimes," he said. "But the way they go about it is humiliating. And it prevents any kind of gay community from grouping."

On Zachy's recommendation, I went and sat in the lobby of the Nile Hilton. Despite the fear engendered by the police crackdown, the hotel was still the spot to meet homosexually inclined men. The Nile Hilton is the most international meeting place in the Arab world. Saudi princes in full regalia and vacationing Kuwaitis in designer leisure wear rub elbows with tour groups of German tourists and American travel agents. Wealthy families hold lavish weddings there, and business groups and service clubs entertain themselves at luncheons and banquets. One wall of the lobby is dominated by a massive carved frieze brought from the Temple of Karnak in Luxor. The lobby is air-conditioned and quite pleasant, featuring comfortable lavender-and-gold couches, bronze coffee tables with vases of fresh flowers, and a view of the Nile through the glass doors.

As Zachy promised, a number of men circled the couches and chairs of the waiting area, attempting to appear as unobtrusive as possible. I bought a copy of the *Egyptian Gazette,* the English-language daily. The paper reported that the prices of gasoline and of butane gas cylinders, widely used for cooking, were going up. So was the price of cigarettes. Meanwhile, the Sultan of Oman, Qabus Bin Said, had just concluded talks with Egyptian president Hosni Mubarak.

Near me, a lean, kinky-haired young Egyptian with a face out of an ancient tomb painting was glancing nervously at his watch and chain-smoking cigarettes. He looked in my direction and smiled. He was waiting for a Dutch friend who was almost an hour late. "Do you drink beer or whiskey?" he asked, and offered to have a drink with me at the Taverna. "You go first," he said, not wanting to attract attention. "I'll follow."

The Taverna was located on the ground floor, right off the lobby. The bar was full of heterosexual couples, many of them Japanese; the police sweeps had apparently scared everyone else off. I found an empty table toward the back and ordered two beers. A few minutes later, the young Egyptian sauntered in.

The man, whose name was Ahmed and who, like every other

young man in Egypt, claimed to be a student, was twenty but looked older. When I told him that, he beamed. Ahmed didn't want to be twenty; he wanted to be a man of the world. He also fancied himself quite irresistible to women. He related the story of a Spanish woman with whom he had spent four consecutive days in bed. She demanded sex every few hours; after such nonstop exertion, Ahmed began developing heart problems and had to go to the hospital. He was now married to an Englishwoman who had returned to London. "We have sex maybe three times a night," he said. "That's enough." His wife was older than he and pregnant, and Ahmed was waiting for her to send him money so he could join her. He talked about her with great affection. "We get along so well because we have the same tastes," he said.

Without much prodding, Ahmed told me that he had short affairs with foreign men—Belgian and French mostly—whom he had met at the Hilton. He was a devout Muslim, though, and sometimes felt bad after sex. "I do it because I'm horny," he maintained. "My wife knows all about this."

Was his primary attraction to men or to women? I asked.

"It isn't like that," he said.

I suggested that perhaps it depended on the person.

"I'm not gay. There is another word in English for me."

"Bisexual?" I asked.

"Maybe that's it," he said.

Ahmed was contemptuous of gay men; he made lewd jokes about them, and generally tried to distance himself from them as much as possible. When I told him about a gay church in the States, he made a mock sign of the cross that ended at his genitals. Unlike Ali, Ahmed offered to introduce me to some homosexual men. He obviously knew his way around.

He wouldn't let me pay for his drink. He was proud. Male hustlers sometimes hung out at the Hilton; he wanted to make it plain he wasn't one of them. Ahmed was the person who made me the ten-dollar wager that I wouldn't find any lesbians in Cairo. In Egypt, the status of women was extremely low; they didn't have the economic independence to surmount family and social expectations. "If you meet any, you can be sure they will be very rich," he said.

• • •

In Egypt, and the Arab world in general, the model of sexuality and homosexuality was different from that of the West. Gustave Flaubert discovered this when he traveled down the Nile during the middle of the last century. "Here it is quite accepted," he wrote in a letter from Cairo, dated January 15, 1850. "One admits one's sodomy, and it is spoken of at table in the hotel. Sometimes you do a bit of denying, and then everyone teases you and you end up confessing. Traveling as we are for educational purposes, and charged with a mission by the government, we have considered it our duty to indulge in this form of ejaculation. So far the occasion has not presented itself. We continue to seek it, however. . . ."

Flaubert, although not gay himself, was part of the long line of Western literary travelers, ranging from André Gide to E. M. Forster to T. E. Lawrence, who observed that Arab men tended to be far more relaxed about homosexual relations than their European counterparts were. "Man in all things lived candidly with man," wrote T. E. Lawrence in *Seven Pillars of Wisdom.* So it was in modern-day Egypt.

Zachy, the Americanized Egyptian, suggested that Arabs were less "conditioned" than Westerners regarding sexuality. Because they were more in touch with their sexual feelings, he said, Egyptian men tended to find both sexes attractive. "That is the way all of us would be if we didn't have that conditioning," he contended. He did admit, however, that the more Westernized Egyptians were, the less tolerant they tended to be regarding same-sex relations. "The working class and the peasants are more accepting," he said. "At least, they follow their desires more."

Indeed, the prevailing sexual mode for Egyptian men seemed to be the polymorphous perverse. A Western anthropologist who had lived for many years in Cairo (and who talked to me on condition of anonymity) put it this way: "Egyptian men desire any kind of sexual outlet. The idea of the real Arab man is to become immediately erect and to come quickly. They don't particularly like masturbation. Women are off-limits, and men are in close physical contact with other men. So men have traditionally had sex with other men until marriage and sometimes after that. There is no sense of guilt about it. This is a shame culture. Shame comes about when something becomes public.) So, in the case of sex between men, the Arab world prefers to look the other way."

The nature of a "shame culture" was one reason why Western notions of gay liberation and gay identity had failed to make an impact in the Arab world. In the West, the anthropologist maintained, "the gay liberation movement faced the guilt issue. People were told, 'Don't feel guilty.' That was the key. Here there is no guilt. Doing this is not wrong. What is wrong is being public about it. In this culture, homosexuality cannot be an open issue. People don't want to be told about it at a public meeting."

Historically, the attitude of Islam toward homosexuality has been equivocal. The Koran condemns same-sex relations but does so without imposing a specific penalty, as it does for other offenses. In Islam, sexuality in general has traditionally been viewed with less horror and distaste than in Christianity, and the Koranic view of heaven is flagrantly hedonistic. In the next world, the righteous are to be attended by bashful virgins "as fair as corals and rubies" and "by boys graced with eternal youth, who to the beholder's eyes will seem like sprinkled pearls" (Koran 76:15). And although some of the *hadith* (sayings attributed to Mohammed) imposed the death penalty on sodomy, the American historian John Boswell notes that "in medieval Islam one encounters an even more overwhelming emphasis on [male] homosexual eroticism than in classical Greek or Roman writing. It is probably fair to say that most premodern Arabic poetry is ostensibly homosexual, and it is clear that this is more than a literary convention."

In contemporary Egypt, the puritanism of the most influential political and social movements—Arab nationalism and Islamic fundamentalism—has served as a barrier to any open discussion of homosexuality. Under Gamal Abdel Nasser, the army colonel who became the ruler of Egypt in the early 1950s and was the idol of the Arab masses, there was a clampdown on prostitution. Belly dancers were forced to wear body stockings so that their midriffs would not be visible. "Remember Egypt is a country that experienced a revolution," said the anthropologist. "This revolution included censorship and thought control and, one could say, 'gay' oppression. Maybe there was a real homosexual scene here a hundred years ago,

difficulty in creating a gay movement

with dancing boys. But the pendulum has swung the other way in the Arab world."

The situation was changing at approximately the same time as Europe and America were undergoing the sexual revolution and the emergence of women's and gay liberation. By the 1980s and 1990s, with the rise of Islamic fundamentalism, Western-style sexual freedom and gay liberation were viewed, in the Muslim world, as signs of decadence. The countries in which more traditional, easygoing attitudes toward sex between men persisted were those where nationalist and religious movements hadn't made significant headway, such as the Gulf sheikdoms and Morocco. By contrast, in Shiite Iran, where fundamentalist, anti-Western elements gained political control after the overthrow of the shah, large-scale executions of homosexuals were reported. When a United Nations committee took up the 1991 application of the International Lesbian and Gay Association to become a member of the U.N. council that monitors human-rights issues, it was a delegate from Libya who led the opposition, denouncing the gay group as "sexually immoral." (The application was deferred.) Between the two poles of the Muslim world's conflicting attitudes toward homosexuality, Egypt lay somewhere in the middle.

In Egypt, because there was so little sense of homosexuality as an identity, what position you took in bed defined all. Between men, the only sex that counted was anal sex. "I like to fuck but I don't like sixty-nine," volunteered Ahmed, the man I met at the Hilton. In the minds of most Egyptians, "gay," if it meant anything at all, signified taking the receptive position in anal sex. On the other hand, a person who took the insertive role—and that seemed to include virtually all Egyptian men, to judge by what my acquaintances told me—was not considered gay. (This was the characteristic pattern throughout the southern Mediterranean and much of the non-Western world.) Many of the insults in the Arabic language concern being penetrated anally by another man. The anthropologist explained that ingesting semen, whether through the mouth or the anus, was seen as defiling oneself in a way akin to taking poison. "A man who would agree to be polluted is allowing himself to be used by other men, allowing himself to be taken advantage of," he said. "So it is okay for younger boys, who are weaker and inferior. They don't have wisdom or control. They are like girls. As they grow up, they become men. They might want to fuck boys. That is okay. But if they continue to want to get fucked, something is wrong with them. But this is forgiven if they are upper-class, because in Egypt class status overrides all."

For his part, Zachy estimated that of the Egyptian men who had sex with other men, ninety percent took the "active" role, five percent the "passive" role, and the other five percent took either. And no Egyptian man, he insisted—with the exception of what he termed "a handful of very obvious queens"—would ever allow himself to be anally penetrated by a foreigner.

For exactly that reason, Zachy theorized that it was unlikely that AIDS would make a significant impact in Egypt, even though safe-sex practices were virtually unknown. His theory was based on two assumptions: that the receptive partner in anal sex was the one more at risk for AIDS (the view of most medical authorities) and that it was foreign tourists who would bring HIV to Egypt. "The dynamic between Egyptian and foreign men is such that the Egyptian does the fucking," he said. "Sure, at the *hammam,* at the baths, you might see an Egyptian getting fucked by another Egyptian, but never, ever by a foreigner. The fantasy is fucking a foreigner—the soft, white skin. Sex roles are very rigid in this country. Perhaps that will be to our benefit in the end."

So far, there was only a handful of reported cases of AIDS in Egypt, but that might reflect a lag time before the epidemic fully manifested itself. Zachy's theory also didn't take into account the possibility of East African heterosexual transmission eventually making its way into the country. And I was baffled by that ninety percent "active"–ten percent "passive" sex-role ratio that he (and others) ascribed to Egyptian men. For that to be true, the ten percent must have been keeping very busy.

Meanwhile, the Egyptian government was at least fitfully aware of AIDS, although in a country where open discussion of sexuality was socially unacceptable, it adopted an approach that emphasized repression rather than education. The anthropologist told me that the previous year the Ministry of Health had ordered the mandatory testing of all resident foreigners for HIV; he himself had been tested. The ministry's intention was that every time a foreign resident left and returned to Egypt, he would be retested. But, in fact, the tests were never repeated. "In Egypt there are often campaigns for a variety of things," the anthropologist observed. "There was one a few years ago to get people to stop honking their horns."

In the evening, on the downtown streets and in the coffeehouses of Cairo, you saw only men. Men were continually throwing their arms around one another, slapping one another's hands at a joke, holding hands as they walked down the street. None of this meant that they were necessarily having sex with one another, of course. But the warmth and the degree of physical intimacy between Egyptian men made the West seem stuffy and repressed. "The way Egyptian men are with one another is the way gay men in Europe and the States try to be," a British resident of Cairo told me.

Ali's wife, Caroline, hated Egypt, hated the "man's world," particularly hated the way Egyptian society treated women. She had been in Cairo for eight months, teaching high school, and couldn't wait to get out. Caroline was proud of her independence and self-reliance, proud that she had studied philosophy and played squash in college and had spent a month cycling around Scandinavia. All this was threatened by Egyptian social norms and by her marriage to a man whose views on relations between the sexes, while enlightened by Egyptian standards, were not enlightened enough to give Caroline the scope she needed. She felt pushed into marriage, which was the only acceptable way a man and a woman could live together in Cairo. Caroline didn't know much about Ali's sexual past. In a patriarchal society, you didn't tell details like that to your wife. The fact that I, Ali's friend, was writing a book about gay life didn't seem to raise her suspicions either. To her, I was just another American and therefore automatically on her side.

One night, before her mother's visit, I went to dinner at Caroline and Ali's apartment. Caroline was wearing jeans and a sleeveless blouse. Ali, dressed in his usual Israeli drawstring pants and blue Russian T-shirt, was upset that Caroline's arms were visible to another man; it offended his standards of feminine modesty. His other main concern seemed to be that Caroline's dislike of Egypt would "poison" her mother's mind.

At sunset, we ate dinner on the roof, which offered a panoramic view of Cairo and the surrounding desert. On the roof, nine stories up, Caroline felt free, she told me. But on the streets of the pious neighborhood where they lived and under the watchful eye of their apartment building's *bawab,* it was quite different. "The *bawab* is the most important person in your life in Cairo," said Caroline. You had to cultivate him, ply him with baksheesh. In addition, Ali and Caroline's neighbors kept careful track of everyone who came and went. For example, there was the young woman from the Gulf sheikdom of Qatar who came alone to visit Caroline and Ali and stayed later than was deemed appropriate. One of the neighbors rang the doorbell and told her it was time to go home.

Most women in Cairo wore a head scarf when they went out, an indication of the rising influence of Islamic fundamentalism. Modesty in appearance—a head scarf, a blouse that covered one's upper arms, at the minimum—was essential. When women, even Westerners like Caroline, flouted these conventions, insults were shouted at them on the street. Some Cairenes tended to minimize the significance of all this. Zachy, for instance, insisted that "the biggest whores in town wear scarves on their heads." (He also claimed many women wore scarves to avoid having to go to the hairdresser.) Yet one rarely noticed a woman driving a car, and only once in Cairo did I see two women sitting together in a café unaccompanied by a man.

Interaction between the sexes was extremely limited prior to marriage. Dating was viewed with disapproval in a society where arranged marriage was prevalent. Outside of educated, middle-class circles, it was unusual to see sexually mixed groups or male-female couples in public.

And this segregation of the sexes was continuing beyond the traditional adolescent premarital period. For the middle class, the cost of marriage was increasing dramatically, and the influx of people into Cairo had created a massive housing shortage. As a result, young people had to put off marriage until they were well into their thirties. Men would go off for years to work in Libya, Saudi Arabia, and the Gulf States to earn the money required for themselves (or their children) to marry.

The delay in the marriage age had far-reaching consequences in terms of sexual mores. It tended to encourage people to find sexual release with members of their own sex, if they were so inclined. Those not so inclined found other solutions. A Cairo accountant related to me how an unknown woman had taken to calling him at his office every afternoon, and that the two had begun to have a sexual relationship by way of the telephone. Random telephone sex, the latest fad among middle-class heterosexual Cairenes, was one solution to the sexual problem of a society that was advancing technologically even as it was retreating socially to the Middle Ages.

When I asked an American-educated, feminist Egyptian physician about the possibility of a gay couple living together, she threw up her hands. "It's impossible, impossible," she said. The reasons for this had due to with economics as much as anything else. Given the housing shortage in Cairo, she said, you had to wait years to get an apartment and when one finally did become available, it was often prohibitively expensive. Young heterosexual couples couldn't afford to set up house without financial help from both families. "It isn't just the flat that is expensive," the doctor pointed out. "To marry you have to have a flat and every appliance for the next fifty years—a washer, a mixer, everything. It has to be complete. Those are the rules. The house has to be entirely ready: a dining room set, a living room set. All this entails a vast amount of money." The way it worked, she said, was that the boy's parents paid for the flat, while the girl's parents paid for everything in the flat, except, oddly enough, the kitchen utensils and the electrical appliances. The boy's parents paid for these.

In the case of a homosexual couple, it was unlikely that they would receive that family financial help—unless one or both of their families were exceedingly rich and exceedingly enlightened.

For men who were homosexually inclined, these economic and social trends proved a double-edged sword. Men who preferred to have sex with other men could remain unmarried for years and plead economic hardship as the explanation. But because the economic situation made it impossible for gay couples to live together, in the manner of the West, it perpetuated the traditional Egyptian model of same-sex intimacy without gay identity.

How did all this affect lesbians? I asked the doctor, who moved in very upper-class and sophisticated social circles. "I have never met a lesbian in Cairo," she said.

Caroline's mother had arrived and had at last been informed about her daughter's marriage. Mrs. Morrow appeared to take it quite well. In fact, she had bought Ali an expensive gold bracelet that Caroline thought made him look like a drug dealer. Then, it all seemed to catch up with Mrs. Morrow. She went to dinner at Ali's parents' house and, somewhere between the main course and dessert, became quite ill. Ali summoned a doctor—the diagnosis was dehydration—and wound up paying her medical bills; like a good son-in-law he refused her offer to reimburse him. As a result, he was absolutely broke. He was thinking about selling the gold bracelet and telling Mrs. Morrow he'd lost it. That was better than accepting her money. In Egypt, how you appeared to the world was everything.

One evening, I was sitting at Wimpy's in downtown Cairo with three married men—Ali, Ahmed (the man with whom I'd had a drink at the Hilton), and a friend of Ahmed's we called Mr. Hassan. There was a Tom and Jerry cartoon on the TV. I had expected to meet the three at some coffeehouse with chess and backgammon going on around us, and the players shouting and slamming their pieces on the table. Instead, here we were at the British version of McDonald's, drinking 7UP and watching American cartoons.

"Don't you love Tom and Jerry?" Ahmed asked me. The entire restaurant seemed engrossed in the antics of the animated cat and mouse.

Meeting Mr. Hassan had an air of mystery about it. He was a schoolteacher who lived in a Cairo suburb with his wife and children. Ahmed had told me to telephone him at seven in the morning, before he went off to work, and to say that I was calling on Ahmed's behalf and that Ahmed wanted to meet with him. "He might not remember me," Ahmed cautioned. It all sounded odd but I went along with it. On the phone, Mr. Hassan was quite friendly. "I would like to see Ahmed again," he said, and proposed we meet that evening at Wimpy's.

Mr. Hassan turned out to be a short, stocky man in his forties with a Saddam-like mustache. He dressed in Cairene civil-servant garb: a white short-sleeved shirt and dress pants. He had three children in their early twenties. Mr. Hassan spoke good English, the result of summer visits to the United States. On those trips, he went to gay bars.

"I have been to the United States ten times," he said, proudly. "This summer I am going to Orlando, Florida, for my vacation."

If people inquired why his wife didn't go along with him on these trips, Mr. Hassan would reply that it was too expensive, and that she didn't like to travel, anyway. (His wife had no idea of his sexual interests.) I was puzzled at how he could afford these excursions himself on the meager wages of an Egyptian schoolmaster.

In many ways, Mr. Hassan's life was similar to that of married gay men anywhere in the world. On Fridays, the Muslim sabbath, he would go to the Hilton health club to work out and perhaps to meet someone. Sometimes, he would go to the *hammam*. Recently, however, he had been afraid to go downtown in the evenings, because of police sweeps and violence. Three years ago, he had been picked up for questioning by the police following a murder. He had also been robbed at knifepoint while standing on a street corner at Talat Harb Square in the city center.

Mr. Hassan referred to himself as gay. He said that he became aware of his sexual inclinations when he was quite young, but that at that time in Egypt, it was impossible for a young man to avoid marriage. These days it was more socially acceptable to remain single, he thought, because of the high cost of getting married. "Today the idea of an unmarried man in his twenties and even his thirties is not so strange," he said. "In fact, it is quite understandable."

He wanted to find a young man and to live with him. When I pressed him on how that would work out in view of his family responsibilities, he became vague. He had just met a twenty-seven-year-old engineer through mutual friends, and they had gone to bed together. It was the other's first experience with a man, and Mr. Hassan had high hopes for the relationship. "I will teach him everything," he assured me.

He noted the difficulty of introducing a male lover to his social circle, which consisted chiefly of other teachers. But the engineer was different, he thought. He was well educated and presentable and might fit in.

Mr. Hassan led an active sex life, much of it revolving around quickie sex in hotel rooms and a downtown cinema (now shut). He told me that just the previous week he had met an Italian man at the Hilton health club and gone to his hotel room, along with two other men. "I like group sex," Mr. Hassan said. He always used condoms, he maintained, but most Egyptian men he came in contact with knew nothing about AIDS and safe sex.

I asked Mr. Hassan if anyone else knew about his sexual orientation, whether he had any friends in whom to confide. "No. Absolutely no one knows. Except the four of us," he said, indicating himself, me, Ahmed, and Ali.

Ahmed and Ali turned away from Tom and Jerry, if only for a moment. They were impressed that Mr. Hassan spoke so openly about being gay. They had never met anyone like that before. "He is not shy," said Ali afterward.

After a while, Ali suggested that we go to a coffeehouse in Islamic Cairo and hear some Arabic music. But Mr. Hassan declined. "That is the kind of place where the police come and check your identification papers when there is trouble anywhere in Cairo," he said. We finished our 7UPs, and Mr. Hassan returned to the suburbs.

It was a journalist named Samir who convinced me to go to the desert. Samir lived in a hotel and, when he wasn't on deadline, wrote fiction. His journalistic articles often focused on Cairo's marginalized groups—the homeless, prostitutes, Gypsies, Jews, Armenians—and he had also written a short story about a love affair between an officer and a conscript set during the 1973 Israeli-Egyptian war. Samir, who was thirty-one, wouldn't identify himself as gay but told me that he had a "special friend," a student who was ten years younger than he and shared his interest in social issues.

Samir was interested in history and philosophy—and, like many journalists, he was also interested in gossip. Did I know that Julius Caesar was gay? And did I know about the sultan of Oman? According to Samir, the sultan had ninety male concubines, aged fifteen to twenty. When they reached the age of twenty, the sultan replaced them. And he was absolutely mad about Gilbert and Sullivan.

I was intrigued but skeptical. "How do you know this?" I asked.

"I am a journalist," he replied, with dignity.

"So you see, you must go to Oman," he went on. "There, all men have sex with other men. No one thinks anything about it. It is totally accepted. Perhaps Egypt was like this a hundred years ago, before the English and the French came here. I think there is no place like Oman in the Arab world."

I went to a few travel agencies and looked into airfares to Oman, but they were too expensive.

Samir told me he had first encountered homosexuality when he was an army officer. A soldier had deserted and then was brought back; everyone said the soldier liked sex with men. Samir interrogated him and asked him about these reports. "What is this?" he demanded. "It is very strange. It is not normal." The deserter, who came from a remote desert oasis, replied, "In my village, it is normal."

"If you don't go to Oman, then you must go to the desert, to the oases," Samir told me. "There, you will find what you are looking for."

Ali proposed we go to Baharîya, an oasis town about a hundred and seventy-five miles southwest of Cairo. He had been there once before and said he knew someone who could introduce me to some gay men. Caroline and her mother were traveling to Luxor and Aswan to look at antiquities. They wanted him to accompany them, but he had begged off, insisting that he had to study for his exams.

"My friend Hani will go with us," he announced. "He is my neighbor. Our families are like one family." Ali had never mentioned Hani before, but then again, Ali was always coming around with somebody new.

"Isn't he handsome?" Ali asked when the two stopped by my apartment. "He can fix anything."

Hani immediately showed me how to recharge my typewriter batteries, get some extra turns out of my typewriter ribbon, and fix the adapter of my tape recorder. He was studying mechanics at Cairo University. He loved motorcycles and had nearly been killed in an accident a year before. His English was limited, but he had his

own brand of charming expressions, which I came to call Hani-
isms—"A flat is freedom," for instance, or "The sky cries," meaning, "It's raining". Tall, dark, with a mustache and sad eyes, Hani
was loyal and trusting. His father was a "millionaire" living in Abu
Dhabi, on the Gulf, with an Indian wife; Hani hadn't seen him in
fifteen years. Hani was engaged to be married—at his family's
request—but he enjoyed having sex with men.

Then, the day before we were to start for the desert, Ali called to
say he couldn't go. His grandmother had died suddenly and he had
to go to his family village in the Nile Delta for the mourning period.
Hani would accompany me to Baharîya. "He knows what I know,"
Ali said, although Hani had never been to Baharîya before. Ali gave
Hani a letter to give to someone named Mohammed.

We took the bus through the bleakest desert. Hani told jokes.
"Egyptian people are joking, always joking," he said. "I know a
hundred jokes." Many of these jokes were self-deprecating, poking
fun at Egyptians as thieves or incompetents. There was, for example, the one about French president François Mitterrand, Britain's
Margaret Thatcher, and Egypt's Hosni Mubarak flying around the
earth in a plane. When they fly over Paris, Mitterrand puts his hand
out the window and says, "I can touch the Eiffel Tower." When
they pass London, Thatcher follows his example: "I can touch Big
Ben." As the plane approaches Cairo, Mubarak reaches out the
window, too. "Someone stole my watch!" he shouts.

Six hours and innumerable jokes later, Baharîya emerged—a
place of staggering beauty. There were palm groves and rice fields;
hot springs where the water got as warm as a hundred and fifteen
degrees Fahrenheit; and always in the distance, the vast desert. The
town had a population of about fifteen thousand and was constructed of one-story mud buildings. Many of the houses were
painted with childlike red and blue designs to indicate the residents
had gone on hajj, the pilgrimage to Mecca. Sand covered everything, as if the town had received a dusting of snow. In the business
section, old jeeps were parked along the main street, and goats and
chickens wandered about. Antique safes were piled in front of one
shop, next door to a row of equally antique washing tubs. The
inhabitants wore blue galabiyas and had the dignity of desert people with their elaborate courtesies.

There was trouble in paradise, though. On our second morning in town, we watched a fight on the main street, involving about fifty people. The police arrived, but the crowds lingered half the day. The dispute had to do with tomatoes. Someone from another oasis had apparently bought land near Bahariya, grown tomatoes, and sold them at a price that antagonized some of the locals.

When we first arrived, Hani and I had no trouble finding Ali's friend Mohammed. He was waiting for the bus, as he did every day. Mohammed was a schoolteacher, who took tourists around in order to augment his meager salary. (He made ninety Egyptian pounds a month, about thirty dollars.) It was blisteringly hot. We sat in the shade of a palm grove and ate *mish-mish* (apricots), which fell off the trees when Mohammed shook them. Water buffalo dozed in the rice paddies.

The way Mohammed viewed it, Egyptians thought about one thing: sex. It was an addiction, he said. However, sex between men had to remain hidden. You didn't want to be seen with people known for such proclivities, of whom there were six or seven in Bahariya. According to Mohammed, they walked up and down the main street at one or two in the morning.

Mohammed had never heard the word "gay" (which, to him, was synonymous with "male prostitute") and didn't know what "homosexual" meant either. Still, he admitted that many men in Bahariya, including himself, had sex with other men. His philosophy was one of homespun tolerance: "One person may plant rice, and the person with the field next to him may plant wheat."

Mohammed was a troubled person. He was twenty-nine, quite intelligent, and was well respected in Bahariya, but he worried about money and health problems; he had been complaining of dizziness for the last four months, but no doctor could figure out what was wrong. Mohammed described how, as a small boy, he had peered through a window and seen a woman masturbating. This made a tremendous impression on him. "I couldn't stop thinking about it for many years," he said.

He would never marry, he said, and it wasn't just because of the problem of money. There was simply no need. "Why buy a cow when there is milk in the shops?" he asked.

But sex in Bahariya was apparently not as readily available as Mohammed made it sound. Sometimes he resorted to sex with donkeys and sheep. In the desert, he said, that wasn't strange at all. In fact, he rather enjoyed it.

He seemed most interested in foreign women, though. "Would you write to a woman in Germany for me?" he asked. "She wrote me very nicely when she left Baharîya but she has not answered my letters." He immediately brought out paper and pen. The longer I stayed in Egypt, the more convinced I became that I could earn a living as a go-between for Egyptian men and their Western girl-friends.

Hani tried to bring Mohammed back to the subject of our interest. Couldn't he introduce us to one of those men who walked the streets at one in the morning? Or anyone else in Baharîya whom he knew to have sex with other men? Mohammed was reluctant. "I wouldn't know how to explain to them what you wanted, and they wouldn't talk to you," he said. "You must understand: In Egypt, everything about sex must be a secret."

We headed back to the main street of town. Everyone knew Mohammed. He stopped and greeted passersby. "Tomorrow, there are many things we can do," he said. "We can go to the white desert, to the gazelle area. We can arrange for you to go camping for a few days. There is an ancient tomb near here. It is never opened. But I can get a special permit."

We lingered in Baharîya a few days. The following night, at one A.M., while Hani was snoring in the next room, I stumbled out of doors for a walk down the main street in hopes of encountering one of the late-night strollers. The cafés and the falafel seller had closed up shop long before, and there wasn't a soul around. The stars were so close you could touch them, and it was perfectly still, except for the howling of a dog and the distant, scratchy whine of a phonograph record intoning a song of longing and passion. I took a couple of turns up and down the street and crawled back into bed. The desert kept its secrets.

Back in Cairo, against the odds, I met a lesbian. Hani had a class-mate named Methat who had a friend named Karima. And so it was arranged. "We know about her but she doesn't know about us," said Methat, who described himself as gay and had a long-term lover. We met at an outdoor café along the "Little Nile" in Manial, a haunt of university students and a place where men and women could sit together.

It was early evening when I arrived with Hani and found a table. Karima and Methat were there already, but it was fifteen or twenty minutes before they joined us. Karima was too embarrassed, Hani explained. Even when she and Methat finally sat with us, Karima giggled, laughed, joked nonstop. At each joke, she would slap hands with Methat in the Egyptian coffeehouse manner. It was the first time I had seen an Egyptian woman do this.

Karima was twenty-three and quite striking, with wide dark eyes. Her hair was neatly coiffed and she wore makeup and nail polish. Except for a pair of flaming red sandals, she was dressed quite properly, in a gray skirt and a long-sleeved white blouse. She had just graduated from university and was hoping to find a job teaching history. She lived with her parents and had seven brothers and sisters. Karima spoke no English; Hani and Methat translated, but this was not necessarily much help.

Hani had suggested that I proceed gingerly, and I did, although there really was no need. Karima was quite forthright.

Do you have a boyfriend or a girlfriend? I asked.

"My girlfriend is my sister," she said.

I was confused. Perhaps Hani's translation wasn't right. Or perhaps she was talking about sisterhood? But, no, in fact, as she confirmed, and Hani and Methat confirmed afterward, Karima was having a sexual relationship with her eighteen-year-old sister. They had apparently had sex for the first time after watching an American porn video.

There was more to the relationship than just sexual release, Karima insisted. She had been in love with a man who had died three years before, but now she said she was attracted exclusively to women. That was her true nature. Of course, she added, lesbianism in Egypt was a "secret."

I asked if her parents didn't want her to marry, and Karima responded with jokes, most of which had to do with her marrying *me*. In fact, pressure for her to marry didn't seem to be an issue, because her parents simply didn't have the money. She was free from such demands, at least for now.

It was impossible for a woman alone or two women together to rent an apartment in Cairo, Karima said, unless they had no family or their family was elsewhere. It was considered improper. Obviously, for her this wasn't a problem, because she and her sister shared the same roof.

Are there many lesbians in Cairo? I asked her.

"Many, many," she assured me. But a minute later, she conceded she didn't know anyone else.

It had been an unusual week—tales of sex with animals in Baharîya and, now, incest of the sisterly sort. The façade of sexual uniformity that Egyptian society presented to the world concealed some curious variations that to many Westerners might seem shocking and repellent. The more I thought about Karima, though, the less surprising her relationship with her sister appeared. In a world where the sexes were kept totally separate, where women couldn't rent a flat or go out to a restaurant together, where they were always under the watchful eye of relatives, the family circle, ironically, might be the place—perhaps the *only* place—where it was possible for a woman to have a sexual relationship with another woman. I had no idea how typical Karima was of other lesbians in Cairo. But there was a familial and familiar quality to same-sex relationships in Egypt—it was adolescent sex, it was "messing around" between friends and classmates and next-door neighbors—and perhaps between sisters, too?

I had almost forgotten my ten-dollar bet with Ahmed. I hadn't seen him since our evening at Wimpy's. Later, I heard that his wife had sent him an airplane ticket and he had gone off to England.

On my last day in Cairo, Hani and Methat dropped by my apartment. They brought along another friend, Walid, who was half Filipino and half Egyptian. Walid had graduated from university the year before, but couldn't get a job, primarily because he wasn't an Egyptian citizen even though he had lived in Cairo all his life. He spent most of his time playing chess and cards and reading Hemingway and Margaret Mitchell. Like Methat, Walid identified himself as gay.

We were waiting for Ali, who was supposed to return from his grandmother's funeral that afternoon. We ate melon, and everyone smoked cigarettes. The TV was on, as was always insisted upon whenever Egyptian friends came to visit.

As we waited, Methat and Walid talked a little about themselves. Methat had a lover with whom he rented a tiny room in Old Cairo for twenty Egyptian pounds a month; they would go there and have sex. He maintained that all gay men in Cairo had both male and female lovers. Both he and his boyfriend were involved with women. Methat had two girlfriends—one older and one younger—although it was unclear to me if their relationship was really sexual in nature. His boyfriend, also a student, was involved with the daughter of the *bawab* of the apartment building where he lived with his parents. "I'm gay," Methat said. "But I like girls, too. All Egyptian gays have girlfriends, too. Isn't it like that in America?"

When I said it wasn't like that, Methat seemed surprised.

"What about Walid?" I said. "Walid doesn't have girlfriends."

"But Walid is not Egyptian," Methat replied.

Walid did have a boyfriend, with whom he had been involved for eight years, since he was fifteen. They met once or twice a week for sex and occasionally took trips together. He insisted the boyfriend wasn't really gay. "He can't marry because he has no money," Walid said. "So he tries to find someone to have happiness with. In this country, there is a big difficulty about getting married. It is so expensive. This makes many people have homosexual sex. My friend is a normal man. But now, sex with men is a habit for him. It is in his blood."

Walid got up to make tea. Methat whispered to me, "His boyfriend is really gay. Don't believe him!"

The fact was that, even though Walid was their close friend and confidant, neither Methat nor Hani had never been introduced to Walid's boyfriend.

I turned to Hani. Wouldn't he like to have a boyfriend?

"I have a boyfriend now," he said. "My friend Ali."

I was quite surprised.

"I would go to the end of the earth for Ali," Hani said, gazing at me with those sad eyes.

"Ali teaches me English," he went on. "Ali is very good to me. Our families live next door to one another. We met when we were fishing. I have known Ali a long time."

Ali hadn't let on about any of this, although, when I thought about it, there had been some hints along the way. Was it just a question of spending weeks with people, of getting them to trust you, before you could finally discover a few of Egypt's secrets? And was one of those secrets that virtually every Egyptian man was bisexual? I had thought that was a cliché. Now I was beginning to believe it was a fact, and that sexuality in Egypt really *was* very different from sexuality in the West. I was curious, too, if Ali's wife, Caroline, had any inkling of what she was getting into.

How did you feel when Ali got married? I asked Hani.

"I felt bad," he said. "Because I lost Ali." In fact, Ali's marriage hadn't meant an end to their sexual relationship, which was continuing, albeit with less frequency. Typically, Ali had his schemes. He had suggested that Hani marry an American woman so both he and Ali could go to the States—with their wives. That way they could continue to be together.

"Is there any place in the world where two men can marry?" Hani wanted to know.

I mentioned Denmark.

"Gays can marry in Denmark!" cried Hani. "Let's go there!"

We stayed around all afternoon, drinking more tea, smoking more cigarettes, and watching thirties movies on TV, about the Egyptian upper classes. But Ali never showed up. My plane was due to leave the next morning at seven-thirty, and, long after I had given up on him, Ali arrived at my apartment. It was five A.M. He was clutching his wife's and mother-in-law's passports. He hadn't slept all night and seemed quite agitated. It developed that Caroline and her mother had arrived home from Luxor about the same time Ali had arrived from his family village, only to discover that the apartment had been broken into and Mrs. Morrow's clothes and jewelry stolen. Ali wanted to go to the airport with me, but had to go to the police station to report the robbery instead.

My clothes were laid out on the bed, ready to be packed, and I excused myself to take a shower. Over the sounds of rushing water, I could hear Ali rattling on about his week in the family village but mostly about his mother-in-law and this latest trauma. "How can I ever explain this to Mrs. Morrow?" Ali asked despondently. "She will never have a good impression of Egypt now."

Finally, my taxi arrived. "I know I will see you again soon," Ali said.

"Maybe in Libya," I joked.

"Yes, maybe in Libya."

When I got to the airport, I discovered that both my credit cards were missing.

3

HONG KONG
THE RED ARMY
AT THE DISCO

Virtually the entire population of Hong Knog was plotting their departure, even though July 1, 1997, was still years away. On that date Britain would turn over the Crown Colony of Hong Kong— the city that the travel writer Jan Morris described as "the busiest, the richest, and the most extraordinary of all Chinese cities"—to the government in Beijing. Although the Chinese Communists had solemnly promised to respect Hong Kong's capitalist system (and legislature and judiciary) for fifty years, no one quite believed them, especially since the People's Liberation Army had slaughtered pro-democracy demonstrators in Tiananmen Square. So everyone in Hong Kong who could afford it was trying to obtain a passport, any passport, as insurance against the uncertainties of 1997.

I woke up my first morning in Hong Kong to eight articles in the daily *South China Morning Post* concerning passports, visas, and emigration. There was an ad for a condo development in Vancouver and a full-page promotion for Melbourne, "City of Gold." At the dock where the green-and-white boats of the Star Ferry transport a hundred thousand passengers each day across the harbor and back from Hong Kong Island to Kowloon (Hong Kong's Brooklyn, with a dash of Ghirardelli Square), a newspaper billboard trumpeted: FAMILY TIES FAVORED OVER SKILLS FOR VISAS TO CANADA. Stories were circulating about pregnant women going off to Canada, Australia, and the U.K. to give birth so their children would be eligible for foreign passports.

I had come to Hong Kong for a glimpse of what it was like to be gay in a predominantly Chinese city. Ninety-eight percent of Hong Kong's six million inhabitants are ethnic Chinese, as many as half of them refugees from the mainland. Once you get away from the central business district, on Hong Kong Island proper, and the apartment high-rises behind it that lead to the Peak, the city's much-vaunted international character all but vanishes. Off the main shopping streets of Kowloon across the harbor and in the concrete-block suburbs of the New Territories, you rarely see a Western face; in the less expensive restaurants, waiters dusted off English-language menus that looked as if they had been moldering in some drawer for years. Hong Kong's status as the last British colony in the East doesn't signify much, either. During my first few days in Hong Kong, I didn't lay eyes upon a single representative of the late empire, save for the statue of George VI in the Zoological and Botanical Gardens. Finally, in a downtown bookstore, I heard a patrician voice ask, "Do you knew where I can find the Jockey Club?" It was oddly reassuring.

Still, the longer I spent in Hong Kong, the more I began to feel as if I were in Shanghai in 1949 or Saigon in 1975 or (in view of the passport frenzy) Vienna in 1938. I was witnessing the collapse of a civilization. Collective action seemed fruitless, in view of the overwhelming proximity and power of China; the crown colony had little tradition of democracy or participation in civic affairs, anyway. It was simply a question of saving oneself. And the lives of Hong Kong's homosexuals, I soon found, were inextricably linked with the uncertain future of Hong Kong.

Gays and lesbians had as much reason for getting out as the rest of the population, if not more. The city's future rulers, the Chinese Communists, did not have a very good record on the subject of gay rights. Homosexuality officially didn't exist in mainland China; like divorce, premarital sex, and other so-called social ills, it was viewed as evidence of Western contamination. When I left for Asia, newspaper reports told of gays in Shanghai being arrested in one of the government's periodic sweeps, and forced to undergo shock treatments. There were rumors of disappearances of Chinese homosexuals. All this hardly inspired confidence.

As it was, Hong Kong didn't offer a very congenial environment for homosexuals. According to a legal code derived from the British, consenting sexual relations between adult males carried a maximum penalty of life imprisonment. (Following the British legal tradition, there were no laws punishing sex between two women.) Although Britain had reformed the sodomy laws at home, efforts at reform in Hong Kong had failed up till now—in part, some asserted, because of opposition from Beijing. Regulations forbade known homosexuals from being appointed to the civil service, irrespective of rank; if convicted of a homosexual offense, serving officers faced immediate dismissal. In the 1970s, the authorities reportedly kept a list of gay men; as recently as the early 1980s, police raided the colony's gay bars.

I had lunch at a Kowloon shopping arcade with Albert, a Chinese graphic designer of about thirty, and two of his friends who were visiting from London. His friends—a Hong Kong–born Chinese doctor and his Scottish lover—had arrived a couple of days before. All, including Albert, were suffering from the effects of food poisoning. They were eating congee, a local version of porridge, to settle their stomachs. I asked the doctor if he found Hong Kong different this time around. "Yes," he said. "The only subject anyone talks about is leaving."

After lunch, Albert and I strolled through crowded streets toward the Hong Kong Cultural Centre, the creamy brick building on the harbor that had been built to rival the Sydney Opera House but whose interior looked more like a Hyatt Regency hotel. The gay population in Hong Kong was barely a community, Albert said. Lesbians were totally separate and quite invisible; many were married. The gay movement was weak. "Chinese are shy, less willing to stand out in a crowd," he said. "Our way of handling a crisis is to keep quiet and hope that eventually a better day will come." Nonetheless, he thought, educated gay men like himself were less willing to remain in the closet than had been the case in the past.

Albert described what he called his gay family—a group of Hong Kong Chinese men who had all come out at about the same time. Two, including his friend the doctor, were exclusively attracted to Caucasians. The first became involved with a Swiss man and moved to Zurich; the doctor went to London for medical school and stayed. Another preferred Asian men; he now lived in Taiwan.

Albert, who was attracted to both Westerners and Asians, re-mained in Hong Kong. His current lover was a British-born archi-tect; they had been together for eight years. In Hong Kong, sexual taste was destiny.

Albert's parents were relocating to Los Angeles that summer and he planned to move with them. His lover would stay on in Hong Kong; he had the security of a British passport, and was earning fifty thousand dollars a year, a comfortable salary in Hong Kong. Albert thought that their relationship could weather the separation. He himself came from a family with ties to Chiang Kai-shek's Kuomintang, ousted from power on the mainland by the Commu-nists in 1949; he feared for his safety when the Red Army marched into Hong Kong. "If I could have my present life, I would stay in Hong Kong," he said. "It is a dreadful place. There is nowhere to go. The people are arrogant. They shout at each other. They spit on the floor. But I love it."

I had a hard time imagining Albert in Los Angeles. The idea of him—with his overly refined English and Sunday blue blazer and gray flannels—on Venice Beach or at a gay bar in West Hollywood seemed incongruous, even poignant. "I don't know how to drive," he admitted.

At the Cultural Centre, the two-week Hong Kong International Film Festival was in progress. Hong Kong was a city totally in-fatuated with the movies. Its film industry was the largest in Asia outside of Bombay; movie cameras and tripods were almost as ubiquitous on downtown streets as the portable telephone business-men ostentatiously carried on their lunch breaks. Albert himself was seeing five movies in two days at the film festival; when I first telephoned him, he told me he could only meet "between films."

All the movies Albert was attending had gay themes. In fact, the film festival featured eight gay-oriented movies altogether, ranging from *Common Threads,* the Oscar-winning U.S. documentary about the AIDS Memorial Quilt, to *Joan of Arc of Mongolia,* a German film about four Western women traveling across Asia on the Trans-Siberian Express who are abducted by matriarchal Mon-golian tribeswomen. The festival catalog touted this one as a "les-bian *Lawrence of Arabia.*"

Significantly, the films sold out in advance were the Hong Kong–

made films—and the gay films. Even a forty-eight-minute gay romantic comedy from New Zealand, *Beyond Gravity,* was booked for all three showings. An acquaintance of mine was so baffled by this that he insisted on telephoning the New Zealand consulate. "Did you buy a block of tickets for a film at the Hong Kong Film Festival?" he asked. No one at the consulate had any idea what he was talking about.

For each showing of the gay films (and they mostly seemed to be scheduled for the nine-thirty and eleven-thirty time slots, when children would presumably be at home in bed), you saw long lines of gay men winding up the stairs from the Cultural Centre lobby to the auditorium. "They are all closeted," I was told. "They think that because this is a government-sponsored festival, it is all right to be seen."

Hong Kong gays were positively starved for lesbian and gay culture—and for gay life in general. The major gay male social center seemed to be the public lavatories. In the entire city, there were two gay bars and two bathhouses; one of the latter was deep in the recesses of Kowloon. (Another ostensibly gay bar, called Waltzing Matilda, was of a dubious character and attracted a crowd that consisted of down-and-out expatriates and what appeared to be members of teenage gangs and their girlfriends.) There was no lesbian bar or meeting place.

The two major bars were located around the corner from each other on Hong Kong Island on the steep, fashionable streets behind the central business district. One of the bars, a snazzy place with a large dance floor and an international flavor, was called Disco Disco, although everyone referred to it simply as "the disco." There, on a crowded Saturday night, I met Philip, a twenty-three-year-old Chinese man who had returned to Hong Kong a few months earlier after six years in the United States, mostly in Albuquerque, New Mexico, but also at the prestigious Kennedy School of Government at Harvard University. He had a brother in Albuquerque, a sister in Vancouver, and another brother scouting out emigration possibilities in Australia. Philip was personable and enthusiastic. The world was still his oyster. After all, he had gone to Harvard, if only for a year.

Philip went to the disco every weekend. It was his only contact with Hong Kong gay life, except for the film festival. (He had bought tickets for all the gay films.) He was living with his parents, who didn't know he was gay. Philip had come out in Boston the year before—really the only year of his life when he had not been living with some relative. Now he was back in the family orbit once again. "In Hong Kong, people say you have to lead two lives," Philip told me. But he sounded as if he had convinced himself such restrictions wouldn't apply to him. He carried around a copy of E. M. Forster's novel *Maurice.*

One day I went along with Philip to a few job interviews at small financial-services companies downtown. The offices all looked identical—gray wall-to-wall carpeting and maroon couches, beige textured wallpaper, and fresh-faced men and women working behind glass partitions. One place, a currency-trading outfit, offered Philip a job on the spot. He took me walking around the city, speculating about what street names the Communist Chinese would change when they took over. "Queen's Road. That one will really have to go," he said. We wandered into a bookstore, where he spotted a copy of a new magazine called *The Emigrant.* The cover stories included "How to Help Your Fiancé Apply for Canadian Citizenship" and "Fiji Warms to Investors with Residence Permits, Passports." "Pathetic," he pronounced with that Harvard self-confidence. "Just pathetic." I suspected Philip, too, would be gone within a year.

As you gaze across the water toward Hong Kong Island from the Cultural Centre in Kowloon, 1997 seems far away. Bank buildings and concrete office towers and apartment high rises extend along the harbor; behind them, dominating everything, is the Peak, wooded and shrouded in mist. The harbor is full of tugboats and trawlers and ferries and cruise ships. By night, the scene is serene. The Hong Kong side is illuminated by neon advertisements for Japanese companies—Hitachi, Canon, NEC, Sharp; the flickering lights of the homes of the taipans, Hong Kong's elite, outline the Peak. In the bricked-in park next to the Cultural Centre, couples are embracing and teenagers are hanging out. Amid the lapping of waves, the smell of the sea and of prosperity, it is hard to believe that in those high-rise apartment buildings Hong Kong people are dreaming of Vancouver and Melbourne, maybe even Fiji.

One evening I took the ferry over from Kowloon, where I was staying, to the Hong Kong Island side to meet Julian Chan. Julian was the city's leading—some said, its only—gay activist. We met at the dock. Julian had just come from work and was dressed in a suit, with a company pin on the lapel. As we walked through the business section, deserted at that hour, toward the gay bars, Julian immediately assured me that he at least had no plans to emigrate. "When people ask me if I will go away," he told me, "I say, 'Look at Canada. Look at all the Chinese there! Look at Australia!' Here, I have a better opportunity to be successful in my career. Here, there is less competition. Also, because everyone is going away, there must be at least someone to stay here and do something for those who cannot go. Everybody is going away so there must be someone to stay here to watch, to keep an eye on the house."

Julian had taken on the role of guardian of gay Hong Kong. He was the president of the Ten Percent Club, the only gay group in the city. Twenty-eight, bright, and well spoken, he had been a hairdresser. Now he worked for a life insurance company, a profession that required him to take the long view.

He took me to Dateline, the gay bar just around the corner from the disco. (Just as everyone called Disco Disco "the disco," so Dateline was referred to simply as "the bar.") Dateline was located in a gloomy basement and tended to attract an older and less stylish crowd than the disco did. The bar was essentially segregated between Chinese and Westerners. In one room, Chinese who were with Chinese friends or there in hopes of meeting other Chinese sat at booths and tables; beyond a doorway, Westerners—and Chinese men interested in meeting them—stood around the bar. There were no women. Julian and I sat down at a table in the "Chinese" section. On weekends, he explained, people would go to the bar first and then, toward midnight, move over to the disco. The price tag for all this was twenty U.S. dollars in cover charges alone.

Historically, Julian said, the Chinese, like the Arabs, had no concept of heterosexuality or homosexuality. They believed that "sex is sex and love is love but marriage is marriage." In ancient China, a man married and carried on the family line, but there were many cases of men who had a male lover apart from marriage. "It was an easy life," Julian said. Then, Western culture and Christianity arrived, bringing concepts like "a love affair is no good, that marriage and love are the same thing."

In modern-day Hong Kong, under the twin influences of Victorian moralism and Chinese Communist puritanism, people had taken up the traditional Western notion that homosexuality was "dirty, nasty, evil," he said. As products of the culture around them, Hong Kong gays tended to believe this, as well. Their poor self-image and lack of awareness slowed down the adoption of a more affirming attitude. Only a small percentage of homosexuals in Hong Kong had been exposed to the ideas of gay and lesbian liberation; these were largely people who had studied overseas or had contact with foreigners in Hong Kong. Those who frequented the disco or the bar generally fell into this group, but they were still a small number. "If you go to the disco or the bar three or four times, you will see the same faces," Julian noted. "There are probably three hundred to four hundred people who go there. And that is such a small percentage of the number of gay people in Hong Kong."

The government, he said, estimated the number of homosexuals in Hong Kong at about thirty thousand to fifty thousand. But if one applied the generally accepted rule of thumb that homosexuals make up about ten percent of a given population, the figure would be more like six hundred thousand. Julian thought a more accurate figure was somewhere around three hundred thousand.

Whatever the numbers, where were they all? Julian assumed the men were "hiding at home" until they were desperate and would then make a foray to a public lavatory or perhaps a bathhouse. The women were just hiding at home, period. In crowded Hong Kong (in Kowloon, the average inhabitant had exactly nine square feet to himself), most gay men lived with their families. "Your friends are all around you," Julian noted. "Your colleagues are very close to you. If something is known, the news passes quickly. Mostly, people are afraid of their sexual orientation being known, so they try not to go to the disco or the bar. These places are known to outsiders. So you meet others at the public toilet, instead. A quickie. But what about the mental need? The spiritual need? You just keep it inside your heart. Closet! That is the word!"

In such a society, you couldn't talk about liberation or action— you could barely talk about getting together for a party. People were too frightened. "They don't even dare to go to the disco or to the bar," Julian said. "Just imagine how much more difficult it would be for them to come out, organize something, or fight for rights."

For men, parental pressure to marry was intense, especially when they reached their mid- to late twenties. Some, like Julian and the others who went to the bar and the disco, were able to resist. Living away from one's family made it easier to remain unmarried, so some Hong Kong gay men shared an apartment with a Western lover or with gay friends. But most didn't have the money to do so. And it was also hard to convince one's family that moving out was appropriate in a society where custom dictated that a son or daughter should stay at home until marriage, and sometimes after that, as well. Many gay men would find a girlfriend in order to pacify their parents. Some, the lucky ones, would find a young woman who knew they were gay and understood their predicament. But often a gay man wound up deceiving his female friend. "He will pretend he is in love with her and bring her home," Julian noted. "And some who surrender to the pressure will really get married."

He himself had left his family apartment at age eighteen to move in with a Western lover. Because he worked in Hong Kong proper at the time, and his family lived far away in the suburban New Territories, they didn't object too strenuously. He had been living on his own since. Julian had never told his parents that he was gay, and the previous year, when he turned twenty-seven, his parents began to pressure him to marry. They introduced him to a girl who had "traditional Chinese women's thoughts," he said—namely, that at a certain age one married. "With my parents' introduction, she started to go around with me, saying she quite liked me and quite liked my mom," he said. Julian tried to keep his distance. But his parents demanded to know how he could go out with her and then ignore her. He continued to see her until finally, unable to continue the charade any longer, he told her he was gay. "She got very surprised," he recalled. "She said, 'I thought you didn't like me. I had no idea you are gay. I thought you didn't like me!'" That revelation didn't end the young woman's interest in Julian. She would promise him, "I can heal you. I can correct you." Eventually, she gave up.

The way to to combat parental and societal pressure was to be firm, Julian insisted. First, you had to live by yourself, away from your family. Secondly, he said, you had to be sincere and honest and stand by your own principles. "I have my whole life ahead of me," he said. "I don't want to do something I don't want for my entire life. I don't think it is good for the girl. If I get married to her, I lie to her. If we have kids, it will create more problems. It gets worse and worse!"

Julian was leading the fight to repeal Hong Kong's sodomy laws and was optimistic. Public opinion had shifted since the early 1980s, when there was strong opposition to liberalization, he said. Eighty percent of those polled in a radio survey thought the anti-sodomy laws were too harsh, and a member of the Hong Kong Legislative Council had told Julian this was the logical time for reform. Nonetheless, there was always the Beijing factor. It remained unclear whether the Communist Chinese were actively opposed to law reform, as Hong Kong gay activists believed, and were putting pressure on the Hong Kong government to scuttle the idea.

The shadow of 1997 made law reform all the more urgent. "We need to get as many rights as we can before we fall into the Communists' hands," said Julian. "After 1997, it will be too late for us to make any changes." The important thing, he believed, was to organize now. Once homosexual relations were legal, gays would have more freedom to establish strong organizations and publish their own material; it would be easier for people to come out.

The problem was that, instead of galvanizing people, 1997 made them still more cautious, and made organizing more difficult. This reflected the situation in Hong Kong in general. At present, Julian said he couldn't find three people to sign their names in order to register the Ten Percent Club with the government, as required by law. Everyone was afraid that signing on behalf of a gay organization would make it difficult to obtain a passport or could have negative consequences once the Communists took power.

And homosexuals, like so many others in Hong Kong, were busily planning their escape routes instead of organizing for Hong Kong's future. It was relatively easy for gay men to leave, Julian thought; usually, they didn't have a wife and children, and they often had savings of their own. The conservative nature of Hong Kong society was almost as great an impetus to leave as the prospect of the Red Army arriving at the disco. "They all go away,"

Julian said mournfully. "No one stays here to fight for liberation."
He noted that his organization's first chairman had left for Canada,
and two other leading activists were trying to get out. "Even if
physically they are still here, their hearts are not here," he noted.

There remained Julian, the guardian, the watchdog. He attributed his activism to his tenacious character and to the fact he
had moved out of his parents' house when he was so young. The
lover whom he had moved in with was an American, from whom
he learned a great deal about being independent. "It helped my
character," he said. "I learned to have concern about my rights and
my space." At age twenty-four he had gone to England for a year
and had come into contact with the gay movement there. "I remember Gay Pride Day in London in 1986," he said. "We went to a big
park. There were speakers, singing, games. Gay men and lesbians
were talking happily. A policeman came up and put his arms
around a few people. I thought, 'This is how the world should be!'
Then I thought about Hong Kong and I got very sad. I thought I
must go back, do the best I can do."

Was Julian afraid for his own safety after 1997? He had been on
radio and television talking about gay rights, although always with
his voice disguised and his picture in silhouette. But he noted that
when he went to lobby legislative councilors, he had to put his name
down in writing. Tapes existed of his radio and TV interviews. "If,
after 1997, there are some secret police interested in rounding up
gay people, they can very easily get me," he said. "Sometimes, I
think about that, too. But, on the other hand, think about all those
students who got away from China after Tiananmen Square. And
they were facing tanks and guns!"

The Chinese characters that spell out "crisis" mean "danger"
and "chances," he noted. "With the crisis, there are hidden opportunities, too. There is no rush to go away."

There was crisis in the air of Hong Kong, and fear and panic and
passport frenzy, but there were visions, too. "Just think of it—a
hundred million gay Chinese!" rhapsodized Sam Sasha, over tea in
a Kowloon restaurant. "Ten percent of the population. We could
have our own People's Republic." That's the way the future begins,
I thought—with a dreamer.

Sam had studied at the University of Texas and in Germany,

where he had been exposed to Western notions of homosexuality. By day he worked for a financial-services company; by night he wrote movie criticism. He had also written a book called *25 Questions About Homosexuality* and another that was a compilation of Chinese historical documents about same-sex love. "I want to be the Magnus Hirschfeld of Hong Kong," he said, referring to the gay sexologist of Weimar Germany.

Of all the gay men I met in Hong Kong, Sam was the one who professed the greatest attachment to mainland China. He considered himself a socialist, although a democratic socialist. Like Julian, he was determined to stay in Hong Kong. "I can have more influence by remaining here and writing in Chinese," he insisted.

He had begun to collect his historical documents because he felt that gays "were being treated as animals, not as humans. The reason was because we have no history. So I wanted to study gay history." He found accounts of scholars who preferred members of the same sex, of "a street during the Manchu dynasty that was like a gay ghetto," of male brothels, and of operas where men played women's roles. He blamed nineteenth-century Western missionaries for bringing to China the view that homosexuality was immoral. "We adopted Western values and denied our past," he said. "Chinese gays are the victims."

Like Julian, he viewed contemporary Hong Kong as a big closet. "We are geographically blocked," he said. "There is simply nowhere to be anonymous. You can't drive to Shanghai like you could in the 1930s." Some of the symptoms of the closet were letters he had received after his books was published. One reader wrote to Sam using his left hand, so his script couldn't be identified. Another letter was composed of Chinese characters cut out of a newspaper, for the same reason.

"Here there are no choices, no alternatives.," he said. "All there is to do is to get drunk and cruise." As for AIDS, Hong Kong Chinese thought it was "only happening out there. They believe it is only the white man's problem." In public lavatories, men were still having unsafe sex.

In the public lavatories, too, the police were harassing and humiliating gay men: "They will come in and ask you, 'What are you doing here?' You say, 'Pissing.' And the policeman looks at you and says, 'Piss for me.' You say, 'Shitting.' The policeman looks at you and says, 'Shit for me.' "

Sam had traveled widely in China and had many contacts there. Gays on the mainland were totally cut off from the world. "All they know about being gay is a character they might see on *Dynasty*, if they can get Hong Kong TV," he said. On the mainland, if you weren't married by the time you were thirty, you were viewed as having a "personal problem." Parents and neighbors would force you to marry. That didn't only happen in China, of course. "It happens among lower-class families in Hong Kong, too," Sam said.

He was giving a lot of thought to how to "introduce" the concept of gayness to the mainland in a way that the Chinese could accept. "Gay liberation doesn't just mean having sex with everyone of the same gender," he said. "It doesn't just mean bars and saunas. We have to find our own Chinese way of gay liberation." Someone needed to write a gay *Das Kapital*—a book that would look at homosexuals in the light of Chinese history and the contemporary Chinese economic and political situation.

Gays could contribute to China in a number of ways, Sam thought—by helping to reduce the population, for instance. In terms of population control, homosexuals could become "the queens of modernization," he contended. "Chinese gay people could come out and use their energy positively for the benefit of society, instead of resisting or fighting pressure all the time. Chinese gays are like the Jews were in Nazi Germany. They are prevented from using their energy for the good of society."

Sam returned to his vision of a hundred million homosexual Chinese—gay Manchus and gay Muslims and gay Tibetans. "We don't need a bar, we don't need a disco, we just need a normal life," he said. "I have hope. When I am old and in a wheelchair, gay people will be marching from Hong Kong to Beijing!"

Sam drew me a map showing the public lavatories where gay men cruised and had sex. "If you want to understand gay life in Hong Kong, that is where you will find it," he said. Taking his advice, I wandered into one of the designated spots, but found nothing. I stuffed the map into my pocket and figured I'd stick to the bar and the disco.

On the evening of Easter Sunday, when most Hong Kong homo-sexuals were with their families or perhaps getting ready for the late-night showing of an American gay movie, *Fun Down There,* at the film festival, I headed off to see if the disco or the bar might be open. There were no signs of life. It was a warm night after a rain and I sat down on a bench, opposite the Beverly Hills Deli and the California Restaurant. Perhaps the disco might eventually begin to stir. As I was waiting, a young Chinese man dressed in jeans and a black polo shirt joined me and struck up a conversation. His name was Tom. He was in his early twenties, lived with his family, and worked at the university. He seemed thoughtful, a little introverted perhaps, and spoke the best English of anyone I'd met in Hong Kong. Did I want to take a walk? he asked.

We climbed toward the Zoological and Botanical Gardens, past expensive shops that sold Persian carpets and Chinese vases. The windows of one building were floodlit. "They are trying to make it look like daytime," Tom said. "This is where they make movies. It's Hong Kong's Hollywood." Tom described his taste in food—he liked Thai cuisine—and music—he went for everything but hard rock. He had grown up in Hong Kong, spent his high school and university years in Toronto, and had returned home two years ago.

We walked for a while in silence. In the Zoological and Botanical Gardens, the trees were glistening after the rain. Pink flamingos strolled on the lawn.

"Has it been hard being back in Hong Kong after all those years in Toronto?" I asked.

"No," he said. "Well, actually, yes."

As we started back down the hill, he began talking rapidly and excitedly. He had been living a double life, he said, trying to hide from his family, his friends, and, above all, from his girlfriend. At work, he made sure to avoid gay people, who might have seen him near the bar or disco; he feared that talking to them might give him away. He couldn't introduce his gay friends to his girlfriend. "What would I say? 'This is my Canadian friend'? 'This is my New Zealand friend'? What would she think?"

Was he attracted to men and women equally? I asked.

"I am exclusively attracted to men."

His girlfriend knew he wasn't serious about her, but she still had hopes. Meanwhile, his family's emigration papers for Canada were being processed. He would be back in Toronto soon enough.

When he had lived in Toronto the first time around, it had been the same, he said—public girlfriend, secret boyfriends, his family, keeping one part of his life shielded from the other. I mentioned that in Toronto, it was rather easy to be openly gay. "But what makes you think I want to live like that?" he asked.

Would he marry?

"If I stay close to my parents, I will," he said.

By now we had reached the bottom of the hill, and were back in the central business district. There were people on the streets. As we turned the corner onto Queen's Road, Tom abruptly changed the subject and started telling me about his trip to New Zealand. He looked at his watch. "I have to catch my train," he said. Without so much as a good-bye, he was gone.

I wandered back up the hill toward the disco, half hoping I'd run into Tom again. With his combination of Western knowingness and Chinese family loyalty, he seemed in many ways to sum up the contradictions of gay Hong Kong. Then I remembered the map in my pocket. I turned up a side street and found myself facing the public lavatory. Inside, there were two neat, clean rows of toilets, perhaps ten on each side, and a strong smell of disinfectant and after-shave. Two or three men, young and well-dressed, paraded up and down, as if the lavatory were a bar. No one spoke. A few men sat in stalls, waiting. That was the geography of gay Hong Kong, I thought: bar, disco, public lavatory. I washed up, combed my hair, trying to look as if I belonged there. That subterfuge exhausted, I prepared to leave. As I approached the door, I nearly knocked over another man who was coming in. I excused myself. It was Tom. He nodded vaguely, as if I were someone he had passed on the street once, not the person to whom he had been telling the intimate details of his life ten minutes earlier. I turned around to speak, but he didn't pay me any mind. He was heading for the stalls.

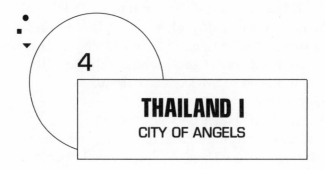

4

THAILAND I
CITY OF ANGELS

Bangkok

I was sitting around the downstairs lounge of the gay baths in Bangkok, reading *The Great Gatsby*. The Babylon sauna had a terrific library of books in English: Fitzgerald, Henry Miller, Gore Vidal, Doris Lessing, and Plato. I was wearing only the gray-and-black robe given to me by the attendant and waiting for Noi, a Thai real estate developer, and Paul, his American-born lover, to arrive. Thai men, mostly in their twenties, filed past on their way to the changing rooms. A few *farang,* as Westerners are called in Thailand, filed past, too. It was the gay middle class of Bangkok at leisure on a Sunday afternoon.

In *The Great Gatsby,* the characters were talking about golf; on the Babylon stereo, Louis Armstrong and Ella Fitzgerald were singing "Gee, Baby, Ain't I Good to You." The lounge walls were decorated with traditional Thai scroll art; the chairs and couches were made of rattan; sculptures of Buddhist mythological figures adorned teak end tables. On the floor-to-ceiling bookcase, next to all those great works of literature, were a television, a VCR (*Road Warrior,* with Mel Gibson, was promised for the evening), stacks of a Thai magazine called *Hi-Class,* and a pile of issues of *Architectural Digest.*

The Babylon itself looked right out of the pages of those magazines. Occupying four floors of a converted Art Deco town house in the part of Bangkok where the wealthy lived behind high walls covered with bougainvillea, Babylon was the closest thing to a designer bathhouse that I had ever seen. I had been a little surprised when Noi—a friend of a friend of mine in Boston—suggested we meet at the Babylon. When I arrived, I realized it made sense. The Babylon was one of the few gay establishments in Bangkok where the commercial sex trade was not in evidence. There was plenty of sex available at the Babylon—in the cubicles and mazes on the third floor and in the dark and crowded steam room (which was named "Gathering Essence"). But the bathhouse was as much a social meeting place as a sexual one and it was suitably elegant for the reception of foreign guests.

The real triumph of the place was the roof garden. Filled with potted plants and flowers, it was open to the sky and overlooked the lush grounds of the Austrian Embassy. There, you could eat dinner on marble-top tables and drop your crumbs on parquet floors. The food was superb: American-style barbecued chicken, fish from the Bay of Siam, and Thai stir-fry. Moreover, the roof garden offered the only cool breeze I encountered in Bangkok, a city where the temperature climbed daily to ninety-five degrees Fahrenheit and the humidity was suffocating.

The Babylon was an oasis of sorts. I met two Dutch tourists who claimed they came there each day as soon as it opened to enjoy the breeze and to get some relief from Bangkok. For Bangkok wasn't the most pleasant city in which to spend time. Besides being hot and humid, the Thai capital was noisy, congested, and polluted. Every major artery was constantly clogged with six lanes of traffic—cars, buses, trucks, motorbikes, motorcycles, and little three-wheeled taxis called *tuk-tuks;* at most hours of the day, the only way to cross the street was by an overpass. The Thai name for Bangkok, Krung Thep, means "City of Angels," but in comparison, that other City of Angels, Los Angeles, seemed a pedestrian's paradise. Bangkok smelled of satays and curries mixed with exhaust.

Thailand was enjoying one of the highest growth rates in the world—more than twelve percent the year I visited—and the number of cars and pickup trucks in the country had tripled in three years. There was so much construction going on that cement was in short supply. The infrastructure, which had been created for the capital of a remote kingdom, not a booming world-class city, hadn't caught up. The Thais themselves seemed unfazed, however. They walked around impeccably groomed, emerging from crowded, airless buses in perfectly ironed clothes, radiating Buddhist calm and equanimity. The entire time I was in Bangkok I never heard a raised voice or a heated argument.

When Noi and Paul finally made their appearance, they looked particularly well-groomed and meticulous. They were, after all, rich. Noi's father was a high-ranking military official, in a society where the military had great influence and privilege. It was hard getting accustomed to seven servants, Paul confided without irony. Paul, who was in his mid-thirties and hailed from Minnesota, was blond and affable and openhearted. He had met Noi when the latter was studying in the United States, and had returned with him to Bangkok. I wasn't sure what Paul did for a living, if anything; when I asked him, he changed the subject. Noi worked for a large commercial real estate development company. He was muscular and appeared to spend most of his free time strapped to a Nautilus machine. He was very proud.

"Homosexuality has a low valence in this society," Paul said. "In Thailand, the difference between homosexuality and heterosexuality is like the difference between rock salt and table salt." The three of us were sitting in the lounge in our identical robes, savoring our ice teas and the air-conditioning. Friends of Noi and Paul stopped by our table to say hello. Ella and Louis had given way to Ravel's *Daphnis and Chloé*. Paul continued to expound. Homosexuality wasn't talked about much, mostly because Thais were reticent about their private lives, he said. Back in Minnesota, Paul's parents didn't talk about his sexual orientation because they were ashamed; here, Noi's parents didn't discuss it either, but for another reason: To do so violated conventions of privacy. When Noi had returned to Thailand with Paul in tow, Noi's mother put her arms around both of them and said, "Welcome home, my sons."

The two men painted a picture of a society accepting of homosexuals and homosexuality, buttressing their contention by naming prominent people who they said were "openly gay"—two former prime ministers and a speaker of the house, actors, actresses, business leaders. But to them, the expression "openly gay" had a different significance than I was accustomed to; it primarily meant having one's initials listed in a newspaper gossip column. That had been Noi's experience. "The newspaper also included the name of my company, so everyone knew," he said. It hadn't affected his career in any way, however. He mentioned an incident some years back when a candidate for political office tried to make an issue of the fact that the prime minister was gay. The English-language *Bangkok Post* published an editorial denouncing the politician for bringing up the subject. After the prime minister left office, Noi said, the king appointed him to his privy council, his closest circle of advisers, essentially granting him the royal imprimatur.

Noi had been first in his class at one of the country's leading schools, Paul told me. That fact made him an object of respect. At the same time—and this was the only negative aspect of being gay, Paul added—Noi was no longer close to his school chums and at the same time was somewhat distant from the people he worked with. He didn't join in group gatherings, which invariably included dinner followed by a visit to a (heterosexual) massage parlor. Noi insisted this was not because of prejudice on the part of classmates or colleagues. It was just that he didn't want to accompany them to the massage parlor, so he was less than eager to get involved in the eating and drinking that preceded it. "I wouldn't invite them to a gay bar," he noted.

Then it was back to a Who's Who of gay life in Thailand. Did I know, Noi asked me, in a voice that sounded more like a challenge than an imparting of information, that the wife of the crown prince had recently attended a party given by a Bangkok transvestite, a fact that was dutifully reported in the society gossip columns? "Where else in the world could that happen?" Noi demanded.

I was becoming increasingly restive under this public-relations barrage. So when Noi announced he was going off to the gym and Paul to the steam room, I was quite content to wander up to the roof deck. There, the Dutch tourists were eating fish and drinking beer. The Dutchmen, both computer programmers, had been to-gether for twenty-five years. One was quite fat. The other, who looked like a marathoner by contrast, had grown up in Indonesia during the days when it was a Dutch colony; he was on his way there to search for his roots. I related my conversation with Noi and

Paul. "Sex, yes," said the heavyset one. "But the real sign of gay liberation is whether gay people can be in a couple together and live together. I don't see that in Thailand."

The heavyset man knew how to enjoy life—and Thailand. Thai men would come up to him in the corridors of the Babylon and grab at his enormous belly, amazed that such an anatomical marvel existed. At age fifty, he was delighted at all the attention. "Do you know the bar My Way?" he asked me. "We were there last night. I paid for this lovely boy. It was wonderful. And the dancers were wonderful, too."

A few nights later, I found myself at My Way, in the heart of Patpong, the "sex tourism" district of Bangkok. Young men in briefs with numbers pinned on them were go-go dancing on a raised stage in the middle of the bar. The stage had three firemen's poles. As part of the act, the performers shimmied up the poles, sometimes hanging across the stage, grabbing one pole with their hands and another with their feet. It was part acrobatic dance, part sexual come-on. While some of the other gay bars in Bangkok offered nudity, even onstage sex acts, by comparison the entertainment at My Way was tasteful and restrained.

Several "barboys" wearing robes stood off to the side, ready to take their turn onstage; still others, whose talents apparently lay elsewhere, sat along the wall in jeans and flowered shirts. My Way had the reputation of having the handsomest boys in Bangkok. Most appeared to be somewhere between eighteen and twenty-two. One gay guidebook described the employees at My Way as "collegiate," and indeed the atmosphere at the bar was a little like that of a fraternity house. Out in the audience, well-heeled, mostly older *farang* watched admiringly from their tables; some were regulars, others tourists fresh from a morning at the Floating Market or a bus trip to the River Kwai.

My Way was essentially a brothel. If a customer wanted to have sex with one of the barboys, he made arrangements with the bar captain. Rooms upstairs were available for liaisons, or, if he preferred, a customer might take the boy back to his home or hotel. The bar charged a hundred and twenty baht—about six U.S. dollars—for each transaction; boys expected a tip of somewhere between three hundred and five hundred baht, depending on customer satisfaction, and sometimes demanded as much as a thousand.

If sex in Egypt was elusive, the same could not be said of Thailand. The sex trade had long been a feature of Thai culture. One recent survey found that seventy-five percent of Thai men patronize prostitutes. Over the past thirty-five years, Bangkok had increasingly acquired a reputation as the Asian center of "sex tourism" (read: prostitution, mostly heterosexual, aimed at the international market). International sex tourism in Thailand began after Japan banned prostitution in 1958 but received its biggest boost from the Vietnam War, when American GIs would make the short hop from Saigon to Bangkok for rest and relaxation. These days, Bangkok sex tourism attracted not only Germans, Scandinavians, and North Americans, but also large numbers of Japanese and Taiwanese, to say nothing of the Thais themselves. From five hundred thousand to a million young women were estimated to be engaged in the sex trade in Thailand. And despite rising numbers of cases of AIDS and apocalyptic predictions of HIV spread, prostitution continued to flourish.

Gay sex tourism was not as developed. The Thai Ministry of Public Health estimated that some four thousand to five thousand men were employed as prostitutes, including some fifteen hundred in establishments like My Way. (This estimate of the number of male sex workers came from the ministry's HIV testing program.) The first gay bars were established in the early 1970s, an outgrowth of heterosexual sex tourism. Since then, there had been a veritable explosion in the number of gay bars, up from twenty a few years before to sixty when I visited. With only a couple of exceptions, all featured male prostitutes, the barboys.

In a country that was still underdeveloped despite the prosperity of the last few years, the government saw the influx of sex tourists as an economic asset. An additional reason for the increase in gay sex tourism, in particular, was that in Thailand, sex between men traditionally did not carry the same stigma it did in the West. The country had no laws against same-sex activity. Unlike other countries in Southeast Asia, Thailand had never been colonized by European powers, so the antihomosexual influence of Christianity had failed to take root. Buddhism, the religion of ninety percent of the population, never actively encouraged the persecution of homosexuals.

As a result, gay travel services organized tours to Thailand, and gay-oriented guidebooks extolled the country. One book aimed at the gay male tourist, *The Men of Thailand (Noom Thai),* instructed the reader in a variety of Thai phrases ranging from "I like your smile" to "Please use a condom" and offered a number of suggestions, such as forgoing meat and dairy products for a couple weeks before arrival to prevent potential Thai sex partners from finding one's Western odor "offensive."

Books like *The Men of Thailand* put forth the notion that Thai prostitution was somehow different from prostitution in the West, that Thai "working men" were actually incurable romantics, proverbial whores with hearts of gold. "To the Western man," the authors of *The Men of Thailand* wrote, "it may seem foolish that a working man would get involved with a foreigner—and vice versa. Yet when the carefree tourist returns to the bar where they met, his Thai friend immediately comes to sit beside him, with awesomely beautiful eyes and big yim [smile]. It is then [that] the gay tourist may also uncomfortably recognize those mounting waves of emotion. Even the suspicious and cynical might dare to be soft-hearted, faced with such affection." An acquaintance who had spent much time in the Far East insisted that the Thais viewed prostitution as an extension of "hospitality." And back home, one American who had spent a few days with a Bangkok barboy recounted how the barboy accompanied him to the airport at his departure and burst into tears.

Some of this seemingly relaxed attitude toward sexuality in its many variations—heterosexual and homosexual, commercial and noncommercial—had to do with the easygoing nature of Thai culture. Unlike China and Japan, Thailand is generally described by social scientists as having a "loose," or relatively permissive, culture. In the case of homosexuality, however, it was a mistake to confuse looseness and permissiveness with acceptance. Nukul Benchamant, the editor of *Neon,* one of five glossy gay-male monthlies published in Bangkok, put it this way: "Thai people have adopted the beliefs of Buddhism for thousands of years, in their breath, their soul, and their mind. They have been taught to be peaceful, kind, generous, not to be aggressive or to scold or to curse. They might think homosexuality is bad, but they won't criticize it. Still, a relative or parent might tell you it is not a good thing. They might say *kathoey* [transvestite] is bad, for example, but the point is they won't say aggressively or directly that you are bad because you are gay."

Traditionally, the concept of gay or lesbian identity had never really existed in Thailand. The dichotomy between gay and straight was something new and far from universally accepted. As in Egypt, it was hard to determine who was heterosexual and who was homosexual; at least for men, bisexuality seemed commonplace. In his book *Male Homosexuality in Thailand,* the Australian sociologist Peter A. Jackson suggests that traditional Thai culture had no concept of homosexuality beyond that of transvestism. There were two roles a man could play—that of the "complete man" (in Thai parlance) or the *kathoey* (transvestite). The "complete man" always took the insertive role in sex and never considered himself homosexual, even if his primary, or even exclusive, attraction was toward other men. A *kathoey* always took the sexually receptive position. (The terms "king" and "queen" were also used to denote "active" and "passive.") To this day, in the villages, "marriages" were said to exist between "complete men" and *kathoey*s.

In contrast to Egypt, today a Western notion of gay identity (and, ever so slowly, lesbian identity) was beginning to make an impact on the younger Thai generation. This concept of identity had nothing to do with transvestism. There was "a change of consciousness," even an "anti-*kathoey* feeling," among the Bangkok gay middle class, according to Eric Allyn, the coauthor of *The Men of Thailand,* who lived in Bangkok and was an insightful observer of Thai gay life. Relationships between men that did not mirror the traditional "complete man"-*kathoey* model were becoming more common. If gay identity—as distinguished from simple homosexual behavior—was socially constructed, as some theorists argue, that social construction seemed to be taking place in Thailand. Contact with Western gays—not only sex tourists, but also visiting gay activists and men like Allyn who lived in Bangkok—had helped bring this about. Interestingly, so did Western imports like gay male pornography. Eric Allyn argued that gay male porn videos had taught Thais that the same person could be both sexually "active" and "passive." He believed such videos helped foster more equal relationships, breaking down the rigid dichotomies between "king" and "queen," "complete man" and *kathoey*.

But in the Buddhist kingdom that was Thailand, hierarchical values persisted, despite the veneer of democracy and development. Allyn believed that the widespread prostitution in Thailand might be a leftover from a more traditional worldview. "The traditional patronage system," he said, "was to associate yourself with a figure of higher social or economic status. Prostitution is the last vestige of this." That, he thought, was why villagers often approved of sending their daughters to Bangkok to become sex workers. Perhaps it also helped to explain why what passed for gay life and gay community in Thailand so often involved the unequal relationships of prostitution, instead of the more "democratic" couplings that flourish in the West.

The bars—gay and straight—that cater to Western sex tourists are mostly located between between Silom and Surawongse roads, in a several-block area known as Patpong, after the street of the same name. Patpong is the most international part of Bangkok, a fact that says much about Thailand's relationship with the West. Airlines like Qantas and Swissair have their offices there, and a number of expensive hotels, shops, and restaurants are within walking distance.

To some extent, Patpong manages to avoid the seedy feel of red-light districts in most other world capitals. It is difficult to ignore the touts who try to entice you inside the bars where women wearing G-strings dance on tables. And lest you forget where you are for even a moment, there are signs to remind you: "Supergirls" and "Thigh Bar" and "Cherie Massage and Body Massage: Hundreds of Pretty Girls Available to Service You. All Clean and Polite." But there are also Buddhist shrines, garlanded with flowers, on street corners and in parking lots, as well as signs that conjure up more innocent associations: DAIRY QUEEN, for example. Beginning at six in the evening, Patpong Road turns into a giant open-air shopping mall, where elderly ladies from Manchester and Melbourne haggle over hand-painted umbrellas and silk scarves and teak Buddhas, and where display tables of Calvin Klein shirts and Benetton shorts and fake Rolex and Cartier watches block the sidewalks so thoroughly that it is a wonder anyone makes it to the fleshpots at all.

Pushing through the crowds toward My Way that evening, I stopped to buy a fake Cartier watch from a street vendor. As part of the deal, I threw in my scratched American timepiece, with its broken second hand, which I had bought at a trendy shop in Harvard Square. "I like antique," the vendor told me. I paid him one hundred fifty baht, the price of a couple of beers at a Patpong bar.

When I arrived at My Way, a gray-haired, fiftyish Caucasian man from Montreal sat down next to me. He had been in the textile business in Hong Kong for twenty years and used to travel to Bangkok on business; he liked the place so much he'd moved here. His Thai lover was spending a few months at a Buddhist monastery. Although the Canadian was just a customer, he acted as if he had a proprietary interest in the place. He joked that he was the "father" to My Way's captain and to some of the barboys. The barboys were "ninety-nine percent straight," he informed me, as if this were a selling point. "They work here for a year or two, save up some money, marry, and forget they ever set foot inside My Way at all," he said. "They all have girlfriends." About fifty boys worked at My Way, although they weren't always at the bar, he explained. They might go off with a client to Pattaya, the beach resort south of Bangkok, or to Chiang Mai, the large city in the north. A successful barboy could earn more in a month than a physician could.

"What places have you been to in Bangkok?" he asked me.

"The Babylon," I replied.

He waved his hand dismissively. "You don't pay for it there. It is a different experience when you pay!"

Most of the boys at My Way came from the poor, rural northeast of the country, he said. He pointed in the direction of the young men standing along the wall in their flowered shirts. "I've had that one and that one and that one!" he announced, like a pasha showing off his harem. He called over one boy who had only been working at the bar a few days and put his arm around him. The boy, who couldn't have been more than eighteen, seemed ill at ease. Then, the Canadian pointed at a Chinese-looking boy who had just walked in the door. "His cock is this big," he said, indicating with his fingers. "You can't even get your mouth around it." The boy sitting with us, who didn't understand any English, smiled deferentially.

"What kind of boys do you prefer?" he asked me. "King or queen?" I tried to sound noncommittal. "Somewhere in between," I replied. He shouted in the direction of the bar captain. "Did you hear that? He wants a boy who can do everything!"

With that he excused himself and went back to his table, dragging the new boy and the Chinese boy along with him. He sat between them, his arms around both, beaming. A Frenchman at a nearby table approached the captain and motioned toward one of the boys standing against the wall. The captain called the boy over. Within seconds—and without a word being exchanged between them—customer and barboy were heading upstairs to the private quarters. As they passed his table, the Canadian—his arms still around the two boys—called out, "Regardes, mon ami! J'en ai deux ce soir!"

The show was starting. I went over to the bar and sat down next to some of the boys. One began to massage my shoulders. He then demanded forty baht. A young man in a denim jacket and blue jeans, who looked like a teen idol, leaned toward me. He pointed at my watch and at his denim jacket. "Trade?" he asked. When I told him what I had paid for the watch, he quickly lost interest.

I looked out at the stage where the dancers with numbers plastered on their briefs clambered up fire poles to a disco beat, at the tables where *farang* sat with with their arms around Thai boys who could have been their grandsons. Sex tourism was colonizing Thailand in a way the European powers never had. Still, the boys seemed to rise above it all somehow, like those crowds in their perfectly ironed shirts crawling out of buses in the ninety-five-degree heat. Hospitality? I doubted it. More likely, just commerce.

I wanted to look at the effect of the sex trade on the Thais themselves. So I got as far away from Patpong as I could. Someone suggested a bar called Moonstruck, located on a small *soi*, or side street, off Sukumvit Road, a forty-baht ride by *tuk-tuk* from Patpong. Most of Sukumvit was an upmarket, Westernized area, where signs in Thai and English offered custom-made suits in twenty-four hours and VD and AIDS testing day and night. But as you went further along Sukumvit toward where Moonstruck was, the English-language signs faded and the avenue was lined with furniture shops and tailors, most of which closed their heavy metal grates by six or seven at night.

At Moonstruck, Mr. Wut (pronounced "Vut"), the owner, showed me a photographic album of his "boys," a shopper's catalog really, his version of L. L. Bean or J. Crew. In the pictures, virtually all the employees were fully clothed. One photograph caught my eye: that of an engineering student who was working at Moonstruck to pay his way through university, or so Mr. Wut said. He was in a dress shirt and slacks and standing on the steps of a Buddhist *wat.* I tried to imagine a call girl in the States photographed for advertising purposes in front of St. Patrick's Cathedral.

Moonstruck was a cozy place, with decor intended to suggest the Oscar-winning film of the same name about an Italian-American family in Brooklyn. A series of moons was pasted on a large mirror on the wall, and everything was checkerboard—the floor, the tables, the border between the walls and ceilings. The place was furnished with couches of black imitation leather. On a shelf in the back were seven or eight gold-leafed trophies, with ribbons, that Moonstruck had won in "handsome boy" competitions to which the various gay bars sent contestants. Moonstruck had only been open six months, and Mr. Wut was still a little insecure about it. "Do you think it is too dark?" he asked me. I suggested it was. "I think that makes it sexy," he said.

When I first arrived at Moonstruck early in the evening, Mr. Wut wasn't around. "Mr. Wut is at Pih-zuh," a woman behind the bar told me. She led me bravely across the twelve-hour-a-day traffic pileup of Sukumvit Road to the local Pizza Hut. Mr. Wut was sitting alone, drinking Coca-Cola. He was about thirty-five, dressed in an open-necked shirt and khaki pants. He had large, doelike eyes and looked like a salesman of something innocuous and quite respectable—Toyota pickups, perhaps, or insurance. A waitress in blue visor, prim pink blouse with Pizza Hut logo, and blue skirt took our orders. The restaurant was full of Americans showing off the splendors of fast food to their Thai friends. At the next table, an older American couple—the husband in shorts (attire frowned upon by Thais), the wife chain-smoking cigarettes—were asking the manager for four Pizza Hut T-shirts as souvenirs. The woman who had guided me from Moonstruck across the avenue to Mr. Wut turned out to be a man.

Mr. Wut stressed that Moonstruck was different from the tourist-oriented bars of Patpong. In this part of town, the authorities didn't allow go-go dancing and sex acts onstage. Sukumvit was an affluent neighborhood with many important residents. The minister of education lived a couple of streets away. Here, a bar had to be quiet and unobtrusive. As a result, Moonstruck was predominantly a call-boy service; clients usually reserved boys in advance, by telephone. "We sell boy *di*-rectly," he said. Unlike Patpong, where employees might be hired for a variety of reasons—such as an ability to dance—at Moonstruck the most important attribute was physical attractiveness. Mr. Wut generally chose tall, brawny types. He was convinced these were what his customers preferred, for their novelty value, if nothing else.

Ninety percent of his clients were Thai, he said, with the remainder Taiwanese and Japanese. Almost no Westerners came to Moonstruck; they preferred Patpong's mix of souvenir shopping and entertainment, along with sex. Here, his customers were interested in sex, and sex only. Out of fear of being seen, many Thais wouldn't go to Patpong gay bars; even at Moonstruck, they would often wait outside in the car. "Thai people lose face if they go into a gay bar," Mr. Wut said. "They are ashamed." Many of these customers were, in fact, married men. "Deep in his mind he is gay, but he must marry," said Mr. Wut. "This kind of person may wait in the car, even let the captain choose a boy for him."

Another reason Thai men preferred a bar like Moonstruck to the bars in Patpong was that they believed it was safer. "Thai people are really scared of AIDS," Mr. Wut explained. "They think it comes from the foreigner. They don't want to go to bars that foreigners go to." He himself wanted to achieve a mix of fifty percent Thai customers and fifty percent *farang,* but conceded that wasn't realistic. If the numbers of Westerners patronizing Moonstruck increased, he would lose corresponding numbers of Thais.

The boys at his bar were between seventeen and twenty-five years old. They all came from up-country, usually from the impoverished northeast. While, according to Mr. Wut, about half the boys at Patpong bars were gay, he claimed that all *his* employees, by contrast, were straight. (A 1988 survey published by the Thai gay magazine *Morakot* reported that thirty percent of Bangkok barboys were gay, thirty percent straight, and the rest bisexual.) Mr. Wut had worked as a manager at My Way for a number of years and assured me he knew what he was talking about. "My Way was my school," he said. At My Way and other Patpong bars, he said, it was difficult to control the boys. There were so many, for one thing. Some worked just for fun; they might not show up for work when they were supposed to. At Moonstruck, the boys were more reliable, because their primary motivation was money, or a step up in the world. "They know there are many famous gays who could make you a model or a movie star," he noted. "They hope to meet someone like this."

Some of the boys were sexually inexperienced when they first came to work at Moonstruck. Mr. Wut used porn videos for instructional purposes, and sometimes the captain would be assigned to have sex with a new boy as a kind of initiation. Nonetheless, many of the boys were limited in what they were willing to do sexually. They refused to be the receptive partner in anal sex, believing it beneath their dignity. Only five percent were comfortable performing all roles, he said. Mr. Wut would "guarantee" to his customers in advance what each boy would or would not do.

As for AIDS, it wasn't a problem, he assured me. He required his boys to use condoms and told them to insist the customers do so as well, although it wasn't clear what a boy was supposed to do if the customer declined. Once or twice a month they were tested for HIV infection, Mr. Wut claimed. If he was aware that it could take six months or even longer for HIV infection to show up in a blood test, he didn't let on.

We finished our pizzas and returned to Moonstruck. Mr. Wut was constantly being called to the telephone. It was nine o'clock, and prime time. On the weekends, the bar was crowded, Mr. Wut said, but during the week most transactions were arranged over the phone. Many clients were regulars; they knew exactly whom and what they wanted. At a table across from us, a young Taiwanese businessman was entertaining one of the boys. The businessman, who owned a travel agency, wanted to take a boy back to Taipei to live with him. I asked Mr. Wut if the barboy he chose would work in the Taiwanese man's business. "No," he said. "He will be—how do you say?—like a housewife. Thai people are very good at taking care of others."

Mr. Wut introduced me to a couple of the boys. Neither spoke any English. Mr. Wut served as translator. Bob, the first boy, was tall, thin, and very shy. He was dressed in dark clothes, with his belt tied so tightly around his waist it seemed as if it would cut off all his circulation. The other boy, named Chit, was giving Mr. Wut a massage as we talked. He was tall and broad-shouldered—Mr. Wut's "type"—and wore jeans and a white T-shirt. Chit was one of the most sought-after employees, Mr. Wut said, a fact he attributed in part to Chit's very masculine appearance. Chit averaged ten clients a week, sometimes two per night. He appeared somewhat Caucasian, as well, which might have been part of his appeal. Bob wasn't as successful; he had only two clients a week.

Both Bob and Chit had come to Moonstruck from the northeast of the country. Chit, now twenty-one, had been a farmer. A friend had told him about the possibility of working in the sex industry in Bangkok, and it interested him—"for the money and the experience," he said. Chit had never had sex with a man before starting at Moonstruck; Mr. Wut sent him to a *kathoey* to initiate him into same-gender sex. When I asked him whether he preferred men or women sexually, Chit answered, "Fifty–fifty." Bob, on the other hand, had had sex with a male schoolteacher in his village before coming to Bangkok. He preferred sex with "a [female] virgin or a man." He was twenty and lived with a *kathoey* with whom he had been involved in a relationship. Now they were just friends. He said that he enjoyed the "feelings and emotions" of his work, although he never got involved with clients. For his part, Chit preferred customers who didn't "demand too much."

Both wanted to get out of the sex industry within a year and open small businesses in their hometowns. (Bob fantasized about a grocery store.) Chit was putting money away in the bank each month. For Bob, it wasn't so easy, perhaps because he had fewer clients. He was spending all his money on food, he said.

What did they do if they didn't like a customer? I asked.

"I do my duty," Chit said.

His boss beamed.

Neither Bob nor Chit would identify himself as gay. So I was surprised when one of the captains, a man named Rak, informed me that he was gay and had told his parents. His parents also knew what kind of establishment he worked in. "In Thailand, it is not like before," he said. "Now, everybody accepts." He was twenty-three and was sending part of his paycheck home each month for his sister's schooling. He noted that a captain didn't make anything resembling the kind of money the barboys did. (Captains didn't engage in sex with clients and thus didn't have the opportunity to receive tips.) He seemed bored with his work, which mostly constituted determining which employee met the sexual tastes of a particular client.

"What means 'moonstruck'?" asked Rak.

"It is difficult to explain," I said. "Something about being crazy for love, maybe."

"Ah, crazy for love," Rak repeated, uncomprehendingly.

As the evening progressed, Mr. Wut was able to relax a bit. By now, I had become his great friend. (I suspected that every *farang* was his great friend.) "Deep in his mind, the Thai doesn't accept homosexuality," he told me. "They say they accept, but they don't really." There were still "too many *kathoeys*" he said; *kathoeys* had a terrible reputation and lowered the dignity and esteem of gays in general. As a result of social attitudes, gay people tended to stay in the closet. So, although, in Mr. Wut's view, male same-sex behavior was "increasing" in Thailand, closeted behavior remained the norm, especially among his generation.

It was rare to find gay male couples in Bangkok, Mr. Wut asserted. Gay and gay couldn't live together, he said, even a gay "king" and gay "queen." "If two men walk down the street holding hands, people look at them strange," he said. "So gay couples must hide themselves." As a result of all this, gay men didn't go to the bars in search of a potential lover or couple relationship. "They come just for fucking, that's all," he said. Gay relationships were viewed as "second-class," another version of the concubines or "minor wives" still commonly kept by Thai married men.

There was another reason why gay relationships failed to flourish. "Gay men won't stay with one another," Mr. Wut said. "They always want someone new." He himself had been involved with another gay man until he discovered the man was seeing someone else. "I lose my face," he said, moving his hand up and down from his forehead to his chin. "I lose my dignity." Although this had taken place ten years ago, it had driven him into the arms of straight men ever since (although, in the Thai manner, they were apparently not *too* straight). "With a straight, I don't lose my face!" he said, becoming extremely agitated. A straight man might have sexual relations with a woman but could at least be relied upon not to get involved with another man. Mr. Wut had recently been in a relationship with a predominantly heterosexual man with whom he had made an agreement that the man could have sex with a woman once a week. That seemed to have worked out well for both.

"Do you know what means 'butterfly'?" he asked. "It is difficult to find a gay who likes only one man. They never stop with one, but fly on to the next. I have heard that in America this is not so, but in Thailand it is the way."

There was another side to the City of Angels, and to its gay life. I glimpsed it one evening at the Thai Red Cross Fair, a sprawling event that is one of the country's major outdoor festivals and attracts tens of thousands of visitors. The Red Cross Fair was really a twenty-ring circus, with singing, dancing, nightclub acts, and costume dramas all going on at the same time, to say nothing of restaurants, T-shirt sales, blood-pressure taking, and throngs of people of all ages promenading about. On one of the many stages at the festival, the White Line dance troupe was performing. As part of the dance, two men dressed in black, wearing grotesque masks and covered with white bandages smeared in red, are on the sexual prowl. A group of women, dressed as angels and holding condoms in their hands, try to ward them off. The men represent AIDS; the women symbolize Bangkok. The music in the background was the hit song "Krung Thep Mahanakorn."

One of the apparitions in black was a man named Natee Teer-rarojjanapongs, the founder, choreographer, and lead dancer of the White Line troupe. After the segment, Natee gave a short speech about AIDS. The AIDS dance was only a part of the White Line program, though. A quick costume change and the motif switched to country-and-western. Natee himself was the consummate showman. In one segment, he was dressed in white pants, lavender sash, tuxedo shirt, and red bow tie. In another, he was all glitz—black trousers and a woman's spangled top. Sometimes, he reminded me of a Thai David Bowie; at other times, he was the friendly, non-threatening boy next door.

Natee was also Thailand's first Western-style gay activist. "I am one of the few openly gay men in Thailand," he'd told me earlier that day as rehearsal was winding down at the White Line studio, a large room with a gymnasiumlike floor and mirrored walls, located upstairs from a Bangkok aerobics club. Natee was wearing a T-shirt that said, in English, AIDS KILLS. DON'T BE SILLY, PUT A CONDOM ON YOUR WILLY. At thirty-three, he had jet-black hair and boundless energy. In Thailand, the prevailing view, he told me, was that "gay is not so beautiful, so we should keep quiet. Coming out is brave. People want you to be straight. The reputation of the gay community is bad. People only think about *kathoey*. And now sex workers make a bad impression. People only think about *kathoey* and screaming and selling sex on the street. We are trying to give a different view that shows the public we are good-quality people who do good things."

Natee had lived for a short time in Boston, where he studied jazz dance, worked in the kitchen of a Thai restaurant on Massachusetts Avenue, and acquainted himself with some of the options available to gay people in the United States. When he returned to Thailand, he formed the White Line troupe. His aim was to fuse traditional Thai dance with contemporary jazz movement. The group, which was mixed gay and straight, started off by performing for a variety of charitable foundations—one for homeless children, for example. At the same time, Natee came out publicly as a gay man; his openness "shocked the media," he said. He wanted to show that "a gay person could do something for society." Soon after, he began to integrate dance and politics in another way. He started an all-gay dance troupe called Purple String to educate barboys and the gay population about AIDS and safe sex, using dance as the vehicle.

Despite Buddhism's surface tolerance, Natee concurred that many Thais were fundamentally uncomfortable with homosexuality. "Thai people are easygoing, but deep down there is a kind of discrimination," he maintained. "They don't hit you but they don't like it if you speak and rally." Still, he believed that Thais could recognize "good people," regardless of sexual orientation. "They might not accept homosexuality but they are not strongly against it," he said. "They can be persuaded if they perceive gay people are good people." While the major purpose of his dance troupes was AIDS education, Natee hoped that his efforts would help change how society viewed homosexuals. "If we deal with AIDS, we can help our society and we can gain recognition from straights," he said.

AIDS had come late to Thailand. At the time of my visit, the number of reported cases of AIDS was relatively low, at least by North American standards—45 altogether, with 145 others diagnosed as having AIDS-related complex. But close to 20,000 had tested positive for HIV, and government estimates of the number of HIV-infected individuals seemed to climb month by month—from 50,000 to as high as 300,000. There was talk of the numbers reaching 3 million by the end of the decade. Of the reported cases of full-blown AIDS, half were gay and bisexual men. But those who tested HIV-positive were overwhelmingly intravenous-drug users or heterosexual women. Gay and bisexual men made up less than one percent of the HIV-positive total. Testing of 98 customers at the Babylon sauna had turned up 3 who were HIV-positive—again, a relatively small percentage, compared to the scope of the epidemic among gay men in other countries.

These figures were somewhat reassuring to Thai gays because they indicated that Thailand was following the demographic pattern of Africa with its heterosexual spread, rather than that of San Francisco or Sydney. But the numbers reflected only those gay and bisexual men who had come forward to be tested. As for the clientele at the Babylon, the men there tended to be mostly middle-class and would be likely to have been informed about safe-sex practices. Many men who had sex with other men would never classify themselves as "gay." Consequently, it seemed logical that the number of HIV-infected gay and bisexual men was probably far greater than the figures might suggest.

In any event, there was a widespread perception that AIDS had reached a dangerous "takeoff point" in Thailand. The traditionally relaxed sexual mores and the widespread prostitution made the situation extremely worrisome. As a result, Natee had started an organization called FACT (Fraternity for AIDS Cessation in Thailand), in an attempt to educate gay and bisexual men—as well as prostitutes, male and female—about the disease. The group met every Sunday, published a newsletter (the gay bars advertised in it), and was planning to set up an AIDS hotline aimed at gay and bisexual men. Group members went out in "cruise squads" to the parks of Bangkok to offer pamphlets and condoms to the men who met male partners there but rarely, if ever, read a gay magazine or went to a bar or sauna where they might come into contact with safe-sex education. According to Natee, seven out of ten men who cruised the parks were now using condoms.

Natee had a larger vision that went beyond fighting AIDS to creating a close-knit gay community in Bangkok. One of the major barriers to the creation of that kind of community, he argued, was the sex industry itself. In addition to the phenomenal increase in the number of gay bar–brothels in Bangkok, there were now twenty such establishments in the seaside town of Pattaya, ten in Chiang Mai in the north of the country, and four on the island of Phuket. It was a "new trend to work in such places," Natee said. He feared such bars would "destroy gay society" and make it impossible for gays to be accepted by the larger community. Thai gay men were using barboys as a way of staying in the closet, instead of forming relationships based on mutuality, he argued. So he wanted to set up alternative social options. FACT was one such option.

Natee was the only gay person I met in Bangkok who dared to speak critically about the sex industry and the "disease, hurt, sex without emotions or feelings" it engendered. "Gay men want to be proud," he said. "They need role models. They don't want to be whorehouse keepers."

He wanted to start an educational campaign to make becoming a barboy in the capital less alluring to impoverished young men from the countryside. He had already given it a name—the "Deglamorize Project." Natee contended that barboys often got little in return once they became sex workers. "At first," he said, "it looks like a lot of money. But they wind up spending it on gambling and alcohol, instead of studying. Then, after three or four years, it is too late to study and they have ruined their lives."

He had introduced the concept of the "*kula* gay," the good gay. "*Kula* gay means to behave good, use the time to help society," he said. "It is against too much promiscuous behavior in the street. It is about not being stereotypical in your behavior."

The idea of activism—whether for gay rights or women's rights or human rights in general—was something quite new in Thailand. In the past, there had been only Buddhist social-work organizations. "The gay community never did good things," Natee said. "We need to be a community. We are starting to realize we need to come together. In two years we will be very strong. The gay scene is not just in the bars. We are ready to move the earth!"

Nonetheless, Natee believed that if gay Thais were perceived as being rude and aggressive in their quest for equality and recognition, it could be counterproductive. "You can't come out in the street," he said. "It won't work. You have to do things little by little. Being a good person has to come first. Then people will accept you as a gay person."

As much as he talked about making changes slowly, Natee's activism—and particularly his attitudes toward prostitution—had raised suspicion. He pointed to stitches on his face, the result of an altercation in which two bar owners had thrown an ashtray at him. He was concerned that as he spoke out about the sex trade, such incidents might be repeated. "I worry," Natee said, "that I might be assassinated."

A few nights later, I returned to Moonstruck. Mr. Wut promised to take me to a party, the opening of a new bar called the Hippodrome. He ordered a large bouquet of flowers, the traditional gift of bar owners upon the opening of a new establishment. He also chose one of his most attractive employees to accompany us, fitting him with a conservative cotton sport coat; openings of new bars often included the "handsome boy" contests in which Moonstruck had gained all those trophies.

At the last moment, Mr. Wut decided he couldn't leave Moonstruck after all. Things were just too busy. So he sent me off with Rak, the captain, and the young man who was to be the contest entry. When we arrived at the Hippodrome, far on the other side of town, we found a small, crowded room, furnished with a couple of couches. It was uncomfortably hot. Someone was up on the ladder trying, without success, to get the newly installed air-conditioning to function. Bar owners and barboys wandered in. The *kathoey* owner of Twilight, the most notorious bar in Patpong, whose show consisted of onstage sex acts, made a grand entrance. A representative from My Way showed up with more flowers. Mangoes and pineapples were offered around, but the handsome-boy contest was shelved because of the heat.

All in all, the evening was rather disappointing, not the splashy affair Mr. Wut had promised. It was just a group of older gay men, elaborately dressed *kathoeys*, and barboys sitting around sweltering. The man next to me introduced me to a *kathoey* sitting across the way. "Would you believe she is a teacher by day?"

What does she teach? I asked.

"Social studies."

The image of that evening remains fixed in my mind—barboys in sport coats and *kathoeys* who were teachers by day; mangoes and flowers; and the extreme heat. The gay bar scene in Bangkok did have its soft edges; prostitution here was "different" in its way. One certainly couldn't begrudge young men from the countryside coming to Bangkok and getting a job in the sex industry that paid as much as a doctor or university professor. But, in other respects, Natee's criticisms were accurate. The pervasiveness of the bar-brothel scene did seem to perpetuate closeted attitudes and unequal relationships, offering few options to younger gay men and assuring that older gay men remained "butterflies," moving from one "handsome boy" to the next. Behind it all lurked the specter of AIDS, despite the bar owners' protestations about regular HIV testing of employees, despite the fledgling efforts at safe-sex education.

Mr. Wut complained that Natee "is wanting us to be good gays, but gays in Thailand are not like that." Yet something *was* changing in Thailand. One could see the earliest beginnings of a movement away from the sex trade and toward community. "We are ready to move the earth!" Natee had promised. Six months later, when I came back to Bangkok for another visit, I learned some of the difficulties that moving the earth entailed.

5

THAILAND II
MR. MINAMI DANCES

Bangkok

When I returned to Bangkok to attend the Third Asian Lesbian and Gay Conference, the heat was more bearable, even though it was August. The concrete buildings seemed blacker from car exhaust than I had remembered, and the congestion even more horrendous. Teenagers in their school uniforms still dominated Siam Square in the afternoons—the girls in black skirts and white blouses, with gold pins in the shape of a sailing ship hanging from their collars; the boys in white pants and long-sleeved white dress shirts, and blue or red or green club ties.

On my first visit, I had amused myself by jotting down slogans on T-shirts the young people wore: CALVIN (as in Klein), DETROIT LIONS, ASK ME ABOUT FLORIDA, and HARVARD UNIVERSITY ATHLETIC DEPARTMENT. I immediately spotted a new one to add to the list: SPAM. In Siam Square, you could watch American major-league baseball games on a large outdoor video screen. *CNN Headline News* in English was now on Thai TV several times a day, although whenever I found it, the announcer was always in the midst of signing off. *Total Recall* and *Die Hard 2* were playing at the movies. For me, too, it was Bangkok: The Sequel.

I had realized something wasn't quite right when, up to the very day of my scheduled flight to Bangkok, I had no idea where the conference was to take place. I joked nervously that I knew the hour-by-hour schedule, which largely consisted of what the program referred to as "coffee brakes" *(sic),* but not the location. Finally, the morning before I was to leave for the airport, I received an express letter, postmarked Tokyo. It announced that the conference would be held at the YWCA in Bangkok. No address was given. The letter also provided the phone number of Natee, the dancer and activist whom I'd met on my previous visit. He and his organization, the Fraternity for AIDS Cessation in Thailand (FACT), were running things from the Bangkok end.

One of my purposes in attending the conference was to meet lesbians. I hadn't had much success contacting women on my previous trip to Asia. But when I climbed the stairs to the second-floor lounge of the YWCA on that first morning of the conference, I saw exactly one female face. She turned out to be a reporter for a Bangkok English-language daily called *The Nation.* Though sympathetic, she was quick to inform me she was not a lesbian. As for the men, there were as many Caucasians as Asians. The program had listed workshops on a number of Asian nations—including South Korea, Taiwan, Hong Kong, and Malaysia—but their representatives were nowhere in evidence.

I greeted Natee, who didn't seem to remember me, and then introduced myself to a gray-haired Japanese businessman in a white suit. He was Teishiro Minami, to whom I had sent my fifty-dollar registration fee a month earlier. "Ah, Mr. Miller," he greeted me. I was relieved. Mr. Minami, at least, knew who I was. He then proceeded to inform me that my money order couldn't be cashed at a Japanese bank. Would I mind handing over the fifty dollars in cash? Reluctantly, I agreed. I reminded him that I would be coming to Japan soon and hoped to meet with him and members of his organization. Mr. Minami looked at me blankly (he spoke little English), gave me his card, and returned to writing the agenda on a chalkboard.

Mr. Minami's organization, ILGA/Japan, the Japanese section of the International Lesbian and Gay Association, was cosponsoring—and financing—the conference. The main concern of the Japanese contingent was to make sure things ran smoothly. This was a reasonable concern, given the casualness of the Thais about almost everything, and the fact that, as I was to learn later on, the conference had come perilously close to being canceled. (It was the first gay conference ever held in Thailand.) The Japanese were in charge of the agenda and the microphones. Right from the beginning, I saw the conference as a cultural conflict—not between East and West but between East and East. It was Japanese efficiency and organization-mindedness versus Thai informality and charm.

"Instead of the scheduled session, we'll start with a coffee break," Natee announced. Charm had won the first skirmish. Demure young women in starched white-and-blue uniforms served beverages and pastry. I scanned the faces of the Japanese; if they were dismayed at this breach of schedule, they were careful not to betray their feelings.

There were three Japanese altogether: Mr. Minami, who was the publisher of *The Adon,* one of Japan's largest gay magazines, and the financial benefactor of the country's fledgling gay movement; a bald, burly man named Mr. Nakayama; and a younger man named Mr. Hashimoto, who worked for a Tokyo securities firm. Mr. Hashimoto, who was rather high-strung, served as Mr. Minami's attentive aide-de-camp and translator. (The official language of the conference was English.) The Japanese were always addressed as "Mr." followed by their surname, according to Japanese custom; the Thais, by contrast, were called by their first name, or by "Mr." before their first name—example: "Mr. Natee."

The Japanese were all attired in dress slacks, white shirts, and ties, the uniform of the Tokyo salaryman. Natee was in jeans, orange sneakers, suspenders, and the DON'T BE SILLY, PUT A CONDOM ON YOUR WILLY T-shirt he had been wearing the first time I met him. He was even more exuberant than previously, perhaps because he had a new boyfriend, an Australian AIDS researcher. Natee had met him the month before, when his dance troupe performed in Canberra.

I asked Natee, who was now beginning to recall details of our first meeting, what countries would be represented at the conference. "We're hoping that Malaysia will send someone, but we're not sure," he said. "And we hope more people from Thailand will come on Sunday. Today is a working day, you know."

On the verandah, I struck up a conversation with a fortyish Caucasian man with a north-of-England accent. His name was

Stephen Bowdell and he had been a supervisor at the National
AIDS Helpline in London. He had come out to Bangkok to set up
a gay and AIDS hotline for FACT. Currently, he said, if you called
up the government-run AIDS hotline, they told you that one way
to prevent AIDS was to avoid *all* homosexual contact. The FACT
hotline planned to take a different approach; it would be aimed
specifically at gay and bisexual men and would promote safe sex
and help callers confront coming out and identity issues. Some
wealthy friends in London had given him seven thousand pounds
to pay for office space, telephones, and air conditioners. Meanwhile, he was trying to persuade the Thai government to pay his
salary so he could stay on and supervise the project for a year; he
had asked for two hundred fifty thousand baht (about ten thousand
dollars) and was optimistic. He had a friend who worked for the
World Health Organization (WHO), to whom he sent copies of all
his correspondence with Thai officials. "If the government says no
to me too many times, they'll hear about it from the WHO," he
asserted.

The coffee break over, we filed into the conference room for the
first session. The room was quite large (it was obviously intended
for more impressive gatherings than our little band), and the air-
conditioning was turned up so high you needed two layers of sweaters to feel comfortable. There were several rows of tables, each
covered with a white-and-blue ruffled tablecloth. At the front of the
hall was a lectern, a screen for slides and transparencies, and a large
banner that said, in English and Thai, THIRD ASIAN LESBIAN AND
GAY CONFERENCE, AUGUST 24–26. I took my place next to the Thai
journalist.

Mr. Nakayama opened the conference with a formal welcome in
Japanese.

There we were, fourteen of us: the three Japanese; three Thais,
not counting the reporter; and the rest *farangs*. In addition to
Natee, the Thai contingent was made up of a quiet and studious-
looking man in his twenties, plus an older gentleman who owned
two Thai restaurants in San Francisco and had returned to Bangkok, where he collected antiques and dressed in traditional embroi-
dered shirts and shawls. The *farangs* included Bowdell, the British
hotline consultant; an ACT UP member from Los Angeles; a law

professor from Vancouver; a man from Guam, who set up a display of the island's travel folders on the front table; Eric Allyn, the coauthor of *Men of Thailand;* and myself.

Natee rose to give his welcoming address. He projected a transparency of the Kinsey scale onto the screen. In the 1948 study that has remained the definitive examination of sexual variation (at least in the United States), sex researcher Alfred Kinsey had classified men on a continuum according to their sexual experiences—from exclusively heterosexual (0) to exclusively homosexual (6), with everyone else somewhere in between. "This makes me feel secure that we have a lot of people in different situations but they are all friends," said Natee, pointing at the transparency. He then proceeded to rate various men in the room according to Kinsey. "I think most of the people here are at six on Kinsey's scale. Eric is there, I know," he said, indicating the author of *Men of Thailand,* sitting in the front row. "Stephen is there, too," he added, nodding in the direction of the British hotline consultant.

Natee repeated much of what he had told me when we spoke some months before. "In Thailand, we have always thought of gay as *kathoey,* or transvestite," he went on, "until we had a new word called 'gay' ten years ago. Now we have more alternatives. There are lots of men who sleep with men but say they are not gay. When they wake up in the morning, they just say, 'Mai ben rai.' That means 'Never mind' or 'It doesn't matter.' I want to convince people to feel comfortable about being gay so these men can come out and say they are gay."

One thing that FACT was campaigning for was to persuade gay men that heterosexual marriage wasn't a necessity. "It is not the right thing to use women in this way," Natee said. He added, "I think we have more than ten percent gay men in the country. But I think we have fifteen percent of men who sleep with men." Or did he say fifty percent? I wasn't sure.

Then Mr. Minami gave a presentation called "The Gay Liberalization Movement in Japan," tracing the development of Japanese gay life from the end of World War II to the present. The text was full of sentences that emerged in English completely fractured: "The age of the belief that man is liberalized by the personal consumption of sex started, resulting in the start of the civil movement that gays can be liberalized by their group activities."

Toward the end of Mr. Minami's talk, there was a stir in the room. Four men entered. Three were ethnic Chinese; the other was darker, with a mustache, and looked vaguely Middle Eastern. All wore slacks and polo shirts. "The Malaysians," whispered the Thai reporter.

Conference participants were called upon to read letters received from gays in the various Asian countries whose representatives never made it to the conference. A letter from South Korea, read by the Vancouver law professor, painted a depressing picture. There were no gay social groups or magazines in Korea, and Korean homosexuals were frequently pressured into marriage by their families. "That is bad, but worse is the Korean gays' cowardice" in not trying to change the situation, the writer concluded. The letter from Taiwan noted that gays accounted for fifty percent of all suicides and seventy percent of all suicide attempts in the country.

I was chosen to read the letter from Hong Kong. It was written by Julian Chan, the activist I'd met on my visit there. Julian's letter brought good news. The month before, the Hong Kong Legislative Council had voted to decriminalize homosexual acts between consenting adults in private, a major victory for the colony's gay community. The vote was thirty-one to thirteen. The decision proved, Julian wrote, "that we are not different from them, that we cry like they do, laugh like they do, love like they do, even hate like they do, and like them, we are human beings, too."

There were no communications from the People's Republic of China or North Korea.

I went to lunch with the Thai reporter and asked her if Thai attitudes toward homosexuality were as accepting as so many people made them out to be. "Oh, you mean, 'Mai ben rai' ['It doesn't matter']," she replied. She then related how the male reporters in her office made antigay remarks when she told them she was covering the conference. Then there was the recent case, reported in the newspapers, of a Catholic school in Bangkok that tried to bar homosexual students. (It was fashionable for the Buddhist Thai elite to send their children to Catholic schools.) "That school was getting a reputation," she said. Un-Thai prejudices were clearly making inroads among the middle classes.

Still, the subject of homosexuality was fascinating to a number of people, including the reporter. "I have a friend—and not a gay friend either—who tried to convince me that the Buddha was actually gay," she said. "He had a good argument for it."

What about lesbians in Bangkok? I asked hopefully.

"There is a small group that is just starting," she said. "We asked them if we could interview them, and other newspapers in Bangkok did, too. But they won't talk to anyone. They don't want any publicity at all."

When we reconvened, the Malaysians took center stage. They were members of Pink Triangle, a group that had been established in Kuala Lumpur two and a half years before as an AIDS telephone-counseling service. Male homosexual sex was still illegal in Malaysia, a legacy of the country's years as a British colony. Malaysian society, an uneasy ethnic stew of Muslim Malays and Chinese and Indians, was quite conservative. Pink Triangle was unable to declare itself a gay organization, lest it be accused of promoting an illegal activity.

Nonetheless, the group's members were almost all gay men. They published a campy newsletter called *Pink News* (Pink Triangle volunteers were called Pinklers) and raised money through variety shows with names like "A Pink Affair" and "Painting the Town Pink." The helpline averaged sixty calls a month, and while almost half dealt with AIDS information and testing, another large chunk included subjects such as loneliness, self-acceptance, and relationships. (According to government figures, ninety percent of the three hundred twenty-one people who had tested HIV-positive in Malaysia were prisoners and intravenous-drug users.) Pink Triangle offered pre– and post–HIV test counseling and had a buddy system in place, and also sponsored a version of the "Eroticizing Safer Sex" workshops popular in the United States and Australia. "We are not a gay organization, but many of us are gay and I am gay and proud," said Hong, the "official" delegate of the contingent.

Hong looked like a Chinese matinee idol of the 1930s. He was tall and strikingly handsome and slicked his hair back; he projected an intriguing combination of worldliness and earnestness. He had lived in Sydney for a number of years and had returned to Kuala Lumpur to enter the family business. One of the Thais at the conference asked him if he was aware that he resembled a well-known Thai actor. "People keep telling me that," said Hong. When the same man said with characteristic Thai directness that he regretted not having had the opportunity to go to bed with Hong, Hong very graciously apologized.

The Malaysians passed out buttons that said in English, "We care about AIDS. Do you?" and featured a pink triangle. Hong showed examples of pamphlets and posters, in Malay, Chinese, and English, which the organization had exhibited at the Central Market in Kuala Lumpur, in conjunction with World AIDS Day. Then he passed around a Ministry of Health pamphlet on AIDS. It was standard stuff, as such pamphlets go, but one recommendation caught my eye. "Avoid unsafe homosexual sex," it said, but "unsafe" was stamped on the page, obviously an afterthought. I asked Hong about it at question time. The government, Hong said, had in fact initially printed the recommendation as "Avoid homosexual sex." But Pink Triangle had refused to distribute the pamphlet if the Health Ministry didn't include the word "unsafe." The government finally agreed.

These days, health officials increasingly worked closely with the Pinklers. Although the government had not been officially associated with the World AIDS Day exhibit, it had helped with printing costs and audio-visual materials. A Ministry of Health representative had recently given a workshop at a gay disco—a first. "It hasn't always been so easy," Hong added, noting that an early Malaysian government warning about the epidemic had shown a man running away from a transvestite who carried a purse labeled AIDS. Now things were different. "We are fearless because the government cannot do without us," he said. As an indication of its credibility, Pink Triangle had even been the recipient of foreign assistance: a twenty-thousand-dollar grant from the Australian Federation of AIDS Organizations.

The Vancouver law professor was impressed. "It amazes me," he said, "how in country after country, fighting AIDS is bringing about gay respectability and creating gay community." In Malaysia, as in Thailand, he added, "an AIDS organization is becoming a gay organization."

Interestingly, in both countries, thus far, AIDS had not exacted a significant toll within the segment of the population that identified itself as gay. Members of Pink Triangle were already beginning to complain that the organization was spending too much time on AIDS, to the exclusion of other issues more pressing to Malaysian gays. "We are not a high-risk group," one of the Malaysians said during Hong's presentation. The situation of gays in Thailand was far more disturbing, given the scope of the epidemic in that country. However, in their AIDS presentation, the Thai gays offered Ministry of Health statistics to prove *they* were not a high-risk group, either.

When the time came for the Japanese to talk about AIDS, they passed.

The following day we went on a specially hired bus to Pattaya, a beach resort south of Bangkok that is known as a center of the sex trade, gay and straight. One guidebook called it "the perfect place for a sailor on leave." Traffic tie-ups were so massive in and out of Bangkok—and along the route to Pattaya, as well—that we wound up spending most of the day inside the bus. As we sat in traffic, Natee joked that he was "a little bit feminine but not too bad." In Thailand, he said, gay men tended to fall in love with straight men because the more "masculine" gays were all in the closet. In addition to persuading people to come out, he wanted to encourage Thai gays to be "less feminine," he said. That, he seemed to think, would help create equal relationships between gay men, not just unsatisfying affairs with straight-identified men. Natee had attended the annual conference of the International Lesbian and Gay Association in Stockholm earlier that summer, and there, for the first time, he had learned "to love gay [as opposed to straight] men," he said. A month later came his whirlwind romance in Australia. He said that he and his Australian lover planned to get married in Denmark, where gay unions were legal. (In fact, the law requires that one partner be a Danish citizen.)

The famous gay beach in Pattaya turned out to be a few hundred feet of sand, littered with thatched huts and beach umbrellas. Older European men sat with Thai boys on their laps. "It's an invasion," one of the Europeans could be heard complaining as we arrived. Local women offered us manicures and massages, which were politely declined. We spent most of the time in group picture-taking. After an hour, we left to return to the traffic jam.

That evening, conferees were invited to Super-Lek, one of Patpong's most popular gay bars, to attend a handsome-boy contest.
The place was packed. Lek Matsuda, the owner of the bar, appeared on stage looking like an Oriental princess: He wore a black-
and-white kimono and combed his hair in a bun from which three
sticks protruded. There were twenty-six contestants altogether,
each a barboy at a different gay establishment. The boys paraded
on stage in slacks and oversized sport coats; next, they emerged in
briefs; the third go-around was the "personality" contest, in which
they were asked a few questions, largely about where they were
from and what bar they represented. While the boys changed
clothes, a *kathoey* who bore a striking relationship to diva Joan
Sutherland ate fire and played with snakes onstage. I sat toward the
front, next to Eric Allyn, who was one of the judges. The Japanese,
watching intently, were seated in the middle of the crowd. I couldn't
tell whether they were enjoying themselves or just doing their duty.

At intermission, I chatted in the courtyard with the Malaysians.
In Kuala Lumpur, shows called "Painting the Town Pink" might
be acceptable, but handsome-boy contests were not. Even Hong,
with his worldliness and many years' residence in sybaritic Sydney,
seemed a little shocked. "After a while it loses any erotic thrill it
might have," he said. "The boys just don't seem to have any charm
or personality up there."

After the winner was announced, there was yet another contest.
In this one—sponsored by FACT—the same contestants were
paraded out and asked the question, "Are you afraid of AIDS?"
The winning answer was given by a broad-shouldered lad with a
wholesome quality: "I'm not afraid because I know how to protect
myself against AIDS." Natee later explained that each participant
had said more or less the same thing, but this particular young man
said it with "more confidence." His award was a framed (and very
graphic) Australian safe-sex poster.

The following morning a representative from Anjaree, Bangkok's
recently formed lesbian group, addressed the conference. She was
the first lesbian to make an appearance. *Anjaree* means "those who
have different behavior"; in the Thai language, there is no word to
signify "lesbian." The speaker, Kai, was well known as an activist
for a group that worked to rescue young women forced into prosti-

tution. I wondered what she might have thought of the beach at Pattaya or the previous night's activities at Super-Lek. "Please don't mention to anyone I was here," she told the reporter, who knew her from her other political activities.

Even addressing an audience of presumably sympathetic gay men, Kai was reticent. She refused to disclose any information about Anjaree beyond that it comprised about twenty or so women who met at various people's homes. "I don't want to talk about Anjaree," she said rather sternly, as she took the microphone. "I want to talk about building alliances." Anjaree was sponsoring an all-lesbian conference in Bangkok a few months later; she hoped the audience would help disseminate information about the event.

The mood was one of uneasiness. I noticed that there wasn't a single Thai man present, not even Natee. It was eleven o'clock on a Sunday morning after the handsome-boy contest, but somehow everyone else had managed to make it out of bed. Still, those in attendance tried their best to be helpful. Hong mentioned how incorporation as a counseling service had given Pink Triangle a distinct identity. Perhaps that approach might work for Anjaree. I feared the conversation might take an unpleasant turn when Hong suggested that lesbians and gay men had nothing in common except that they both suffered from discrimination. But Kai didn't take offense.

At the end of the hour, Kai announced she had to go to another meeting. Mr. Minami jumped up, camera in hand. "Picture?" he asked, seemingly oblivious to the tension in the room. Kai declined.

I accompanied her to the door and asked her if she could help arrange for me to meet some of the women from Anjaree. "I'm going off to Amsterdam on Tuesday," she said, "but I'll mention it to the others in the group."

In fact, it wasn't until I was in Tokyo that I actually got to talk with a Thai lesbian. She had moved to Japan in order to come out and had an American girlfriend named Fred. She was teaching a course in elementary Thai to Japanese lesbians in preparation for the Bangkok conference that Kai was touting. About Thailand, she would say only, "As a lesbian, I could never go home to live, because of my family. I could certainly never bring Fred!"

• • •

Despite the hectic round of meetings, traffic-snarled sight-seeing expeditions, and handsome-boy contests, I did get an opportunity to reflect on the conference—and on my travels thus far. Almost everywhere I had been outside the West, the issue of identity loomed large, creating uncertainty and confusion when it came to issues of sexuality and sexual orientation. In the black townships of South Africa, isolated from the rest of the world by apartheid, people weren't sure if gay men were really men or women or a third sex. They weren't even sure if perhaps gay men couldn't have babies. In Egypt, where the polymorphous perverse ruled, all the men I met seemed to be bisexual, even the handful who courageously referred to themselves as "gay." In Thailand, Natee was using a scale of behavior devised by an Indiana sex researcher forty years ago to make some sense of his own culture, which was dominated by the casualness of *mai ben rai.* Only in Hong Kong, where there had been a long history of Western colonial rule, was there perhaps a surer sense of sexual orientation—and greater social hostility, too. In all these cultures, the status of women was so low that the notion of women existing apart from men—let alone in lesbian relationships—was barely comprehended.

In such societies, Western dichotomies of "gay" and "straight" just didn't seem to fit. Attempting to build a Western-style gay and lesbian movement in cultures where categories based on sexual identity were traditionally unknown was a dubious venture, at best. It was significant that in many of the countries I visited, the leaders in creating a gay movement—Zachy in Cairo, Julian Chan in Hong Kong, Natee and Kai in Bangkok—had all spent time in the West. It didn't seem enough to urge homosexually inclined men to come out of the closet, as Natee had done at the conference; in much of the non-Western world, there were just very different ways of thinking about sexuality that resisted fixed labels.

Significantly, Western notions of individualism and personal freedom were largely absent as well. Communal values—those of family and maintenance of family—were dominant. The idea of carving out an identity that was at variance with family responsibilities was virtually unthinkable. Women clearly suffered from this more than men, who could have their "minor wives" and their sexual liaisons. Hence the Thai woman in Tokyo, who felt that she could never go home to live in the midst of her family and certainly could never bring her girlfriend.

In Thailand and throughout Asia, economic development and Westernization were having an impact. Yet even among the emerging middle classes, deeply rooted cultural traditions could not be dismissed. During one of the multitudinous conference coffee breaks, I chatted with an accountant from Kuala Lumpur who attributed the pressure to marry brought to bear by ethnic Chinese families like his own to ancestor worship. If children remained unmarried, they wouldn't produce grandchildren to pray for and offer food to the spirits of parents, grandparents, and relatives long dead. That was a major reason why in Chinese culture, marriage—and procreation—were so crucial, he believed, and why a gay identity that might preclude them was unacceptable. How could you oppose the wishes not only of living relatives but of generations past, as well?

Given all these factors, it wasn't really surprising that attendance at the Bangkok conference was so sparse, the proceedings often verging on the bizarre, the entire enterprise so seemingly quixotic.

The final session centered around planning the next conference. When should it take place and where should it be held? The consensus was to hold the conference in two years in Kuala Lumpur. The Malaysians were hesitant, worried about how the idea of a gay conference would be received by the Malaysian authorities. They agreed to take the proposal back to their membership. There was also talk about sponsoring representatives from poorer countries, such as the Philippines, who perhaps couldn't afford to come this time.

In the middle of this discussion, suddenly and unexpectedly, Mr. Nakayama took the microphone and made a closing statement in Japanese. The business portion of the Third Asian Lesbian and Gay Conference was officially over.

Afterward, everyone went out for dinner at a garden restaurant in a nineteenth-century mansion in Patpong. We had our own "private" area, a long table off to one side. The Thai man who owned restaurants in San Francisco ordered a variety of dishes for the entire table; the food was sumptuous—coconut soup, Thai pancakes, chicken and pork satay, endless varieties of fish, and mango and pineapple for dessert.

Following dinner came the entertainment, a performance by Natee's dance troupe. People from the other tables stood around to watch. The troupe did a traditional Thai dance, in costume, and the "City of Angels" segment I had seen at the Red Cross Fair on my previous visit. Then came a number that was unfamiliar to me. "When we did this in Australia, some people objected to the ending," Natee said. "I'd like to know what you think." In this number, a young Thai man and woman are approached by a Western sex tourist dressed in a clown costume. "I love Patpong. I love mankind," sings the sex tourist, mockingly, in English. In the end, the Thais turn on the sex tourist and kill him.

When the clown removed his mask, he was revealed to be Natee himself.

"How many of you like the ending?" Natee asked. Most of the audience, swept up by the enthusiasm of the dance, raised their hands in favor. The Malaysian accountant dissented, however. "It would have been much better if they could have just pushed him away, instead of killing him," he said. Lest the evening deteriorate into controversy, Natee turned off the gramophone, lined everyone up, and handed each of us a cucumber and a condom. There was nothing like a little safe-sex instruction to bring people together.

Finally, Natee put on the music again and called upon Mr. Minami to dance. The Japanese businessman, who had been last seen leaving the conference in white pants, seersucker jacket, and bow tie, and carrying a briefcase, was suddenly in the middle of the floor in a green lamé jacket and yellow sash, dancing with one of the women in Natee's troupe. Mr. Minami seemed to be enjoying himself more than I had seen him do since the weekend began. Charm had won the day.

6

JAPAN
THE EMPEROR'S NEW CLOTHES

Tokyo, Kyoto, and Osaka

I didn't call Mr. Minami when I arrived in Tokyo. I wanted to try things out on my own first. I took a room at a business hotel in Shinjuku, a neighborhood where department stores and expensive cafés lay cheek by jowl with massage parlors and peep shows. After work, salarymen got drunk at sushi bars. On every street corner stood vending machines that dispensed iced coffee, Earl Grey tea, orange juice, and beer—and a soft drink called Sweat. Some sold porn magazines, even porn videotapes. (There were estimated to be 5.3 million vending machines in Japan, one for every twenty-three people.) Behind my hotel were lanes so narrow that a car couldn't pass. Mostly, they were lined with "love hotels," places where prostitutes and their customers (as well as Japanese couples in search of privacy) could spend a few hours. Many of the love hotels had Continental-sounding names, such as La France, Valencia, and the Alps. My hotel room didn't have a closet or a dresser, but everyone assured me that Japanese business hotels were all like that.

I had expected Tokyo to be a frantic megalopolis, but in some respects, it had a small-town flavor. Old folks rode bicycles on sidewalks, even in Shinjuku; bicycles were parked everywhere and rarely locked. No one crossed the street until the signal changed. Every morning, Tokyoites armed with tiny brooms swept the patches of sidewalk in front of their houses. The city was an aggregation of neighborhoods surrounding subway stations. The subways went everywhere and, on most lines, trains ran every four minutes without fail. I was in a truly well-run country.

Still, the odd juxtapositions couldn't help but make the foreign visitor feel disoriented. When I dropped a hundred-yen coin into a vending machine to buy my morning orange juice (*orenji jusu* to the Japanese), the machine obliged by playing the tune "Camptown Races." "Mr. Sandman" blared out of the Meiji Gun Shop; at Le Chat coffee shop it was "Moon River" and "Days of Wine and Roses"; when my hotel put telephone callers on hold, the background music was "Home on the Range." In the window of the Arajin video store was a large caricature of Audrey Hepburn, in a black evening gown and heels, carrying home an armful of videotapes.

All the transpositions from the North American to the Japanese context made me uneasy. Where exactly was I? What year was this?

I decided to ring up Mr. Minami.

Mr. Minami was friendly and much less preoccupied than he had seemed in Bangkok. He invited me to stay at the office of ILGA/Japan, the organization he headed, in nearby Yotsuya. Meetings took place there for a couple of hours most evenings, but otherwise the place would be mine, he promised. There was a futon to sleep on, a kitchenette, a bathroom, and plenty of English-language books. He also offered to take me on a tour of Tokyo's gay bars.

There were said to be some three hundred gay bars in Tokyo, each usually consisting of a counter, a few stools, a tape deck, and the obligatory video screen. (There was virtually no such thing as a disco or dance bar in gay Tokyo.) Most were in Ni-chome, Shinjuku's second ward, an area of three- and four-story buildings where laundry dried on balconies and plastic branches with fake red-and-yellow leaves hung off telephone poles to indicate autumn. Square neon signs, one on top of the next, climbed the sides of buildings, creating the effect of a tower made of children's blocks. There was a park where men cruised, and a couple of gay-oriented variety stores that sold everything from back issues of gay magazines to plastic caricatures of Charlie Chaplin and Superman.

For the visitor, particularly the non-Japanese-speaking visitor,

Ni-chome was a closed world. The bars were almost impossible to find. They were located along lengthy corridors in what appeared from the outside to be small office buildings; sometimes there were three or four bars to a floor. There were virtually no street signs in Tokyo and, even where there were, street numbers signified nothing. The neon signs that advertised the bars were invariably in Japanese. Someone gave me directions to GB, a bar popular with *gaijin* (Westerners): "Turn left at the fruit stand a couple of blocks past the coffee shop, go down the alley, and make a left and go down the steps to the basement. But if you go on Sunday, the coffee shop will be shuttered and you will get completely lost."

Mr. Minami was the ideal guide. The bar owners, or masters, as they were called, all treated him with great deference; most advertised in the pages of his magazine *The Adon* (as in Adonis). Mr. Minami always paid his bill scrupulously, even though he drank large quantities of alcohol, and Ni-chome bars were not cheap. A beer and a "side" of pickled relish went for close to ten dollars.

Like the other bars in the city, Tokyo's gay establishments were highly specialized. There were bars for English-speaking *gaijin* and Japanese interested in meeting them; bars for Germans and Scandinavians and their Japanese friends; bars for eighteen-year-olds, where everyone wore white T-shirts, and strobe lights pulsated incessantly; bars where transvestite comics performed; and *karaoke* bars for noisy and hyped-up teens, and still other karaoke bars for Westerners and older Japanese.

In a 1983 magazine article about Tokyo, the American author Frances Fitzgerald speculated, "There is surely a bar for composers who have lost their manuscripts, a bar for actors who want to be dentists, a bar where baseball players discuss the works of Jean-Paul Sartre." I was told there had been a gay nightspot in Ni-chome where a scale stood at the entrance. Each potential customer was obliged to weigh himself before entering; if you were *under* two hundred pounds, you were denied admittance. Although the story might have been apocryphal, it caught the flavor of Ni-chome, where there was a bar for every taste.

The gay bars were rigidly segregated by sex. Only one, called Kinsmen, attracted both men and women. There were three lesbian bars in Ni-chome, all of them relatively new.

Mr. Minami took me to Daytime, a glary spot that was decorated with translucent fish and sailboats hanging from the ceiling. The decor was seasonal, Mr. Minami told me; in the spring, mobiles of cherry trees hung over the bar. It was still early, and the place was empty. As we drank, Mr. Minami's English began to improve. He told me how he had worked for ten years as a writer and photographer for a magazine devoted to the Kabuki theater. He had been married for twenty-six years (although he and his wife had been separated for most of that period) and had two grown children. When he was younger—he was fifty-two now—it was not considered "abnormal" for gay men to marry, he explained. He had founded ILGA/Japan in 1986 after a visit from a group of Swedish representatives of the International Lesbian and Gay Association. Since then, he had taken a paternal—some said paternalistic—role in the organization, and continued to pay the rent for the ILGA office, which he treated as if it were his own.

At a *karaoke* bar, someone was singing "I Left My Heart in San Francisco." Mr. Minami introduced me to the master, a crew-cut, athletic-looking man who had played tennis at the international Gay Games in Vancouver the previous summer. The master brought over a photo album. The Japanese had sent a team of four to Vancouver, Mr. Minami explained; Mr. Minami was among them.

"What was your sport?" I asked Mr. Minami.

"Darts," he said brightly.

We went to Kronos, a place favored by the gay intelligentsia. There were large posters for the movies *Cabaret* and *Birdy* on the wall. A row of framed photographs of allegedly gay luminaries stared down from above the counter—Sir John Gielgud, Leonard Bernstein, Montgomery Clift, Rock Hudson, Cary Grant, Cole Porter, and Burt Lancaster. "Burt Lancaster!" I exclaimed. "He's not gay." Mr. Minami repeated this to the master. The master insisted, despite my protestations, that Lancaster was bisexual.

Mr. Minami ticked off the names of novelists and poets who came to Kronos, though I didn't recognize any of them. He pointed out someone who he said was a Kabuki critic. Older, bohemian-looking customers who sat along the bar poured glasses of beer for me, shouting "Kampai!" No one spoke English. Mr. Minami dragged me to the other end of the bar to show me a book displayed under glass in a recessed area on the wall. "It is by Yukio Mishima's brother," he said. (Mishima was a gay Japanese novelist and right-wing nationalist who took his own life in a ritual suicide in 1970.)

As we left, I tried to figure out, through an alcoholic haze, exactly where the bar was located. Kronos, I reminded myself, was on the third floor, and I noted a sign downstairs advertising a soft drink. I was convinced I had stumbled into the heart of a Japanese gay culture with a long and rich tradition. But I feared Kronos was like Shangri-La—in the labyrinth of Ni-chome, I would never find it again.

From Kronos, we went to a bar called the M and M, where *War and Peace,* starring Audrey Hepburn, was on the video screen. Audrey Hepburn was Japan's favorite actress, said the master, a *gaijin* who had been principal of a Vancouver high school for thirty-five years before retiring to Ni-chome's night life.

Who was Japan's favorite male actor? I asked.

"That's easy," he replied. "James Dean. And do you realize that if James Dean were alive today, he would be one year older than I am?"

Mr. Minami insisted on taking me to one last place. As soon as we entered, I knew there was something different about it from the other bars we had visited. Three muscle-bound men, naked to the waist and wearing tight jeans, greeted us. The ashtrays on the tables were made from wood and adorned with carvings of erect phalluses. A pornographic video was showing on the movie screen that dominated one wall; because of Japanese obscenity laws, images of genitals were scrambled, creating a bizarre effect.

"This is Bangkok-style," Mr. Minami said.

I was puzzled.

The bar was a small room, with only six tables. Except for us, the sole customer was a young man of thirty or so, dressed in slacks and a polo shirt. On the floor beside him, he had put a couple of shopping bags. The young man, who seemed nervous, was conferring with one of the "waiters." After a few minutes, the waiter motioned for him to move to the next table, so he was no longer sitting directly across from us. A lacquered screen was brought out and arranged to surround the table and the young man, creating a kind of room within a room. The muscled waiter then disappeared behind it. It was impossible to see anything and, because of the ecstatic groans emanating from the video soundtrack, impossible to hear anything either.

By now, I had no doubts as to what "Bangkok-style" meant. Mr. Minami called over another employee, who brought him the price list. Ten minutes behind the screen with one of the waiters cost ten thousand yen (seventy-five dollars). Two hours in a hotel was fourteen thousand yen; the price for an entire night was twenty-eight thousand yen (two hundred dollars). "Most like ten minutes only," Mr. Minami explained.

Sure enough, after precisely ten minutes, the waiter emerged and removed the screen, revealing the young man sitting at the table, fully clothed, not a hair out of place, his drink in front of him, as if nothing had happened. For one skeptical moment, I wondered if anything had. But Mr. Minami had no doubts. He appeared astonished and delighted. "*Very* interesting! *Very* strange!" he kept exclaiming. As for the young man, he no longer seemed nervous.

Japan was a culture of hierarchies, of compartments, of rooms within rooms. These characteristics often made it seem impervious to analysis or understanding. "They say a Japanese man has six faces," a Canadian woman who lived in Tokyo told me. "You never see every one of them. In fact, you are lucky to see three." There was a rigid demarcation between public and private, between the outer façade of social convention (*tatemae*) and one's inner feelings (*honne*). They were expected to be separate. You followed the rules and otherwise thought or did what you wished; in exchange, people (and society) left you alone. As a Japanese academic put it, "Japan is a country of double standards, of multi-standards, really. You can say you are straight in public and be gay in private. That is acceptable."

For many Japanese gays and lesbians that meant there was no urgency to come out and to tell family or friends about one's sexual orientation; it also meant there was no need to avoid marriage. You could divide your life. You could have sex behind a screen in a public place, and people were supposed to pretend it wasn't happening, as long as when the screen was removed you were sitting there perfectly composed with your tie on straight.

• • •

Japanese culture has a long historical tradition of male-male sexual relations. During the feudal period, samurai warriors pledged themselves to one another in "brotherhood bonds," in the manner of ancient Sparta. The Buddhist clergy was rife with homosexual relations: Saint Francis Xavier, the first Portuguese missionary to Japan, wrote in the sixteenth century that, among Buddhist monks, "the abominable vice against nature is so popular that they practise it without any feeling of shame." Among the urban classes of the Tokugawa, or Edo, period (1603–1868), a "cheerful bisexuality" was the norm, according to American historian Gary Leupp.

As in Thailand, traditional Japanese same-sex relations never implied a gay identity. The closest word the Japanese language offered was *"nanshoku-zuki"*—"lover of *nanshoku*"—*nanshoku* being what Leupp calls the "role-structured male homosexual behavior" that flourished during the Edo period and whose culture centered around *nanshoku* teahouses and the Kabuki theater. In a society characterized by often loveless arranged marriages, *nanshoku* offered the possibility of romantic love. Given the rigorously hierarchical social structure, male homosexual relationships in Edo Japan were almost exclusively between older men and boys, and often involved a difference in social status as well. And in view of the patriarchal character of that social structure, there appears to have been little or no outlet for lesbian relations—or at least no writing or records to document them.

If, in seventeenth- and eighteenth-century Japan, male-male relationships were an accepted part of the sexual landscape, that began to change with the accession to power of the Westernizing Meiji dynasty in 1868. *Nanshoku* was increasingly regarded as an embarrassment, a feudal holdover in an era when Japan desperately wanted to industrialize and catch up with the West. Negative Western medical views about homosexuality became influential. Even the laws began to reflect this change in perception: Anal intercourse between consenting males was briefly prohibited, between 1874 and 1882. (Homosexual sex has been legal since then, however.)

By the mid-twentieth century, the traditional *nanshoku* had faded from public view. A new word became part of the language: *doseai,* or "same-sex love." *"Doseai"* applied to both men and women, so it had fewer connotations of pederasty than *"nanshoku"* had. But *doseai* was still *shumi*—a "hobby," or "pastime," or "personal interest," something that could be taken on and put off at will. It wasn't serious and certainly didn't constitute an identity. For women, *doseai* was *"S"*—nonsexual schoolgirl crushes, which involved holding hands and exchanging love letters. *S*—the letter stood for "sister"—received wide attention in the Japanese press in the 1930s after a series of suicides among infatuated schoolgirls. By and large, *S* involvements ended when school was over, and young women yielded to parental and societal pressure to marry.

By the late 1980s, a concept of gay and lesbian identity began to emerge. In part, this was the result of Western cultural influence. Postwar Japan imported dress, music, and youth culture from Europe and North America. Why not ideas about sexuality, as well? As a result of increasing affluence, many young people were no longer forced to live with their families. Women began to enjoy a degree of economic independence and social freedom. The proliferation of gay bars, following the 1964 Tokyo Olympics, and the emergence of gay magazines enabled gay men to feel less isolated, to communicate with one another, and hinted at the possibility of community. In the mid- to late 1980s, the first gay organizations were established in Tokyo: Mr. Minami's ILGA/Japan; a gay youth group, OCCUR; and a lesbian organization, Regumi Studio. "Dyke weekends," started by a group of Western lesbians living in Japan, were held four times a year at a women's educational center near Tokyo. Because of the still unequal status of women in Japanese society, lesbians have lagged far behind gay men in developing a sense of identity and community. But that was changing, as well.

Nonetheless, in contemporary Japan the overwhelming majority of gays and lesbians remained in the closet. In Tokyo and Osaka and other major cities, there were no gay neighborhoods; no one on the streets or subways appeared visibly gay or lesbian; few, if any, businesses apart from the bars, sex establishments, and variety stores of Ni-chome, catered to a gay or lesbian community.

Homosexuality remained a subject unsuitable for academic study. The media continued to equate male homosexuality with transvestism; lesbians were ignored completely. Although there were few signs of overt hostility, Japan remained an extremely homogeneous society, with little tradition of tolerance for minority groups. As one Osaka lesbian put it, "The policy of our society regarding something it doesn't like or feels uncomfortable with is to ignore it. People don't criticize it or say it's bad. They just pretend it isn't there. Japanese don't think about themselves or examine themselves. They don't ask the question, 'Who am I?' So it is hard to develop a sense of identity. And without a sense of identity, a minority group cannot survive."

As a result, to many Japanese, homosexuality was still an alien concept, something that belonged to the West, not to modern-day Japan. One Japanese woman told me that when she had made some mention of Ni-chome's gay bars to a friend, the friend said, "No Japanese go there, right? Only foreigners!"

The formation of gay identity, Japanese-style, was precisely what was going on one Sunday afternoon in my newly adopted living room—the ILGA office. "I Flat," as everyone called the place, was sleek and high-tech, with a computer, a TV, a conference table, and neat rows of audiotapes and videotapes. It was located in a neighborhood of fake brick- and-stucco-fronted residences on a little lane down from a Baskin-Robbins ice cream parlor; at night you heard crickets and air conditioners and the chanting of Buddhist prayers in living room shrines.

The occasion was a discussion group on homosexuality, attended by a handful of young Japanese men and led by a mild-mannered American named Michael. Michael was assigning reading—an early account of the U.S. gay liberation movement and an academic-sounding Canadian tome that was unfamiliar to me. He had been in Japan for ten years and taught history at a university in Tokyo. Today he lectured in English, primarily for my benefit.

In Japan, Michael said, sexuality as a category that defined a group of people was a new idea. "I don't say to my friends that I am gay," he noted. "I say, 'I like men.' One of the problems in Japan is this lack of definition. To most people, saying 'I'm gay' is like saying 'I masturbate.' It still represents an act, not an identity." This was "troublesome" when it came to gay liberation. "For this reason, Japan is a laboratory for the social construction of homosexuality," he said.

While in the United States, Michael went on, there was a "gut reaction" against homosexuality that led to gay bashing, in Japan, this wasn't the case. "There is no feeling of hatred against gays," he contended. "What there is is discomfort. The main Japanese concern is 'How should I act?' So when it comes to homosexuality, it is not that they hate gays but that they are afraid of embarrassing themselves. They are uneasy; they prefer not to talk about it."

In Japan, Michael said, "the cowardly thing is to be yourself. Conformity is considered the strong thing to do, the admirable thing."

Most of the Japanese in attendance were silent as Michael talked. He was the professor, after all. Then someone spoke up—a tall man dressed in blue jeans and an epauletted denim jacket, with plastic bangles hanging from his wrist. "Michael is right when he says that Japanese people don't say homosexuals should be killed or anything like that," he said. "They don't bash them. If anything they find them funny. Not immoral or evil, but cute!" He added, with a trace of bitterness in his voice, "As cute as dogs."

The speaker's name was Masonari Kanda and he was fierce. He was argumentative and critical of everything. In fact, he behaved in such an "un-Japanese" manner that he admitted people found him rather "scary." He was proud of that, except that it made for difficulties in finding a boyfriend. "Japanese people want everything to be calm and quiet," he maintained. "They don't want to do or say anything that is different, shocking, confrontational." I thought Kanda would be happier in North America, in an organization like ACT UP or Queer Nation, than he was in Japan, where compromise and consensus ruled.

Kanda, who was in his early twenties, worked as a high school English teacher. He was active in OCCUR, a gay youth organization that had gained notoriety earlier that year when it was barred from meeting at a youth facility run by the Tokyo Board of Education. OCCUR was suing the board, charging it with antigay discrimination, the first case of its kind ever brought in Japan. Litigation in itself was a very un-Japanese thing to do.

OCCUR was having a dinner party that evening, in honor of my visit and that of a gay man who had come to Tokyo from the southern island of Kyushu. The dinner was to take place in the apartment of one of OCCUR's members in Asakusa, an older part of Tokyo. Kanda, Michael, and I took the subway there together.

On the way, Kanda related his experiences as a high school exchange student in Salt Lake City. He had converted to Mormonism but lasted about a year in the church—he was a "Jack Mormon," he said, which meant he was lapsed. The family he lived with in Salt Lake made fun of how he slurped his noodles, in the Japanese manner. It was in America that he realized he was gay, and when he came out to his host parents, they expressed disapproval. He had had no idea that that the Mormon religion considered homosexuality a sin. "I couldn't wait to get back to Japan," he said. "I thought I would feel free here." In fact, he didn't. That made him all the more rebellious.

Kanda joked that "people say that Michael is really Japanese and Kanda is really American."

When we arrived at the party, food was laid out on a tablecloth on the floor: sushi and boiled potatoes and cabbage, two kinds of tofu, and chicken in deep-fried rolls. There was beer and sake and Coke to drink. Although Kanda had said the apartment was large by Tokyo standards, it was essentially a single room (plus a kitchen), furnished with low futon couches. From the window, one could see the modernistic corporate headquarters of the Asahi group, with a large gold abstract sculpture that was illuminated at night. "Everyone's reaction to that sculpture is the same," said Kanda. "They say it looks like a giant turd."

There were about seventeen people present, all men and mostly Japanese. They were generally young: OCCUR membership was officially limited to those between sixteen and twenty-six years old. Many were students. Mr. Hashimoto, the man who had been Mr. Minami's translator in Bangkok, was present, although Mr. Minami was not—OCCUR members had split off from ILGA three years previously to form their own organization. Someone told me that the other honored guest, the young man from Kyushu, had arrived in Tokyo with a suitcase containing two hundred thousand yen (about fifteen hundred dollars). He was apparently looking for a job and a place to live in Tokyo, although no one knew for sure.

I chatted with OCCUR's twenty-three-year-old president, Hiroshi Niimi, whom I had met previously on a visit to the group's office. He immediately began to pepper me with questions. Kanda translated, since Niimi, like almost all the Japanese in the room, spoke little English. Niimi had just seen Harvey Fierstein's film *Torch Song Trilogy* and wondered whether the increasing focus on domestic life was undermining lesbian and gay liberation in the United States. Niimi was well informed and curious about everything. "We just received some videos in the mail of gay town meetings in New York and San Francisco," he said. "I'd like to know your opinion about 'outing.' "

Niimi was on the stocky side, with his hair in a flattop; he invariably wore a black T-shirt and black jeans. The first time I met him, he expressed surprise that an American would be interested in the Japanese gay movement. "I thought Americans didn't care about the rest of the world," he said.

When Niimi reached nineteen, he decided not to go to university but to devote his time to gay activism instead. To support himself, he worked part-time at a menial job.

Once, when I asked Kanda what was important to to him, he responded, "My personal life comes first, OCCUR second, and my teaching job third."

What about Niimi? I asked him.

"With Niimi, everything is OCCUR," Kanda said. "If he has a personal life, he never speaks of it. And he certainly doesn't care about his job. He just does that to survive."

Niimi was acutely aware of the difficulty of creating a gay movement in a country where there were many social outlets for gays and lesbians, and little public hostility. One difference between the West and Asia, Niimi had told me at that first meeting, was that, in the West, where Christianity was dominant and opposed to homosexuality, "gay people had no choice but to raise their voices. But here you have the influence of Buddhism. Buddha never said homosexuality was a sin. So no one feels they have to stand up and fight."

OCCUR took a gay-separatist view of things. In the opinion of both Niimi and Kanda, Japanese heterosexuals had absolutely no interest in gay people or their problems. Kanda put it this way: "In the United States, 'coming out' suggests the formation of new kinds of personal relationships with heterosexuals. But in Japan, coming out won't accomplish that. Heterosexuals just don't understand us or care about us." What gays needed to do, in his view, was to strengthen themselves personally and as a community and to forget about the rest of society. "I used to have straight friends but since I came out, I don't have any," Kanda said. "I don't want to waste my energy on coming out to straight people."

OCCUR's practice was different from its rhetoric, however. The group gave talks at universities, put out an AIDS pamphlet and poster in conjunction with the Ministry of Health, and had worked with a coalition of organizations to oppose the government's restrictive AIDS-prevention law. Niimi himself had appeared on TV as an openly gay man. I suspected that OCCUR's hostile stance toward heterosexuals might reflect a need to create "enemies" in order to provide a rationale for an identity and a movement. In order to have an "us," OCCUR sensed it needed a "them."

Over dinner, I asked Niimi who his role models were. Whom did he look up to?

"No one," he said firmly.

You couldn't look up to the older generation, he contended. As long as they were able to have sex, that was enough for them. The identity of the entire society had collapsed after World War II; all that the postwar generation cared about was making money. "The gay movement is in its infancy here," he said. "Japanese gays are relaxed but not free. We think the OCCUR discrimination lawsuit against the Board of Education will be fundamental. It will be Japan's Stonewall!"

Niimi noted that Mr. Minami had proposed holding Japan's first gay and lesbian pride parade in Ni-chome in 1995. Niimi believed this could never happen. No gay march or demonstration had ever taken place in Japan. Gay identity was just too weak. "The lack of gay identity is a major difference with the West," he said. "So building a network is the most important thing." One of OCCUR's ideas, he said, was to start a gay restaurant or community center in order to help build up a sense of identity and community. The logical source of funds to do this was money from older gays. But he was reluctant to ask them. "I fear their suggestions," he said.

Why don't you ask the group some questions? Niimi said to me. I asked who had come out to their parents, receiving varying responses. Then, I inquired, "What are some of the problems you face as gay people in Japan?"

No one said a thing.

• • •

In a later conversation, Mr. Hashimoto said, "OCCUR is just so pessimistic."

Mr. Minami said, "They are so young and they don't know about being gay and money. They really have no experience, so they look at things with a dark viewpoint. I have my own business and I know what money and power and the right voting can achieve. People at OCCUR don't own their own businesses. The only people they are in contact with are people whom they have to ask for help. So they are always in a weak position. They are pessimistic because they are weak. I have been to other countries and seen exactly the same situation as in Japan and seen it change. The gay community doesn't know what power it has."

AIDS was a factor in Japan—and then again, it wasn't. When I asked Mr. Minami what ILGA's greatest achievement had been, he paused and responded, "AIDS services." The AIDS crisis had played a role in gay community-building; Tokyo's gay and lesbian organizations had been founded shortly after the first cases of AIDS were reported in Japan in 1985. That was no coincidence. For many people, including many gays themselves, the arrival of AIDS was the first indication that there actually were homosexuals in Japan.

Yet the reality was that, thus far, Japan—and the country's gay community in particular—had been spared the worst of the AIDS epidemic. Most of the reported cases were among hemophiliacs, infected by blood products imported from the United States. Forty percent of the nation's hemophiliacs were estimated to be HIV-positive; a group of hemophiliacs was suing the government and five pharmaceutical companies for $1.6 billion in damages. As of April 1990, a total of only thirty-eight homosexual men had been diagnosed with AIDS, and another seventy-nine had tested postive for HIV infection in a country of 120 million people. A study of the prevalance of HIV among gay men in Tokyo from 1985 to 1989 had found an infection rate of three percent; half of those who tested positive were *gaijin*. A similar study of gay men in cities other than Tokyo revealed a rate of infection of less than one percent.

The effect of these numbers was that the overwhelming majority of Japanese gays didn't personally know anyone infected with HIV.

No gay man in Japan had gone public to offer himself as a "role model" for living with the disease. In my conversations with Japanese gays, the subject of AIDS never came up unless I raised it. AIDS just wasn't viewed as a serious problem. As a result, there was little awareness of safe sex among gay men. Gay saunas barred Westerners (but not other Asians), and that was viewed as all that was needed to combat AIDS. Safe sex was sex with another Japanese—whatever his sexual practices or however many times he had traveled abroad. Although Japan had the highest rate of condom use in the world (condoms were the leading method of birth control in the country), gay men weren't exactly lining up at drugstore counters.

Even Mr. Minami, who was more aware than most, seemed to imply that safe sex really wasn't necessary in Japan. According to him, Japanese gay men by and large didn't engage in anal intercourse. "For many Japanese gay men, sex equals hugging and mutual masturbation," he told me. "The number of people doing anal sex is very small. It is seen as a variation of heterosexual sex. Men are afraid to take the bottom position. That is why the AIDS problem is not so great in Japan."

For his part, Mr. Hashimoto recalled the moment at the Bangkok dinner party when Natee instructed the guests in placing condoms on cucumbers. "I was so embarrassed," Mr. Hashimoto said. "That was the first time I ever touched a condom in my life. I didn't know how to do it. Everybody had the impression that I don't practice safe sex. Natee was saying, 'This is terrible.' I said, 'It's not terrible. We don't need it in Japan so much because we don't practice anal sex.' "

These comments seemed odd, because in Egypt and Thailand I had found that, between men, the only sex that counted was anal sex. According to historian Gary Leupp, the same had been true in Edo Japan. Later, when I asked a Japanese friend if it was true that Japanese men rarely engaged in anal sex, he laughed. "Whoever told you that!" he demanded. "My friends all do it."

Did he use condoms? "I guess I should," he said, sheepishly. "You really can't tell if someone has AIDS just by looking at them, can you?"

It was unclear why there were so few cases of HIV infection

among gay men in Japan. The Japanese government and media offered the explanation that there were few homosexuals in the country. An article in the English-language *Japan Times* claimed that homosexuals made up half of one percent of Japan's population. Usually, the government gave out a figure of one hundred thousand, or one-tenth of one percent of the population. But these figures were not based on any scientific survey, and smacked of wishful thinking more than anything else.

More likely, the reasons for the low HIV infection rate lay in some combination of the late arrival of AIDS in Japan, Japanese sexual xenophobia, and the absence of the complicating factor of intravenous-drug use. The sexual practices of Japanese gays may have played a significant role, as well. But when a research fellow at the Japanese Foundation for AIDS Prevention did a survey of four hundred Japanese gay men to explore that very issue, Mr. Minami successfully pressured him not to publish his findings—and actually tried to expel him from ILGA. And this despite the fact that *The Adon,* Mr. Minami's magazine, had originally published the survey questionnaire in its pages. Mr. Minami's second thoughts apparently stemmed from his fear that publication of the survey findings might put the gay community in a bad light and further the connection in the public mind between AIDS and gay men. Even OCCUR's Kanda was critical of the survey. "That researcher asked the Japanese all kinds of personal questions they are not used to," he said. "He equated homosexuality and AIDS." Meanwhile, questions about the spread and prevalence of the disease among Japanese gays remained unanswered.

I had heard that one of *The Adon*'s rival publications, a monthly magazine called *Barazoku,* had printed an article advocating that gay men and lesbians should marry each other and present a heterosexual front to the world. Barazoku's publisher, Bunaku Itoh, supposedly wasn't gay himself but had often served as a media spokesman for Japanese gays. I made an appointment to see him. Kanda volunteered to serve as translator. He was as curious about Mr. Itoh as I was.

Kanda and I arranged to meet at Shibuya Station, in front of the statue of the dog Hachiko. Everyone in Japan knew the story of

Hachiko. Hachiko's master was a professor of agriculture at the Imperial University in the 1920s. The professor would go off to work each morning and leave Hachiko at Shibuya to await his return. One day, the professor was taken ill at the station and never returned. Each morning, for the next ten years, Hachiko would go to Shibuya and remain there all day, awaiting its master. The statue of Hachiko was a favorite meeting spot for Japanese, but it was an odd place to meet Kanda. Hachiko's docility seemed to exemplify everything Kanda claimed to despise about the Japanese.

We took the subway to a café that Mr. Itoh owned in an unpretentious Tokyo neighborhood filled with small shops. The café was rather grand. It was furnished with red plush velvet couches and antique furniture and decorated with gilt-framed nineteenth-century prints. Smartly dressed women drank tea. We could have been in any European capital.

I was uneasy about taking Kanda along, given his reputation for abrasiveness. It was a little like bringing a bomb thrower into a cathedral. Sure enough, as we sipped our coffee and awaited Mr. Itoh's arrival, Kanda began to offer some comments about our host. "He makes money off the gay community and puts nothing back!" he exclaimed loudly in English. None of the smartly dressed customers paid him any mind.

Once Mr. Itoh arrived, Kanda was unfailingly polite and respectful.

Mr. Itoh was a charming and sophisticated man in his fifties, graying at the temples. "Do you like the paintings?" he inquired. "They were done by a French artist who was quite well known in New York at the turn of the century."

Mr. Itoh was in the family business. His father had owned a publishing company and, after World War II, handed it over to the son. In 1961, Mr. Itoh published a book called *A Single's Sex Life,* essentially a how-to book on masturbation. It turned out that many of the book's readers were gay and wrote letters to him. He was surprised. Here, clearly, was an untapped market. Eventually, he decided to publish a gay magazine. In 1971, he launched *Barazoku* meaning, literally, "tribe of the rose." *Barazoku* featured erotic stories and pictures of mostly naked men, a formula Mr. Itoh had continued (and all other gay magazines in Japan have imitated) to this day. "Right after the first issue was published, the number of readers reached twenty thousand," he said. "The number is the same today. It hasn't changed at all."

I asked if it was true that he had suggested that gay men should marry lesbians.

Mr. Itoh was forthright on the subject. Many gay men, he replied, had traditionally married heterosexual women. It was hard to stay single after thirty, especially in the countryside, because of the pressure to enter into an arranged marriage. Parents and friends of gay men looked out for possible wives for them, and they couldn't refuse the arrangement. "This has been hard, often disastrous," Mr. Itoh went on. "But if the woman was a lesbian, it could be a little more successful. I wrote about it in the magazine, and the response was rather good. So I started a section in which lesbians and gay men interested in marriage could correspond by letters. Some of them have married. The number of those who have married is small but there are several happy cases."

I asked Mr. Itoh what he thought of gay rights organizations like ILGA and OCCUR. Kanda hadn't revealed anything about his association with OCCUR; in translating, he posed the question without a hint of personal interest. Mr. Itoh wouldn't state outright that he opposed such organizations. But he did contend that because there was no law or religious prejudice against homosexuals in Japan, there was little reason to organize in this way. "Over and over again, I tell readers that every gay person has to start a revolution in his own mind, to change himself," he said. He insisted that for a number of years he had tried in the pages of *Barazoku* to encourage gay people to come out but without much success. So he had changed his strategy, focusing instead on attempting to convince society that homosexuality was not bad or abnormal.

He had wanted to publish a magazine for lesbians similar to *Barazoku* and had even come up with a title: *Eve and Eve.* But lesbians were absolutely invisible in Japan, he said. It took a lot of courage for gay men to buy *Barazoku;* he concluded it would even be more difficult for lesbians to buy *Eve and Eve.* So he finally rejected the idea.

Was he gay himself?

"I've been asked the question any number of times," Mr. Itoh replied. "But I am in a happy, monogamous, heterosexual marriage."

He insisted that his heterosexuality worked in his favor. Certain homosexuals preferred younger men, or perhaps older men, and because of such inclinations, they couldn't discuss the subject objectively, he claimed. "I am the one who can discuss it without passion because I am not gay," he said.

He had been influenced strongly by gay people, however. "Look at this coffee shop!" he said. "I think it has good taste. A gay man from San Francisco helped me decorate it. Many gay people have extremely good taste and I have benefited from knowing them."

Mr. Itoh was called to the telephone. When he returned he announced he would have to leave soon to pick up the latest edition of *Barazoku* at the printer's. "Americans think that all Japanese are very rich," Mr. Itoh said. "But I have to drive copies of *Barazoku* around in the car myself. And gas is extremely expensive in Japan."

He then related his difficulties with censorship laws. In Japan, he said, you were not permitted to show male or female genitals in the media. However, *Barazoku* had done so and, on four different occasions the previous year, Mr. Itoh had been called to the police station; issues of his magazine had been seized. As his punishment, Mr. Itoh had been compelled to write a letter of apology. This year he had only been called to the police once. "I envy American magazines," he said.

I asked him about the differences among the various gay magazines in Japan. Mr. Itoh was characteristically gracious. "*Barazoku* is the magazine which contributes to the happiness of all gay people," he said.

With that, he pulled out a shopping bag full of gifts for me—mostly pornography. There were innumerable back issues of *Barazoku;* a series of prints of men in provocative poses, their bodies covered with tattoos; a book of S/M porn; and still another volume that would undoubtedly have gotten me arrested for purveying kiddie porn if I tried to bring it through U.S. Customs. I suspected that as Mr. Itoh didn't know me or my sexual tastes, he was trying to cover all the possibilities, from leather to twelve-year-olds.

"Thanks for letting me be a spy," Kanda said, as we walked

toward the subway. The bag of gifts was so heavy I could hardly lift it. I wondered how I would ever get it home.

I asked Mr. Minami about Mr. Itoh. Mr. Minami had gotten his start in gay journalism working on *Barazoku.* "He is a businessman," he said, dismissively.

Mr. Hashimoto said, "Of course, Itoh knew who Kanda was. Everyone knows Kanda!"

I said, "Mr. Itoh lives in his own world. I don't think he knew."

Mr. Itoh was right in one respect. In a country with little manifest antihomosexual prejudice, where gays were "cute as dogs" and AIDS was primarily a disease of hemophiliacs, marriage remained the central issue for Japanese homosexuals. The formation of lesbian and gay identity was inextricably linked with it. It was unclear which created more problems—to be gay or to refuse to marry. "The sole obstacle Japanese gays would face in coming out is the marriage system," as one gay man put it. "You can live with things as they are, as long as you clear up the question of marriage with family and bosses."

Although still strong, the marriage system was beginning to weaken. *Omai,* or arranged marriage, was in decline, particularly in the cities. Japanese were marrying later than in the past; today the average age was twenty-five for women and twenty-eight for men. A survey of Japanese men had shown that one-third wanted to postpone marriage, while another third didn't want to marry at all. "The whole social mood is changing," one woman told me. These changes—particularly the delay in the marriage age—presented gay men and women with a little more room to maneuver, a window of time in which to take control of their lives and stave off marriage, if not avoid it completely.

In Japan, gay men and lesbians were suddenly discovering that lover relationships, long-term partnerships, were possible, instead of the "hobbies" of a previous era. "Right now, one of the major changes is that people want to have *koibito,* a lover," OCCUR's Niimi told me. A Tokyo lesbian named Minako made the same point. "Today, it is the hottest thing—to have a lover," she said. "Before, it was difficult. There wasn't a real community. You were in a heterosexual world, and your lover might become lovers with a man. You were no match for that. You were in a tug of war and you were on one side and the rest of the world was on the other side. So you let her go. Now, it is lover, lover. Everyone is talking about *koibito, koibito.*"

A gay academic related that when he was at university ten years before, he and a male friend tried to rent an apartment together and found it wasn't possible. At that time, students were expected to live in dormitories; the idea of two unmarried men sharing a flat was not well accepted. Today, living with a roommate was increasingly common, especially in the large apartment buildings run by absentee company landlords. "You have to understand that the idea of gay couples is really a new idea," the academic added. "The traditional combination was a rich older man, usually married, and a younger man. And the younger man was replaceable—the older man could always find someone else. These were short-time relationships. Today, it's different. Relationships are possible that are *real* relationships."

Nonetheless, it was easy to overestimate change. In Japan, there was always the tension between *tatemae* and *honne,* between the outward acquiescence to social convention and one's inner feelings. Sometimes, the façade one presented to the world was sleek and high-tech and seemingly Western, and at other times it was traditional. But what people really thought and felt—the *honne*—was often quite different and difficult to fathom. So, while long-standing social arrangements appeared to be undergoing change, at the same time deference to the wishes of one's parents remained a powerful countervailing force. Young people were extremely hesitant to offend parents or to make them unhappy in any way.

That was especially true when it came to marriage. A Westernized Tokyo gay man in his early thirties reported how his parents were "dying" to ask him about marriage but wouldn't do so directly. When his mother had visited his apartment recently and saw how neat he kept his kitchen, she commented, in an oblique reference to his unmarried state, "It looks like you can take care of yourself!" He had taken his parents on a trip to Europe and, at one point, when a button fell off his jacket and he sewed it on himself, his mother said, "You don't really need anyone to take care of you, do you?" These comments were obviously intended to elicit some kind of response, to open up the subject of marriage for discussion. "I know I will have to face the issue eventually," the man said. "The question is when." Friends had suggested that he consider living abroad as a way of avoiding the issue.

Clearing up the question of marriage with bosses posed additional problems. Many Japanese companies traditionally encouraged employees to marry. If one didn't do so, chances of promotion beyond the level of middle management were slim. Although some companies—department stores and securities firms, for example—were becoming more liberal in this regard, others, such as banks, were as strict as ever. At the OCCUR dinner, I met Kato, a man in his early thirties who had been working for eight years for a large Tokyo bank. At OCCUR meetings, he was typically the only person in salaryman "uniform"—dress pants, white shirt, and tie.

"At my bank, no one says that unless you get married, you're fired," Kato told me. "But the pressure is there. It's just unspoken. When we have drinks after work or in ordinary conversations during lunch, people ask, 'Why are you not married? Are you not interested in this girl, that girl?' There are some people who remain single, although it is not clear if they are gay or not. And they are not treated well. They are not promoted as high."

Besides the issue of homosexuality, Kato emphasized, "All gay people face one problem—the problem of marriage."

One reason the bank cared so much about marriage was because a major task of its employees was to negotiate with officials from companies with which the bank had financial dealings. The negotiators on both sides of the table were almost always men. "In Japan, it is very hard for men to take part in negotiations or just to talk in a friendly manner if they are not married," Kato said. "Single men are not considered grown-ups. The banks want to send people to negotiate who look capable in their jobs and capable in other parts of their lives, like taking care of their families."

For his first seven years at the bank, Kato's job had been to engage in such negotiations. But recently, he had been shifted to another area. "I am now one of those who take care of odd jobs, paperwork," he noted. "So now I really don't have to talk with people from different companies." He emphasized that in his bank it was not uncommon for employees to be moved from one area to another. "I have not been demoted," he insisted.

How would his co-workers react if they knew he was gay?

"Some of them know," he said. "I was constantly being asked, 'Why are you not married?' and 'Aren't you interested in any girl in this company?' I was sick and tired of this. So, one day at lunch, I just said it—'I'm gay!' "

After that revelation, some co-workers stopped bothering him. But others either didn't understand what he was talking about or thought it was simply irrelevant. They continued asking the same question as before: "Kato, tell us, when are you going to get married?"

For Japanese lesbians, the formation of identity and relationships—to say nothing of the avoidance of marriage—was a far more difficult process than for gay men. Japan, after all, was a society only fifty years away from the time when women were expected to stay behind their husbands when walking down the street. Despite the advances women had made, they were less economically independent than men and far more susceptible to family and social pressures. For many, being a lesbian was just not a viable option, even today. As Mr. Minami put it, "For women, before taking the position of a lesbian, they have to take a position as a woman. And, in Japan, the position of women is weak."

Nonetheless I had an easier time meeting lesbians in Japan than anywhere outside the West. This probably had to do with the higher status of women there, at least compared to the rest of Asia. Perhaps it was simply that my contacts were better. In Boston, I had been introduced to a Japanese lesbian who had met a woman named Yoko at Regumi Studio, the Tokyo lesbian group. The Boston acquaintance, who was barely twenty and rather meek, found the women at Regumi intimidating. But she didn't feel that way about Yoko.

I took the subway out to the quiet Tokyo neighborhood where Yoko lived with her New Zealand lover of five years, a photographer. Their apartment was a typical Japanese fusion and confusion of East and West: tatami mats for Japanese guests to sit on and Western-style tables and chairs for *gaijin*.

Yoko was forty and taught physical education at a university outside Tokyo. She had her hair cut short and and insisted she never wore a dress or makeup. "My students say, 'You are like a man,' " she told me. "I say, 'So what!' Students understand that you have the right to your freedom." She added, "Of course, there are some who won't talk to me at all." Yoko looked robust and healthy, as a physical education instructor should. In white shorts and a lavender polo shirt, she might have been off for a morning at the tennis court.

She painted a rather dreary picture of being a lesbian in Japan. You couldn't come out, she said, or you'd lose your job and friends. Most lesbians with little education wound up marrying men. Others, who refused to marry and became involved with another woman, often wound up taking on the stereotypical roles of heterosexual couples, with one partner playing the "husband" and the other the "wife."

Yoko had had a long struggle to accept herself as a lesbian. While at university, she had a lesbian relationship that lasted for four years. "We always quarreled," she said. "It was because of this feeling of sin every day—that we should not be doing this. We were miserable. We felt that everything we did was the result of sin!"

She went off to England, where she lived for nine years. There, she was involved in a relationship with another woman; they were constantly debating whether or not to have sex. They never did.

Back in Japan, she met an American lesbian who told her it was "good to be gay." Yoko visited her in Honolulu, spending time at the women's center there; in that environment she felt comfortable with her sexuality for the first time. Shortly after she returned home, she met her current lover.

Within the past four years, there had been significant changes in Japan, she said. The lesbian group, Regumi Studio, had started up in Tokyo; in Osaka, the country's third-largest city, there was a women's coffeehouse. The first book about lesbians in Japan was published; this documentation of a previously hidden subject enabled greater numbers of women to consider the possibility that they might be gay.

The four times yearly "Dyke Weekends" were instrumental in the creation of a sense of lesbian solidarity and community, as well.

"I remember that first weekend so well," said Yoko. "Women were crying. It was like a new world had opened." The weekends, which attracted sixty to seventy women—half *gaijin* and half Japanese—were still rather clandestine. The women's educational center where the events took place refused to allow the organizers to use the term "lesbian." They called it the "International Women's Conference" instead.

Networking was in a relatively rudimentary state. Yoko showed me a telephone tree ("Dyke Denwa," *"denwa"* being Japanese for "telephone") that was used to organize dinners and social events. One person would telephone someone else, who in turn would call the next person on the tree. One woman was the link to Osaka; she made the call that activated the Dyke Denwa in that city.

I noted that most of the twenty or so names on the list were foreign women.

"That's true," said Yoko gloomily. "Most Japanese lesbians are isolated and alone. They find a lover and they stay by themselves."

Despite her own five-year lover relationship and the evolving support system, Yoko admitted that even now she couldn't totally accept herself as a lesbian. "Some part of me resists," she said.

Sometimes, she would go and have a drink with a male colleague who had repeatedly asked her to marry him. "I ask myself why am I going out with him," she said. "I won't marry him. But I feel it's bad not to. I can't get rid of this cultural feeling that I should marry, that I shouldn't be a lesbian. I am getting better, but I still feel this way to some extent."

She wanted to tell her mother that she was gay but just couldn't manage it. "If I told her, she would be desperate," Yoko said. "I am ready to tell her. Really I am. But she is relying on me. I just can't do it."

Living abroad throughout most of her twenties had enabled Yoko to resist pressure to marry. She believed that being involved in a relationship with a foreigner was helpful, too. Japanese had an "inferiority complex" regarding *gaijin,* she said. Living with a Westerner afforded Yoko a degree of status that somewhat counterbalanced the stigma of being an unmarried woman (to say nothing of being a lesbian). And the fact that she had lived in England for nine years also made it more understandable to colleagues and neighbors why she might live in a way that appeared unconventional by Japanese standards.

"Actually, I am quite lucky," she said. "I live with my lover. I work at a university. My behavior is that which is expected of a physical education teacher. I have friends who have to put on makeup and dresses for their jobs. I don't have to do that." Still, she said, "being a lesbian is not easy in this country." She wanted to leave Japan and move to New Zealand with her lover. She was studying osteopathy at night school in order to enhance herself professionally and thus make emigration easier.

Whatever her conflicts about her sexuality, Yoko, as she herself pointed out, was in a far better position than Japanese lesbians of her generation who had less education and fewer skills. "Their parents are powerful, and so these women get married and then divorced," she said. "They wind up working at the supermarket checkout counter. It isn't surprising they want another woman to be their 'husband.' Or maybe they wind up remarrying with a man. That is the lesbian pattern. There are a few brave ones who won't marry and keep on working at the supermarket."

A few days later, when I met Yoko's friend Minako and Minako's lover, Atsuko, it was a virtual continuation of the same conversation. Minako was describing how *koibito* relationships, even long-term ones, often fell apart under family pressure to marry. "Not to marry is like erasing all the culture and tradition that the Japanese have concentrated on building," she said. "It is such a different way of living for us. We feel that. A lesbian can have a relationship for many years and then marry. The reason she gives is that her parents want her to get married. Or that her father is dying and his last wish is that she get married—in costume, or something! She makes clear these are not her wishes but they are stronger than her wishes. There is no way to fight against that. You can't blame her for going the other way.

"It is like taking hostages," she continued. "People use your ailing mother or your ailing father to keep you in place. We always have to choose between respecting our ties with our original family and our new relationship. It is always one or the other. It is real psychological pressure and you get mixed up."

Even if women were more independent than in the past, one's economic freedom was precarious. "Let's say someone in your family gets sick," she said. "Then you have to go and take care of them. Women are caretakers. Many will quit their job for this reason and then it is hard to get a job back." All that put tremendous stress on lesbian couples. "If you have independence, you can create new relationships," Minako said. "But if something happens to someone in your original family, questions arise: Are you going to live all together with your family, for example?"

That is exactly what Minako had done. Minako, Atsuko, and Minako's nine-year-old daughter, Sakura, all lived together with Minako's mother in her childhood home. Her mother occupied half the house; Atsuko, Minako, and Sakura lived in the other half. This arrangement was a way of short-circuiting some of the difficulties Japanese lesbians faced.

Minako was short and rather pretty, with a cosmopolitan air. She was thirty-four, had been a reporter in the Tokyo bureau of *El País,* the Madrid daily newspaper, and currently worked as a Spanish and English translator. Before becoming involved with Atsuko, Minako had lived for three years with a Colombian man, who was the father of her daughter. Atsuko, forty-five and graying, was warm and sporty and had her own small business, an insurance agency. She was also an artist.

We were sitting at the office of Regumi Studio, a couple of subway stops away from Shinjuku. Regumi (pronounced "Le-Goomy"—it means simply "Lesbian Organization") shared space with two other women's groups. It had its own small room, with books, file cabinets, and a "Lesbians are Everywhere" poster.

I noticed a box of onions and garlic in one corner.

"One of our members who lives in the countryside sent it in place of dues," Atsuko explained.

On the wall was a calendar with the monthly Regumi hikes circled. The hikes were Regumi's most popular activity. There was also a pile of back issues of the Regumi newsletter, which Atsuko edited. Issues of the newsletter were never more than thirty-five pages; Japanese lesbians had nothing resembling the professionally produced, book-size magazines that Mr. Minami and Mr. Itoh published. One back issue included drawings by Atsuko and an advice column she and Minako had written about lesbian relationships.

Social options for Tokyo lesbians were expanding. All-night dance parties now took place once a month in Shinjuku, with as many as a hundred and fifty women in attendance. "Some women arrive with sleeping bags," Atsuko said. She also noted that feminist gatherings increasingly featured workshops about lesbian sexuality. These workshops always drew the largest crowds. "In a way, the pressure we get is very strong but we have more places to talk about our issues than gay men do," Atsuko said. "Women have a lot of different networks. Men have bars, but we have a lot of gatherings where we can be open about being lesbians."

Relationships with Tokyo gay men were strained, the women told me. A few years before, lesbians and gay men had worked together to oppose the government's coercive AIDS-prevention bill. Among other provisions, the bill slapped a hundred-thousand-yen fine on any person a physician suspected of being HIV-positive but who refused to be tested. But when gay men drew up an alternative bill which seemed to protect the civil liberties of homosexuals but not those of female prostitutes, the women were incensed. (The government proposal was approved, in any event.) Today, although Minako and Atsuko praised a group of Osaka gay men who were strongly influenced by feminism, they had little interaction—or patience—with gay men in Tokyo. Organizations like OCCUR and ILGA/Japan were insensitive to women's concerns, they felt. "For us it is too much work to educate gay men," Minako said.

We went to the corner soba shop for lunch. On the wall above us was a large poster of a Western woman in a bikini. The anti–"Miss Contest" movement was catching on in Japan. (Japanese always referred to beauty contests by the English expression "Miss Contests.") In fact, the leader of the gay group in Osaka had just participated in a parody of a Miss Contest that had been reported in the newspapers. "These contests are mushrooming now," Minako said, disapprovingly. "Every town or city is organizing one—with taxpayers' money. Even banks are starting to use women on their posters. Before, that was unthinkable. So, the antiporn movement is getting strong here."

Take Back the Night marches (to focus attention on rape) and issues such as incest and wife-beating were gaining attention, too. Lesbians were prominent in working on all these issues, although they often kept their sexuality quiet. Minako was involved with the first large-scale study of incest in Japan. "Now, there is a lot of interest in these subjects," said Minako. "Lesbians are finding some expression because of this, and women welcome it. They say, '*Gam batay!*' That is when you do something and people support you. It means 'Keep it up!' "

If relations between lesbians and Tokyo gay men were problematic, those between lesbians and the younger generation of straight feminists were relatively good. "Still, not many heterosexual feminists come to the women's dances," Minako said. "They are more used to discussing or reading a book. Many lesbians are the same way. They are just starting to find they can have fun, too. Maybe it is just a question of opportunity. We think that we have to create different kinds of activities."

Atsuko agreed. "We need to create a new kind of person who can enjoy many things. A more versatile lesbian!" She laughed. "I'm used to dancing and playing sports. I'm not used to discussions. Minako is different. She is one of those more used to discussions. But she is learning, too!"

In Japan, many of the new political and social ideas didn't emanate from Tokyo but instead from Osaka and Kyoto. Osaka was the commercial and industrial hub of southwest Japan and an international business center. Kyoto had been the imperial capital for nearly a thousand years; today it was a university and tourist town, surrounded by green hills and dotted with Japan's most beautiful and spectacular temples. If Tokyo was Rome, and Osaka was Milan, Kyoto was Florence—artistic, intellectual, proud.

Today, Osaka and Kyoto constituted a single metropolitan area, with the two cities about thirty minutes from one another by Shinkansen, the Japanese bullet train. In Osaka and Kyoto, Minako said, there was more "popular culture" and less "official culture" than in Tokyo. The influence of feminism was greater there. In the southwest of Japan, they were determined to do things their own way, without slavishly following Tokyo's lead—and that determination extended to gay and lesbian issues, too.

I took the Shinkansen to Kyoto. The train was clean and graceful and traveled at a speed approaching a hundred and thirty-five miles an hour. It offered all the excitement of flying, but none of the anxiety. Mr. Minami had given me the name of a Kyoto University graduate student who was interested in gay issues. We met at the Yasaka Shrine, a bright orange-colored temple dedicated to the Shinto god of medicine, who was supposed to protect the city from epidemics. Each New Year's Eve, people came to take a flame from a bonfire lit at the shrine. According to tradition, if you ate a New Year's breakfast cooked with a flame from that fire, you would be free from disease for the coming year.

The graduate student was lanky, half-shaven, his shirt hanging out of his trousers. He arrived on a motorcycle. He had wanted to do his master's thesis on the development of the gay movement in Japan. But even at Kyoto University, considered the most radical in the country, his proposal was rejected. Homosexuality was not considered a fit subject for sociological research. He was doing his thesis on the subject of obedience to authority instead.

The graduate student informed me that he wasn't gay. He was, however, married to the daughter of a well-known Tokyo gay bar owner and political figure, which might have explained some of his interest. Curiously, he had only met his father-in-law twice in his life.

Over dinner, he noted that virtually no academic work had been done in Japan on the subject of homosexuality; data were extremely limited. He suspected that this lack of information—and the absence of legitimacy that scholarly interest conferred—was a major cause of the difficulty Japanese gays and lesbians faced in constructing their own identity. (It also enabled the government to make patently ridiculous claims about the number of gay people in Japan.) "There just isn't any gay studies in this country," he lamented.

The graduate student was fascinated by the subject of how and why gay identity developed in Japan. The Japanese traditionally had little notion of sexuality or sexual orientation, he thought. They only understood homosexuality in terms of hobby, or *shumi*. When did gay identity in Japan begin? he wanted to know. Was it around 1950, did I think? "I don't believe that that gay identity existed during the eighteenth or nineteenth centuries," he said. "Maybe the identity of a pederast existed, but not a gay identity."

What about a more contemporary figure like Yukio Mishima? I asked.

"Mishima wasn't gay in the modern sense," he replied. "He viewed himself as a pederast. That's something different."

He took me to buy a comic book, an example of *genesto,* a genre that idealized male homosexual love and was extremely popular with junior high school girls. The comics, unabashedly homoerotic, featured androgynous young heroes called *bishonen.* One reason for the popularity of such comics seemed to be that the view of sexuality they presented was nonthreatening. The graduate student thought their appeal was also related to the equation of male homosexual love with romance and chivalry that had come down through Japanese history. In the Japanese mind, same-sex love had an aesthetic connotation; it was associated with devotion and sacrifice and suicide, all of which had a great attraction to teenage girls. We bought a comic that featured a love triangle consisting of a sister and brother who were both involved with the same man. In the pictures, it was hard to distinguish between male and female.

We went off to a gay bar, C'est Bon. It was a small place, where regular customers would purchase a bottle of whiskey, leave it behind the counter with their name on it, and order from the bottle each time they came in. The graduate student seemed comfortable there. The bar master was in his fifties. Most of the gay men of his generation were married, he told us. He had only avoided that fate because his parents had died when he was young.

On the counter was a slick, book-length Japanese gay magazine called *Samson.* In addition to stories and personal ads, it featured pictures of naked, overweight men, many of whom looked to be in their fifties. Their genitals were covered by a white cloth. "We don't have this kind of magazine in the United States," I said to the graduate student.

The master, who didn't look much different from *Samson*'s models himself, was offended. He handed me a magazine published in California that was clearly aimed at the same audience. I apologized profusely.

We talked some more and I walked the graduate student back to his motorcycle. "Please send me some books, articles, catalogs about homosexuality from the United States," he pleaded. "There is just nothing in Japan! Send me anything!"

Gay Osaka had its rebels. I went to see Hiroshi Hirano, the head of the Osaka Gay Community (OGC), the city's gay organization, who had been a participant in the mock "Miss Contest" that Minako had described. At an ILGA meeting I attended in Tokyo, someone passed around a newspaper clipping about the contest, featuring a photo of Hirano—in an evening gown. A long and rather grave discussion had ensued. I never could determine exactly what was said, although I assumed it was not complimentary.

Hirano made Tokyo gay activists uncomfortable. They tended to dismiss the OGC, which had split off from ILGA and today had a membership that was almost half women—lesbians and heterosexual feminists. "They should call themselves the Osaka Feminist Community, instead of the Osaka Gay Community," said OCCUR's Niimi, huffily. But the women in both Tokyo and Osaka spoke highly of Hirano. They liked his critique of accepted notions of gender roles, the fact that he was trying to play with the Japanese tradition of transvestism and to use it in the service of feminism and gay liberation.

I waited for Hirano in the lobby of a hotel next to the Osaka railway station, under a large mural painted to look like Seurat's "Afternoon at the Grande Jatte." It was one of those quasi-official meeting places that were so popular in Japan. Businessmen and students paced up and down, glancing at their watches; everyone was expecting someone. In a country where virtually every male dressed identically, Hirano wasn't hard to spot. He was wearing stretch pants and a purple floral-print jacket over a T-shirt, plus an assortment of jewelry—an earring in the shape of a cat, a choke necklace, bangles, rings. His hair was pulled back and tied with a rubber band. The effect was androgynous but not at all flamboyant, recalling Haight Ashbury in 1965, rather than Kabuki theater or the Jewel Box Revue. Hirano himself was shy and unassuming.

We sat in the hotel coffee shop. Hirano, who was thirty and taught Japanese at an evening school, was more interested in talking politics than fashion. In Tokyo, he said, "gay people will say they are gay in a gay context only. Otherwise, they stay in the closet. In Osaka, we believe our meetings should be open to nongay people. We feel that communication between gays and heterosexuals is important."

OGC viewed gay men not as "males" but as "persons," Hirano explained. As long as gay men remained closeted and pretended to be heterosexuals, they received the privileges of the dominant gender. Only by coming out, renouncing their privileges as men, and allying with women could gay men transform themselves and society.

Most gay men didn't understand this point of view, he conceded. In fact, while the number of heterosexual women in OGC was growing, the number of gay men stagnated. But Hirano refused to modify his principles to recruit more gay members.

I asked Hirano about the "Miss Contest." The intention, he said, was to reverse the situation of the traditional beauty pageant: In this case, the men were the contestants and the women were the judges. There were four contestants altogether, and an audience of some five to six hundred people. "We wore evening dresses and high heels and also bathing suits," Hirano said. "It was a kind of a comedy."

Who was the winner?

"Didn't you know?" Hirano asked. "*I* was!"

The trouble was, however, that, with the exception of a Kyoto newspaper, the media treated the contest as an example of tranvestism. The element of feminist social criticism was lost. "One of the TV stations called me a 'professional gay,'" said Hirano. "The media has the idea of gay people wearing dresses and pretending to be female. They missed the point of what we were trying to do."

Hirano always went to work in the androgynous style of dress he favored the afternoon of our meeting. On a couple of occasions, while riding his bicycle, people had shouted *"Okama!"* (the Japanese term for transvestite) at him, but he was rarely harassed. The purpose in dressing the way he did was not to indicate he was gay, he emphasized. "I want to break down established ideas," he said. "I want to break down the idea of separate male and female clothing." His reasons were aesthetic as well as political. "I hate male clothing," Hirano said. "Male clothing is not beautiful." As for women's clothing, "the contest was my first experience in dressing as a woman," he said. "I don't have much interest in women's clothes." What did interest Hirano was creating his own eclectic style, one that challenged accepted notions.

Midway through our conversation, another OGC member, named Kawamura, joined us. He was twenty-eight and, like Hirano, was also a teacher of Japanese. He was dressed in the conventional salaryman manner. Even if you couldn't have picked him out in a crowd, Kawamura was trying to challenge established ideas, in his own way. He wanted to change how Japanese gays viewed relationships, to undermine the concepts of hierarchy that had determined the way Japanese had interacted with each other since time immemorial.

Kawamura was putting theory into practice, starting with his relationship with his lover. The couple, who had been together two and a half years, were currently living separately, but Kawamura's lover wanted them to move in together. Kawamura resisted the idea, partly because his lover, who was younger, seemed incapable of doing any household tasks. "I am afraid if we live together, he will become too dependent on me," he said. "I don't want us to be husband and wife. When gay couples don't imitate husband and wife, they imitate older brother and younger brother. I want him to think about his role!"

Japan is a society where relationships have traditionally been based on hierarchical dependence—parent-child, husband-wife, older brother–younger brother, older sister–younger sister. Equality was an alien notion. All models for relationships were family models. Age traditionally determined one's place in the schema. This was true in gay and lesbian relationships, as well. In the brotherhood bonds of the feudal period, one samurai took the role of older brother and the other that of the younger. In *S* relations between schoolgirls, the traditional model had been that of older sister–younger sister. Even Minako and Atsuko had argued in their advice column in the Regumi newsletter that an age difference between partners was crucial for the success of a relationship.

In Japanese gay and lesbian couplings, "the first thing that two people do when they meet is to find out the other person's age," one gay man told me. "It is a quasi family, really. You are looking for an older—or a younger—brother or perhaps a father or son. In Japan, you have to know the role first or you can't communicate with the other person. That is different from the U.S., where you develop roles as the relationship goes on."

Even Kanda, OCCUR's enfant terrible, said that in relationships he preferred to call his partner "Younger Brother" and to be called "Older Brother." "It makes me feel a sense of intimacy," he said. "If we just call each other by first names, I just don't feel comfortable." A study of 514 personal ads in *Barazoku* found that forty-one percent of the advertisers used the term "big brother" to describe themselves, while another eighteen percent referred to themselves as "little brother." Only ten percent used the terms "lover" or "friend." As the American anthropologist Ruth Benedict noted in her book *The Chrysanthemum and the Sword:* "When the Japanese want to express utter confusion, they say something is 'neither elder brother nor young brother.' It is like saying that something is neither fish nor fowl, for to the Japanese a man should keep his character as elder brother as drastically as a fish should stay in water."

So here was Kawamura, trying to create a different basis for a relationship, and merely sowing utter confusion. "My lover thinks that because I don't want us to live together, because I don't want him to be dependent on me, I don't love him," Kawamura said. "And that isn't true!"

In trying to reformulate another hierarchical relationship—that with his parents—Kawamura was finding matters equally troublesome. His parents lived in Osaka, but he had rented an apartment by himself in Kyoto. Since he was the only son, his decision to leave home had caused a rift. "My parents see living by myself as rejecting them," he said. "In their view, dependence equals love." At this point he only saw his parents once or twice a year, even though they lived a short train ride away. Telephone conversations degenerated into arguments about his decision to live by himself. "I want to come out to them," he said. "I have confidence in myself and in my relationship. But there has been so much arguing and fighting about my living away from them that I don't dare."

One effort at breaking down established roles had been more successful, though. Kawamura and other gay men in OGC occasionally provided child care for the women in the group. That way, gay men got a chance to develop relationships with children; the women got an evening of freedom.

"There is a big difference between us and OCCUR," Kawamura explained. "They're very political, too political, I think. We emphasize personal issues." In other respects, the differences between OGC and the Tokyo groups reflected differing strategies for building a lesbian and gay movement in a country where, in OCCUR's Niimi's words, gays were "relaxed but not free." OCCUR was trying to establish a stronger sense of gay identity by creating, somewhat questionably, the idea of heterosexuals as the "enemy." Mr. Minami's ILGA/Japan was trying to replicate San Francisco or Scandinavia through an equally questionable Western-style display of gay political and economic muscle.

In Osaka, by contrast, the emphasis was on cooperation between gay men and heterosexual and lesbian women. The Osaka approach had its drawbacks—a tendency to take an orthodox feminist line on certain subjects (Kawamura, for instance, seemed under the sway of the American feminist Andrea Dworkin) that made it difficult to build grass-roots support among gay men. But in a country where the issue was not so much homophobia as the pressures of family, marriage, and hierarchical roles, it seemed sensible to view gay men and heterosexual and lesbian women as allies, fighting the same battles.

When I returned to Tokyo, I went to Minako and Atsuko's house for dinner. It was a friendly and appealingly disordered place, with none of the chilly minimalism that characterized much Tokyo interior decor. At one point, Minako's extended family had lived there: uncles, aunts, cousins. There, she had cared for her aged grandparents when they were ill. "When I was growing up, this was all fields—and cows," said Minako. "Now, it is the middle of Tokyo."

The main course was eel, a Japanese delicacy.

Before dinner, Minako spent a long time on the phone. A lesbian couple she was friendly with was breaking up, and she was dispensing comfort. Minako and Atsuko had been together for six years, which made them one of the longest-running lesbian couples in Tokyo. Other women relied on them for advice. "Do gay men in the

States talk to other gay men about their relationship problems?" she wanted to know.

Minako's nine-year-old daughter, Sakura, dressed in a black sweatshirt that said HOT PEP, made a brief appearance and then vanished. (Sakura means "cherry blossom.") She returned again when her father telephoned. But she had only a moment to spare for him. "She is watching her favorite TV show," her mother explained. "Nothing else has any importance to her."

The eel was delicious. We discussed the difficulties of finding the right terminology to describe lesbian and gay partners. Minako and Atsuko had decided that the Japanese word for lover, *"koibito,"* didn't suit them or their relationship. They had come up with a new word: *"nakayoshi,"* which means literally "good relationship" and which children use to signify "buddy" or "chum." It was a word that Sakura and her friends used. "Usually your childhood friends are very important," said Minako. "We want to get closer to that kind of experience."

Atsuko put it this way: "After six years, our relationship is changing, and we need something—a word—to describe what it is. There are few words that describe what we experience or feel, so we have to create our own. Then, we tell our friends and hope it really becomes a word."

I was curious about what it was like for Sakura to grow up with two mothers. "Sakura doesn't think she is a child, you know," said Minako. "She thinks we are all friends. It is only when someone else comes in that she considers us to be her mothers." Sakura called them Mother and Acha (the latter being short for Atsuko). When people asked her if Atsuko was "her sister or her aunt or what?" Sakura would respond, "She's just Acha!"

Sakura had created a fantasy that enabled her to believe she had a special relationship with Atsuko. She had convinced herself that she had actually met Atsuko before her mother had, that she and Atsuko had become friends, and that it was Sakura had actually introduced Atsuko to Minako. In the fantasy, Sakura and Atsuko were at the beach; while Minako was asleep, the two went off to get an ice cream. Then, Minako woke up and she, too, became friends with Atsuko.

"The truth is," Minako said, "that Atsuko and I met at a party. But we don't want to destroy Sakura's fantasy."

I felt at home visiting Minako and Atsuko. In many respects, it wasn't much different from visiting lesbian friends in the United States. Of the non-Western societies I visited, I thought that Japan had the greatest possibility of creating a Western-style sense of gay and lesbian identity and community. Of course, in Japan, the visitor had to be wary: How things appeared on the surface was not necessarily how they were deep-down. There remained that weak sense of identity and the pressure to marry. But if Japan was a rigid society, it was also a pragmatic one. Japanese gays and lesbians had a number of advantages: nonjudgmental religious traditions; a high standard of living, which increasingly enabled younger people to live on their own; the rising social and economic position of women; and an infatuation with anything Western, particularly anything American. And that infatuation extended to Western ideas about sexuality and homosexuality and women's roles.

When it was time to leave, Minako accompanied me to the door. I noticed a large pile of wood on the front porch.

"What's that for?" I asked.

"We're hoping to build several houses in the countryside," Minako explained. "Japanese-style, you know—just wood, no nails. We want to start a lesbian commune."

She dug out a couple of pieces of wood from the pile and cradled them in her arms as she might have held Sakura when she was a baby. "You know, they say that whatever happens in the United States happens ten years later in Japan," she said, smiling. "We're beginning to catch up."

7

ARGENTINA AND URUGUAY
HEARTBREAK TANGO

Buenos Aires

When I arrived in Buenos Aires, inflation stood at two hundred percent for the month. The austral, which had been valued at $1.10 a few years before, was now worth ⅟₆₅₀ of a dollar. The newly elected Peronist government was pardoning the generals who had been imprisoned for presiding over the torture and disappearance of more than nine thousand of their fellow citizens during the Proceso, the years of military rule between 1976 and 1983. And the electricity was out.

I was staying with two friends: an American named Chris and his lover, Osvaldo, an Argentine who had fled the country in 1979, hiding out in the bathroom of a Pan Am jet. Both now lived in Boston and were spending the summer—the Southern Hemisphere's winter—in Buenos Aires. Chris is a novelist who was writing a book about Buenos Aires and Montevideo, the Uruguayan capital just across the River Plate; Osvaldo was working on his doctoral thesis on the gay novel in Argentina. He was spending much of his time videotaping gay Argentine writers, most of whom, curiously, were in their sixties or seventies.

Chris greeted me with a flashlight. Buenos Aires relied on hydroelectric power, generated by a series of dams near the Paraguayan border. There hadn't been any rain in months. So power was being rationed in the form of rotating blackouts. The elevator, of the ancient bird-cage variety that seemed out of a forties French movie, had been among the victims of the power outage. We carried my bags up seven narrow flights of stairs in the pitch dark. Neighbors opened their apartment doors to let some light into the windowless stairwell. "Buenas noches," joked one, even though it was eleven o'clock in the morning. "Bienvenidos a la colonia," muttered another, which translated as "Welcome to the colony" or, maybe, "Welcome to the Third World."

Out of breath, we arrived at Chris and Osvaldo's apartment, the penthouse. The French doors were thrown wide open; the brilliant sunlight and mild breezes of Buenos Aires winter filled the apartment. Osvaldo led me to the terrace. Before us lay the entire city: a panorama of monochromatic cream and gray buildings, with the dome of the Congreso building off to one side and the River Plate (and, barely visible, the coast of neighboring Uruguay) on the other.

Later, when we went out for a walk, the streets of San Telmo, Chris and Osvaldo's neighborhood, were deserted, the shops shuttered. On Saturday afternoon in Buenos Aires, almost everything seems to close down; the fact that the price of gas had quadrupled the week before led most people who had cars to keep them at home. San Telmo is a splendid though decaying late-nineteenth-century neighborhood, with narrow cobblestoned streets and stone-faced French and Italianate buildings, many with wrought-iron balconies. Virtually every façade was covered with graffiti, mostly urging a vote for Carlos Saúl Menem, the Peronist presidential candidate elected the month before, but also touting heavy-metal rock bands like Mötley Crüe. San Telmo was probably best known for its Sunday-afternoon outdoor antiques market, where you could purchase old gramophones and stuffed armadillos, silver and brass items, and tango scores.

At nearly midnight, dinner hour in Buenos Aires, we went out to a neighborhood restaurant, the Almafuerte. We ate *achuras*— tripe, kidneys, and cow intestine—and other standard Argentine dinner fare. Osvaldo took charge of the menu. He would insist, "Try this," and decline to identify precisely what he was recommending. It would taste good, but the consistency would be just a little disconcerting. Then he would inform me gleefully that I had just consumed some part of a cow's innards. "Now, wasn't that good?" he would demand, in a show of national pride, and I would reply bravely, "Yes, it really was quite delicious," trying to concentrate on the possibility of dessert.

We took a cab downtown. As a consequence of the latest devaluation of the austral, a taxi ride cost less than a dollar. Most of the cabs in Buenos Aires—and there seemed to be an endless number of them—were riding around empty. Argentines couldn't afford them, and there weren't enough tourists to pick up the slack. You could put your hand out on virtually any street corner in town and a taxicab would stop instantly. "Every New Yorker's dream," said Chris.

Like Paris, Buenos Aires is a city of grand avenues, of train stations built to resemble palaces, of cafés and *confiterías* on every corner. Like Paris, too, it is a city of lights, from the gleaming Obelisk, meant to recall the Place de la Concorde, to the sea of neon down the Avenida Corrientes, with its theaters and restaurants and book and record stores. But that first evening, something seemed wrong. Buenos Aires resembled Paris, but a wartime, down-at-the-heels Paris. There were still people on the streets, lining up in front of darkened theaters or trying to make out the prices of items in barely lit store windows. But the crowds seemed a little dazed, the lights dimming; and their money was worth less and less each day.

All this was particularly galling to Porteños, as the inhabitants of Buenos Aires are called, because, as the children and grandchildren of Spanish and Italian and Eastern European Jewish immigrants, they consider themselves displaced Europeans. In 1928, after all, Argentina boasted the eighth-highest gross national product of any country in the world. That today they should have to endure the same hardships as much of the rest of Latin America was the ultimate humiliation.

By the time I departed Buenos Aires, some weeks later, the drought had ended, and the neon lights on Corrientes were back on again. Inflation had stabilized, too, at least for the moment, and the major news story was not the economy but an incident in which a man with a gun entered a suburban health club and forced the aerobics instructors and their customers to have sex with one another as he watched. Still, my initial impression of a city in crisis lingered. Even with the lights blazing and the prices remarkably steady, incomes were worth only a fraction of what they had been a few months before. I was constantly hearing stories of people being laid off, and meeting others who worked two or three jobs or supplemented their incomes selling sneakers door to door.

After our stroll downtown, Osvaldo went home, and Chris and I headed to a gay bar named Teleny (after a story attributed to Oscar Wilde). It was a small place, just off the Avenida Santa Fe, the middle-class shopping boulevard that is the heart of gay Buenos Aires. In contrast to the bars and restaurants in the downtown area, the place was brightly lit and the tables were crowded with young men, their hair slicked back in the manner of thirties tango idols; they were all dressed in sweaters and blue jeans and matching jean jackets. Decor consisted of framed photos of the usual gay icons— Garbo, Lauren Bacall, Montgomery Clift, and Marlon Brando. Chris and I ordered anise, which was brought in large tumblers. We stood on the fringes, crushed between other customers, most of whom were smoking cigarettes and drinking wine spritzers.

On a small stage toward the front, drag queens in blond wigs and ruffled red dresses were singing tangos. One queen, her hairy shoulders visible just above her dress, sang one of the most famous—and melancholy—of the genre:

> Verás que todo es mentira,
> Verás que nada es amor,
> Que al mundo nada le importa . . .
> Yira! . . . Yira! . . .
> Aunque te quiebre la vida,
> Aunque te muerda el dolor,
> No esperes nunca una ayuda,
> Ni una mano, ni un favor.
>
> (You will see that everything is a lie,
> You will see that love is nothing,
> That in the world, nothing matters . . .
> Wander! . . . Wander! . . .
> Even if life breaks you,
> Even though pain eats away at you,

Don't expect any help,
Neither a hand, nor a favor.)

The song's refrain, "Yira! Yira!," meant "Wander! Wander!," but it also signified wandering in the sense of "cruising" the Avenida Santa Fe just down the block—and the double meaning was lost on no one at Teleny. It was an anthem of gay misery that could have come directly out of *The Boys in the Band.* Yet despite the pre-liberation atmosphere, Teleny didn't really seem gloomy. Perhaps it was that everyone was too young to really feel the disillusionment of the tango, that they were just playing at being "all the sad young men." Or maybe it was just Argentina, where pessimism and fatalism were the prevailing worldview—the lights could go out, the government or the economy could topple in an instant, but you ate and drank and stayed up till dawn, nonetheless. Shortly after three A.M. one of the drag queens did a climactic tango with an older man, and the customers began to drift out, no doubt to "wander" the streets of Buenos Aires, in search of the lover who, the tango warned, could only disappoint.

Democracy had been restored in Argentina, but, for gay people, it didn't appear to have much meaning. There hadn't actually been a revolution, just the fall of one of the more brutal of one of Argentina's periodic military regimes, which have dominated the country for most of the century. The institutions of repression—the military and police—remained intact, as did many of the social and cultural attitudes that sustained them.

Argentine militarism, in particular the military government that ruled during the Proceso, had actively persecuted homosexuals. Peronism, the populist-cum-fascist political movement founded by the dictator Juan Perón in the 1940s and now in the saddle again, had traditionally taken a very conservative position on sexual issues. A powerful Catholic church and a macho culture, where women were kept in their place and gay men viewed with contempt, rounded out the picture. In Argentina, we were back in the familiar world of Western notions about sexual orientation (although, as in Egypt, the man who took the "active" position in anal sex was usually not considered gay). The issue wasn't identity, rather an entrenched, often violent, and socially sanctioned prejudice against homosexuality and homosexuals. The military might have returned to barracks, and a civilian government might have been installed in the Casa Rosada, but it was no wonder that a sense of insecurity and hopelessness dominated the worldview of many Argentine lesbians and gays.

On Monday, I went down to the offices of the Comunidad Homosexual Argentina (CHA), the country's leading, and virtually only, gay and lesbian organization. Chris came along to translate. Osvaldo was dubious. He had been a member of the first gay group in Argentina—the Frente de Liberación Homosexual (FLH)—which was established in 1971, during a short respite between military dictatorships. Members of the FLH, an all-male group, took women's names; Osvaldo's was Lucrecia Borgia. The FLH had been influenced by the youth culture of the time and the radical ideas of gay liberation emanating from the United States and Western Europe. It went underground as the country moved toward repression and extremist violence under the rule of Isabel Martínez de Perón, the former chorus girl who became Juan Perón's third wife and, upon his death, the president. The FLH formally dissolved when the military overthrew Isabel in 1976 and it was never revived. Osvaldo was convinced—as were many other gay people in Buenos Aires—that the members of the CHA did little but sit around and talk and drink *mate*.

Osvaldo tended to take things personally. "Why don't they march in the streets the way we did in the FLH?" he demanded. Chris thought he was being unfair. "It's not the 1970s anymore," he insisted, with the objectivity of the outsider. "Then, all the young people of this country were in the streets. Today, it is a totally different situation."

The CHA was located in a brownstone on a street of fading elegance lined with photocopy establishments; the other tenants of the building were primarily notaries and accountants. The offices, open for "drop-in" every evening from six to eight, consisted of a few small, high-ceilinged rooms. The walls of the main reception area were decorated with an Italian safe-sex poster and another featuring two handsome soldiers and the slogan FATE L'AMORE, NON LA GUERRA. Also on the wall was a copy of the CHA constitution.

A list of the addresses of each police precinct in the city of Buenos Aires covered the side of a file cabinet. Detentions of gay people by the police were an ongoing problem.

The offices were crowded, with a variety of meetings going on. Members greeted one another with an affectionate "Qué tal?" and a kiss on the cheek. Chris and I were ushered into the office of the group's president, Alejandro Zalazar. Zalazar was a rather harried-looking man in his early thirties who supported himself managing property. He spoke no English. Dressed in a militarylike shirt and khaki pants, with pomaded hair and an authoritarian manner, Zalazar cut an odd figure for the head of a lesbian and gay group. "All he needs is a swagger stick!" Chris observed.

His appearance aside, Zalazar was courteous and helpful. The CHA, he told us, was established in 1984, shortly after the military regime fell victim to its disastrous war with the British over the Falkland Islands, and democracy was restored. In the first heady days of freedom, many gay people—like members of other social groups that had been persecuted by the military—believed that democracy would solve all their problems. They soon learned otherwise. In March of 1984, police raided a popular gay club and arrested a large number of people. A week later, at a mass meeting at a Buenos Aires disco, the CHA was formed.

Zalazar emphasized that the CHA was very different from the old FLH. It included both men and women (although lesbians made up only about twenty percent of its members) and eschewed the leftist, gay-liberationist ideology of the earlier group. The CHA viewed itself as a human-rights organization, but one that was distinct in that it put particular emphasis on the free expression of sexuality. It was careful to remain independent of political parties—a difficult task in Argentina, where interest groups not under the aegis of political parties have historically been rare.

I asked Zalazar what he considered his organization's major accomplishment. "Just continuing to exist," he said, an allusion to the divisions that had rent the organization. Beyond that, there had been "small victories," he said. In the province of Buenos Aires, outside the city, a law barring homosexuals from voting had been repealed; the CHA claimed some of the credit. The CHA was one of many organizations that played a role in successfully pressuring the country's Supreme Court to guarantee the right of everyone detained by the police to a telephone call. But the group had been less successful in its effort to overturn the police edicts that allowed people to be held without charges in the first place. And the CHA itself was still campaigning to achieve legal status as an organization. "Remember that in Argentina, democracy is only six years old," Zalazar cautioned.

Because democracy was so new, the CHA had to contend with the fear and intimidation that were the legacies of military rule. Fear remained a generalized feeling in the country, Zalazar noted. But because the gay population existed on the margins of society to begin with, the effect of that fear on homosexuals was more profound. As a result, the CHA held few marches or demonstrations; only a very small number were willing to participate in such a public manner. "If things were right, the CHA would have over a million members," he said.

Zalazar went back to work, and the CHA's vice president, Rafael Freda, invited us for mate. Mate is the bitter-tasting herb that working-class Argentines drink incessantly as tea; it is steeped in a small cup or gourd, and passed from person to person like a joint of marijuana. It was fashionable for intellectuals and people on the left to drink maté, a way of demonstrating one's social and political allegiances.

Rafael told us—with some pride—that he was addicted to the stuff. It gave you a lift and dulled the appetite, he said. Rafael was a youthful-looking, fair-haired man of forty-one, wearing an aviator jacket; he gave the impression that he didn't eat enough. He was a high school literature teacher and a writer for one of the country's major television stations. He spoke a good, if somewhat rusty English, from his days as a graduate student at the University of Denver fifteen years before.

As the mate was passed—each person sucked it through a long silver tube called a *bombilla*—Rafael offered a semiologist's analysis of the outer office door. When the CHA had rented its first office, he said, the organization deliberately chose an office that had two doors—one to enter and one to escape. In its current location, there was only one door. He had been afraid it would be dangerous, but Zalazar hadn't agreed, and Zalazar had been right. "When that

door opens," Rafael said, "you never know who will enter. Will it
be an anxious youngster? A person carrying the AIDS virus? Someone who has just left the police precinct after being detained? The
police? The mailman saying there is no money for us? All the ones
I have listed have occurred."

A week or so later, Rafael dropped by Chris and Osvaldo's to talk.
The police had begun raiding the gay bars, he said. These weren't
the huge, wholesale raids that Buenos Aires had experienced in the
past, when entire bars were emptied out and their patrons brought
to the nearest police precinct. Instead, Moralidad (the vice squad)
would come and pluck five or ten or twenty or even forty people off
the dance floor. Moralidad usually chose the ones who appeared
the most stereotypically gay or the least likely to protest or to fight
back. (Some bars were mixed, so not everyone arrested was necessarily gay or lesbian.)

Rafael promised that if I came down to the CHA offices the next
evening, he would introduce me to someone who had been detained
in one of the raids. In the meantime, he left me with a list of bars
and numbers of arrests:

Saturday, August 19

Contramano	8	Precinct 25
Bunker	40	
Confusión	??	

Friday, August 25

Soviet	25	Precinct 15
Experiment	5	
Maximum	10	

Saturday August 26

Contramano	??	Precinct 19
In Vitro	3	
Quiero Lola	??	

Homosexuality wasn't illegal in Argentina, Rafael emphasized.
There were police edicts in Buenos Aires regarding *escándalo*—the

soliciting or offering of oneself for a sexual act—that had traditionally been used against homosexuals. But two judges had challenged
the use of these edicts. So, today, the police would merely detain
people for a maximum of twenty-four hours on the pretense of
checking their records and then release them. This functioned as a
very effective form of intimidation. It also provided an easy means
for the police to fill their arrest quotas on a quiet night.

When I arrived at the CHA offices for my second visit, everything
was in an uproar. The furniture had been moved around in such a
way as to make the place almost unrecognizable; what had been the
reception area had been turned into the president's office. The CHA
constitution hanging on the wall was now covered over with a
purple cloth.

What was going on? I asked Rafael.

"This all has a political purpose," he explained. "We don't want
people to get too comfortable with the structure or the leadership."

I felt as if I had stumbled into Shanghai in the middle of the
Cultural Revolution.

Rafael introduced me to Miguel Kurylko, the CHA treasurer,
who was among those arrested. Miguel was a husky, mustachioed
man who managed the office of a small firm. He was relaxed and
good-humored and had spent most of the period of the Proceso
living in Brazil. "I love Brazil," he said. "I love the people, the
music. At Carnival, you can feel the sensuality in the streets. Argentina is so boring, don't you think?"

On the night of one of the raids, Miguel had been at Contramano, a popular disco that had been the first gay dance club to
open after the restoration of democracy. Today, it drew a mostly
middle-aged crowd and was decorated with fake brick walls, mir-
rors, and strobe lights. Miguel wasn't generally a bargoer. The
CHA was planning a benefit dance at Contramano, and he was at
the bar trying to work out last-minute details with Contramano's
owner.

It was two-thirty in the morning, the peak hour for Buenos Aires
nightlife. Miguel was in the owner's office when an employee rushed
in. Moralidad was in the bar, he announced, and they were taking
people away. "Fuck, not again!" said the owner, and rushed out of
the office. Miguel followed.

For a few moments, Miguel stood and watched. Most people were going about their business. They were dancing, talking to one another, pretending nothing was going on. Plainclothes policemen passed Miguel a couple of times without demanding to see his identification papers. He stepped up to talk to the arresting officers. Perhaps being in the bar in his organizational capacity emboldened him in a way that wouldn't have been the case if he had been there just to have a good time. He identified himself as an official of the CHA and demanded to know what was going on. The officer in charge informed him that what they were doing was perfectly legal. "But you arrested people last week, too," Miguel said. The officer hadn't been aware of that; there had been a new directive, he said. "What is the new directive?" Miguel demanded. "More repression now?" The officer became angry. He ordered Miguel brought to the police station with the others.

This hadn't been Miguel's first brush with the police. In the late sixties, when he was a long-haired musician, the police would often drag people to the station and force them to have their hair cut. Miguel was fortunate; he got off with a lecture, not a haircut. Later, toward the end of the Proceso, Miguel was arrested coming out of a restaurant with a friend who was rather flamboyant in his appearance. Miguel was jailed for twelve hours. When the police asked him if he was gay then, he denied it.

This time, Miguel didn't deny his homosexuality. As he got into the police wagon, he began shouting to the other detainees, "Don't sign anything. I am a member of the CHA." The only problem was that many of the other detainees didn't know what the CHA was. The group was brought to the central police station. There, in the main courtyard, some eighty people—half of them women—were lined up. It was pouring rain. As the crowd waited to hand in their documentos, one man had an epileptic seizure. The police took him away. Someone else was pacing nervously up and down, refusing to stand in the line with everyone else. According to Miguel's account, a policeman slapped this man and twisted his arm; then two plainclothesmen removed him, as well. Miguel himself was shaking so much that he kept his hands in his pockets so no one could see how afraid he was.

The men were divided from the women and each group put in

separate cells. The men's cell was small and dark; you had to ask your neighbor's pardon every time you moved your feet, Miguel said. Everyone was afraid, especially people who had been arrested before. Some said they wouldn't go out "by night" in the future. Miguel tried to argue with them, saying that was exactly what the police wanted. He urged everyone to come to the offices of the CHA at a certain time the following week to initiate joint action against the police.

Seven hours later, Miguel was freed—the first of the group to be let go. The CHA's lawyer had persuaded a judge to issue a writ of habeas corpus, which authorizes the release from jail of someone who has not been charged with a crime. As Miguel was leaving the station, a policeman asked him where he had been picked up. "Contramano," said Miguel. The policeman looked surprised. "You don't look like most of them," he said.

A few days later, Miguel waited at the offices of the CHA at the hour agreed upon for his former cellmates to file a protest against police tactics. But no one showed up. He was disappointed but not entirely surprised. "The gay community has lost its fear of policemen a little bit," he said. "But now that fear is being renewed. Our work is just at the beginning stage." He added ruefully, "I thought I was more powerful than I was."

Rafael, who was acting as interpreter, suggested that the sudden upsurge in police raids was connected to the inauguration of the new Peronist government the month before. The raids didn't bode well for policies of the new regime. But Rafael maintained that abuses of this kind were systemic, related to the unchecked powers of the police in Argentina, no matter who was in power. He believed that being victims of this kind of discrimination was the primary thing gay people had in common. "I don't believe gay identity is a cultural one," he said. "The only thing that unites us, the only thing we share, is that the police can arrest us whenever they have a particular quota of arrests they have to fill."

A woman named Deborah joined us. She was a physical education instructor in her early thirties, with long, sandy hair; she dressed in jeans and a jean jacket. Deborah recalled an incident that took place the year before when she and three other women were leaving a bar called Confusión. As they stood talking on the sidewalk, they observed a white Ford Falcon—a make of car well known in Argentina as a police vehicle—heading in their direction. A taxi was parked in front of the bar; they jumped in. The Falcon followed, but they lost it. The police, Deborah said, were after them simply because they were coming out of a gay bar.

Deborah claimed there were actually more detentions of women than of men, but that they were rarely reported. One lesbian she knew had been stopped walking home from a gay bar, put in a cell with three prostitutes, and kept for sixteen hours. Another woman was picked up in front of a bar and forced into a patrol car. When she tried to resist arrest, the policeman told her he would let her go only if she would have sex with him. She acquiesced, and he kept his word.

Naturally, this kind of harassment created an atmosphere of insecurity. "The problem," she said, "is that you are having a good time and you are thinking that at any moment, someone can come in and spoil the fun. There is no way to avoid the knowledge of that reality. There is no way to be at peace."

Argentina was a country obsessed with death and history. During the weeks I was in Buenos Aires, the papers were full of controversy about whether or not to bring the remains of the nineteenth-century dictator Manuel de Rosas back to Buenos Aires from their exile in England. On the Calle Florida, the pedestrian mall that stretches the length of downtown, street vendors sold stickers with a picture of Evita Perón and the slogan "¡Volveré y seré millones!" ("I shall return and be millions!" [of people]). Every Thursday afternoon, at the Plaza de Mayo, in front of the presidential palace, the mothers marched as they had been doing for years now, keeping alive the memory of their children, the *desaparecidos* of the Proceso.

I quickly familiarized myself with the history of twentieth-century Argentina—the military governments that dominated the country for most of the preceding sixty years; the ascension to power after a 1943 military coup of Juan (and Eva) Perón and the political movement they created, which even today retained the allegiance of the country's working class; Perón's overthrow and exile in 1955, his return to power in 1973, and the disastrous reign of his wife Isabel after his death; the state terrorism of the Proceso;

the restoration of democracy under Raúl Alfonsín in 1983, and the election of the Peronist Carlos Saúl Menem in 1989.

"The history of some countries is a history of class struggle. The history of others is a history of original sin. The history of Argentina is a history of repression," one silver-tongued lawyer told me. I wasn't quite sure about original sin, but the rest sounded accurate.

Argentine gay history was certainly one of repression, as sketched by the eminent sociologist Juan José Sebreli over coffee at a downtown bookstore café. Sebreli had written a long and definitive article, "Historia Secreta de los Homosexuales Porteños" ("Secret History of the Homosexuals of Buenos Aires"). It was a story almost entirely of gay men, however. "Lesbians don't exist—in the eyes of the rulers or the police or the church," he said. "Women count for nothing in this country." Unless you were a wife of Juan Perón, of course.

Sebreli recounted a series of scandals in the 1940s that brought the gay subculture into public view. One involved the dramatic arrest of a national idol, the notorious Spanish singer and dancer Miguel de Molina. The arrest took place in the middle of a performance. Molina was charged with the corruption of minors and was expelled from the country.

Then there was the spectacular raid in the late 1950s in which bathhouses, gay cinemas, and the entire subway system of Buenos Aires were shut down simultaneously in a crackdown on male homosexual sex. That raid took place during the legally elected civilian government of Arturo Frondizi. "In terms of the antigay repression, there is a tendency to assume that the military governments were the bad guys," Sebreli noted. "That is not necessarily true. In fact, many of the policies specifically directed against gay people were the products of civilian governments."

According to Sebreli, Perón himself was a master at using antigay prejudice for his own purposes. For example, in 1955, feuding with the powerful Roman Catholic church, he permitted the reopening of the brothels of Buenos Aires. Almost simultaneously, he began a campaign of persecution against gay men, claiming that the lack of prostitution in the city had been leading Argentine men into homosexuality. After fifteen days of banner headlines, however, everything was back to normal. "Policies regarding homosexuality were often incoherent," Sebreli noted, "because they had to do with other things."

Perón's antigay campaign took place three years after the death of his wife Evita. Among the many myths that had grown up around Evita was that, during her lifetime, she had been a kind of protectress of Argentine homosexuals. While I was in Argentina, a newspaper had carried an interview with Evita's dress designer, who had talked openly about being gay and bragged of his Peronist connections. "I am an Evitista," a supporter of Evita, he told the interviewer. Buenos Aires lesbians carried a placard at an International Women's Day march that read: ¡SI EVITA VIVIERA, SERÍA TORTILLERA! ("If Evita had lived, she would have been a dyke!"). Sebreli, who back in 1966 had written the first Argentinean book to take Evita seriously as a political figure, thought this view of her was exaggerated. "Evita had been an actress and she had the same attitudes you find so often in the entertainment world," he said. "They like homosexuals but they deprecate them at the same time. She reflected that kind of ambivalence."

In the last days of the government of Isabel Perón, the short-lived flowering of sexual liberation in Argentina gave way to right-wing reaction. In February 1975, a front-page article in a magazine published by the president's most influential adviser called for the incarceration of homosexuals in concentration camps. The headline was ACABAR CON LOS HOMOSEXUALES ("Finish off the homosexuals"). This proposal was never put into effect, but the article signaled open season on gay men.

When Isabel was overthrown by the military in 1976, open season began in earnest. Gay bars were closed—the last in 1980—and no gay or lesbian organizations were permitted; movies were heavily censored for any hint of homosexuality; harassment of gay men on the streets intensified, particularly at the time of the 1978 soccer World Cup in Buenos Aires. "The whole mechanism for antihomosexual repression was now in place because repression was generalized throughout the entire society," Sebreli said.

I heard repeatedly that gays and lesbians "disappeared" during the Proceso simply because they were gay, but I was never able to confirm this. A friend of the CHA's Rafael Freda told of giving asylum in his apartment to a gay man who used to frequent train-station lavatories; he and his lover hid the man for fifteen days before an acquaintance in the police department helped smuggle him out of the country. This same friend said he knew of three cases in which people disappeared for being gay and other instances in which they were tortured for that reason. But if he had anything other than anecdotal evidence, I never saw it.

"People tended to be disappeared on the basis of political militancy, rather than homosexuality per se," maintained the CHA's Zalazar. "The FLH members who disappeared, disappeared as leftists. Still, after being arrested, the fact of being homosexual exacerbated the punishments these people were subjected to."

Nonetheless, everyone who survived the period had stories to tell. Rafael, for example, had been the principal of a primary school in the early days of military rule; three members of his staff disappeared. On his way to work each day, he would pass an area where, he said, the military dumped the bodies of the *desaparecidos.* He himself was arrested three times during the Proceso, stopped while walking down the street with gay friends. On two of those occasions, he was detained for only a few hours. The third time, the police kept him and his friend for two days, trying to persuade each to accuse the other of soliciting sex.

People coped in a variety of ways. Some gay men married women. Others tried to appear as straight as possible. "You imitated traditionally masculine characteristics," one man told me. "It was common for gay men to involve themselves in sports."

With the bars closed and no places permitted for gays to gather, many experienced a strong sense of isolation. New ways of keeping in contact emerged: gay and lesbian literary, musical, and creative-writing groups, for example. *Café-concerts,* small clubs where performances took place, proliferated. "There was a tango singer who wasn't gay," one woman recalled. "But she developed a large gay following. Word got out and gay people would pack every performance."

A Buenos Aires man who ran a travel agency in those days told me how he would host dinner parties at his apartment every weekend for ten or twelve gay men. Because some of his regular guests were the sons of military officers—and one, he claimed, was the son of a former president of the country—he never worried about a police raid.

Others who didn't have the luxury of weekend dinner parties adopted other strategies. "There were raids on gay cruising areas, so we chose cruising areas far away and changed areas frequently," a student at the time said.

Although there was no shortage of recollections, it was difficult to evaluate the impact of the Proceso on gays and lesbians. If you were gay and not a known leftist and didn't go out at night or spend time at gay cruising spots, you may have experienced a sense of isolation but probably were not afraid for your life. Lesbians generally fared better than gay men; as Sebreli noted, they were invisible in the eyes of the authorities. And they never spent time cruising the Avenida Santa Fe, even in more congenial times. On the other hand, life—and death—was a random matter. A person could disappear simply because his or her name appeared in the address book of someone the military suspected of being a subversive. "You might get arrested for cruising the Avenida Santa Fe," Sebreli pointed out, "but you also might get arrested for standing on a street corner for too long waiting for a cab." As a result, it is hard to know which acts of persecution were directly targeted against homosexuals and which weren't.

Today, there was a degree of amnesia about that time. Rafael admitted that for three years he completely repressed the memory of his morning journeys past the dumping ground of the bodies of the disappeared. Just how much other people chose to forget regarding the persecution of homosexuals in particular was anyone's guess.

But Rafael emphasized that the most recent period of military dictatorship had to be seen in a larger historical context. "We have been deprived of civil rights for sixty years or more," he said. "In many ways the Proceso was simply more of the same. It was more dramatic, of course. But my grandfather was expelled from Argentina seven times because he was an anarchist. This is a country with no tradition of civil rights. When there is a time to lose your life and your freedom, you lose it."

San Lorenzo had just been defeated by Rosario, and Rafael was disheartened. San Lorenzo used to be the best soccer team in Argentina—what had happened? We were sitting in a *confitería* in Caballito, where the suburban train lines come together, waiting for a lesbian couple named Pochi and María. Buses roared past constantly. Rafael had just come from the game, to which he had taken his seventy-seven-year-old father along with him. He was still wearing his San Lorenzo hat.

Pochi spoke to me in English. "I learned it from the songs of Frank Sinatra and Nat King Cole," she said. "My first love was Hedy Lamarr, then Rita Hayworth." Pochi ran a small workshop that made shoes. In her early forties, she dressed in jeans and boots and a checked sweater with patches on the sleeves. María was thirty, with dark curly hair and dark eyes and a sweatshirt that said PIN BALL. She was a grammar-school teacher and helped out at the workshop. The couple had been together for two years.

Pochi entertained us with humorous stories of trying to outwit the authorities. Early in the Proceso period, before the military closed the gay bars, she was at a bar when Moralidad arrived and ordered all the customers to lie down on the floor. The police detained one of Pochi's friends, a woman she said was very beautiful. The policeman asked the woman, "Are you a *torta*?"—Argentine slang for lesbian. She said she was. An hour or two later, a macho-looking gay male friend went to the police station to try to get her released; he claimed she was his girlfriend. "That girl is homosexual," said the officer in charge. "Who says she is?" demanded the indignant "boyfriend." "*She* does!" replied the policeman. The woman remained in jail.

More recently, Pochi said, the CHA had held an art show in a Buenos Aires park. A policeman arrived to investigate what was going on and spotted Pochi. He assumed she was a woman who lived in the neighborhood and was merely passing by. What did she think of the display? he asked. "I think everyone should have the freedom to express their ideas," she said. Assuming her to be the voice of public opinion, the policeman left, and the exhibit continued unimpeded.

These days, Pochi didn't have any problems with the police. She had no fears about going to bars, although she didn't patronize them very often. Her main difficulty seemed to be harassment by a butcher in the neighborhood where she and María lived. Whenever he saw Pochi, he would shout, "Here comes the *torta*!" She was sure it was a matter of envy on his part. "He once asked me, 'Where do you get all those beautiful girls working for you?' I think he is just jealous," she said.

Her lover María said that no Argentine man would accept the idea that a feminine woman could be a lesbian. Nonetheless, she believed that if a woman accepted her homosexuality, other people would let her alone. She had a friend who was twenty-seven and complained that family and friends were constantly asking her why she didn't marry. The problem, María thought, was that her friend hadn't really accepted herself. "People never ask *me* why I haven't married!" she said.

Still, while some of her fellow teachers knew she was gay, others suspected she was being kept by a rich man. María didn't disabuse them of this idea. "Teachers are so underpaid," she noted. "But I have a car and tennis shoes and my clothes have designer labels on them. So they suppose someone is taking care of me."

Neither Pochi nor María had told her parents she was a lesbian. María was twenty when she moved out of her parents' home to live with her first lover, one of her teachers at the university. Her parents were angry. When she visited them, they ignored her. Her mother told her lover she didn't mind that she and María were friends; what concerned her was María's living away from home. The nature of their relationship was never discussed. After the couple broke up, María returned to live with her parents. Now, she had left home again to live with Pochi but still hadn't told her mother directly she was a lesbian. "I am sure she must know, because history has repeated itself," she said.

The fact that they were living together—in a room attached to the workshop—was significant, they felt. "The men are living with their parents, whether they are sixteen or forty-five," Pochi told me. "But the women are leaving home. The women are very brave."

In Argentina, as in many of the countries I had visited, economic pressures made it difficult for gay people to live independently. Given the current state of the economy, few young people could afford to rent their own apartment. Even when they had the money, finding an apartment in Buenos Aires was almost impossible: Most apartments were for sale, not for rent. In addition, time payments on furniture were structured in such a way that if you missed one, the rest increased dramatically. With inflation and currency devaluations, missing a payment at some point was virtually inevitable. As a result you could get locked into paying for furniture for years.

There were cultural factors, as well. While pressure to marry was perhaps not as great as in Asian societies, there *was* tremendous pressure to continue to live with one's parents even as an adult. In Argentina, Rafael said, if an unmarried child left home, the implication was that the family was not getting along. There would be no other conceivable reason why one would leave. He himself had moved out of his parents' home at age thirty and it was a very traumatic event, he said. Even once he had moved, the break was far from complete: His mother had a key to his apartment. He was living with another man and tried to keep the fact from his mother. If he knew she was planning to drop by, he would ask his lover to come home late or pretend he was just visiting.

So it wasn't surprising that so many young people, gay and straight, continued to live with their parents for years. Often, younger gays or lesbians tended to become involved in relationships with someone older and more established who might have his or her own place to live, as in the case of Pochi and María. In general, though, these barriers to living on one's own blocked the development of a strong, cohesive lesbian and gay community that could stand up for itself to the authorities. The situation also encouraged homosexuals to remain in the closet. If you lived with your parents, you didn't want to hurt them by coming out, or run the risk of getting thrown out of the house.

Years after leaving home, with his own apartment and an income from a number of different jobs, Rafael was as intertwined with his family as everyone else in Buenos Aires was. His mother had died recently, and his father had asked Rafael's married sister to move back to the family home to care for him. Rafael was insulted that his father hadn't asked him, instead. He attributed it to his father's homophobia. In Argentina, he insisted, tradition dictated that the unmarried child live with the surviving parent. After his long battle for independence, I was surprised that he would even consider returning to his father's house. "You have to understand," he said. "This is Argentina."

•   •   •

Chris and I had barely met Rafael that first evening over maté at the CHA office when he began to talk about sex. He was telling a story about picking up a young working-class man on a bus. The man was so unfamiliar with the rules of street cruising that he asked Rafael if he had to pay *him* for sex. "Can you imagine?" he asked, incredulously. "And he was half my age!"

It wasn't long before Rafael became my guide to gay Buenos Aires. He was the grandson of Italian immigrants; his father had been a high school principal and his mother the first woman chemist in Argentina. In addition to his jobs as high school teacher and TV writer, he put together a monthly newsletter for a health maintenance organization, did translations from the Italian for a religious publishing company, and was superintendent of the apartment building where he lived. He also spent something like twenty hours at week at the CHA offices, played the piano, had completed two unpublished novels, and wrote sonnets that he admitted were hopelessly out of fashion.

I never quite understood how he found time for sex. But to hear him tell it, he was constantly meeting men on the streets, buses, and subways, and dragging them home to bed. In Buenos Aires, street cruising was a way of life for gay men, dating from the days when there were few bars in the city and few other ways to meet a sexual partner or lover.

Aren't you afraid of AIDS? I asked. "Of course I am," he said. "I have been to Brazil—twice." He showed me a drawer full of condoms and assured me he used them without fail. The CHA had recently received a shipment of condoms from a European gay organization. One Sunday, Rafael and other CHA members had handed them out to the well-heeled crowd at the San Telmo antiques fair. "You wouldn't believe the looks on people's faces," he said.

Rafael owned his own apartment in San Telmo. It was filled with books and records, particularly classical music and opera. When he played the piano, his four canaries would sing along and virtually drown him out. Still, it seemed symbolic that the street he lived on was once the outermost boundary of the city limits of Buenos Aires. For Rafael's life was filled with insecurity. The key word, for him, was *marginación,* which translates as "marginalization"—being pushed to the fringes of society. While "marginalization" is little used in English, in Argentina it formed the centerpiece of everyone's analysis of society. In Argentina, poor people were viewed as marginalized; young people were marginalized; so, largely, were gays and lesbians. In fact, the entire Argentine middle class seemed to be slipping inexorably into a state of marginalization.

Rafael saw himself as fighting a constant battle against *marginación*. At his current teaching job, for example, he didn't have tenure, although he had been at the same school for years. The TV station he worked for provided no job security and would offer him nothing if it had to lay him off. Being gay made you far more vulnerable to *marginación*, he maintained. Society would use you as long as you were valuable and then you would be the first to be let go.

So Rafael was desperately trying to save money against the possibility of losing one or both of his major jobs. He would spend his weekends working on his translations from the Italian to earn some extra income, and dream of the day when he could afford to buy the boxed set of Beethoven's string quartets he had seen at a used-record store. "I haven't gotten up the nerve to ask the price yet," he said.

When I met Rafael's friends Héctor and Carlos, I received a first-hand glimpse of *marginación*. Hector and Carlos were a "typical" middle-class gay couple, Rafael told me; they had been together twenty-one years and lived around the corner from him in San Telmo. A week before we were to visit them, Hector lost his job at a bank. "He is depressed, but told us to come anyway," said Rafael. "Maybe it will take his mind off it."

As he greeted us, Héctor seemed perfectly cheerful. He was a handsome man in his late forties, with graying hair; he dressed conservatively in a cardigan sweater, dark slacks, and sneakers. (Cardigan sweaters seemed to be regulation attire for gay men over thirty-five in Buenos Aires.) Carlos, his lover, projected a different image. A mestizo from the north of the country near the Bolivian border, he wore tight-fitting jeans and a Levi's shirt unbuttoned almost to the waist. He worked in the office of an import-export company that dealt in electrical components. Neither spoke any English.

Héctor and Carlos owned three apartments. They lived in one;

Héctor's eighty-five-year-old mother lived next door in another; and they rented out the third. Their own apartment looked like a comfortable but slightly faded men's club. It was furnished with a matching sofa, chairs, and large cabinet—all made out of the same polished wood. The sofa and chairs had identical maroon leather cushions. There was gray wall-to-wall carpeting, a TV and a VCR, and a large tapestry on the wall, with an Arab motif.

Héctor's family once had some money. He had grown up in Junín, the same provincial town that Evita Perón had escaped as a young girl for the bright lights of Buenos Aires. Héctor left for Buenos Aires, too, but after his father died, he returned home to live with his mother. They survived on his father's legacy until it was exhausted. Carlos, who remained in Buenos Aires, would spend weekends with them. But life was not necessarily pleasant in the provinces. More than once, someone approached Héctor on the street and inquired, "Are you the male prostitute?" It was a way of telling him to get out of town. Eventually, when his mother got older, they moved to Buenos Aires and their present apartment.

I learned these details later, from Rafael. The most that Héctor would say in our conversation was that, in Junín, it was "impossible" to live as a gay man.

I asked Héctor and Carlos whether they were monogamous. They were evasive. "Maybe," said Héctor. Carlos responded that total fidelity "doesn't exist anywhere in this world."

When I asked if they were concerned about AIDS (SIDA, in Spanish), they became offended. "You can send SIDA to hell," said Carlos. Héctor demanded, "Why would we worry about it? We lead a clean life." They had no friends with AIDS; the disease didn't exist in the circles they frequented, they assured me. Héctor added that he thought the country ignored the problem. (There were about four hundred officially reported cases in Argentina at the time.) "Illness is always for other people" was the prevailing view, he said critically. That seemed to to be his attitude, as well.

Later in the conversation, Héctor became more heated. "Your questions are so North American! Asking us about SIDA and things like that!" he said. "Ask us about violence, about blackmail, about our families!"

He then proceeded to describe how, when he was younger, he had picked a man up on the street who later pretended to be a police-man. The man frisked him—as a police officer would—and robbed him. For his part, Carlos related meeting a man in a cruising area who threatened him with exposure if he didn't pay him a large sum of money. "Violence is almost natural in Argentina," Héctor said. "But the police would help a criminal before they would help a gay person. Here, the social idea is that gays are mixed up with dirty affairs and have to be kept down by the police."

In Argentina, Héctor went on, people still believed that homosex-uality was contagious. For that reason, his family had an unstated rule that he was not to talk to or otherwise interact with his neph-ews, nieces, or cousins. His brother hadn't spoken to him ever since Héctor had told him he was gay; the brother believed AIDS could be transmitted through casual contact. His aunts and cousins re-fused to recognize that he and Carlos lived together and for this reason wouldn't visit their apartment. Again, Héctor stressed, this was all unspoken; no one had ever stated any of this to him directly.

As for his elderly mother, Héctor said she had "two faces" re-garding his and Carlos's relationship. For many years, she had rejected it; now, because she was ill and dependent, she had no choice but to accept the situation.

After his outburst, Héctor talked more freely, particularly about their economic situation. Because he had lost his job and because Carlos's position was increasingly insecure (the number of people employed by Carlos's company had shrunk from twenty-five to four), they had decided to move Héctor's mother out of her apart-ment and in with them. That way, they could rent out two apart-ments, instead of one, as at present. "It won't work out," Héctor conceded. "But we'll do it." For his part, Carlos was worried about his and Héctor's sexual relationship. With Héctor's mother living there, they might have to go to a hotel in order to have sex. And what would be the "profit in the whole affair"? he wondered. Still, he agreed, "it is necessary. There is no way out."

The following day, Rafael ran into Carlos at the corner store. Carlos, he related, had been afraid I had gotten a bad impression of them because of their economic worries. "You shouldn't have asked them about their financial situation," Rafael told me. "Argentines are very proud. They want to put a good face toward the world."

Two or three weeks later, Rafael told me that Carlos had lost his job, too. He had been hired for a few days by the French Embassy, helping to put together a van that would go out to the provinces, spreading the glories of French culture. Meanwhile, Héctor had gotten a temporary position working nights at another bank. It was now up to Carlos to take care of Héctor's mother in the evenings and put her to bed. "She is driving Carlos nuts," Rafael said.

Guests were overcrowding Chris and Osvaldo's penthouse on the Calle Perú. So I moved to a *bulín* on the Calle Ecuador, on the newer and more cosmopolitan side of town. *Bulín* is slang for "love nest," and that was how the place functioned for two friends of Osvaldo, a gay couple who both lived at home with their parents. The apartment was on the fourth floor, overlooking a day-care center and a bookstore that specialized in psychological titles. The rent was about to quadruple; the two men were afraid they might have to give up the *bulín* altogether, and they were willing to forgo a few days of privacy in exchange for some U.S. dollars.

I had imagined that the *bulín* would be the "love nest" of the tabloids—piled high with stacks of pornographic magazines, ashtrays filled with cigarette butts, and half-empty wine bottles. In fact, it turned out to be neat and tidy, with a sofa bed, a kitchen table and chairs, a well-stocked refrigerator, a TV, a tapedeck, and plants. On the walls were reproductions of Chagalls and Klees, and there was a shelf of books—a novel by the Italian filmmaker Pier Paolo Pasolini, a volume out of the complete works of Freud, and a copy of Dickens's *Hard Times* (*Tiempos Difíciles,* in Spanish). Cassette tapes ranged from Philip Glass to Stevie Wonder's *Journey Through the Secret Life of Plants.* No matter how loud I turned up the music, it was never enough to drown out the noise of the buses and taxis of the Calle Ecuador below.

Still, I was glad to have an apartment of my own. On the Calle Perú, Chris and Osvaldo were absorbed in creating a salon: writers and painters who lived half the year in Paris or New York; a cabaret singer who sang uncannily like Edith Piaf; wealthy businessmen's wives who spent evenings going off to tango clubs in the suburbs.

All that had an appealingly romantic flavor, but my impression of Buenos Aires, gay Buenos Aires at least, was taking me in a very different direction: I saw it as a city where violence reigned, every sexual liaison was dangerous, and the police would drag you off to jail on the slightest provocation.

Meanwhile, a man named John McCracken was trying to get in touch with me. I had met him through Rafael, and he wanted to arrange a meeting for me with a wealthy gay businessman. The businessman, who was very important and very busy, had invited me to his house for dinner the following evening; that was the only time he could see me. According to McCracken, he made fabulous ravioli. I was trying to put McCracken off. Osvaldo insisted that McCracken was primarily interested in impressing the businessman with the fact that he knew a North American journalist. But McCracken would not take no for an answer. Finally, I agreed to go to the rich man's house for drinks, but begged off on the ravioli.

McCracken was an Argentine of Scottish origin, born in Buenos Aires. He raised Skye terriers and was the president of the local St. Andrew's Society. A man in his fifties who invariably wore a tweed sport coat, McCracken looked like he should be the lord of some vast *estancia* on the pampas. He exuded confidence—and connections. A stalwart of the Radical party, just defeated at the polls by the Peronists, he told me he was a friend of Raúl Alfonsín, the former president. "I owe him a visit," he said. "But, since the election, I haven't had the heart to go."

McCracken had started a company for the Argentine manufacture of the Denver boot, a metal contraption that locks one's automobile wheels in place and is the scofflaw's nightmare. The nearby city of La Plata had already purchased fifteen of McCracken's devices; the municipality of Buenos Aires had ordered sixty or seventy, he said. McCracken was quite optimistic about his new venture. "No one pays their parking tickets in this country," he explained.

McCracken lived with his twenty-six-year-old boyfriend, José, and his elderly parents, both of whom, to judge by my telephone calls, seemed exceedingly hard of hearing. "They know all about me," McCracken said. José was a hairdresser who had come to Buenos Aires from the provinces. He and McCracken wore identical rings, and McCracken had taken José with him to some fifty different Scottish functions. "People aren't blind," he said. "No one in the Scottish community cares very much, as long as you're not ringing bells and throwing feathers."

Before settling down with José (they had been together six years now), McCracken used to patronize "taxi boys," male hustlers. Prostitution in Buenos Aires was unlike that in the States, McCracken claimed. "You take them out to dinner first," he said. "There is friendliness. The sex is less cold and mechanical." He maintained that some taxi boys demanded payment for sex in part as a way of convincing themselves that they were not really gay. They could then claim, "I do it for the money, not because I prefer men." He mentioned one taxi boy whom he would pay for sex; then the two would go out to dinner, and the taxi boy would insist on picking up the tab.

I asked McCracken if this wasn't dangerous. Quite matter-of-factly, he began to tick off the names of people he knew who had been victims of violence, usually in sexual situations. He had a friend, a bar owner, whose lover had been murdered the year before by a soldier he had picked up; recently, the bar owner had been found stabbed to death, too. An attorney he knew had been thrown out a window. A young gay couple had been murdered—found bound and gagged in their apartment. Another friend who had met someone on the street and brought him home for sex had been stabbed in his bed; he fled naked down the steps, and eventually lost a lung, but survived.

Still, McCracken believed that many of his friends who had troubles of this nature—and virtually everyone he knew had been involved in some dangerous situation with street pickups or taxi boys—had only themselves to blame. They weren't cautious enough. He, on the other hand, always made sure to take potential sexual partners out to coffee first.

When McCracken stopped by to take me to the rich man's house, José accompanied him. José was tall and dark-haired; he wore jeans, a blue denim jacket, and a T-shirt that said NEPAL. He spoke little English. I was impressed that McCracken had such a young and handsome boyfriend. "One difference between Argentina and the States," McCracken told me, "is that here younger men often prefer men who are significantly older."

• • •

"I am the finest cook in Argentina," the rich man announced as we arrived at his apartment. He showed off a copy of a magazine that featured some of his recipes. Then he handed me a book by the Craig Claiborne of Buenos Aires. The handwritten inscription read, "To the man who really is the best cook in Buenos Aires . . ." I realized then that I had made a great mistake in saying no to dinner.

On the coffee table, five different kinds of cheeses, plus sausages and red wine, were laid out. The apartment was elegant without being ostentatious. There were parquet floors and Oriental rugs, a glass dining room table, and a large terrace with orange and lemon trees. Paintings in the French impressionist style adorned the walls. Two dachshunds greeted us noisily.

The rich man, who was in his forties, was wearing a cardigan sweater, like everyone else in town, but this one appeared to be by Missoni or a similar Italian designer of wildly expensive garments. He reclined on a couch with a dachshund curled up on his lap. McCracken and José sat quietly, looking pleased.

Speaking in English, the man explained that Hugo, his lover, with whom he lived, was still at work. Hugo was a manager at the rich man's company; they had been together for twelve years. During the day, at work, they acted like employer and employee, he said. When he left at the end of the day, he would say to Hugo, along with everyone else, "Good-bye; see you tomorrow."

He added, "I do all my life after six P.M. I only say to Hugo, 'No trade union in bed. Don't ask me for a raise in salary in bed.' "

Most people, including some members of the board of directors of his own company, weren't aware that he and Hugo lived together. The couple kept the answering machine on at all times, even when they were at home. That way (the voice on the tape was the rich man's), there was no danger of Hugo picking up the receiver and raising the suspicions of the caller on the other end. Still, they spent every weekend together at the rich man's country house and they traveled together in Europe. All his friends accepted Hugo. "No one wants you to explain," he said. "Everyone goes along with it if you don't speak about it." And he added, "When you have a good economic position, people don't investigate. They accept you for what you are. And everyone likes Hugo."

The rich man was somewhat careful about his friends. He preferred "married gay people" (his terminology for gay couples) who were not "flames." When he went out to a restaurant or the theater with his gay friends, he wanted to feel comfortable introducing them to business acquaintances or the prominent people he might encounter. "I am not at home with feathers or with hair that is dyed purple," he said. He had laid down the law to his friends who had become involved with "flames"—either they came alone when they socialized with him, or he wouldn't continue the friendship.

At this point in the conversation, Hugo returned home from work. In a blue blazer and pleated slacks, *he,* at least, was extremely presentable. He was ten years younger than the rich man, spoke no English, and seemed to have a sweet disposition.

The rich man began to joke about his first lover, who had left him after seven years together to become a Catholic priest: "He told me, 'I love you, but God called.' So I asked him, 'Which phone did he use? Are you sure it wasn't the wrong number?' "

He recalled dropping off his lover at the seminary that first time. A massive wooden door stood at the entrance. As the door banged shut, "my heart was breaking," he said. "I never had that feeling before." Over the years, he had remained friends with his ex-lover. But when the priest came to his country home last Christmas, he felt indifferent to him for the first time. "What is the word that is the opposite of 'love'?" he asked me. "I felt, 'If he is alive or dead, I don't care.' " The priest had intense conflicts about being gay, he said, and that was one of the reasons for the current breach.

His mother had liked the priest very much but didn't care for Hugo. He was convinced his mother had been partial to his former lover because he had blond hair and blue eyes. Hugo was darker-complected. When his mother referred to Hugo, she would ask, "Is Blackie coming?" The rich man thought her hostility had more to do with issues of social class than any suspicions that they were lovers.

He hadn't told anyone in his family that he was gay. He was sure his brother would understand. Still, both his brother and his brother's wife felt better if the subject was not spoken about directly. "My brother and his wife are not stupid," he said. "They talk all the time about 'you'—meaning Hugo and me. But no one wants to know what is going on."

How would his mother react if he told her? "She wouldn't be surprised, but it would kill her," he replied.

The rich man was proud—and somewhat defensive about his country. He had been in Germany on business, he said, and some students had criticized Argentina's human-rights record under the Proceso. "How dare they?" he said, his anger rising even now. "After what the Germans did during the war!" He bristled at the suggestion that the situation of homosexuals might be better in any country other than Argentina. Gays in Argentina had "total freedom," in his estimation. Next door in Brazil, despite the country's reputation for sexual tolerance, his gay friends in Rio and São Paulo were "like flowers," part of the decor at the parties of their heterosexual friends. "There is hypocrisy all over the world," he insisted. "There is no open-minded country."

He was a member of an organization called the Christian Association of Entrepreneurs. He recalled going to a luncheon at which the speaker, an eighty-year-old priest, had stated, "God loves divorced people." The rich man went up to him after the luncheon and told the priest how much he appreciated his broad-mindedness. "That man is the last saint in Argentina," he informed me, adding, "The boat of Peter is to rescue people, not to shipwreck them."

On other issues, though, the rich man was rather retrograde. Regarding the CHA, he said, "They did some rather brave things in the beginning, but I haven't heard much about them lately. I hope I'm not on their mailing list." As for AIDS: "When you are in love with a guy like Hugo, you don't worry about AIDS. It is not our problem: We prefer 'married' gay people."

I feared what his ideas on lesbians might be, but I posed the question anyway.

Did he have any lesbian friends?

"No," he said. "Lesbians are not pretty girls."

In Buenos Aires, in many respects, it was still 1969 or so. The first question people asked when they met you was "What's your sign?" Hermann Hesse was everyone's favorite author, just as he had been in the States during the heyday of the counterculture; copies of *Demian* were prominently displayed in bookstore windows, along with Robert Ludlum and the latest Latin American magic realists.

The city was obsessed with therapy and "self-improvement"; psychoanalysis was flourishing (Buenos Aires was said to have the most psychotherapists per capita of any city in the world) and so were Gestalt therapy and all sorts of Gurdjieffian offshoots that combined bodily movement with personal growth. At the lesbian bar in San Telmo, hippie vendors wandered from table to table hawking incense, candles, and jewelry.

Argentina had always been a bit behind the United States and Western Europe in cultural trends. Yet, perhaps because the *Proceso* had brought intellectual and artistic life to a standstill for so many years, here there had never been the reaction against the sixties that had taken place in North America. Culturally, the society was still young and idealistic; it hadn't heard of "post"-anything.

As in the United States and Western Europe in 1969 or 1970, feminism—and lesbian-feminism—was in its first flower. And no one illustrated that better than Ilse Fuskova, a sixty-year-old woman who had come out of the closet at the ripe old age of fifty-seven.

Ilse spoke English with a German accent, even though she had been born in Argentina and had lived there almost all her life. She parted her blond hair in the middle and wore a lavender scarf. Although she was sixty when I met her, she looked twenty years younger, a fact that I attributed to the rejuvenation resulting from her discovery of her sexuality at such a late age. Books by women—Mary Daly, Anaïs Nin, and Doris Lessing—lined the walls of her apartment. There were also plants and wall hangings and paintings by her lover, a filmmaker in her late thirties.

Ilse always called me "Miller." She ended all her sentences with "yes?" her inflection rising—"Women are making so many strides nowadays, yes?" Her parents had been of German and Czech extraction; she was married for thirty years to a German Jew. Ilse thought I resembled her oldest son, who lived in Berlin, and for that reason was constantly looking at me with a slightly perplexed expression. "Doesn't he look like Gabriel?" she asked her twenty-eight-year-old daughter, a psychology student, when she dropped by. Her daughter was unimpressed. Ilse showed me a picture of Gabriel; I didn't see much resemblance.

At a week-long conference of Latin American feminists in Rio in 1985, Ilse fell in love with another woman, a lesbian activist from Madrid. She began writing love letters to her, which she would deliver at breakfast. "It was the first time I experienced that deep attraction which I suppose I had always had," Ilse said. "But it manifested itself there in that tropical climate near the beach and the palm trees. When I came back to Buenos Aires, it was quite clear to me the power this attraction to women had for me." Her affair, however, remained platonic, even when the Spanish woman visited Argentina. "All that happened was that we walked hand in hand down the Avenida Santa Fe and talked a lot," she said. "If she had asked me, I would have gone to Spain. But she didn't ask." Two months after the Rio encounter, she began her first physical relationship with another woman, a photographer.

By that time, Ilse was separated from her husband. She had taken her first confusing steps toward confronting the issues of sexuality and identity several years earlier, in 1978, when she had been married for twenty-eight years and was living with her husband and two teenage sons and her daughter in an upper-class Buenos Aires suburb. Ilse had been quite ill for two consecutive winters; the third year, "trying not to be sick or to die," as she put it, she ran off to Paris with a Uruguayan painter, a man. When she returned to Buenos Aires three months later, her husband and children refused to let her in the house. She borrowed the keys to the apartment of some friends who were away on vacation, and stayed there. Completely alone, she attempted suicide. She spent ten days in a hospital, after which her husband and children reluctantly allowed her to come home.

The decision to run off to Paris was "a craziness you feel at some point in your life," she said. A few months after her return, she met the Uruguayan painter quite by chance (they had ended their affair by then) and she felt "nothing, nothing." "You know, Miller, you can invent yourself a love affair," she said. "Have you ever done something like this? Especially at the end of two illnesses, which were really illnesses of sadness at the end of this long marriage."

Shortly after her flight to Paris, Ilse joined a feminist group. Her marriage continued to unravel; she eventually left her husband and moved into her own apartment. But she still did not feel any particular recognition that she might in fact be a lesbian. Over the years, she said, she had always been interested in women's personal histories, particularly in finding out how women behaved when they were on their own. "That subject was something of great importance to me," she said. "It was something that was separate for me, like a focus, like a light, yes? How are women when they are alone? But the word 'lesbian' never appeared in my mind. There was something that didn't allow for me to feel the attraction."

The year that she finally fell in love with a woman for the first time was no ordinary year, however. It was the year her father died. Ilse thought that fact was crucial. "The powerful image of the father with all that male authority vanished," she noted.

A friend of Ilse's attributed her late sexual blooming as much to the political as the personal, however. The friend believed that Ilse couldn't recognize her lesbianism until feminism emerged in Argentina to give her a context for it, to offer the possibility of a life centered around women.

Now, Ilse was devoting her life to lesbian and feminist activism, in particular, to publishing a magazine, *Cuaderno de Existencia Lesbiana* ("The Notebook of Lesbian Existence"). She didn't have to have a regular job: She had some money from her husband. She wouldn't live with her current lover, the filmmaker, however. "After thirty years of a family, I want to live alone," she said.

At this point, Ilse had no interest in working politically with men. She would have little to do with the CHA, an organization she dismissed as male-dominated. She claimed she didn't know a single gay man in Buenos Aires who was sympathetic to lesbian-feminist ideas. There was no lesbian group to speak of in the city; "Lesbians are absolutely invisible here," she told me. So besides the magazine and the conference of Latin American lesbians held every two years, it was feminism that was the focus of Ilse's activism. The fourth annual meeting of Argentine women had just taken place in the city of Rosario, with three thousand women in attendance, many from political parties and labor unions as well as feminist organizations. Ilse was very excited.

That conference had included a panel on lesbianism, but within the women's movement in Argentina, as in other countries, there had been problems with lesbian visibility. For example, the women's center in Buenos Aires, Lugar de Mujer, had given Ilse permission to screen a film that her lover had made about the Lesbian and Gay Freedom Day Parade in San Francisco. But on its calendar of events, Lugar de Mujer refused to permit the mention of the words "lesbian" and "gay." Instead, the program noted that a film would be shown about "things Ilse saw in San Francisco." The women's center was quite willing to show the film, but they didn't want to be identified in any way with the subject matter.

A more unpleasant event happened at the annual International Women's Day march in Buenos Aires in 1988. Thousands of women were in attendance and, strictly by chance, Ilse and some fifteen friends, marching under a lesbian banner, found themselves leading the entire procession as it traversed the Avenida Corrientes. "Imagine!" Ilse said. "We felt like angels who had just come down from heaven." But their leadership role was short-lived. As Ilse told it, within a few minutes, a group of Peronist women blocked their path. There was an altercation, and the lesbians withdrew. A week later, at a meeting of march participants, one of the Peronist leaders apologized for the incident. "She asked us to be patient and to excuse them," Ilse said. "She said they would call us some time and invite us to come and explain to them about being lesbians." The Peronists never called.

That incident illustrated the gap between the predominantly working-class Peronist women and the middle- and upper-class lesbians who were the sexual vanguard of Buenos Aires. But Ilse wasn't discouraged. She noted that her group and the women of the CHA had been listed as sponsors on the International Women's Day program for two years running. "We feel our space is growing," she said.

Harassment remained a problem for lesbians. Two of Ilse's friends had been on a city bus late one recent evening, when some male passengers began shouting at them, calling them *tortas* and other epithets. The women returned the abuse. The driver ordered the women off the bus, whereupon the men followed and started to beat them. A week later, Buenos Aires feminists organized a protest that blocked traffic at the spot where the women had been attacked.

Ilse hadn't experienced any harassment personally, though. Because she was sixty, and her lover thirty-eight, people assumed they were mother and daughter.

She had a dream, a dream of universal androgyny—of "a time

when nothing in your appearance would give any indication that you are a man or a woman. So when you are attracted to someone and the time comes to go to bed, it is only then that you find out if the other person is a man or a woman. I think it would be wonderful—an attraction based on just one person to another, regardless of sex, yes? For me, it is the ideal." But that remained a vision. At this point in history, in Ilse's view, being involved with a man essentially meant you were placing limits on your ability to question sex roles and sexuality. You wound up compromising certain values. For this reason, she didn't want her daughter to marry. But her daughter wasn't paying her too much heed. "She wants a family," she said.

Ilse had no tolerance for anything that smacked of cynicism. The women's movement was young, the lesbian movement even younger. "Give us some time!" she said. "Don't you think that in the last fifty years, it is incredible how women have changed? Now, we are living what these changes have brought about. In the next twenty years, there will be more insights and changes. You can't change all of six thousand years at once, Miller!"

Meanwhile, Ilse's mind was on something more mundane. There wasn't any real meeting place for women in Buenos Aires (the lesbian bar was too noisy to really talk, she maintained). So the following day, between six and ten in the evening, a number of women were planning to show up at a bar they had picked out—an ordinary bar—on the Avenida Corrientes. They were spreading the word and hoped to make the gathering a weekly event. There was one problem, though. The owner didn't know they were coming. "But the bar is always empty, so I suppose he will be happy," Ilse said. "It is a nice-looking place. Imagine fifty women there in the afternoon. Let's see what happens, yes?"

A week or so later, a march took place to protest the Indulto, the government's decision to pardon the imprisoned former military rulers responsible for all those deaths and disappearances. The march, which took place in the early evening, was one of the largest I had ever witnessed. It lasted for hours—some two hundred thousand people marching down the Avenida Corrientes, around the Obelisk, eventually wending their way to the square in front of the

Congreso building, Argentina's parliament. Many of the contingents in the march, including the state telephone company and the Commission on Atomic Energy, listed the names of the *desaparecidos* on their placards.

There were chants:

> To jail, to jail
> all the soldiers
> who sold out
> the nation

and

> Now there is no pardon.
> Now there is no pardon.
> Even if he goes to mass,
> He is still a son of a bitch.

The largest contingent belonged to the MAS, the successor to the Trotskyist Socialist Workers party. The most spirited was a group of Chilean exiles. Ilse's feminist groups were represented, and I marched with the CHA contingent, about thirty or so people, the largest number that the gay group had ever managed to assemble. CHA members carried a banner that said: "End bar raids. Without justice, there is no democracy." Miguel, the CHA treasurer who had been arrested at the Contramano disco, handed out circulars about police harassment to anyone who would take them. People read them attentively. As we descended the hill from the Avenida de Mayo into the packed square before the domed Congreso building, spectators greeted the CHA banner with loud and enthusiastic applause. It was a moment of hope, even inspiration, in a country that had known few such moments. But the generals walked free anyway.

Montevideo

In Montevideo, they were selling anemones on the street corners. The trees were starting to bud, although it was still raw and rainy. The Communist party daily, *La Hora Popular,* was headlining the death of Perez Prado, "the king of the mambo," on its front page. In the windows of the shops of the money changers, you could chart the relentless fall of the Argentine austral and Uruguayan peso against the dollar. The back streets off the Avenida 18 de Julio smelled of damp wool; on the Plaza Libertad, people drank mate out of thermoses to keep warm.

From Buenos Aires, you reach Montevideo, the Uruguayan capital, by a forty-five-minute plane flight or an overnight "slow" boat across the River Plate or a five-hour combination boat and bus trip down the Uruguayan coast. The "slow" boat was sold out for weeks in advance, so I took the less atmospheric boat-and-bus. The Plate was muddy and so wide it seemed like an ocean; belowdecks, passengers were playing bingo.

When I reached the Uruguayan shore, no one bothered to stamp or even look at my passport. Indeed, during my stay there I often felt as if I was still in Argentina. The currency was different, it was true; prices were higher; and the people were more subdued. But Montevideo's population was of the same European (mostly Spanish and Italian) stock as Buenos Aires's; one had the same sense of a middle-class city going down the tubes.

In Montevideo, as in Buenos Aires, democracy had been recently restored. The military dictatorship that ruled the country from 1973 to 1985 with its own brand of state terrorism and its own *desaparecidos* had relinquished power. But Montevideo had never quite recovered. Some three hundred thousand to four hundred thousand Uruguayans—mostly of the generation that today was in its thirties and forties—had gone into exile and not returned. In a country of three million, that was a substantial number. Perhaps as a consequence, Montevideo was a sleepy place, provincial, all tattered charm and Art Nouveau buildings with funny cupolas and curlicues, with the deserted and appealing melancholy of a seaside town off season.

Uruguay had a different historical tradition from Argentina's. For most of the century, the country had been a model of democracy, with the most advanced welfare state in Latin America; the dictatorship had been an aberration. The Roman Catholic church wasn't as powerful as in Argentina. (Unlike in Argentina, for example, there was no legal requirement that the president be a Catholic.) And there was, I found, a small-town sweetness about the Uruguayans. If the Argentines seemed to know the violence and evil lurking beneath the façade of ordinary life, here it was not so. Buenos Aires might be a city of Ford Falcons—the automobiles the military used to take people away during the Proceso, and which still had ominous associations—but Montevideo was a city of cozy little Fiats and VW bugs.

For gay people, the years of military rule in Uruguay had been grim ones. The police raided the bars, denied passports to gays and lesbians, reportedly kept a list of homosexuals. One man related a story of a 1981 bar raid that sounded right out of Buenos Aires at the height of the Proceso—and also out of contemporary Cairo. A hundred and twenty men were rounded up at one of the bars, brought to the police station, and separated according to presumed sexual roles—"active" and "passive." When the police believed someone had incorrectly declared his preference, an officer would hit him. "I passed as 'active,' " said the man who told the story. "Of course there was no way the police could really tell the difference. They didn't believe 'active' men were 'real' homosexuals. They released us first."

Today, the democratic and secular traditions made Uruguay somewhat more congenial for gay people than Argentina, or so Uruguayan gays claimed. (The Uruguayans were always trying to present themselves as more enlightened, more "European" than their neighbors across the River Plate.) But I wasn't convinced. In my view, Montevideo, even more than Buenos Aires, was a city of marginalized gay people.

When my bus pulled into the main square of Montevideo at eleven in the evening, Clever Velázquez was there to meet me. Clever, a friend of Rafael, was involved in a fledgling gay group called Homosexuales Unidos (HU). We went off to the Café Sorocabana, one of those old cafés full of character that can still be found in Buenos Aires and Montevideo, much as they were fifty years ago. Sorocabana had wood paneling and marble-topped tables, aging wooden chairs with green leather upholstery, ceiling fans, and waiters who looked as if they had been there since the place opened. By day it was filled with elderly gentlemen in gray suits and scarves and overcoats, intently studying their newspapers. On my first visit—it was close to midnight—the café was largely populated by gay men. Someone Clever vaguely knew came up, introduced himself, and gave me a small amethyst as a souvenir. Speaking in French, he told me how his mother and his lover had gotten married, for reasons I couldn't exactly ascertain but had something to do with wills and inheritances.

Clever, thirty-seven, was a little on the husky side, with dark hair, a squarish face, and a wispy beard. He lived with his parents, his grandmother, his sister, and his sister's two children. Clever had lived in Buenos Aires for a couple of years but returned home once he proved to himself he could survive away from Montevideo and his family. Shortly before my arrival, he had lost his job at the office of a food-processing plant. Politically, Clever was to the left and, like almost everyone I met in Montevideo, passionately anti-American. (Uruguayans blamed American military advisers for the 1973 military coup and the ensuing dictatorship.) His main interest was music: His room was filled with stacks of Bob Dylan and Frank Zappa records and he was taking percussion lessons. I never saw him dressed in anything besides an overcoat and a tweed cap; he smoked and coughed incessantly.

Clever had become active in Homosexuales Unidos a couple of months before. The group had just moved into a couple of rooms in a building not far from the university, where it shared space with an organization that worked rehabilitating prisoners. A mysterious wealthy Uruguayan paid HU's rent; he also funded the prisoners' group and an organization for prostitutes' rights. The prisoners' group was apparently less than enthusiastic about sharing quarters with HU. It hoped that prisoners would be permitted to come to its offices on furloughs and was concerned that the presence of a homosexual group might make the authorities less inclined to permit this.

The HU office was sparsely furnished, with only a table, some chairs, and a single-size mattress on the floor. On the bulletin board were sign-up sheets for volleyball and soccer games. HU thought sports were important, Clever said, a part of the "de-marginalization" of gay people. On the wall was a poster that said:

HU es:
Compañerismo
Lucha
Libertad
Solidaridad
Apoyo
Conciencia

("HU is: /
Comradeship /
Struggle /
Liberty /
Solidarity /
Support /
Conscience.")

Clever emphasized that the group was very "clear in its mind" about its political goals, although I was never quite sure what these were. When he lived in Buenos Aires, he had been active in the CHA, but he said that a major problem had been the reluctance of many people, including CHA leaders, to come out publicly. That wasn't the case at HU. "Most people in our group have assumed their gay condition," he said.

The group's president, Luis Carlos, was a bearded man in his late thirties with a head of wild, graying hair. He worked as a dress designer and was a visionary of sorts. Luis Carlos wanted to start a small dress factory in the HU office space in order to fund the group's activities and to offer employment to gay people. "Homosexuals often have a relationship to dress designing," he explained. He was quite serious about the idea; the man who paid their rent wanted the groups he supported eventually to become self-sufficient. All HU required was a few sewing machines.

Toward the end of the dictatorship, there had been a large gay group in Montevideo, but it destroyed itself as a result of internal squabbling and the emigration of its leaders. Now, in its initial stages, HU seemed to attract unassuming and isolated people, many of whom worked in shops or at supermarket checkout counters. Most were young—Clever and Luis Carlos seemed to be the only members of the group over twenty-five—and there were virtually no women. Clever himself was a loner who spent most of his time involved with his music; he had very few gay friends in Montevideo and his only relationship had been a two-year involvement with a man almost twice his age. Another HU member, who worked at a dress factory doing ironing, told me had been sexually abused at age fifteen and had been unable to have sexual relations with anyone since. He was reluctant to go to a therapist about this problem because he was convinced any therapist would be judgmental about his homosexuality. HU provided him with some social support. Another man I met there had grown up in Montevideo, moved to Buenos Aires, and returned shortly after his lover had been killed in an automobile accident. There were a couple of young lovers, charming and militant in their own way, who used the HU offices as their *bulín,* making love on the mattress when no one else was around.

And then there were the transvestite prostitutes, Michelle and Fanny. In fact, of the people I met at HU, Michelle and Fanny were the ones for whom the organization seemed the most important. Scorned by the gay community, they were the most marginalized of the marginalized; the HU offices represented their clean, well-lighted place (bare light bulb notwithstanding). At HU, they could experience a sense of acceptance and belonging they found nowhere else.

It was a particularly cold and wet evening when I talked with Michelle and Fanny at the HU office. One window was missing a pane of glass, and gusts of wind and rain periodically swept through the room. I wore my winter jacket; Michelle huddled under her fur coat. Both Michelle and Fanny dressed as women "twenty-four hours a day," and for that reason said they had no alternative but to earn their living as prostitutes. They couldn't find any other employment. Michelle, thirty-eight, was tall and broad-shouldered and had started cross-dressing—and prostitution—at the age of sixteen, in a small town down the coast. She was working that evening; under her fur coat, she wore a low-cut black lamé dress, fishnet stockings, and heels. She had on a blond wig, and the cleavage between her silicone-implanted breasts was quite visible. Michelle didn't like her work very much. Her main concern, she told me, was for transvestites to be accepted in occupations other than prostitution. She wanted HU to provide some public education on the subject. "I hope this group can help us with the authorities," she said.

Fanny told me that when she first took up prostitution, at age twenty, it had opened a whole new world for her. She made a good deal of money and enjoyed the sex. This evening, however, fourteen years later, she was mostly dreading having to go out in the rain. Pretty and waiflike, Fanny was dressed in a tight-fitting maroon acrylic sweater and matching pants. She too had breasts of silicone; her hair was blond, but it was her own, with the brown roots visible. If Michelle was responsive but a little distant, Fanny was engaged, smart, and lively.

Michelle viewed herself as a gay man who liked to dress as a woman. She wanted to feel like a gay man, not a woman, she said; she was involved in a three-year relationship with another man and had had other same-sex relationships over the years. Fanny, on the other hand, saw herself as transsexual. "If I could be a woman, I would," she told me. But a sex-change operation cost two thousand dollars (in Chile), a sum beyond Fanny's means. Even if she had the surgery, she might continue prostitution, she said, but thought she would have greater opportunities to work in other fields. She believed society might be more open to accepting her as a transsexual than as a man who dressed as a woman. "People tell me that transsexuals don't have much pleasure in sex, but I don't care," she said. "Sex isn't the only thing."

Both said that few of their customers ever mistook them for biological women. They knew what they were getting. "They want a different experience," explained Fanny. Michelle's customers usually wanted her to take the "active" role in sex, even though they were often married and presumably heterosexual. She had about four clients a day, she said, and would have sex with them in cars or hotels.

These days, under the new democratic government, transvestism was legal in Uruguay, while prostitution was punishable by a fine and a twenty-four-hour stay in jail. In the days of the military dictatorship, it had been quite different, however. Then, Fanny and Michelle spent as long as seven days in prison at a stretch. Fanny asserted that she was tortured by the police during this time, but she declined to talk about the experience. In fact, during the dictatorship, she spent more time in jail than out, she said. Because Uruguay's economy was in better shape in those days, spending all that time in jail—as unpleasant as it was—didn't destroy her livelihood. "Today, even without jail, I am making less money than I did when the military was in power!" she said.

Michelle recalled the period of 1979–1980 as particularly difficult. There were constant arrests. She would come home at night and enter her apartment through a rear window in order to make it appear she wasn't there, and she would keep the lights off at the front of the apartment. In prison, there was a special area for transvestites, she said. Prison authorities made her dress in men's clothing and, when she was released, she was given men's clothing to wear. To get her original female clothes, she had to return to the prison dressed as a man.

Today, despite the improvement in the situation, there was still reason for caution. Fanny said the police knew where she worked and often impersonated clients in order to entrap her. She had spent a day and night in jail just three weeks before. In the taxi on the way to the HU offices, she and Michelle had hidden their faces, she said; when they left, they would make sure to be accompanied by some of the men in the group so as not to call attention to themselves.

In addition to police harassment, there was something new to worry about: AIDS. Fanny asked her clients to use condoms, but many refused and she didn't insist on it. "I prefer dying of AIDS than dying of hunger" was the way she viewed it.

Transvestites faced other day-to-day difficulties. Fanny said that when she tried to rent a room, landlords often demanded an exorbitant amount of money. In Uruguay, in order to rent an apartment, you needed someone who owned property to guarantee the rent; for Fanny, it was hard to get that guarantee. At one point, she had squatted at an abandoned house. All the attention she received because of her appearance troubled her, as well. She had gone to the doctor recently and said that the doctor's secretary and other people at the clinic had stared at her as if she were a freak. At one point, she had been ill for a long time but to avoid ridicule hadn't sought medical attention. Situations of this kind increasingly disturbed her; she wanted to go to a therapist to learn to control her anger.

There were some sixty to seventy transvestites in Montevideo, Fanny and Michelle told me, all of them gay and most of them prostitutes. But competition was increasing. Nowadays, transvestite prostitutes were coming from Buenos Aires to Montevideo to work. "They work here for fifteen to twenty days a month and then they return to Buenos Aires, where the prices are lower and they live better," Michelle said. "Besides, in Buenos Aires, transvestite prostitutes [who solicit] have more problems. They can be put in prison for forty-five days."

I mentioned to Fanny that her life sounded extremely stressful—the fear of arrest, the financial insecurity, the annoying stares of passersby. She agreed; she didn't have much energy to do other things because her life was so full of anxiety. "My dream is to live peacefully," she said. She was a devotee of a Brazilian spiritual cult that claimed an ability to summon spirits from the dead. The cult had given her a reason to live, she said. Now HU offered her another reason. "I feel a sense of freedom here, that we can gather together and demand our rights," she said. "Many gays don't understand the problems of transvestites. Some of them do, though. The way to make changes is to join together and fight."

On my last evening in Montevideo, I went to one of the two gay bars in the city, a dark cave of a place called Arco Iris. At close to two in the morning, I headed back to my hotel on foot along the Avenida 18 de Julio.

Because of the hour, the *avenida* was rather deserted, although it was the main boulevard of the city. The sidewalks were wet after the rain; a couple of blocks were completely blacked out. After walking for about ten minutes, I was stopped by a dark-haired man dressed in a sport coat and trousers, heading in the other direction. He looked like a football player slightly gone to seed. He asked me, in Spanish, if I knew where I was going. I explained, as best I could, that I was on my way back to my hotel. He continued walking with me. Where was I from? Did I like Montevideo? Was I gay? Yes, I replied uneasily to his last question. Then, he said something that I didn't quite understand, although I recognized the word "*amor.*"

"Where are you staying?" he asked.

"The Hotel Richmond," I replied.

"Could we go there?

"I don't think it's a good idea," I said.

We continued walking for a block or so when, suddenly, his tone changed. Homosexuality was illegal in Uruguay, he told me. (This was not true.) He flashed some kind of identification card with his picture on it. I couldn't see it well in the dark. "Soy policía," he announced. There was a danger of AIDS in Uruguay, he said; he was going to have to take me to the police station and have me deported. I told him I didn't understand, but he persisted. I said I was leaving for Argentina the following day anyway; couldn't he just let me go? It flashed through my mind that the Uruguayan authorities hadn't stamped my passport when I arrived in the country. I was in Uruguay illegally, as it was.

"*Bien,*" he said, "if you pay me some money, I won't take you in." He repeated his line about AIDS and was becoming increasingly unfriendly, if not menacing. We were coming into an area of late-night restaurants and pizza joints; there were people on the streets. I wondered what would happen if I just walked away, tried to melt into the crowd.

He led me across a plaza in the direction of the central police station. I had better give him some money, he repeated. "*No tengo dinero.* I don't have any money. Let's go to the police," I said, with as much finality in my voice as I could muster. Without quite realizing it, I had called his bluff. He gave me a shove, said good-bye, and went on his way.

I felt a sudden surge of relief and freedom. When my mind cleared, I realized that the man hadn't resembled a football player after all; he was more likely an off-duty policeman trying to make an extra peso. Here was an unpleasant glimpse of the danger, the insecurity, the potential for violence, that I had heard about so frequently in Buenos Aires but had never experienced firsthand. Clearly, I was in a privileged position—my U.S. passport (even without the required Uruguayan stamp), the extra cash stashed under my pillow—but that didn't make the whole incident any less frightening. In these countries, if you were gay, you were vulnerable, and that was that.

When I described the incident to Clever the following morning, he assured me that the man hadn't been a police officer at all. "I know exactly who he is!" he said. "He's been doing this sort of thing for years. He once went to prison for impersonating a police officer." When the man had stopped me on the street, I hadn't any inkling of that, of course. I had returned to my hotel and slept fitfully, half expecting a knock on the door at four A.M. I did awake the next morning to the sound of knocking, but it was only the chambermaid, bringing me the breakfast coffee I had ordered the night before.

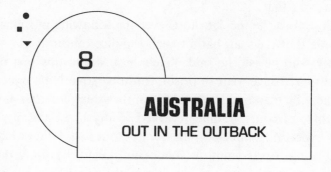

8

AUSTRALIA
OUT IN THE OUTBACK

Brisbane and Sydney

The "ocker," the Australian version of the "redneck," was dead, the country's leading newsmagazine proclaimed, with a combination of smugness and surprise. "Contemplative, cultured, creative, eclectic—recognize the typical Australian?" went the headline. A poll had asked twelve hundred Australian adults what they wanted to do on their holidays. One-fifth wanted to organize a vacation around cultural activities, and an equal number around food and wine. An even bigger chunk wanted to pursue nature and conservation activities. Only a minority preferred to "go fishing." What was happening, one analyst asserted, was the "the softening, the intellectualising of Australians and the extraordinary push to the environment . . . the thoughtful Australian coming out of the old ocker."

It was the vastness and the diversity of Australia that dazzled and eventually tripped you up. Australia is a continent and a whole world: the stunning harbor and the bleak western suburbs of Sydney; the cafés and retro-clothing stores of Melbourne (a.k.a. Cappuccino City); the afternoon cream teas and the vituperative antigay rallies on the northwest coast of the island of Tasmania; and the empty and seemingly endless center of the country that, from the air, looks like a planet abandoned millions of years ago. Australia is made up of descendants of convicts and English gentry and of newer immigrants—Greeks, Yugoslavs, Hong Kong Chinese. It is also its Aboriginal people, the heirs of the continent, now dispossessed, desperately poor. It was difficult to get hold of Australia or make a single statement about it that seemed true. I tried: Australians had the civility of the British and the unpretentiousness of Americans, I would say whenever anyone asked me about the place. An American woman who had spent a long time there had another view. "Australia is the most sexist, racist country I've ever been to," she contended. "They don't even speak English!"

Australia was a place where you could impose your own fantasies and come up with whatever you wanted. Australians turned almost every word into a cozy diminutive to get some of that vastness under control—Australia became "Aussie," Tasmania was "Tassie," university "uni"; even aggravation became just "aggro." They also shortened Australia to "Oz."

It was that vastness, I suspected, that might work to the benefit of gays and lesbians. Like the United States, Australia was a country where you could move around, leave your old self behind, and call your family only at Christmas. You could migrate from Perth on the west coast to Sydney on the east, or vice versa, a distance much like that from California to New York. Even Sydney and Melbourne, the country's two largest cities, were sixteen hours apart by car. Australia was very different from the claustrophobic, tradition-bound societies I had visited so far. It was still a frontier country, and if "flat is freedom," as my friend Hani in Cairo put it, frontier is freedom, too.

The best place to begin was the Australia of myth and caricature. So I started out in Queensland. Queensland is the tropical state, larger than California, Nevada, Texas, and Oregon combined, and extending for fifteen hundred miles along the country's northeast coast. It is Australia's Sunbelt, with an economy that depends on agribusiness, tourism, and mining. For thirty-two years, Queensland was governed by the right-wing National party, led by Sir Johannes Bjelke-Petersen, the son of a Danish rural pastor. Sir Joh was famous for banning strikes, rallies, and marches and for bashing Aboriginals and gays. Women went south for abortions. In liberal circles in Sydney and Melbourne, Queensland was referred to as "the Deep North," "the Banana Republic."

Queenslanders were forever telling Sir Joh stories. One of my favorites related how a man applied to march with his dog for a hundred meters at two A.M. on April Fool's Day in a suburb of Brisbane. He was denied a permit. Man and dog marched anyway, shadowed by four police cars. "It is the thin edge of the wedge," said Sir Joh, with gravity.

When I visited, the sodomy laws, making sexual behavior between two men a crime punishable by seven years in prison, were still on the books in Queensland. There was also a law that made it illegal for pubs to serve prostitutes, thieves, drug pushers, child molesters, persons of ill repute, or sexual deviants—i.e., homosexuals. The police were all-powerful. Until a corruption scandal had forced the National party out of office a few months before my arrival, entrapment of gay men had been commonplace. During one particularly nasty period, as many as ninety policemen were reportedly assigned to patrol gay cruising areas. The powerful Special Branch, "Sir Joh's SS," as it was known, kept files on gays.

Brisbane, Queensland's capital and the country's third-largest city, was my first stop in Australia. It was midsummer, which in Brisbane means heat and humidity of an extremely uncomfortable sort. The city was originally founded as a place for convicts from Sydney to be sent if they committed a second offense. Today, it is a boomtown reminiscent of Dallas or Houston in its heyday, "a place of bare legs, big hats, intuitive judgements, and moneymaking," as Ross Terrill wrote in his book *The Australians*.

Not everyone in Brisbane fit the mold, though. One of the first gay men I met was a twenty-six-year-old primary-school teacher who listened to the Smiths and the Dead Kennedys, got around Brisbane on a ten-speed, and spent most weekday evenings climbing the floodlit cliffs along the river. His students were all underprivileged—many of them were Aboriginals—and he was using rap music to teach them Tennyson. He had come out after reading Edmund White's novel *A Boy's Own Story*. He worked on a weekly gay and lesbian radio show on an alternative station. The evening I met him, he was asking his listeners, "We've all heard gay jokes. Does anyone out there know any straight jokes?"

Brisbane was experiencing the euphoria of post–National party liberation. The city's first-ever gay march had just taken place; three hundred people showed up, an act of supreme courage in Queensland. Manifestations of freedom often took odd forms, though, as I found when I attended a gay backyard barbecue. In many ways, the barbecue was a typical suburban gathering. The fare was the usual Australian sausage ("You have to eat it with ketchup, that's the only way it has any flavor," one guest explained). Toward midnight, the host, fully dressed, was thrown into the swimming pool. The theme of the party was "beats," the Australian term for parks and public toilets where gay men met one another for sex. The backyard featured a directional sign that said ALBERT PARK— after one of the major cruising spots in Brisbane. Then there was a life-size papier-mâché box, meant to represent the outside of a public toilet, "Stone's Corner" by name. Guests were invited to scrawl graffiti, as they might on a bathroom wall, and many availed themselves of the opportunity: "For a good time, call Paul" and "All faggots go to hell." I had the feeling I was in a basement theater in pre-revolutionary Prague or Warsaw, with the forces of repression finally on the run.

Then I went to visit a man in prison.

I took the bus down to the Gold Coast, a high-rise beach resort an hour and a half south of Brisbane. During the recent Queensland election campaign, the National party premier had warned that if the opposition Labor party won, the Gold Coast would become the gay capital of Australia. That certainly hadn't happened. The place boasted the "biggest T-shirt store in the Southern Hemisphere"; it was crowded with Japanese tourists. Michael Browne, a Brisbane gay activist, met me at the bus station and drove me out to the prison farm to meet Stephen Watson.

Officially, Stephen was in prison for defrauding his aged grandmother. But he had also pleaded guilty to twenty-one counts of "carnal knowledge against the order of nature" (sodomy) and thirteen counts of "gross indecency" (oral sex). His was a complicated story, one part family feud, another part antigay prejudice. It was also what Michael Browne called "a Gothic horror story."

Michael had been deeply involved in Stephen's case from the moment when the gay community in Brisbane took it up as a cause célèbre. A large man with a dark beard, Michael was a former Roman Catholic seminarian. (The gay movement in Australia seemed to be made up largely of ex-seminarians and former left-wing activists.) He had spent four years working as a mortician in Cairns, the tourist town opposite the Great Barrier Reef. He now taught marketing at a university in Brisbane. The year before, at the Gay and Lesbian Mardi Gras in Sydney, he had paraded with bananas in his hair to call attention to Queensland's "Banana Republic" politics.

As he drove, he interspersed his conversation with imitations of Dame Edna Everage (Barry Humphries), the Melbourne-born grande dame of female impersonation: "Did you hear about Dame Edna's visit to the Queen?" and "Did you hear what happened when Imelda Marcos came on Dame Edna's TV show? Dame Edna screamed, 'She's wearing my shoes!' Of course, it wasn't really Imelda. . . ."

Stephen's case, he explained, was not the only one in recent memory in which the Queensland sodomy laws had been applied. Eighteen months before, on the Gold Coast, the police had gone to question two men on a routine matter. The police noticed there was only one bed and asked why. The men, naïvely, said it was because they were gay. The police then asked what they did in that bed. The men, naïvely, told them. They apparently had no idea such activities were against the law in Queensland. The couple were prosecuted for sodomy and released on a two-year "good behavior" bond (the Australian counterpart of a suspended sentence). One of the conditions of that bond was that they were forbidden to see one another as long as they remained in Queensland. They moved to Sydney.

After Michael and I had driven for an hour and a half or so, the country suddenly opened up. The hills became rough and spectacular, covered with gum trees. We were entering the grounds of the Numinbah prison farm. "It isn't too bad as prisons go," Michael assured me. "The National party built it so it would have a place to send its crooks." We entered an open pavilion, signed our names in the guest book, and sat down at a picnic table to wait for Stephen. Around us, other prisoners sat with their visitors; one man was locked in an embrace with his girlfriend for almost an hour. There was an ice chest full of cold drinks, the smell of cow manure in the air, and a view of the green hills. It was at the Numinbah prison farm that I became aware of the majesty of the Australian landscape.

Stephen greeted us with a wide grin. He had been out repairing prison fences. At twenty-four, he was short and a little stooped, with deep-set hazel eyes and rough hands, the result of years of outdoor work. He was dressed in his prison garb, a light-blue work shirt and jeans. He amused himself describing pranks that he and the other convicts had played on prisoners they didn't like. "There was this new bloke that showed up," he told us. "He thought he was better than anyone else. We decided, 'We'll fix him.' So we put jam and sugar on the roof of his cabin. The roof is tin, you see. You wouldn't believe the racket the birds made when they discovered it in the morning. Then, there was this other bloke—we put a nine-foot carpet snake in his bed!" Stephen thought this was all quite hilarious. Michael asked him if he was having any sex. Stephen became red in the face. It sounded strangely like summer camp.

Throughout most of our visit, however, Stephen seemed tense and distracted. He was angry at his family, whom he held responsible for his predicament, and resentful that few of his gay friends from Brisbane, who had been so eager to embrace his case, had come to visit him in prison.

Stephen had left school at fifteen. When he was seventeen he began to work for his eighty-one-year-old grandmother on the family farmstead near Roma, a town of nine thousand in flat, dry country about seven hours west of Brisbane. He and his grandmother would go out on his motorcycle to muster cattle, with Stephen driving and the grandmother sitting behind, shouting at the cattle to keep in line. Stephen also shot kangaroos and sold their hides.

As she got older, Stephen's grandmother apparently grew unwilling to pay for certain things necessary for the upkeep of the ranch. So Stephen would have her write out a check for, say, three dollars, and then he would add two zeros to the figure. Whether Stephen was really looking out for the ranch or taking advantage of his grandmother was unclear; Michael preferred to believe he had just acted "stupidly."

About four months prior to his arrest, Stephen's lover, nineteen-year-old Darryl Barton, moved in with him at the ranch. The family was outraged. Eventually, Stephen's uncle went to the police in Roma and accused Stephen of taking financial advantage of his grandmother. He was arrested and released on bail. The following week, Stephen's stepsister handed over to the police a photo album that included pictures of Stephen and Darryl, naked.

On a Saturday morning, Stephen and Darryl were brought to the Roma police station and accused of having sexual relations with one another. Darryl confessed; despite several hours of interrogation, Stephen refused to admit anything. Neither had a lawyer. The two were charged with one count of sodomy and kept overnight. The next day, they were charged with a total of sixty-six counts of sodomy and oral sex.

Meanwhile, the police had searched Stephen's house and discovered a diary. A third man, mentioned in the diary, was also arrested and charged with six sexual offenses. All three men were ordered to undergo HIV tests.

On Monday, Stephen and Darryl appeared before a magistrate. The police opposed bail. Darryl and the third man got lawyers and were released on bail at midweek. But Stephen still refused to admit any guilt, and he remained without a lawyer. By Thursday, he was alone in jail; he hadn't been allowed to take a shower or to change his clothes. He told the officers he was ready to confess. But they wouldn't give him the opportunity. The same thing happened the next day. Finally, on Saturday, he was permitted to give a full confession. The following Wednesday, after ten days in jail, Stephen was released on bail. Under the conditions of his bail, he and Darryl were barred from seeing one another; in addition, Stephen was required to report to the police twice a week.

Upon his release, Stephen went to a nearby town to stay with a pensioner friend named Harry. He was frightened; they hung blankets over the windows and never went out at night. Meanwhile, Darryl's family were doing their best to keep him out of jail. They had found him a girlfriend and even set a wedding date. He appeared in public with love bites on his neck. Then Darryl attempted suicide. For the first time since Darryl's release, Stephen was permitted to see him.

"You have to imagine Stephen's situation at that time," Michael said. "His family has turned on him. He hears that Darryl is getting married. He still doesn't have a lawyer. He is a complete wreck. And none of the gay people in Brisbane, myself included, know anything about this."

Harry, the pensioner, finally went and got a lawyer for Stephen. The lawyer immediately called the Queensland AIDS Council. That was when Michael Browne got involved. Michael used his religious contacts to arrange for an Anglican priest who lived nearby to visit Stephen. The priest brought him to Brisbane. It was the first time Stephen had ever been to Brisbane in his life.

He arrived the night of the annual Queen's Ball, a drag event that is a major date on the Brisbane gay calendar and is said to attract some three thousand to five thousand people. Michael brought Stephen along with him. Toye de Wilde, a drag entertainer and community leader who had run unsuccessfully for Parliament the year before, got up and related the outlines of Stephen's case. "He is not alone," Toye said, as the crowd cheered. Money was raised for Stephen's defense. "Stephen was bawling," Michael remembered. "I was bawling. Stephen didn't know what hit him."

The following morning, Michael awoke and peered into the living room, where Stephen had spent the night. Stephen was sitting on the couch, rolled up in a ball and shaking. He was listening to a cassette tape that featured an electronic organ, a drum, and a out-of-tune sax, playing an arrangement of "Dream a Little Dream of Me." He would play the same tune over and over again.

The Brisbane gay community took Stephen under its wing. The location of his pretrial reporting requirement was changed from Roma to Brisbane. He worked at a grocery shop–café owned by a local activist, in the inner suburb of New Farm. "He loved working at the store," Michael said. "He began to get better."

Stephen's new friends hoped his grandmother would settle the case out of court. But that didn't happen. The family was determined to punish him. Finally, he was sentenced to six months in prison on the fraud charge and granted two years' good-behavior bond on the sex charges.

Four months into his sentence, Stephen was sitting at the picnic table at the Numinbah prison farm, relating boyish pranks and worrying what it would be like once he got out. Would he see Darryl? Would his grandmother take him back? Where would he go if she didn't? When Michael mentioned that he and his lover were considering buying the grocery store–café where Stephen had worked during his Brisbane idyll, suddenly the solution seemed in sight. The tension vanished; Stephen wasn't distracted any longer. "I'd work for nothing," he said. "I really would. I wouldn't care. I'd do anything to get back there."

A couple of days later I was on my way to Sydney. Michael Browne drove me. We were just in time for Sydney's twelfth annual Gay and Lesbian Mardi Gras. Toye de Wilde was supposed to have come with us, but at the last minute she decided to fly instead. I was disappointed. To arrive in Sydney for Mardi Gras alongside Brisbane's most famous drag queen would have provided an entrance in the spirit of the event.

Toye had told me that on returning from Mardi Gras to Brisbane, one felt a "sense of doom." Going in the opposite direction felt like a dash for freedom. Certainly this was the road taken by countless refugees, gay and otherwise, from Sir Joh's tyranny. Not everyone wanted to take that road, of course; some, like Stephen Watson, were backwoods boys who wanted to muster cattle and shoot kangaroos and, failing that, work in a grocery store–café in the "big country town" that was Brisbane.

Soon enough, we were over the border and into the state of New South Wales. I didn't see a sign, though. If there had been one, I imagined it might have read:

Welcome to New South Wales.
Sodomy laws abolished.
Discrimination on the basis of homosexuality illegal.
Gay and Lesbian Mardi Gras party tickets $40 per person.

After thirteen hours of driving, sometimes on two-lane highways that were virtually country roads, we finally reached Sydney. Sydney was Australia's version of Fun City, a sort of San Francisco (the hills, the views, and the harbor) combined with New York (the brashness, the polyglot ethnicity). Sydney had a reputation for hedonism and unpretentiousness—but also for toughness and corruption. It had started out as a prison; at one point, rum was the local currency. All of this had produced a particular culture which was "very much a good-time town," as one transplanted Queenslander told me. "It is a city with a heart. You scratch a Sidneysider and they are down-to-earth, friendly, straightforward. The bus drivers will run you down on the street but if you get on the bus and say, 'Shit, the weather's terrible,' they'll talk to you."

I had mixed feelings about Sydney. Oh, yes, it had its beaches and its arched iron bridge that looked like a rainbow over the harbor, and the famous opera house which, from the outside, resembled a series of nuns' wimples. At the first intermission at the opera, while it was still light, you took your drink out on the terrace and felt as if you were on a ship in the middle of the harbor. At the second intermission, as the sky darkened, you stood in the same spot and watched the lights of the city come on. At moments like that, there was a magic about Sydney. But, if you couldn't afford a harbor view, Sydney could seem rather seedy. My view was a back alley. I was staying at King's Cross, the city's red-light district, where most of the less expensive hotels were located. It had once been the bohemian center—and the gay heart—of Sydney. Now it was noisy, dirty, inhabited by down-and-out characters and raucous teenagers.

Sydney was where Australians and New Zealanders came to be gay and, in Australian parlance, "to rage." As long ago as 1966, in his book *Profile of Australia,* Craig McGregor wrote, "Homosexuals are very much in evidence in Australian cities, and overt homosexual behavior surprisingly common in view of the communal intolerance with which it is regarded; an English acquaintance remarked after two days in Sydney that it was 'the campest city I have ever seen.' " A gay New Zealand lawyer told me he burst into tears every time he got on the plane to return home from Sydney to Christchurch.

Sydney's homosexual life took many of its cues from San Francisco, the American city where you also went in order to be gay. Like San Francisco, Sydney had had its clone scene in the late 1970s and early 1980s. With its emphasis on outrageousness, Sydney's Gay and Lesbian Mardi Gras most resembled San Francisco's Lesbian and Gay Freedom Day Parade. Sydney had its version of the Castro, San Francisco's gay ghetto, and a thriving commercial scene. There was a real gay communal life in Sydney, with newspapers, bars, restaurants and cafés, political organizations, and—during Mardi Gras at least—lesbian and gay music, theater, and comedy. Sydney gays hadn't established themselves politically quite as firmly as their counterparts in San Francisco had, but increasingly the gay vote was a factor in city and parliamentary elections. For Sydney's emerging lesbians, San Francisco was the model, too. The Dykes on Bikes contingent at Mardi Gras was the direct result of a visit by two Sydney lesbians to San Francisco. When San Francisco lesbians scuttled their separatist politics, it wasn't too much later that Sydney began to do the same.

But if Sydney was reminiscent of San Francisco, it was reminiscent of San Francisco before AIDS. Not that Sydney hadn't been hard hit by AIDS; the city accounted for almost three-quarters of Australia's thirteen hundred cases. Estimates were that twenty-five to thirty percent of Sydney's gay men were infected with HIV; that statistic was comparable to a American city like Boston but represented half the estimated rate of HIV infection in San Francisco. Sydney had some advance warning: AIDS arrived a few years later than in San Francisco, and the city had time to prepare itself for the onslaught of the epidemic.

For whatever reasons, Sydney never lost the hedonistic flavor that had characterized San Francisco ten years ago. The bathhouses were still open—and crowded—although safe-sex educational material was everywhere. The city was mad about dance parties, which were usually held in large warehouses; you could go to a gay dance party virtually every weekend of the year. The parties, in fact, were so popular that tickets were now available through mainstream ticket agencies; as a result, straights were beginning to take them over, to the dismay of many in the gay community. I met a couple of gay tourists from San Francisco in town for Mardi Gras who were amazed that Sydney was "so up," as they put it, compared to "depressed" San Francisco.

The commercial heart of gay Sydney is Oxford Street, a thoroughfare of two-story, turn-of-the-century buildings with garishly painted signs that is a short walk from the downtown business district. Oxford Street was lined with black flags that said GAY AND LESBIAN MARDI GRAS and featured colored triangles. The Green Park diner, where you could get egg, bacon, pineapple, and cheese sandwiches, had cut-out fairies hanging from the ceiling and twelve years of Mardi Gras posters on the wall.

Garry Wotherspoon took me on a brief tour. He taught economic and social history at Sydney University and had just completed a book on Sydney's gay subculture since the 1920s. Garry was in his late forties and dressed in a cream-colored suit over a black T-shirt; he wore his hair long. His lover was a black South African.

He arranged to meet me at the piano bar at the Albury Hotel. The Albury was the most popular gay bar in Sydney, known for its weeknight drag shows, which attracted crowds that spilled out onto the street. As we walked down the Oxford Street "strip," Garry pointed out other gay establishments, all within a few short blocks of one another: the Oxford, a clone bar out of San Francisco circa 1979; the Exchange, a punky, trendy dance club; the Midnight Shift, a late-night cruise bar; and the baths. There was a gay bookshop, and a photographer's shop where, the Monday after Mardi Gras, people lined up to buy color prints of various floats. The street had declined somewhat since its heyday in the early 1980s, but it still offered a concentration of gay venues and businesses that no other Australian city, including Melbourne, could match. In this case, "gay" definitely meant "gay male." Except for the lesbian section at the bookshop, a stroll down Oxford Street betrayed few signs that the gay community included women.

Garry indicated the cheap Thai restaurants (the influx of Asian food had transformed a country that had taken its cuisine from London pubs), a place with "the best meat pies in Sydney," another that had good hamburgers. It was eight P.M., but Oxford Street seemed rather deserted. "Where are all those gay tourists here for Mardi Gras?" I asked him. "They're home, putting on their faces," said Garry.

Unfailingly cheerful and optimistic, Garry painted a picture of being gay in Australia that was very different from the one I found in Queensland. The country was highly urbanized, he noted, with nearly half the population living in Sydney and Melbourne. "There is no Middle Australia," he insisted. Because of the lack of a rural base, religious fundamentalists didn't have much power or legitimacy in the country. Melbourne and Sydney did have their religious fringe—the Reverend Fred Nile, arch-opponent of Mardi Gras, was the exemplar of this—but it was only in rural Queensland and isolated Tasmania that fundamentalists had any strength at all. "We don't have the rural crowd you have in the U.S.," Garry said. The country was increasingly multi-ethnic, and gays were "riding the coattails of this," Garry said. Homosexuals were being viewed as just another ethnic or constituency group, along with Greeks, Yugoslavs, and Asians.

All the Australian states except for Queensland and Tasmania had abolished their sodomy laws in recent years. (In December 1990, shortly after my visit, Queensland repealed its sodomy law as well.) New South Wales and South Australia had passed legislation banning discrimination on the basis of sexual orientation; Victoria, the state where Melbourne is located, was expected to follow suit. Under the government's immigration policies, overseas partners of Australian gays and lesbians could become Australian citizens themselves in four years, on the basis of a relationship. All they had to do was to show proof of that relationship—letters from friends, indications of joint assets or shared living arrangements, and such. (New Zealand had a similar policy.) The government was putting a substantial amount of money into AIDS education and services. The statewide AIDS councils, funded entirely by the government, had produced some of the most explicit safe-sex material anywhere in the world.

Australia, Garry insisted, was "an affluent, free, and open society." Because of this affluence, kids could, by and large, leave home and share a flat. This gave gay young people an escape route. There were, to be sure, the bleak, working-class western suburbs of Sydney, where there were few options beyond the local beats. But "any kid in Sydney will see the Mardi Gras on TV," Gary said. "This gives them enormous opportunities. There are gay radio shows in Sydney and you'll find suburban gay kids listening."

We passed the gay bookshop. I remarked that when I had stopped in earlier in the day and asked about books on Australian gay life, the clerk showed me a grand total of one: a compendium of biographical essays called *Being Different,* which Garry had edited. There was a similar book about lesbians, but no fiction of any kind, male or female. When Australian gays and lesbians talked about books, the authors they mentioned were invariably North American or British. Putting his usual optimistic face on things, Garry assured me there were several Australian nonfiction books on gay subjects that were about to be released. "But it is a matter of economics," he said. "The gay audience is just not big enough for publishers to publish very many books."

Gary bade me farewell. He had a number of friends in town for Mardi Gras and had to get back to his house guests. "See you at the parade," he said. "You won't recognize me. I'll have to say hello to *you!*"

On the day and evening of Mardi Gras, the Reverend Fred Nile, a member of the parliament of the state of New South Wales and Australia's most fervent antigay crusader, was praying for rain. The Reverend Nile had his reasons, beyond his opposition to homosexuality and his conviction that Sydney had become the "moral sewer of the Pacific," as he was fond of calling it. The year before, one of the floats at Mardi Gras had portrayed the jowly, double-chinned head of the Reverend Nile on a platter. That was enough, surely, to convince even the most good-natured of men to invoke the wrath of the deity.

And it did rain. It rained buckets, torrents really. Oxford Street was so dense with umbrellas it was almost impossible to see a thing. Flinders Street turned into an ocean of discarded beer cans. It rained so hard that the Reverend Nile took time out from an all-night prayer vigil to announce that his prayers had indeed been answered. "We were hoping it would rain," the *Sydney Morning Herald* quoted him as saying. "We prayed that God would do something to intervene, as the Government and some of the church leaders did not want to intervene."

The Gay and Lesbian Mardi Gras was Australia's largest parade. It was estimated to bring ten million dollars into Sydney's economy. The parade was listed in the New South Wales Tourism Commission statewide events calendar, alongside the Macksville Hoof and Hook Competition, the Cowra Bread Show, and the *Sydney Sun-Herald* Teddy Bears Picnic. Actually, the New South Wales minister of tourism had ordered the removal of the Mardi

Gras from the following year's calendar. But, this year at least, it was still there.

There were three thousand participants, accompanied by forty floats and an estimated two hundred thousand spectators—many of them not gay—all getting properly drenched. By eight in the evening, along Flinders Street, in front of the Bagel Nosh and Budget Rent-a-Car and a used clothing–cum—taxidermy shop that featured a stuffed kangaroo in the window, the crowds were three and four deep. I had a front-row spot. The first floats were passing, and the theme was, inexplicably, hair. There was a larger-than-life aerosol can with GAY GLOW, HAIR MIST written on it, and then a float of hair curlers, with a bewigged drag queen sitting in the middle of it. Next to me was a thirtyish, mustachioed man who had stumbled onto the parade by mistake. "I didn't know this was going on," he said. "I just went out for a drink." He had wanted to come the year before, he said, but his then-girlfriend had vetoed the idea. "Anything gay was a no-no to her. She was very conservative." He then went on to chat about the universal topic of the decade: real estate.

It was beginning to rain harder, and I gave up my spot to a man with a three-year-old child. I clambered on top of a parked car, but even from there it was difficult to see. A brigade of about fifty Dykes on Bikes passed, engines revving, as well as an all-lesbian float with a country-and-western motif. They were followed by a group of Ethel Merman impersonators (with a huge cardboard mouth) called the Ethel Mermansons. The Sisters of Perpetual Indulgence—a group of Sydney gay men dressed as Roman Catholic nuns, who performed mock blessings and exorcisms at gay events—made their inevitable appearance. Music ranged from Verdi to Afro-pop, and virtually every historical era seemed to be represented—ancient Rome, seventeenth-century France, the American West. Interestingly, there seemed to be no references to Australian culture at all.

The biggest applause of the night went to the float of the AIDS Council of New South Wales, which used white umbrellas and pieces of fabric to give the impression of silhouettes. The council's slogan was "Keep it up. Safe sex. We're winning against AIDS."

In many respects, the affair was similar to a gay pride parade in the United States. Virtually every major homosexual organization in Sydney was represented—the Gay and Lesbian Counselling Service float featured a life-size telephone booth; the Gay and Lesbian Immigration Task Force advertised itself with a giant disco globe. But Mardi Gras differed from many gay parades in the States in that carnival and spectacle were as important as gay pride and affirmation. In Sydney, the aim was to be as outrageous as possible. That's what they believed that gay meant. There was no attempt to make a "good" impression or to avoid stereotypes: the event reveled in drag and naked torsos, in this case thoroughly soaked ones.

Abruptly, the rain halted. It was time for the party at the Sydney Showgrounds, one of the most sought-after tickets in this dance-party-crazed city. With fourteen and a half thousand tickets sold in advance, the party offered almost as much spectacle as the parade itself. There was a huge dance floor inside the Showgrounds hall; it had taken two days to lay the plywood. As I entered, a performer was swinging from a rope in the middle of an abstract mobile, doing dives and other circus acts. Outside, thousands of people were milling about or sitting at picnic tables, the men in sleeveless T-shirts and spandex bicycle shorts or jeans, some of the women still in their country-and-western outfits. There were outdoor stages that offered everything from transvestite fashion shows to sitar music.

The year before, virtually every female impersonator in Australia had gotten up on stage to sing Jerry Herman's "I Am What I Am," bringing the entire evening to a smashing finale. Nothing quite so memorable happened this year, but there was still an orgiastic quality to it all, as if New York's legendary symbol of seventies sexual license, The Saint, had been reborn Down Under in the nineties. Everyone seemed to be on something, particularly Ecstasy, Sydney's most popular drug; by the end of the evening, some twenty-five to thirty people had been taken to the hospital with drug reactions.

At three in the morning, still wet—and tired—I decided to depart, even though stragglers continued to arrive. The whole idea of the Mardi Gras party was to stay up till dawn; when I told people afterward that I had left before the sun rose, they looked at me disapprovingly, as if I had transgressed some cardinal rule of Sydney society. Near the exit, I noticed a pile of condoms on a table, courtesy of the AIDS Council of New South Wales. The packets said, DANCE PROUD, FUCK SAFE, SHOOT CLEAN. Near the door, too, in a heap on the floor, walkie-talkie in hand, lay Cath Phillips, the Mardi Gras president. She smiled a smile that managed to combine radiance with complete and utter exhaustion.

"Mardi Gras is the only thing the community cares deeply about," Cath had told me a few days before. "It transcends politics and political differences." Cath, a redheaded New Zealander in her thirties, was busily signing checks amidst banners and papier-mâché costumes in the warehouse that was the Mardi Gras office. On the bulletin board were signs for artists specializing in Mardi Gras transformations. "Hair, imagination, makeup," went one. "Marlene Dietrich. Dolly Parton. Joan Crawford." On the floor was a box filled with red armbands; people who had been harassed or bullied were urged to take one to wear during the parade. Outside, in the parking lot, a group of fifteen or twenty men and women were practicing dance steps. The phone was ringing constantly. There was a sense of excitement of a winning political campaign the day before election.

Cath was laying down some stiff rules on tickets for the Mardi Gras party. By then, all the tickets had been sold, except for a few that had been put aside for people coming from outside New South Wales or from abroad. "Tell people we have to see a bus or a train ticket with a date on it," she was saying. "*Anyone* can have a bus ticket. And if they drove here, we need to see *dated* petrol receipts." Out in the lobby, ticketless would-be partygoers were taking a fatalistic attitude. "If it's meant to be, it's meant to be," sighed one young man with a large hoop earring dangling from his ear and a guitar strapped around his shoulder.

Cath was dressed in a white blouse, gabardine shorts, and sandals. She was a sculptor, making "the big ones that don't sell," as she put it. The year before, her art work had gotten her two days in jail for obscenity in Mildura, a small town just over the state line in Victoria. The offending work, exhibited in the town's annual sculpture show, was part of a series Cath was doing on the subject of domesticity. She had constructed something akin to a large dollhouse; the viewer could see inside. In the bedroom was a double bed, and on the floor in front of the bed were the words "She ran her tongue like fire across my nipple. She slipped her hand in my cunt and grinned." The show's officials covered up the words with plywood. Cath removed the plywood. Show officials put the plywood back a second time (it was exhibited that way), and off to jail went Cath Phillips. The entire case had dragged on for eight or nine months, and Cath hadn't been able to work on any sculpture since. She was putting her energy into Mardi Gras instead, working sixty hours a week. "I am an all-or-nothing person," she said.

When Mardi Gras first started in 1978, it was more overtly political than today. That year, the parade took place in June, in the midst of the Australian winter, a date chosen to commemorate New York's Stonewall riots. It reflected political activism in the United States at the time—opposition to California's Briggs Initative (a ballot proposal that would have barred gay teachers from the classroom) and singer Anita Bryant's campaign to repeal the gay rights law in Florida's Dade County. As at Stonewall, there was a clash with the police; fifty-two people were arrested. The event had attracted both gay men and lesbians, but by the following year the women had left in droves. Lesbian separatism was in the ascendant. Mardi Gras became an all-male event, dominated by drag, and the date was moved from June to February, when the weather was more pleasant. In part as a reflection of the improving situation of gays in Australian society, Mardi Gras increasingly became a Sydney event and not just a gay community event. In fact, in 1986, someone had actually left the word "gay" off the Mardi Gras T-shirts. It was an error, but it was emblematic of Mardi Gras's changing role.

In 1988, the "Gay Mardi Gras" added "Lesbian" to its title. That year, Cath and two other women were elected to the Mardi Gras committee; the activities that accompanied the Mardi Gras parade—theater, music, sports—began to reflect lesbian interests as well. (Now, six out of the thirteen committee members were women, with Cath the first woman president.) The transformation wasn't easy. Another woman on the committee told me that the female trailblazers had taken heat from both sides—from the entrenched Mardi Gras men, who resisted admitting women to their exclusive club, and from lesbian separatists, who accused them of "going to work for the boys."

Since the name change and the increased participation of women,

Cath contended that Mardi Gras had been "a happier place."
"There had been a small group of men running things," she said.
"A lot of people were disenfranchised and alienated, and not just
women. Now, with the women here, there is more creativity. There
is a real buzz when you walk in here."

To Cath, the parade, the party, and the cultural events added up
to "an incredible political statement." They had made it fun and,
"if people have fun, there is less fear of the unknown," she believed.
"The unknown is a giggle."

She bristled at the notion that the parade encouraged gay stereotypes. "Creativity breaks down stereotypes," she said. "It is uniformity that promotes stereotypes." And she insisted that the fact
that the parade had gained mainstream acceptance did not mean
that Mardi Gras had become "heterosexualized," as some had
complained. With heterosexuals watching the parade and understanding gay culture (in its Mardi Gras guise, at least) would come
recognition and respect. "That is different from tolerance," Cath
said.

The fact that Mardi Gras took place at night was crucial. "Night
is when forbidden things happen," she said. "Mardi Gras is about
sex and raunchiness. When you turn the corner onto Oxford Street
and you enter gay territory, the air is electric. This is not an earnest
event!"

And what about all those earnest, "ideologically sound" Sydney
lesbians? I wondered. How did they feel about a parade that put
such a high premium on drag and frivolity? "They are learning to
have fun," Cath said. "Lesbians are watching the parade and thinking, 'I could do that.' And the next year, they are participating. And
the next year they may even want to go to the party!"

That change in lesbian attitudes reflected some very profound
changes in Sydney's lesbian community, Cath said. For years, not
only had the lesbian community been quite separate from men, but
a "wowser-like"—puritanical—ideology had been dominant. If
you weren't downwardly mobile, you were somehow suspect. Now,
being "ideologically sound" (and on the dole) didn't have the ca-
chet it once had. More and more women had economic resources;
Cath's own lover was a physician. "There is a developing acceptance of different points of view," she said. "A few years ago, if you

worked with men, you were persona non grata. That isn't true today. There is more acceptance of the idea of working in coalition."

"Coalition politics"—gay men and lesbians working together—was the latest buzzword in Sydney. Within a two-year period, virtually every gay organization in town had refashioned itself as a mixed lesbian and gay group. Mardi Gras was only the most visible example of this. The formerly all-male Gay Sports Association was now the Gay and Lesbian Sports Association. The old gay Solidarity group, a left-wing political organization, was now reformed as the Gay and Lesbian Rights Lobby. Separatism—male and female— was not quite dead exactly. But, more and more, it seemed a spent force.

I arranged to see Carole Ruthchild, the co-convener of the Gay and Lesbian Rights Lobby, on the day after Mardi Gras. "Just keep ringing," she said. "I'll leave the phone off the hook until I wake up." Having gone to bed early in violation of Mardi Gras norms, I felt restless and a little guilty the next morning. It seemed as if everyone in Sydney was still fast asleep. I started calling Carole at eleven. Busy. At noon, her line was still busy. At one, busy. Finally, at two, she picked up the phone. An hour later, I was at her doorstep, a worker's cottage on a narrow lane in the very English- looking suburb of Balmain. Carole, a computer programmer in her early thirties, had herself emigrated from England sixteen months before. A poster on the kitchen wall said: "Thank you Fred [Nile] for helping bring lesbians and gay men together. Let's stick to- gether. Let's fight together. Let's win together."

Carole was a major proponent of coalition politics. In the past, lesbian separatists had done important work in areas such as rape crisis intervention, she said. But today separatism wasn't achieving anything politically. "Women who are serious about politics are doing coalition politics," she insisted. She noted the number of lesbian-feminists who had been at the Mardi Gras party the night before. "In previous years, they would never have dreamed of going," she said.

Carole's worldview was the product of class politics in England. Feminism had galvanized her. "Reading about rape ripped the scales from my eyes," she said. She had been angry (she took the name Ruthchild during that period). But you could only maintain a life motivated by anger for so long, she noted. An activist had to be pragmatic. "All movements change with time," she said.

It was in England that she herself had begun to change. In Leicester, where she had lived, relations between lesbians and gay men had been "terrible," she said. There had a row between the two groups in the only gay pub in town over the showing of porn videos and the presence of heterosexual men. She decided to get involved in the Gayline, the local telephone counseling service. She persuaded the organization to add the word "Lesbian" to its title and encouraged women to join. The membership was soon half men and half women. "I learned we could change things," she said. "Before that, I felt I was in a corner. It was stifling. Men and women are much more powerful together. We need to think of ourselves as allies, not enemies."

The political situation in Sydney was less favorable to gays and lesbians than it appeared on the surface, Carole contended. Even though a 1984 New South Wales law made it illegal to discriminate on the basis of "homosexuality" (there was, interestingly, no provision against discrimination on the basis of heterosexuality), no gay complainant had ever won a case before the Equal Opportunity Tribunal. Recently, a gay man had gone into the hospital for surgery and was told he had to take an HIV test. He refused, appealed to the Equal Opportunity Tribunal, but lost his case. "We need legislation," Carole said. "But we also have to be able to take cases forward. And that does not seem to be happening."

How much complacency was there within the gay and lesbian community? I asked.

"Complacency. God!" exclaimed Carole. "Sydney!"

If anything had shaken Sydney, said Carole, it was the recent rash of "poofter-bashings." The majority of incidents had taken place around Oxford Street and in the heavily gay inner suburbs of Darlinghurst and Surry Hills. The Gay and Lesbian Rights Lobby had monitored sixty-seven cases of gay-bashing within a six-month period. In the past two months, especially during summer, the numbers had been "incredible," Carole said. There had been vicious attacks, for example that of "a guy at two in the afternoon who was hit with five blows to the head by someone wielding something extremely heavy. This was not just a quick thump to the chin."

Violence against lesbians was more difficult to measure, although there were two recent cases of women surrounded by groups of men and attacked with razors. "It is more common for a woman to be raped than to be bashed," Carole noted. "Now does that happen because someone is a woman or because someone is a lesbian? Who knows? There isn't one particularly lesbian area in town, and this makes it harder to figure out, too."

When I asked what lesbian issues the lobby was working on, Carole was vague. She mentioned the subject of child custody, but admitted that there had been no recent problem with the New South Wales courts.

Just identifying lesbian issues was problematic. "Lesbians have been so invisible here," Carole said. She noted that there hadn't been any regular lesbian publications until the recent emergence of the monthly *Lesbians on the Loose*. Previously, the sole lesbian publication had been *Lesbian Network,* which had been available only at women's bars and bookshops; the publication maintained a policy barring men from looking at it.

Still, it was clear from a visit to Sydney that the lesbian profile was rising. People talked about a lesbian "takeover" of Mardi Gras, an idea that would have seemed laughable a couple of years before. In a city where weekends were devoted to dance parties, lesbians were now organizing a series of warehouse parties and inviting gay men. Before, it had been the other way around. Women seemed to be gaining confidence and visibility. "Even Fred Nile talks about lesbians these days," said Carole. "That links lesbians and gay men in the public mind. And that makes us less invisible, too."

Sydney was still Sydney, though—brassy, freewheeling "salacious Syd," as a Melbourne acquaintance was fond of calling it. Where else on earth could one find a city where the proposed lesbian and gay community center was to be supported by slot machines? And where the prime mover behind the same lesbian and gay community center was a perennial Communist candidate for mayor who turned out to have, as he so carefully put it, "a talent for business"? I'd originally gone to see Brian McGahen because he had been the president of Mardi Gras in the days before Cath Phillips. But that seemed the least of Brian's accomplishments. Perhaps more than anyone I met, he represented the quintessential gay Sydney.

I met Brian in a tiny café near my hotel in King's Cross. It was early afternoon, and the prostitutes and junkies hadn't made their appearance yet; the crowds of rowdy teens who gathered nightly outside the Hard Rock Café were engaged in more useful pursuits. You might have been in some quiet suburb, not in the midst of the most notorious red-light district south of Patpong. Brian was a slight man with a mustache and the faintest hint of a twinkle in his eye. He had an earring in his ear and a tattoo on his arm and was dressed in a tie-dyed sleeveless T-shirt. He didn't look like he had been Moscow's man in New South Wales.

Nor did he look like the Sydney city councilor he had been from 1984 to 1987, when he represented Surry Hills. Brian had been a rather unconventional city councilor. He got a square named after Nelson Mandela, and received Soviet peace delegations when they came to Sydney. He was openly gay and worked to persuade the City Council to go on record as supporting Mardi Gras. In those days the Sydney City Council was a rather unconventional body. It was populated, in Brian's words, with "gays and Communists." (There were three openly gay councilors, including Brian.) In 1987, the state government abolished it. Today, under a revamped system, the Sydney City Council represented only the central business district, while a number of other councils represented residential areas.

In the 1970s and early 1980s, Brian had run as the Communist party candidate for mayor a number of times, garnering ten percent of the vote in one race. Despite the traditionally antigay stance of the CP in most other countries, in Australia, Brian said, there were many gay members. Recently, the Australian Communist party had abolished itself, but Brian was making good use of his party contacts. He had gone into the import business, bringing in fabric from China, coffee from Nicaragua (during the Sandinista period), and handicrafts made by Palestinian refugees.

Back in 1981, when Brian became the president of Mardi Gras, he immediately put his capitalist talents to work. Mardi Gras had less than two hundred dollars in the bank then. (Today, it had savings of close to five hundred thousand dollars, he said.) Brian's method of putting Mardi Gras on a sound financial basis was to inaugurate the year-round dance parties that eventually became the staple of Mardi Gras fund-raising and Sydney gay social life.

Brian headed Mardi Gras in the days before the emergence of coalition politics. I got the impression he was one of those gay men who had been dragged kicking and screaming into the new era. His most recent project was a lesbian and gay community center called the Pride Initiative; he recalled an occasion when he and a woman involved in Pride went to see a solicitor on organization business. Rather condescendingly, Brian told his companion to "be sure and dress up." He discovered that the woman was more adept at dealing with the solicitor than he was.

The Pride committee was negotiating a lease for a building just off Oxford Street; they wanted to have offices, meeting places, even a gym. Brian, characteristically, had some novel ideas for generating income. For example, at an early planning meeting, he suggested that the first thing that was needed was a bar. "People were shocked," Brian said. After all, a community center was supposed to be an alternative to the bars. Eventually, the group agreed. "It was the lesbians who came around early to this idea," said Brian. "Women have few venues in Sydney, and because it would be a private club, we could keep straights out. That was something they saw as desirable."

Then, Brian floated an even more controversial idea to keep the center going: slot machines.

He insisted that slot machines had a different image in Australia than elsewhere. In the state of New South Wales, under the registered-clubs legislation, only private, nonprofit organizations could legally operate slot machines. "Jewish clubs and Italian clubs have had slot machines for years," Brian said. "They use them to raise money. It is very difficult to raise money in Sydney. The tradition of private philanthropy that you have in the United States doesn't exist here." If all this came to pass, Brian dreamed of twenty thousand dollars in income for the first year and as much as a hundred thousand in five years. Brian—and visions of all that money—had persuasive power. At the most recent meeting, he said, the Pride Initiative committee had voted seventy to twenty in favor of slot machines.

Brian had yet another scheme: He wanted the center to apply to join the Registered Clubs Association, which lobbied the state government on behalf of various social organizations. Members of the association included football clubs and the Returned Servicemen's Clubs (the Australian counterpart of the Veterans of Foreign Wars in the United States). It was as "ockerlike" a crowd as you could find. Brian's desire to join the Registered Clubs Association went beyond a desire to rub shoulders with footballers and Gallipoli veterans. He thought the association was doing a good job. "If we do get a bar and slot machines, we won't have to pay tax," he noted. "The law is the result of lobbying by the Registered Clubs Assocation."

That was when I first noticed the twinkle in Brian's eyes.

When I got back to the States, about a month and a half later, I learned that Brian had taken his own life. He had known for two years that he was infected with HIV, although he hadn't mentioned it to me or shown any signs of illness. He had been a member of the Voluntary Euthanasia Society of New South Wales. Shortly after his death, a friend telephoned the *Sydney Star Observer,* the weekly gay paper, and reported that Brian had committed suicide, "peacefully, surrounded by those close to him." Before Brian died, he placed his own death notice in the *Star Observer.* It went like this:

Brian McGahen

3.3.52 to 2.4.90

Died peacefully at home by
his own hand as a result of
the AIDS disease. He was a
peace activist and communist.
Alderman Sydney City
Council as an Independent
1984 to 1987. President

Gay Mardi Gras 1981 to
1985. Always a fighter for
social justice and liberation
of all oppressed people. To
be privately cremated.

Soon after, I read in an Australian magazine that the gay and
lesbian center had been unable to open because of problems with its
lease. No mention was made of slot machines.

Melbourne

Ava Gardner didn't think much of Melbourne. When the Hollywood actress came to town, in the late 1950s, to star in the film
version of Nevil Shute's apocalyptic novel *On the Beach,* she pronounced the city "the perfect place to make a movie about the end
of the world." Melburnians still remember Ava Gardner, and not
fondly. In those days, Swanston Street, the city's main avenue, was
bounded on one end by the war memorial and the other by a
brewery. But the brewery had burned down. If war and lager had
once defined the parameters of Melbourne life, that wasn't as true
anymore.

I came to Melbourne intending to stay for a few days. Soon, a
few days stretched into a week, a week into two weeks. I liked
Melbourne—the parks and gardens as green as the English countryside; the bohemianism of Brunswick Street, with its bookshops,
cheap and exotic restaurants, and retro-clothing stores; the beach-
colony atmosphere of St. Kilda, with its decayed Luna Park. I even
liked the Victorian suburbs, with their latticework and corner milk
bars. The city is crisscrossed by green-and-yellow trams featuring
conductors who are a match for the most colorful New York cab-
bie. You buy a ticket for the day, and you can get on and off as
many times as you like without paying a penny extra.

Melbourne might be at the end of the world in geographic terms,
but a stroll about reveals a city as sophisticated as any metropolis
of the Northern Hemisphere. Even its detractors refer to it as
"Cappuccino City." As you head down Toorak Road in upmarket

South Yarra, you pass bistro after bistro, all serving trendily identical pastas. Sydney has nothing on Melbourne in terms of multiculturalism: *The Age,* the Melbourne daily newspaper, lists the Muslim prayer times along with the weather forecast and the surf report. Melbourne has a thriving arts scene; during my stay, jazz greats Stéphane Grappelli, Joe Pass, and Blossom Dearie were performing, and you could see the same *Così fan tutte* they saw in Sydney. Ava Gardner probably wouldn't recognize the place.

To really understand Melbourne, you have to see it through the prism of Melbourne-Sydney rivalry. Australia is, in many ways, a tale of two rival cities dueling for a dominant position. If Sydney is a rough, upstart town that began as a penal colony, Melbourne is respectability personified. Its prosperity was based on "clean" money—mining, whaling, the gold fields, and later, finance and banking. It has no convict skeletons in its closet. If Sydney is glitz and "glam" and flash, Melbourne is stateliness and seriousness. If Sydney is New York and San Francisco and Mecca, too, Melbourne is London, Boston, and a little bit of Athens (it has the third-largest urban Greek population in the world).

The lesbian and gay communities of the two cities reflected these polarities. When the American gay writer Armistead Maupin came calling, in Melbourne a hundred and sixty people paid to have dinner with him. In Sydney, a similar event was canceled because of lack of interest. *The Age,* the Melbourne daily, is the most respected in Australia; *Outrage,* the glossy Melbourne-based monthly, is the country's most serious-minded gay publication. In the seventies and eighties, it was Melbourne "Uni" that produced the leading figures of the country's gay intelligensia.

People in Melbourne were constantly comparing their city to Sydney, sometimes defensively, sometimes with bravado. That was particularly true of gay Melburnians, in view of the fact that Sydney's reputation as Australia's gay capital was always threatening to lure away Melbourne's best and brightest. To the Melbourne gay mind, Sydney was either the fount of all good or the fount of all evil; it was either the only place in Australia where any significant gay life or activism could be found, or it was "salacious Syd," frivolous, heartless, uncaring.

Gary Dowsett, a Brisbane-born AIDS researcher who lived in

Sydney, contended you could see the difference between the Melbourne and Sydney gay communities in the imagery the Victorian and New South Wales AIDS councils used in their safe-sex posters and brochures. Melbourne pictured young men who tended to be blond and blow-dried and slightly androgynous. Sydney preferred harder, more directly sexual, and traditionally masculine images. "The state of desire" in Melbourne, Dowsett said, using the term originated by the American author Edmund White, "is gentler, less evoking of the hard-edged gay imagery and performance that seems to be so important in parts of the Sydney inner-city gay community. The sexual stakes are not as high in the venues in Melbourne. To be able to play in the games at Sydney bars like the Oxford or the Midnight Shift you have to be pretty skilled. You have to look right and get it all right in lots of ways. The only way to play is to fit into that specific imagery. It is much more diverse in Melbourne."

The two lesbian communities were different, as well. While Sydney's women had found the utopian future of coalition politics, Melbourne's remained locked in the Stone Age of separatism. Instead of having a Gay and Lesbian Mardi Gras, Melbourne had two separate but equal celebrations—the all-male Midsumma Festival and, for the first time, a highly successful lesbian festival.

Long after it was over, Melbourne lesbians were still rhapsodizing over the lesbian festival, which had included ten days of theater, music, films, and workshops, plus a party that attracted some twenty-five hundred women. The festival had been "the best ten days I've ever experienced," said Jean Taylor, a forty-five-year-old mother of two who was one of the festival planners. "You'd get up in the morning, go off to a lesbian space, watch lesbian music and theater and film, and then come home at two or three in the morning to a houseful of lesbian guests. You'd chat for an hour or two, then go to bed, wake up in the morning, and do it all over again." At the lesbian festival, the debate was over which activities should be "lesbian only" and which should be open to "all women." Gay men—to say nothing of men in general—were beyond the pale.

Still, Melbourne's community didn't really have a focus, a center. The two festivals didn't play the unifying role that Mardi Gras did in Sydney; they lacked Mardi Gras's long tradition and visibility. In Melbourne, there was no Oxford Street, no gay or lesbian commercial and residential core. The city was split in two by the Yarra River; there were inner suburbs with identifiable gay populations (Fitzroy, St. Kilda, South Yarra) but they were scattered about. Bars for gay men tended to be dispersed in out-of-the-way districts of warehouses and light industry. Lesbian social institutions were even more elusive. There weren't any exclusively lesbian bars—just "lesbian night" on Thursdays at one pub, Fridays at another, and the like.

One of Melbourne's few community-wide institutions was the gay (but not lesbian) biweekly newspaper, the *Melbourne Star Observer*. I went to see Chris Gill, the paper's dashing editor, at its tiny, second-floor office on bohemian Brunswick Street. Chris did virtually everything—writing, editing, layout. Melbourne's most famous drag entertainer sold ads. The latest issue of the paper had been put to bed, and Chris could relax a bit. "We're a smaller paper than the *Sydney Star Observer*," Chris said. "They get straight advertising, which we don't. In Sydney, the gay community is at least seen as a market. We haven't even reached that status in Melbourne." At twenty-eight, Chris had closely cropped hair and wore an earring. He had grown up in a Melbourne suburb and started out in journalism working for a Trotskyist newspaper.

He took me off to the Shrine of Remembrance, the memorial to Australians who had died in World War I. It looks a little like the Great Pyramid. The building had been designed so that on the eleventh of November every year, at exactly eleven A.M., the time the armistice took effect, a shaft of light entered the windowless building and moved across the letters of the word "love" chiseled in stone. These days, the shaft of light makes its appearance every half-hour, simulated for tourists. "Disneyland," sneered Chris, always alert to the the incursions of crass American influence.

Chris had an incisive turn of mind—and a turn of phrase that sometimes got him in trouble. When the *Star Observer* received a series of letters accusing Melbourne's major disco, the Sir Robert Peel, of discriminating against women patrons, Chris titled the letters "Peeled Off, I," "Peeled Off, II," and "Peeled Off, III." Sir Robert's owner was more annoyed at the headlines than at the letters themselves; he threatened to pull the bar's advertising.

Chris was critical of gay Melbourne; in his estimation, the city suffered from "woeful" community development. There were two and a half times as many gay establishments in Sydney as in Melbourne, even though the two cities had virtually the same population. The Victorian AIDS Council (VAC) was the only gay-oriented organization in town of any consequence. There was barely a gay political group, and the telephone counseling line had shut down amidst accusations of scandal eighteen months before. "The common wisdom," said Chris, "is that in Sydney they eat mangoes and go to the beach, while in Melbourne we pride ourselves on sitting on committees and getting things done. But why is there no gay political group here? There *is* something called the Gay Electoral Lobby and I can give you the names of the two people involved. Exactly two." Australia was sending a hundred and fifty athletes to Vancouver for the Gay Games that summer. Of that number, one hundred were from Sydney, but only six from Melbourne. "That is pathetic," Chris said.

It was easy to be complacent in Melbourne. Law reform had been achieved relatively painlessly in the state of Victoria. Protection against discrimination on the basis of HIV status had been handed to the gay community "on a plate," as someone put it. The state health minister was a volunteer at the Victorian AIDS Council. There had been three hundred or so AIDS cases in Melbourne (approximately two thousand people had tested HIV-positive), about a third as many as in Sydney. "Young people are not angry in Melbourne," said Chris. "They are not angry that their friends are dying, because their friends are not dying. They can now go through life without knowing anyone with HIV. Anyone with a mustache gets sneered at. There is a real generation gap."

Meanwhile, many 1970s gay activists had moved into AIDS work, often becoming health professionals and public-health bureaucrats. They were doing a fine job, Chris thought, but outside of AIDS, all other areas were being neglected. "There used to be debates and forums on all kinds of political issues," he noted. "Now, there are only safe-sex workshops."

But surely something must be going on in Melbourne, I insisted. "What do you write about in your newspaper?"

"For the past several weeks, bashings," said Chris.

There had, in fact, been six murders at Melbourne "beats" during the preceding twelve-month period, and a raft of summertime assaults. But gay men were afraid to go to the police to press charges, in part because the police themselves had a history of antigay harassment, if not antigay violence. "The Victoria police force are under siege from within and without," Chris said. "*The Age* has been running features about police improprieties and basically the image is coming forth of the police as a 'gang of cowboys.' There have been massive resignations." In this atmosphere, a group of gay men had formed a vigilante squad called the Friends of Dorothy. The name, taken from *The Wizard of Oz,* was a code that gay men used to refer to one another in the more closeted forties and fifties.

When I asked Chris how I could meet the vigilantes, he was circumspect. "If you go to the Porter Street sauna and talk to Colin and Patrick, they might be able to help you," he said. Then he changed the subject.

I went looking for "a friend of Dorothy." When I arrived at the 55 Porter Street sauna, located in the southern fringe of Melbourne, fifteen or twenty men were sitting around the lounge in red towels, watching the Australian version of the Emmy awards on TV. Porter Street's central motif was safe sex. Patrons received a card, with a picture of a naked man and a map of the mazelike premises, that said, "Relax, stay safe and have a great time. . . . Remember it's OK to say NO at any time to anything." The inside of each locker door offered safe-sex information; there were condoms in all the cubicles. On the walls, every ten feet or so, were safe-sex posters. Plum jam was for sale, the proceeds of which went to Australia's AIDS quilt.

Colin, one of the owners, was serving coffee and brownies, as if at a church bake sale. He was in his thirties, curly-haired, wiry, with a bit of the street fighter about him. He had grown up in a working-class family in a country town, joined the navy, and married when he got a girl pregnant. Then, he met Patrick and left it all behind him. They had been together fifteen years. Colin was drinking coffee himself; he was working till seven o'clock in the morning, closing hour at Porter Street.

I told him I had been to Mardi Gras, and he immediately

launched into an exposition of his view of the differences between Sydney and Melbourne. "Sydney is a party scene and has always been," Colin said. "Melbourne was where you had a circle of friends and went to dinner parties. In Sydney, the attitude has been, 'We're gonna die, let's party. Let's take it to the top.' You still get that feeling. In Melbourne, we got health consciousness. When AIDS hit, the AIDS Council got the education out straightaway and got the trauma over. Melbourne adjusted its life-style quickly and went back to being Melbourne again. In Sydney, they get sicker quicker. People who are sick are out partying. I know people in Melbourne who have been positive since 1981. Their friends in Sydney, who got sick around the same time, are dead."

His lover and co-owner, Patrick, arrived, carrying two bags of groceries. He was on the stocky side and wore his hair in a flattop. If Colin was warm and gregarious, Patrick called himself "the cold one, icy, bitchy." He came from a family of high achievers; both his parents were scientists. "I have never had a great deal of appreciation for my fellow man," Patrick informed me. "Working in saunas, I never have had to deal with the world very much." When I asked him the "secret" of his and Colin's long-standing relationship (they had met when Patrick was eighteen) he replied, unhesitatingly, "Drugs, porno, and threesomes." Also, he said, "I don't believe in knights in shining armor."

For the first several years after they met, the two had worked in saunas, including Steamworks, at the time Melbourne's grandest sauna. Eventually, they decided to open their own enterprise. They built Porter Street virtually with their own hands, they said. Five people owned it together—one a silent partner with a forty percent interest. Colin and Patrick each had a ten percent share.

Porter Street opened after the AIDS epidemic hit, at a time when major cities in the United States were closing down their bathhouses. Saunas in Australia learned from the fate of San Francisco and New York's bathhouses; shrewdly, they began to promote safe sex early, establishing good relations with health departments and AIDS councils. Porter Street led the way. "Right after AIDS arrived, attendance at saunas was declining," said Colin. "Steamworks lost half their business. When we opened Porter Street, we created a new crowd—younger, more aware people."

For his part, Patrick admitted that before AIDS, saunas had been "fuck shops." In the 1990s, he thought, the emphasis had to be on services. So Porter Street offered a legitimate masseur, a naturopath (the Australian counterpart of a chiropractor), even a flotation tank. One night each week, volunteers from the Victorian AIDS Council dropped by to do AIDS education and on another night the state Health Department did the same. Patrick argued that people who went to saunas like Porter Street were less likely to have unsafe sex than those who patronized the bars. If you cruised someone at a bar for hours, had a few drinks with him, and then went home together, you became very invested in the situation. In that case, "it becomes harder to resist unsafe sex," he said. The argument was self-serving, to be sure, but it was undeniable that at Porter Street, at least, one couldn't avoid constant reminders about safe sex.

Colin brought up the subject of the Friends of Dorothy. Melbourne's gay community had never been "political," he said. Victoria had gotten sodomy-law reform through backdoor politics, and not a lot had happened since. Recently, however, there had been some "gatherings," as he put it: "People are angry." There had been "just a bit too many bashings and attacks on venues and cars. So a little group has formed called the Friends of Dorothy. They have managed to get information on the bashers, including license-plate numbers. Apparently, they have used some contacts in the road traffic authority to get the names and addresses of the owners of these cars."

He knew all this from "two guys I've never seen before" who had happened to wander into Porter Street one night and started talking. "They have stirred something up that needed stirring up," he said. He didn't know if the Friends of Dorothy had taken any reprisals yet but expected there would be some. There was a new attitude, he said, one of "Fuck it: I don't have to take it anymore." Recently, at a Melbourne beat, a gay man attacked a poofter-basher with a bicycle lock; two "thugs" had invaded Porter Street and were beaten up. "Gone are the days of wimps," said Colin. "We have gained lots of self-confidence from building up our bodies and looking after our health. Today, gay men are more aggressive."

Patrick concurred. "I have purchased a Louisville Slugger," he said and left it at that.

After meeting Colin and Patrick, I presumed that I had just made the acquaintance of the major organizers of the Friends of Dorothy. Mostly, what I took away from my visit to Porter Street, though, was the idea of a safe-sex, socially responsible sauna, one that at least gave the impression of fufilling the educational role that U.S. proponents of bathhouses were always claiming for such establishments.

Beyond the baths, Melbourne was a particularly interesting laboratory in which to look at the role of the AIDS epidemic in community-building in Australia. The city wasn't an AIDS "war zone." Seven percent of the gay men in Melbourne were estimated to be infected with HIV—a figure that put Melbourne on a par with North American cities like Knoxville, Tennessee, and Birmingham, Alabama. Yet a group of gay activists—with the active cooperation of Victoria's Labor party government—had created a highly developed AIDS service infrastructure.

The centerpiece of that infrastructure was the Gay Men's Community Health Centre, the only one in Australia, located in a spruced-up old hotel that had once been run by a gangster. More than any of the other statewide AIDS councils, the Victorian AIDS Council was unapologetically gay-identified, saying in its mission statement that its purpose was to promote the "health and well-being of all gay and bisexual men in Victoria . . . in a manner consistent with the principles and practices of self-empowerment and community development." It was also the most participatory of the AIDS service organizations. Its six hundred volunteers played such a key role in policymaking and even day-to-day operations that VAC general manager Alan Hough was led to say, "In many respects this organization treats its staff as if we were volunteers, not the other way around."

The longer I spent in Australia, the more I was impressed with the country's response to the AIDS epidemic. In the early 1980s, when Australia's cases were relatively few in number, community-based AIDS councils were established in New South Wales and Victoria and then extended to every state and territory. Like AIDS service organizations in the States, they aimed to provide advocacy, education, support, and related services for people who were HIV-positive or at risk. But unlike U.S. AIDS service organizations, the Australian councils received virtually all their funding from the government, half from the federal government in Canberra and half from the individual states. In Victoria, the state government had given the gay community a capital grant to start up the Gay Men's Community Health Centre and continued to fund its operating budget. (Queensland, predictably, was the one state that refused officially to fund AIDS services; until recently, state money had been "laundered" through the Sisters of Mercy, a Roman Catholic order, so National party politicians could contend they weren't subsidizing "immorality.") Some of the AIDS councils became large organizations: The AIDS Council of New South Wales (ACON) had sixty-six paid employees when I was there; the VAC had about twenty-seven.

As part of the effort to confront the epidemic, the AIDS councils saw their role as fostering individual self-esteem and gay community development. The idea was that the better individual gay men felt about themselves and the stronger their community support systems were, the more likely they would be to practice safe sex and to lead healthy lives. The federal government and most state governments generally endorsed this approach to AIDS prevention. As a result, the AIDS councils were using Australian taxpayers' dollars to support all sorts of programs that undoubtedly would never have been approved otherwise—establishing groups for gay adolescents, for example. The AIDS Council of New South Wales had hired two full-time "beat outreach" workers whose job was to spend time in parks and public toilets spreading the safe-sex message. The safe-sex material issued by the various AIDS councils was often astonishingly graphic, the most famous being the AIDS Council of New South Wales' "Six Tips for Hard Cocks."

In Victoria, the notion of community health and community-building extended to IV drug users, as well. The government established needle-exchange programs at thirty-eight sites around the state, one of which was run by the Melbourne prostitutes' collective. The state also funded a peer-education group for drug users.

When I told VAC's Alan Hough how amazed I was by all of this, he replied, "It is amazing to me, too. What we are doing in Australia is extremely innovative, and the fact that it is funded by government is nothing less than extraordinary. For a long time, I was arguing that we shouldn't take on youth issues because the last gay counseling service in Melbourne folded after accusations of pedophilia. Now, I'm not worried about that anymore." He added: "Often we look to the United States. But I think we are doing a better job."

There was a variety of reasons why Australia had reacted to the epidemic in such a forthright manner. First was the societal assumption that it was the government's role to look after public health. The country had a national health-care system; unlike in the States, people with AIDS didn't have to patch together their health care and health insurance. The second was the ruling Labor party's commitment to community-based health care. As Warren Talbot, former head of the Australian Federation of AIDS Organizations (AFAO) and now AIDS consultant to the government of Tasmania, put it: "Community development, community change, community solidarity. The Labor party knows all that terminology. That is part of their political culture." Talbot noted that the opposition Liberal party, traditionally more conservative than Labor, also supported the government's AIDS policy. The Liberals could point to the fact that the AIDS councils were "voluntary organizations, people helping themselves, that it wasn't some government bureaucracy doing things," said Talbot.

Equally crucial was the role of Dr. Neal Blewett, Australia's health minister throughout the 1980s. (He left the ministry in 1990.) "In Australia, we were just lucky," said Talbot. "We had a Labor government, and within the Labor government, we had a center-left health minister [Blewett]. And, for a number of years, this minister had senior staff members who were gay men. It was all quite coincidental. It all came together to give us a reasonably good scenario." Blewett himself had taken a good deal of heat on the AIDS issue. The year before, a senior vice president of the Australian Medical Association, an organization that resented the "demedicalization" of AIDS policy in the country, claimed publicly that Blewett was gay and that he had permitted his alleged sexual orientation to determine policy. Blewett brought a defamation action and won.

As in the United States, AIDS transformed many gay community leaders from radical activists to inside political operators. Warren Talbot remembered gay conferences of ten or twelve years before, "passing resolutions on South Africa and Nicaragua and sending them to the prime minister. We were just a radical fringe looking at government totally from the outside. As a result of AIDS, a number of us realized we had to operate from within, to write submissions, to lobby, to dress up in suits. Quite quickly, people became moderately professional operators within the system. There had been no tradition of that within the gay movement in this country before AIDS."

The cozy relationship between the community-based AIDS organizations and the state and federal governments had its drawbacks, however. From the gay and AIDS activist side, no one was significantly challenging government AIDS policy. People with AIDS were almost invisible in Australia, one reason being that the generally responsive government policies didn't encourage militancy. "There are few who have declared themselves HIV-positive or [who are open about] having AIDS," said Peter Grant, president of the board of VAC. "You can count them on one hand. That has helped make AIDS remote for many people."

That situation was rapidly changing, however. There was increasing awareness that drug trials and treatments were lagging years behind those in the United States. Debate was growing as to whether the country needed an organization similar to ACT UP. Indeed, shortly after I left Australia, an ACT UP group was formed in Sydney. In one of its first actions, it floated helium-filled condoms and safe-sex messages over the walls of a New South Wales prison. Within the year, Melbourne had its own ACT UP. By December 1991, ACT UP/Melbourne was able to turn out three thousand people to protest the government's decision to close a local hospital as part of the "mainstreaming" of AIDS treatment. Among ACT UP's leaders was editor Chris Gill, critic of Melburnian complacency.

Unlike U.S. lesbians, those in Australia had not taken a leadership role in AIDS organizations. There were only two lesbians on staff at the VAC, and the number of lesbian volunteers was small; in Sydney, the situation wasn't much different. "It has to do with the Australian phenomenon of always being several years behind the States," Alan Hough suggested. "When AIDS first arrived here, lesbians were still in the separatist stage, even in Sydney. In the States, lesbians had gay male friends who were dying, and were very moved by that. In Australia, lesbians and gay men just hadn't had that contact."

Lesbians who did work in the area of AIDS ran the risk of criticism from the separatist old guard, particularly in Melbourne. Jean Taylor expressed the commonly held Melbourne view. "Some women are throwing themselves into AIDS work," she said. "But in fact there are more lesbians dying of cancer than gay men are dying of AIDS. Lesbians often view every issue but their own as important. We need to care for our own community as well."

For his part, well-respected Melbourne writer and political scientist Dennis Altman argued that in Australia, AIDS was actually increasing the separation between the gay and lesbian communities. "The AIDS councils are more focused on gay men and gay community and this keeps divisions going," he said.

In Melbourne, one example of the role of AIDS councils in gay male community–building was the VAC's Gay Now! program. Its purpose was to "create peer support for the practice of AIDS prevention behaviors, and to raise individual and group self-esteem," according to its creator, VAC's peer-education coordinator, Richard Clayton. A New Zealander who had studied group dynamics in London and whose lover had died of AIDS the year before, Richard was, in the words of one Melbourne activist, "the closest thing to a California-style guru you'll find in Melbourne." Close to three thousand gay men had gone through the Gay Now! groups, Eroticizing Safe Sex workshops, and the twice-yearly large-scale "Sex Events" that he ran.

Each Gay Now! group met once a week for six weeks and had two dozen or so participants, all gay men, ranging in age from sixteen to seventy-seven. Evenings were organized around a specific theme, and the workshops were, in Richard's words, "a series of carefully elaborated parlor games." The games betrayed a New Age influence: The first evening included "a concrete visualization of a planet where gay and bisexual men were totally healthy." Some exercises were right out of behavioral-psychology texts, asking each person to describe his health strengths and weaknesses and to suggest an "achievable goal"—taking a couple of long walks a week, for example. Other sessions focused on eroticizing safer sex, relationships, homophobia, and self-esteem. Meetings were followed by a social hour; the last get-together was a dinner. Everyone was paired off with another group participant, and the two "buddies" talked by phone each week between meetings.

As a result of his experience leading these workshops, Richard was increasingly convinced that self-esteem was the crucial issue for gay men. In Victoria, despite the relatively favorable political and social climate, the level of gay self-esteem was still fairly low. "People are satisfied with second-rate relationships and with living as if they don't have any rights," he said. "They don't believe they deserve to have real good-quality relationships." Although he had focused on sexuality in his workshops in the past, Richard was now planning to launch a series of programs specifically on the issue of self-esteem.

On Richard's suggestion, I contacted a closeted suburban high school teacher who had "graduated" from a Gay Now! group. The man's name was Tad. I called him on the phone, and explained my interest in talking to him. He seemed a bit suspicious.

"You're not one of my students, are you?" he wanted to know.

I assured him I had been out of high school for many years.

"I'm sorry," he said. "I thought you might be one of my students playing a joke."

When we met for dinner at a Brunswick Street restaurant, Tad began by telling me how startled he had been at one of his first Gay Now! sessions to hear another gay man announce that his main interest was reading. "Of course, I knew that there were other gay men who liked reading, just as I do," he said. "But part of me saw 'gay' as meaning a nineteen-year-old guy who spent his life at the disco. It was a bit of a shock to discover all this variety in gay life, that there were teachers and accountants. Here were a large number of men and we all felt alienated from bars and discos. We were all outsiders in gay culture."

Tad was in his early forties, tall and fair-haired and not unattractive. He spoke rapidly and appeared somewhat nervous. His sense of being an outsider went beyond just the gay scene. "I have never met anyone else with the same name I have!" he said. Tad had grown up north of Brisbane, the son of a prosperous sugar-cane farmer. He left Queensland after finishing university; he had fallen in love with a straight roommate and wanted to get as far away as possible. He had been a child of the sixties, involved in the anti–Vietnam War protest movement (Australian troops fought along-side American GIs in Vietnam, and there was strong opposition at home); he had traveled in Thailand, Indonesia, and India. Now he lived nearly an hour's drive from Melbourne, in a suburb where he taught English and history. In the outer suburbs, he said, it felt as if there weren't another gay person for miles around.

His students were the children of the "upper working class"; many of their fathers were factory managers. They had horses in their backyards but no books at home. Education took second place. You had to "stand on your head" to get them to learn anything. Still, Tad's major satisfaction in life came from the class-room. "I am a teacher first," he said. "During summer vacations, I find it difficult to come down from the high of being with the kids. They have such strong personalities."

None of the other teachers knew he was gay, although Tad didn't believe that coming out would have any significant negative conse-quences. Virtually the only conversation among the teachers was sport, a subject in which he had no interest. He pretended to care about Australian Rules football, picking a team to "barrack for" (root for) on the basis of its colors. He got tips from his students so he could bet in the football pools with the other teachers.

For years, Tad viewed himself as an academic and would spend his free afternoons at a university library "escaping." He had never had a lover, went out to bars but rarely conversed with anyone. Finally, he stopped going altogether. The saunas were his main outlet, even though he never spoke to anyone there either. His gay life wasn't his "real life," he thought; real life was the kids he taught, the suburb where he lived, far from any organized gay community, and those solitary afternoons in the "uni" library.

One time at the sauna, he picked up a copy of the *Star Observer* and read about the Gay Now! groups. He decided to go. He had just returned from a year teaching in New Guinea, where he had been completely celibate. That year made him realize how important sex was to him—and some kind gay identity, as well. But taking the initial step wasn't easy. It was more threatening to go into a Gay Now! group, where men had their clothes on, than to a sauna, where they were naked. "It is amazing how a Gay Now! group can change lives," he said. "It is not therapy. It is not psychological. It is just a discussion group really, a bunch of games. It doesn't seem like a big deal, but it *is* a big deal."

As a result of Gay Now!, Tad was finding friendship and community for the first time. He had become a Gay Now! group leader. He was receiving invitations to dinners and barbecues. These days, when he walked into a bar, he actually knew people.

Still, life had not turned around completely. He was no "twenty-four-hour-a-day gay," he assured me. His gayness was more "real" than it had been, but he still had not completely integrated it with the rest of his life. Maybe he was now a "five-night-a-week gay," he suggested. "I am still gay in the city, but not at home. I haven't brought my sexual partners into my house. In that house, I am not gay."

Some of those contradictions had surfaced recently when Tad received an anonymous phone call from a student who asked him, "Do you want to have sex with me?" He recognized the voice. It was not an obscene phone call, he said; it was a call for help. The outer suburbs of Melbourne might as well be northern Queensland, for a gay kid. The student had started calling him as often as eight times a day; the only assistance Tad could provide was the names of city-based gay organizations. "I felt guilty," he said. "I hadn't created an atmosphere for kids to identify as gay." And he added: "I am only still now identifying myself."

The habits of years die hard, and Ted had long been accustomed to viewing the world through the prism of alienation. These days, despite Gay Now!, his alienation was taking some bizarre forms. He still felt isolated from the gay community, the reason being that he wasn't HIV-positive and didn't have any friends who were. To him, the Victorian AIDS Council was "Control Central" and the "real gay circle" was composed of HIV-positive people.

I found his comments odd, considering that it is HIV-positive men who most often feel left out and ignored. Yet the fact that someone would express this view seemed revealing in a city where, at least at that time, not much of a gay community existed outside of the local AIDS council. AIDS organizing had brought Tad in from the suburban cold. But with few ways beyond AIDS organizing for men to identify with and participate in a gay community, such a skewed perspective was perhaps inevitable.

A few days after my conversation with Tad, I sat in the balcony of the old Greek theatre, in the "nuclear-free" inner suburb of Richmond, looking down at the crowd below. The occasion was the Victorian AIDS Council's Crossfire dance party. A huge VAC banner covered one one wall, and on the movie screen safe-sex messages alternated with clips from old Busby Berkeley films. Hundreds of people were dancing on a slippery floor covered in sawdust and crepe paper. The crowd was mostly men, but there were women, too, and a number of what appeared to be straight couples. The men eschewed the spandex look of Mardi Gras for sport shirts and jeans; the women were largely dressed in black. It all felt somewhat bohemian-trendy.

Downstairs, Porter Street's Colin and Patrick were dancing. The party was scheduled to go on all night, so Porter Street was holding a "recovery" party starting at nine the next morning. I didn't see Tad, although he had told me he would be there. I didn't see lesbian activist Jean Taylor either, but that was to be expected. A group of Melbourne women, including Jean, were planning to form a human chain around a women's prison the next day; probably they were plotting strategy or just getting a good night's sleep. Alan Hough, VAC's general manager, was wearing a SAFE T-shirt. It had been a difficult week, he said. One of the organization's leaders had died of AIDS, the first AIDS death that the VAC had had to face.

Confetti dropped from the balcony. The lights made graceful, semicircular loops from ceiling to floor and back again. For a moment, I could stand back from it all. Out of a terrible epidemic, I thought, has come so much determination and commitment. Just the very idea was a cliché, of course; the same was true in other cities throughout Australia and much of the rest of the world. But I felt it strongly that evening in Melbourne. Perhaps AIDS organizing was the only game in town, crowding out everything else; perhaps it kept men and women apart; perhaps, as some argued, other pressing needs were being ignored. But if the Crossfire dance party was the closest one could get to a sense of community, then perhaps the city at the "end of the world" wasn't doing that badly, after all.

Hobart, Burnie, and Ulverstone, Tasmania

I didn't attend the rallies to oppose sodomy-law reform that were held in the towns of Ulverstone and Burnie, on the northwest coast of the island of Tasmania, in the summer and fall of 1989. But I certainly heard about them and saw videotapes of Australian television coverage. I don't know for sure if the seven hundred people at the Ulverstone Civic Center really did shout, "Kill 'em, kill 'em." Or if there were signs outside the hall that read, STOP AIDS. KILL A POOFTER. Or if local toughs wandered around the streets with baseball bats. People told me all these things, but in view of the intensity of the emotion surrounding the events, it is difficult to ascertain what actually happened. But what was beyond dispute was the mood of the rallies: hate-filled, sometimes frenzied, frightening.

What was clear, too, was that the front lines of the struggle for gay and lesbian rights in Australia were not in Sydney or Melbourne or even Brisbane, but in Tasmania, the Australian island state about the size of West Virginia (population four hundred fifty thousand), just over the Bass Strait from Melbourne. Tasmania offered something stark, simple: a struggle between the forces of good and evil, with life-size heroes and villains.

Little Tassie, as the Australians call it, was an unlikely place for gay and lesbian activism, let alone some provincial version of Armageddon. Poor, isolated, largely rural, Tasmania was the last Australian state where sexual relations between men remained a criminal offense. But unlike in Queensland, where sodomy-law reform had finally been achieved with minimum fanfare, in Tassie the debate over law reform had been a noisy one, sometimes drowning out every other issue on the island. From the blaring front-page headlines to the letters-to-the-editor sections, the island's newspapers couldn't get enough of the subject. The debate had been most heated in the industrial, fundamentalist-influenced northwest—the "heart of darkness," as Rodney Croome, the state's leading gay-rights campaigner, called it. The northwest coast was my destination, but I stopped at Hobart, the capital, first.

Some clues as to why homosexuality had become such a major issue in Tassie can be found in the island's history. Originally called Van Diemen's Land, Tasmania was the last and the most brutal penal colony in Australia. The penal apparatus there was not dismantled altogether until 1886. In the public mind, the convict system had been closely associated with homosexuality; one of the arguments that reformers used for its abolition was that it encouraged sex between men. In Van Diemen's Land, two and a half times as many people had been charged with sodomy as in the entire rest of the country. The one part of Australia where remnants of the penal past were still in evidence—both psychologically and, in the charred remains of the Port Arthur prison, physically—was Tasmania.

If Australia as a whole had an inferiority complex, in Tasmania insecurities were magnified tenfold. It wasn't just that Tassie was isolated; it wasn't merely that it had the highest unemployment, the lowest wages, and the least educated work force in Australia. The island was also a national joke. A columnist for *The Age,* the Melbourne daily, suggested that Tassie be sold to the Japanese, who could then turn it into 37,312 golf courses. If you mentioned Tasmania to a mainland Australian, the first thing he was likely to bring up was inbreeding. Even Tasmanians joked about that. In his book, *Down Home* (its U.S. title is *Behind the Mountain*), the Hobart-born author Peter Conrad wrote, "Tasmanians love to tell stories about the endogamic clans of the midlands, which have intermarried with their animals: I remember hearing when I was a boy about middle-aged women with the faces of pigs, sheep pushed in prams, and children with chains round their necks living in dog-kennels."

Rodney Croome, who left a graduate program in history to head the law-reform campaign, suggested that mainland Australians projected all their own fears, insecurities, and self-doubts onto Tasmania. Australians worried that they were inbred and parochial, so they kidded about how inbred and parochial Tasmanians were. They felt guilty about killing Aboriginals, so they made a point of saying that the one place in Australia where there were no Aboriginal people left was Tasmania. They were concerned that the rest of the world considered them descendants of convicts, so it was easy to deflect attention to Tasmania and its historical role as Australia's gulag.

In the 1970s and early 1980s, the island underwent a transformation. It became the focus of environmental conflict in a very environmentally conscious country. The Tasmanian state government had announced plans to dam the Franklin, the last of the state's wild rivers. The result was a cascade of activism the likes of which Australia hadn't seen since the Vietnam War. Mainlanders flocked to Tassie to protest the dam, and even the usually phlegmatic islanders roused themselves from their torpor; there was a massive campaign of civil disobedience, with more than a thousand arrests. Hobart itself was the scene of some the largest demonstrations that had ever taken place in Australia, outside of Sydney and Melbourne.

In the end, the Franklin was saved, and Tassie was never the same. The island's power structure had been successfully challenged. Many mainlanders who came to protest stayed on for good to enjoy the natural beauty, the unpolluted air, and the inexpensive housing; at the same time, Tassie's youth and new working class (office workers, shop assistants, service-industry workers) had been thoroughly "greened." In the 1989 elections, the state's fledgling Green party received eighteen percent of the vote and found itself holding the balance of power in parliament between the Liberal and Labor parties. To the shock of old-line Tasmania, the Greens signed a coalition agreement with Labor and entered the government, a first in Australia—and the first time the Greens had joined a state government anywhere east of the Rhine. The sole provision of the Green-Labor accord that had no connection with environmental issues was one that provided for the decriminalization of homosexuality. The fact that Dr. Bob Brown, the leader of the Green party and a much-admired hero of the Franklin campaign was openly gay was a key factor in the Greenie embrace of law reform.

The sense of empowerment that so many Tasmanians felt as a result of the Franklin campaign extended to gays and lesbians as well. "If it weren't for the Green movement," said Rodney Croome, "I don't think there would have been any gay politics in Tasmania. Tasmanian society is so homogeneous. But the Green subculture in Hobart provided a refuge to some extent to people who didn't fit into the mainstream. And the Green movement also provided us with expertise and resources." That inspiration and those resources came into play a year before the Labor-Green accord, in September 1988, when the Hobart City Council banned a booth set up by the gay and lesbian law-reform group at the city's outdoor Salamanca Market. It was at Salamanca that the gay struggle in little Tassie really began.

Hobart (population one hundred eighty thousand) is a picture-postcard town of Georgian cottages and corrugated red-roofed Victorian bungalows clambering up wooded hillsides under a four-thousand-foot mountain. The downtown shopping area has a small-town feel to it, the prototype of that "Middle Australia" that I had been assured didn't exist; people look as if they haven't changed their hairstyles and style of dress since the 1950s. Downtown, too, just across from the parliament building, are several blocks of beautifully restored nineteenth-century sandstone warehouses, now turned into yuppie boutiques. There, every Saturday morning, the outdoor Salamanca Market takes place. The hundreds of market stalls offer homemade apricot tea cakes and secondhand books, leather handbags and pottery, vegetables in profusion. A group of Southeast Asian refugees sell embroidery. Greenpeace has a table, as does the Tasmanian Gay and Lesbian Rights Group (TGLRG). The gay and lesbian group offers pamphlets, buttons, and T-shirts, one featuring two men with black strips over their eyes and the words "Steve slept with Mark the night of his 21st. In Tasmania he could be in gaol until he's 42." The "models" for the T-shirts were actually two young Hollywood actors, their likenesses cut out of movie magazines.

The TGLRG table is where all the trouble started. After the City Council banned the display, gays and lesbians and their supporters defied the police every Saturday morning for three months and continued to staff the booth. It became a question of free speech, transcending the gay-rights issue and inaugurating a weekly confrontation with the authorities that resulted in a hundred and thirty-two arrests. To the Tasmanian power structure, the defiance at Salamanca represented another test of their credibility, like the Franklin River dam. Virtually every Saturday while the protests continued, Salamanca was a major, if not the leading, story on the Tasmanian evening TV news. Out of nowhere, Tassie's gay community, among the most closeted in Australia, became the focus of national media attention. For one shining moment, the issue brought together gay men and lesbians, homosexuals and heterosexuals. In fact, a majority of those arrested over the period were not gay; many were active in Green politics. "The atmosphere at the market during those weeks was electric," recalled Biddy Searle, a Hobart social worker involved in the weekly planning sessions. "But it was very stressful in many ways, too. People were frightened because of the visibility. There were cameras everywhere. They were afraid of losing jobs and family. This is a small community. It is amazing that so many people were prepared to come out and to be seen on this issue."

After a three-month standoff, the City Council capitulated. The booth was allowed to stay.

When I arrived almost a year and a half later, the effects of Salamanca lingered in the cool summer air. The controversy had been the turning point for the gay population in Hobart, and to some extent, for gays and lesbians in the rest of Tasmania, as well. In the wake of Salamanca, I found an entire community coming out or on the brink of coming out. Hobart even had a community-run gay and lesbian bar, the only one of its kind in Australia, with proceeds going to four local gay organizations. There was a sense of exhilaration and excitement in gay Tasmania that I didn't find in the rest of Australia, not even in Sydney during Mardi Gras.

But Salamanca was just the beginning of a long battle. With the City Council's capitulation at the marketplace and the signing of the Labor-Green accord several months later, pressure was mounting for the repeal of the state sodomy laws. In the spring of 1990, the Labor-Green government officially proposed repeal. Law reform was a major part of a general strategy to prevent the spread of AIDS; decriminalization, in the new government's view, would encourage responsible sexual behavior. But as the issue gained visibility, Tassie's religious and secular right began to stir. Opposition Liberal party leaders began to see controversy over law reform as a way of weakening the government and torpedoing the coalition.

Then came the antigay rallies, bringing together Liberal party politicians and fundamentalist preachers and attracting large crowds. All together, three meetings were held on the northwest coast, plus a calmer and more sparsely attended fourth meeting in Hobart. The national press and television covered the events as if they were Nazi party rallies. Tassie's image as a national laughing-stock, synonymous with backwardness and bigotry, was reinforced. But it wasn't funny. To watch TV coverage of the events is to understand the power of mass hysteria.

The most emotional and hate-filled of the meetings took place in June 1989, in the small northwest-coast town of Ulverstone. Speakers warned about international gay conspiracies and accused gay men of engaging in bizarre sexual practices. The crowd of seven hundred people was at a fever pitch. Then, at question time, a young man had walked up to an open microphone and said, "I'm twenty years old. I'm gay. And I'm proud." It was, in the words of a reporter for Australian national radio who was on the scene, "one of the bravest things I've ever seen."

The young man's name was Shane Knowles. One evening, several months after the Ulverstone rally, I sat in the living room of Shane's apartment in downtown Hobart. A large model of a Qantas 747 airplane sat on top of a cabinet. Otherwise, the place was almost devoid of furniture, as if it were kept forever ready for a party. We drank red wine. Shane's friend Lee Gwen Booth was there as well, along with her year-and-a-half-old daughter, Jessie, and her lover, Deb. So was a friend of Shane's named Ian, a dark-haired, somewhat puffy-faced young man of seventeen. Ian insisted he was straight. He was drinking a lot.

They had gone up to Ulverstone on the bus, fourteen gays and lesbians from Hobart, including Shane and Lee Gwen, who brought along Jessie. At the rally, Shane and a friend sat apart from the rest, taking places in the middle of the hall. Shane remembered his friend camping it up as the antigay harangues intensified, saying things like, "Oh, I just love that woman's dress." Shane was embarrassed. The speakers were fascinated by anal sex. "I wouldn't put my sexual organs in someone's garbage disposal," one proclaimed righteously. Another described anal penetration by means of cups, saucers, and bottles. "Then I got up at question time," Shane recalled. "When I said I was twenty, it was quiet. When I said I was gay, everyone booed. When I said I was proud, they erupted. It was all on national TV, which I didn't know at the time. Then, someone got up and said to me, 'What about those cups and saucers and bottles?' I said, 'If it wasn't for that last speaker, I wouldn't have known anything about them.' "

At first glance, Shane seemed a typical twenty-year-old, mostly interested in having fun. He was tall, with surfer-blond hair, dressed in loud shorts and a polo shirt. He had trained as a chef, but like many people I met in Hobart, he was on the dole. By coincidence, Shane had grown up in Roma, the same small town in rural Queensland that prisoner Stephen Watson had come from. Shane was high-spirited and had his raucous side; he did a convincing imitation of a Queensland ocker, caricaturing the shrill accent and narrow-mindedness.

Shane didn't have an easy time of it growing up. He and his siblings were subjected to physical abuse by a family member, he said. As a teenager, he'd had two nervous breakdowns and tried to kill himself. Once a fortnight, he'd take the night bus from Roma to Toowoomba, a large town about halfway to Brisbane, where he'd spend the day doing the beats. Then, he'd take another night bus home and start work at six A.M. At the beats, he said, he was less interested in sex than someone to "help me, to talk to me. In Roma I felt like I was the only gay person in the world."

At fifteen, Shane left home. After a spell of living on his own in Brisbane and a couple of other towns in Queensland, he made his way south. "I rung up my mother from Melbourne, and I said, 'Guess what, mum, I'm in Melbourne!' She wouldn't believe me until I sent her a postcard."

It was when he moved to Tasmania—about as far from Roma as he could get—that "things began to sort themselves out," he said. "Tassie brought me out. Tassie is my home."

And then came the Ulverstone rally. "Brave?" Shane asked, when I repeated the reporter's comment. "At the time I didn't think

I was. Everyone says, 'Oh, you done the gay community a good cause.' But I wasn't doing it for them. I was doing it for me!"

Lee Gwen broke in. "He was incredibly brave," she said. "They are chanting, 'Kill them,' and he gets up in the middle and says, 'I'm gay and I'm proud.' I certainly would never have done it!"

Lee Gwen had had her great moment, too—the year before at Salamanca. During the weekly civil disobedience, getting arrested was the badge of dedication and commitment. But Lee Gwen had a hard time convincing the police that she was proper jail fodder. When Salamanca began, she was eight months pregnant; that didn't stop her from attending the demonstrations. Once Jessie was born, she insisted on bringing her along. "We don't want to arrest you," one policewoman told her. "You're too sweet." Finally, when Jessie was seven weeks old, Lee Gwen got her wish; she and Jessie were escorted into a police wagon—diaper bag, bottles, and all. They were brought to the police station, booked, and then released.

"There are some people who don't like that I take Jessie around with me," Lee Gwen admitted. "They feel I am exploiting her. I know that Shane feels that way. But I was taken to Vietnam War moratoriums when I was in my pram. It sort of runs in the family."

Lee Gwen was twenty-one. With her long blond hair, fair skin, and educated accent, she looked as if she could have been a debutante in another life. She grew up in Hobart, went to all-girl Catholic schools, lived in West Africa for a year with her family. She called her lover "dahling" and constantly talked about "Mum." Jessie, her daughter, was a wild, redheaded child. There had been complaints that Jessie was underfed and unsupervised; Community Welfare, the social-service agency, was threatening to take her away.

Jessie's father was an Australian sailor, whom Lee Gwen had met while selling chocolates for the Freedom from Hunger campaign, the day the Tall Ships docked in Hobart for the Australian bicentennial. She went to bed with him with the express intention of getting pregnant. "I barely remember what he looks like now," she says. "He got what he wanted and I got what I wanted. He doesn't know about Jessie. But I know his name and what ship he was on. So if Jessie ever wants to track him down, she could do so."

Lee Gwen talked nonstop. She had met her lover, Deb, a diminutive woman of twenty-three dressed this evening in tux and bow tie, at a Quaker meeting. "Deb doesn't want to say anything!" Lee Gwen informed me. "She's bisexual. She just came out three weeks ago." I suspected that it wasn't that Deb was reticent; Lee Gwen simply wanted to do *all* the talking.

Salamanca had reinforced Lee Gwen's lesbian identity. "I already knew I was gay but that was how I got politically involved," she said. "And it was important to me that Jessie was there because I got sick of people telling me, 'You can't be a lesbian, you've got a child!' "

When the protests at Salamanca were taking place, Shane was eighteen and had only been in Hobart for two months. He wasn't admitting he was gay at the time; in fact, he had two identities— "Robert" was his straight self, and "Shane" was his gay self. After Salamanca, "Shane" won out.

Both Shane and Lee Gwen had become overnight media stars— Shane because of the Ulverstone rally, Lee Gwen as a result of her arrest with Jessie at Salamanca. Shane rattled off his celebrity resumé: "I was on Australian Broadcasting Company seven-thirty report, the Channel Six news, the Sunday current-events program. I was in the *Mercury* and the *Examiner*. They're the two leading newspapers down here."

Lee Gwen did him one better. "Apparently, I even had my picture in *Pravda*!"

"*Pravda*!" I exclaimed. "You're kidding."

But Lee Gwen didn't hear me. Deb had shouted something, and Lee Gwen rushed out of the room. While no one was paying attention, Jessie had wandered out the front door and onto the street. A passerby had brought her back. The incident didn't last more than a minute or two, but Lee Gwen was thrown into total panic.

After Lee Gwen calmed down, we took Jessie home to bed. Their apartment was the most disorderly I'd ever seen. Ian, who had agreed to baby-sit, plopped down on a couch. *Ben-Hur* was on TV. Ian was quite drunk. "I think I'm bisexual," he confided. By then it was past midnight, and the rest of us—Lee Gwen, Deb, Shane, and I—went out dancing.

The following evening I went to what was billed as the first drag show in Tasmania's history. It took place at the Poseidon Adventure (better known as the Ship), the community-run bar. I was staying with Rodney Croome, the law-reform campaigner, and his lover, Nick Toonen, the general manager of the Tasmanian AIDS Council. Earlier in the week, a young man not yet twenty, named Andrew, dropped by to use the stereo. Andrew was practicing for the show—he *was* the show, in fact. He lived with his mother across the street from Rodney and Nick. She didn't know he was performing; he had borrowed some money from her for a down payment on a wig but she didn't know what the money was for. Andrew was calling himself Morgan LeFay. He was practicing Eartha Kitt's song "I Love Men." Andrew played it over and over again, trying to get it perfect. It would be the first time he had ever performed in public.

At a party before Andrew's debut, I met two other gay men who had taken the occasion of Andrew's performance to dress up in drag themselves. Both were novices. One, who had been selling law-reform T-shirts at the Salamanca Market earlier in the day, complained that his brassiere was too tight and that his makeup was making him sweat profusely. "Every time I go to the bathroom I have to hitch myself up," he said. He wore a wig that sat too high on his head. His friend, in a blue chiffon gown, traded his heels temporarily for a pair of slippers. "Five hours to go before the show," he moaned. Despite the discomfort, they seemed to be having a terrific time, shedding former personalities and trying on new ones.

The Ship was located at the back entrance of a downtown hotel; only the initiated could find it. The ceiling was covered with fish-netting. The music was loud and the place was packed. At one-fifteen in the morning Andrew swept in, looking a little like Louise Brooks as Lulu, with his black wig combed in bangs, and wearing a black dress and pearls. "I Love Men" had sounded better in Rodney and Nick's living room, though. On stage, Andrew didn't hold the microphone close enough and was almost drowned out by the music. But that didn't really matter. What Andrew lacked in vocal power, he made up for in enthusiasm and self-confidence. The audience was rapturous. Morgan LeFay was somebody to be reckoned with.

• • •

Then I headed for the "heart of darkness." I took the bus from Hobart to Launceston, Tasmania's second-largest city (population ninety thousand), my jumping-off point. We drove through forests of eucalyptus and stopped for milkshakes in decrepit convict towns with tiny sandstone buildings. Launceston is a treasure trove of Victorian architecture, hilly, with fine public parks and gardens. It was the one major town in Tasmania that hadn't had an antigay rally; Launceston is a snobbish place, and I suspected that the townspeople simply felt it was inappropriate to discuss the subject in public, period.

In Launceston, I rented an aging red Datsun. One headlight didn't work and the horn seemed to grow increasingly faint with each use. The interior reeked of cigarettes. I hadn't driven on the left-hand side of the road in years.

Still, it was a relatively easy hour-and-a-half drive west to Burnie (population twenty-five thousand), the town where one of the major antigay rallies had been held. As you approached the city along the coast, you were greeted by an immense chemical plant spewing smoke; the national TV network had labeled Burnie the "dirtiest city in Australia." Burnie is a working-class town. It has wide streets and wide sidewalks, and many of the buildings are made of concrete; it was a place where a lot of people seemed to be on the dole.

I had arranged to meet Yvette Sneddon, who, along with her lover, Louise Titcombe, was one of the mainstays of the Northwest Gay Support Group (NWGS). I was early. I searched out the local beat, the public lavatory that I had been told was Burnie's major gay meeting place. Ironically, it was located right next door to the Burnie Civic Center, site of the antigay rally. It was the middle of the afternoon, and the beat was deserted. Inside a stall, I noticed a message scrawled on the wall: "D—Can't make it tonight. How about Wed/Thursday—C." Another one read: "Sunday, tonight, 10:45 P.M. Must be under 25—am 24 and very horny." Under this message was what appeared to be a reply: "11-2-90. Here. 10 P.M. Am 24." Plastered on the toilet itself was a sticker in the shape of a condom. "You can beat AIDS," it said. "Use condoms and water-soluble lubricant." The sticker gave the address of the Tasmanian AIDS Council. In addition to everything else, the beat seemed to function as a community bulletin board.

Late in the afternoon, Yvette met me in front of the library. I followed her home, climbing toward the open country overlooking Burnie and the sea. Soon, we were in a world of rolling hills, paddocks, and wonderful views that could have been Scotland. Yvette took the narrow turns and steep ascents with ease; I limped behind in my Datsun. Their house stood alone down a dirt road. Yvette and Louise had five cows, ten calves, and some horses, plus six cats and a German shepherd. The cows had alcoholic names like Whisky and Brandy. A platypus was said to live in the pond on their property.

Yvette brought up some hay from the barn for the cows, and we picked blackberries. "If there is a bully around, you stand up to him," she said in reference to the antigay ralliers. At thirty-one, Yvette was tall and blond, with a commanding presence. She had had a tense day; she was a nurse and quite high-ranking in the hospital where she worked. She took some swings at a punching bag set up just outside the front door. "Try it," she suggested. "It will make you feel better." She was right.

Louise wasn't due home until late, so Yvette made a few calls and arranged an invitation for me to a dinner party at the home of an older gay man a few towns down the coast. It was a cultivated gathering—Schubert string quartets on the stereo, homemade ice cream for dessert, and Scotch after dinner. Among the guests were a schoolteacher and his twenty-year-old lover; they had both come out within the past two months. The teacher had just left his wife and two small children. Another young man told the story of an Anglican priest who had come by to visit late one evening and attempted to seduce him. When the vicar made his move, the man fended him off with "More tea, Vicar?" Everyone thought this was quite funny, particularly because they knew the vicar in question.

As I climbed the steep roads back to Yvette and Louise's house, with no moon and only a single headlight to guide me, I thought that the northwest coast was a curious "heart of darkness"—lesbian couples living in bucolic settings, with a platypus out the back gate; gay men drinking after-dinner Scotch and listening to Schubert quartets; and vicars paying late-night calls on their parishoners, looking for tea, sympathy, and something more. The next day, when I chatted with Louise, I received a very different picture.

"But this really *is* the Bible Belt," Louise assured me, using a term that I wasn't aware traveled beyond Tennessee. "One-third of the families have domestic-violence problems. It is such a small community. One gay man runs into his uncle at the local beat." As for women's relationships, they were totally ignored. When some of the women in NWGS gathered at a local pub, as they did every fortnight or so, the pub regulars would ask, "Where are the kids?" or "Are you a sports group?"

Louise was personable and forthright. She was a research chemist working on her Ph.D. at the local "uni." At the ceremony at which she had received her master's degree, she became so excited that she waved her certificate in the air and gave Yvette a kiss. "It got a lot of looks," she said.

The Northwest Gay Support Group was viewed as radical by other gays and lesbians in the area. Few members were under thirty. "The women here are in couples and leading quiet lives," Louise said. "The young guys don't fit in. They are trendy. Their life-style fits Melbourne, not Burnie. It is very transient here. Once people come to terms with being gay, they want to get out." Louise, who had six months to go before finishing her Ph.D., was eager to leave herself. She had never been gay anywhere but Burnie and was concerned that she was missing out on the lesbian culture of the mainland cities. "Living here stunts your personal development," she said.

Louise described the Burnie rally, which, although not as rowdy as the one in which Shane had featured, was still one-sided and vitriolic. Throughout much of the evening, she said, she had been nervous, even shaking. She had held up a gay-and-lesbian-rights poster. When a man near her complained, she put it down. The man then ripped it up. "Everyone was tense," she said. "I saw the wife of the minister at the church I used to go to. She was pointing at a gay person and saying, 'There's one of *them*!' There was a wall of hatred. It was a little like inviting the Ku Klux Klan to a discussion of blacks." Louise recalled with some amusement one woman getting up and saying, "It is very difficult to speak about a subject I know nothing about." The woman went on to vilify homosexuals.

The evening did have some positive aspects, however. Afterward, Louise was sitting at a local café where people at various tables were discussing the issue in serious and thoughtful tones. "People who are in the middle of the issue are still in the middle," she said. Some women from the hospital where Yvette worked formed an organization called HUGS, Heterosexuals Unafraid of Gays. The name came from a group formed in New Zealand during that country's long and bitter battle over law reform in 1985. HUGS had organized a second meeting in Burnie. That meeting, although not as well attended as the antigay rally, was less emotional and more balanced, "like a university lecture," as someone put it.

All in all, though, Louise believed the rallies encouraged gays and lesbians on the northwest coast to go back into the closet. Some NWGS members stopped coming to meetings when they were moved to the library at nearby Ulverstone; they were afraid of being seen. When Rodney Croome came up from Hobart to establish a chapter of the Tasmanian Gay and Lesbian Rights Group, few came to hear him.

"The rallies really disturbed me," Louise said. "I didn't realize how much they disturbed me until later." In fact, shortly afterward, she developed cytomegalovirus, which sidelined her for several months, forcing her to decline several opportunities to speak in public at a time when there was increased interest in the subject of homosexuality.

If the emergence of such vituperative antigay feeling had a devastating effect on younger and more open people like Louise, the effect on older, closeted people was even more profound. It confirmed all their worst fears—namely, that they had more to lose than to gain by emerging from the shadows.

One gay man in his early sixties told me that the rallies had driven gays and lesbians on the northwest coast "into cupboards." This man hadn't attended any of the rallies and was one who complained that NWGS meetings at the Ulverstone library were too public. Previously, the group used the premises of the Adult Education Center in Burnie and that had been troublesome enough for him. "Half of Burnie knows me," he said. "But when people would ask what I was doing there at least I could say, 'I'm attending classes.' " Now, how could he explain why he would go to Ulverstone, several towns away, to take a book out of the library? "I won't go to public meetings," he said. "I just won't. I am afraid of doors being shut in my face, if it became known. If people found out, I would be more lonely. It is sad to be that way, but that is the way it is."

For many years, this man's sex life had consisted of clandestine meetings at the public lavatory. Like many gays and lesbians I met on the northwest coast, he had been married for a number of years; he was now divorced but still hadn't told his ex-wife he was gay. "At the beat, it was quick, in and out, whiz-bang," he said. "You just got your rocks off and left." Still, various people made friends there and broke off into little cliques. "It can be a lonely life, and the older you are, the more lonely it can be," he said. "I would often ask, What happened to them, the people my age that I used to see at the beat? I just don't see them around anymore. Are they home having a quiet wank?" His tone was elegiac.

The views expressed by this man and by Louise—that the rallies had made life more difficult on the northwest coast—were in contrast to the "official" gay line in Hobart that the rallies had backfired. Perhaps the latter view might have been true on the mainland, or to a certain extent in Hobart, but it didn't appear so when viewed from Burnie. Nonetheless, there was an inexorable quality about the changes in gay people's lives in Tasmania, even on the northwest coast. Most people I met there had been out a short time: three years, two years, even two months. Even the older, closeted man had revealed his sexual orientation to a professional group he was involved with, and that had happened since the rallies had taken place.

These changes were beginning to cut across class boundaries, as well. In Burnie, I met a woman named Sandra McKenzie, whose background was very typical of the northwest coast—lower middle class, family-oriented, religious. She had been married for a number of years to "a good fellow," as she put it, and had three children, ranging in age from eleven to twenty. Then, a year before, she suddenly left her husband—not for another woman, but just to be gay.

Sandra worked as a domestic at a hospital. A trim woman of forty-one, her graying hair parted off to the side, she had the look of someone who had worked hard all her life. She was living in reduced circumstances in a two-room apartment in downtown Burnie. The kitchen was in the living room and some of the chairs were torn. There was a mattress leaning against a wall; Sandra's older son had stayed over the night before. It was grim, but that didn't matter. "If I could just help one more gay person to stop them from getting married!" she said.

While growing up, Sandra fell in love with her girlfriends but got married anyway. There didn't seem to be any other options. "I always thought that gays were uneducated people," she said. She hadn't left her marriage earlier because of health problems in the family. Her husband had open-heart surgery; her older son had a kidney transplant and was on dialysis. Her mother had a stroke and had lived with them for two years before going into a nursing home. When Sandra did come out, many of her friends and family—her husband among them—thought she was just trying to find a way to escape these problems. That wasn't the way Sandra saw it. "For the first time in my life, I haven't cried," she said. "The tears I used to shed! Now, I only cry for my kids. They are different tears. I always used to be in tears. I felt so trapped and I thought it would be like that for the rest of my life."

Sandra had only had sex with another woman once in her life. She attended meetings of the NWGS, but they didn't meet her social needs. All the other women there were in couple relationships. She had heard about the Café Glitz, a once-a-week lesbian coffeehouse in Launceston, and had gone a couple of times. But it was a long drive, and Sandra often had to be at work at six the following morning. She wanted to leave Burnie, to make a new start somewhere on the mainland. "What is there in Burnie?" she demanded. "Nothing! I have to get out, but I can't, because of the kids."

She had grown up in an extremely conservative church. There was a young man in the church named Des, to whom Sandra was drawn. When he was younger, Des had had a brain hemorrhage and the congregation had prayed for him. But all that was forgotten when poison-pen letters revealed that he was gay. The congregation expelled him. "He loved to teach Sunday school so much," Sandra said. "They made an announcement in church that he was gay. They sent the children outside and made the announcement." No one in the church stood by him except for Sandra, who was still married at the time. When she told him she wanted to be his friend,

Des was astounded. He told Sandra's brother, who is also gay, "You've got a wonderful sister." After this, the brother came out to Sandra.

Des had since moved to Hobart. Although his mother had visited him secretly there, birthday presents that he had sent to family members were returned unopened, Sandra said. He was not permitted to attend a reunion of his Sunday school class. Sandra hadn't been in contact with him since he moved away. But seeing the way the church treated Des made Sandra all the more determined to come out. If the church had been an important force in keeping her in her marriage, it was now unmasked as a cruel and hypocritical institution.

Sandra herself was never expelled from the church. She gradually moved to the fringes. But, since she had announced her lesbianism and left her husband, dealing with her children had been quite difficult. Recently, her fifteen-year-old daughter had said, "I hope Dad meets a nice woman." Sandra replied, "I am looking to do the same thing." The daughter became furious. Now, the same daughter was "changing," she feared. While the daughter had previously spent most of her time with girlfriends, she had started hanging out exclusively with boys. Sandra was concerned the daughter might get pregnant to show she wasn't like her mother. "I hope she isn't going to try and prove anything!" she told me. Meanwhile, the son on kidney dialysis was sure that it was *his* medical condition that had somehow turned his mother into a lesbian.

She had attended the two Burnie rallies. "You've got no idea what it was like," she said. "At that first rally, we didn't have a say. They wouldn't let you even ask a question." She could pick the church people out. But the rally—and everything she had gone through—made her feel "so strongly about fighting for other gay people today." At the second and more sympathetic Burnie meeting, someone had gotten up and said, "It's okay to be a lesbian." "Imagine that," Sandra said. " 'It's okay to be a lesbian.' If I'd only heard those words when I was younger!"

To me, Sandra, like Shane, was an admirable, even inspirational figure. But, in Tassie, notions of heroism depended on where you stood. For instance, in its coverage of the Ulverstone rally, *The*

Examiner, the Launceston daily newspaper, had written, "The moment Ulverstone councillor Rodney Cooper stepped on to the stage it was obvious who was the crowd's hero. The organiser of the State's first public rally to protest against the decriminalisation of homosexual acts in Tasmania was given a standing ovation, not once, but twice. He responded, American style, waving and punching his arms into the air. The majority of the 700-strong crowd clapped harder."

On my journey back to Hobart, I stopped to meet Rodney Cooper. Unlike Burnie, where you feel a sense of working-class culture and at least some diversity, Ulverstone is a solidly middle-class, homogeneous, "Christian" town. Most of the people on the streets are elderly women in long print dresses or younger women wearing proper sweaters and skirts and pushing prams. The fortresslike red-brick Civic Center, where the rally took place, sits across the street from the Salvation Army citadel and next door to the City Hall. There, in the City Council chambers where he had served for four years, I met Rodney Cooper.

Decriminalization of homosexuality was just the beginning, he warned me. Next would come antidiscrimination legislation, teaching about homosexuality in the schools, then gay marriages and adoptions. "Once these things start, it is like the environmental issue," he said. "There is no end to it."

Councilor Cooper kept his facts and figures in a folder on his lap. He referred to them periodically. The state of New South Wales had sixty-two percent of the AIDS cases in Australia, he said, and fifteen times as many AIDS cases per capita as Tasmania. And sodomy, he noted ominously, had been decriminalized in New South Wales in 1984. The consequences of sodomy-law repeal were clear: Repeal the law in Tasmania, and AIDS would run amok. "We need a restraining barrier, a bulwark," he said.

The councilor was fond of analogies. He compared homosexuality to murder and rape but also to drunken driving and neglecting to put a coin in the parking meter. If his arguments were dubious and his analogies erratic, he still didn't seem like someone to incite a crowd to a murderous frenzy. I had heard a lot of things about Councilor Cooper—that he drank, that he had himself been arrested for drunken driving. Louise claimed that he beat his wife. In person, he came across as a rather genial, well-mannered, fortyish workingman who had read too many right-wing tracts. He combed his hair in bangs, in the rural manner, and wore blue jeans and a blue polo shirt that matched his blue eyes. The councilor took pains to appear color-coordinated. He made his living as a house painter, which might have had something to do with it.

I asked whether homosexuality wasn't simply a sexual orientation and, if so, why it should be punished. To Councilor Cooper, the terms "weakness" and "inclination" were more appropriate. "We all have weaknesses," he emphasized. "There are many who are prone to adultery. People may have an inclination to commit incest or to rape. And then we have sadists. Who was that fellow in America who murdered the actress?"

"Charles Manson?"

"Charles Manson, yes. Obviously, he was a crank with sadistic tendencies. No one would seriously contend we should decriminalize murder or rape. It is rather ridiculous to eliminate standards, just because we have inclinations in one direction, whether it be adultery or violence or something."

He went on. "The argument is often being put up that homosexuality is a victimless crime. I don't accept that argument. One real argument against that is that a third of the . . . I can't think of the name of these people . . ."

He consulted his papers. "Yes, hemophiliacs, that's the ones I'm thinking about.

"One-third of hemophiliacs in Australia contracted AIDS by transfusions—from homosexuals. That in itself does away with the notion that this is a victimless crime. Anyway, there are many victimless crimes that just because they are victimless doesn't take them off the statute books—there is parking, there is speeding, there is drunken driving."

Was he in favor of criminalizing lesbian sex, which was currently not penalized in Tasmania? Wasn't lesbian sex, at least, a "victimless crime"? He considered the question. Sex between women, he replied, should be against the law, if only in the name of consistency. "It is still female unnatural sex," he claimed. "Again, it is noncreative sex. This has an impact on society. I've read many accounts of lesbians and they aren't the happiest people in the world either. Many are frustrated, macho-type personalities who have lost their way in life."

At points during our conversation I wondered how much the councilor really cared about homosexuality, or whether he wasn't just trying to get notoriety and political mileage out of a subject that had the capacity to inflame public opinion. (He was a candidate for the Legislative Council, the powerful upper house of the Tasmanian parliament, although he wasn't given too much chance of winning.)

In fact, the issue that seemed to rile him the most was the environment—and the Greenies, who, he was convinced, were ruining Tasmania. "All the Greenies want to do is to lock up forests and to hold the virtues of a pantheist religion lifestyle," he said. "This country is becoming hell-bent on becoming a bunch of pagan tree worshipers. You must lock up the forests, you mustn't allow mining, forestry, all this type of thing. I am talking about the Green party!" And the Greenies, he was quick to note, were supporting sodomy-law reform.

As the convener of the Ulverstone rally, Councilor Cooper was dismayed at the way the "biased media" had covered the issue; he accused the national television network, in particular, of deliberately trying to create an unsympathetic picture of the anti-gay forces. "I said right from the beginning it wasn't a witchhunt against homosexuals," he insisted. "That was pure media humbug. They tried to manipulate it all and to make the rally look like a bunch of fanatical, inhumane idiots, religious cranks, wowsers, when in fact none of these things were true."

Did the crowd at Ulverstone shout, "Kill 'em, kill 'em"? I asked.

"Absolutely not," he insisted. "It's true that things did get a bit excited on occasion . . ."

Then he added: "There was a young, twenty-year-old bloke, very good-looking, a real nice specimen of a young man. It was really tragic! That boy could have got a pretty woman any time he wanted. And he stood up and said he was 'young, gay, and proud.' This boy—nature smiled on him—and he has been ensnared into that type of lifestyle. That's tragic."

• • •

When I returned to Hobart, I looked up Shane again. I wanted to tell him what a "nice specimen of a young man" Tasmania's leading antigay campaigner considered him to be. He wasn't at home, although his friend Ian, the seventeen-year-old last seen passing out in front of *Ben-Hur,* was there, drinking too much as usual. Shane was visiting friends, Ian said. He led me along a river and through a series of back alleys. Along the way he left secret signals for his mates and looked for their signals to him. He'd turn over a rock, search for a certain piece of bubblegum, check for a cigarette pack in a special place, then write something in a little notebook hung on the door of an abandoned factory. By this means, Ian and his closest friends knew one another's whereabouts at virtually all times. "Do your friends know that you go to gay bars?" I asked Ian. "They do," he said. "But that doesn't mean that I'm gay."

After about half an hour, we arrived at an apartment where Shane and some friends were watching gay pornography on the VCR. The images were dark and badly photographed. It was hard to get X-rated videos in Australia; they were legal only in the Northern Territory and the Australian Capital Territory (where Canberra is).

Ian left quickly. I reported to Shane what Rodney Cooper had said about him. His face lit up. "Did he really say that?" he demanded. "That I could get any girl I wanted?" Others in the room—some of whom had been to the rallies—told me how condescendingly nice the religious people had been at Ulverstone and Burnie, saying, "We feel sorry for you," "We can help you," and that kind of thing. There was now a movement afoot in Tasmania among fundamentalists to try to convert gays. "After the rally, I got heaps of invitations from these religious people to go and have coffee with them," Shane said.

We returned to the video, and Shane seemed shocked by it all. "That's disgusting!" he'd cry every once in a while, in that high-spirited way of his. Then, he'd go back to watching with rapt attention.

Each place I went in Australia seemed to be at a different stage in the effort to build viable gay and lesbian communities. In Sydney, Gay and Lesbian Mardi Gras flags festooned Oxford Street, and the men and women were finding common cause, at long last. In Melbourne, despite "woeful" community development, AIDS activism was proving a linchpin. Tasmania had its own particular flavor. Here, it was gay pornography that was more often than not an indistinguishable smudge; "I Love Men" in a black dress and pearls, with the words difficult to make out over the poundings of a disco beat; law reform in a heart of darkness. Everything was new in Tassie, and exciting, and a little awkward, too.

By February 1992, however, the political situation in Tasmania was not as hopeful as it had been during my visit, two years before. The Labor-Green coalition was out of office, replaced by a more conservative Liberal party government. And the sodomy laws remained on the books.

Still, Tasmanian gays and lesbians could take heart. As activist Rodney Croome put it, "Until 1988, gay life in Tasmania was as hidden and invisible and as limiting as you could find in this country. Today, we are working on creating a gay Tasmanian identity. In the past, to have a gay identity you had to leave the island. If you stayed, you lived in fear and hiding. We are trying to make it possible to live in Tasmania as a gay person. We are achieving this to a remarkable extent. Sometimes with some help from our opponents, but mostly through our own efforts."

9

AUSTRALIA AND NEW ZEALAND
THE LAND THEY LOST

Melbourne

In Melbourne, I met a man with three names. I called him Gideon, the name by which the white world of Melbourne knew him. He had recently taken the tribal name Banguil, which means "eagle." And, finally, he was known as Elaine, the name his gay friends gave him. Gideon was an Aboriginal gay man, and, in Australia, even in Melbourne with its culture and cappuccinos and nuclear-free suburbs, that was no easy thing to be.

The Aboriginals were the most marginalized group of people in Australia, their social situation not unlike that of American Indians. "They have experienced the most profound social disintegration I've ever seen," one public-health official told me. Many of the country's two hundred thousand remaining Aboriginals had migrated to the cities, and there were Aboriginal communities in virtually every major urban center in Australia. In Brisbane and Sydney, they referred to themselves as "Murrays." In Melbourne, they were "Kooris."

Gideon, who was about thirty, had light skin and blue eyes. He didn't look like most Aboriginals. In fact, when people first met him, they often mistook him for a Pacific Islander or an Indian or Sri Lankan. He was a tentative, somewhat anxious person. He had had a difficult life—foster homes, a nervous breakdown, identity crises, harassment by the police.

We sat outdoors at a café on Brunswick Street, where the area's bohemian charm recedes and it becomes merely seedy. Gideon was working at an Aboriginal social-services agency nearby, mostly doing office work and answering phones. He wore jeans, a maroon pullover, and a blue pin-striped jacket that had once been part of a suit. His head was covered with a red kerchief and he carried a tote bag with Koori colors—yellow, black, and red. He invited me to lunch. "There is a restaurant nearby here, in a gym, where a lot of Kooris go," he said. I told him I'd be pleased.

Among the urban Aboriginal community, gays were accepted, Gideon said. Kinship ties were paramount. "Even if you are gay, you are still someone's brother or their cousin," he maintained. "In the Koori community, you can be a prostitute and still be some-one's auntie." This acceptance had one flaw, however: In his own family, Gideon was treated as if he were a girl. "This is a sexist stereotype, I know," he said. "But Koori men are more comfortable viewing gay men as girls." Aboriginal gays went along with this to some extent: They gave one another women's names. Hence "Elaine."

But if the Koori community was willing to accept homosexuality, being HIV-positive was one thing that was not accepted. "AIDS is viewed as just another thing the white man has brought," Gideon said.

Gideon patronized white gay bars and discos but said that peo-ple's attitudes would change once they realized he was a Koori. "People act differently toward you," he said. "You feel it."

Things were worse on the street. The police frequently stopped Gideon and interrogated him for no apparent reason. He described one incident in which an officer threw him against a police van and called him a "dirty black homosexual." The Melbourne police had been widely criticized for antiblack as well as antigay harassment. "People say black women are the worst treated of any group in Australia," Gideon said. "But I think black gay men are treated worse."

Gideon was raised "upcountry" in a large family, but was sent off to live in white foster homes. This was a typical experience of Aboriginal children of his generation; they had often been placed with white families in order to learn white values. "Kooris get processed through the system," Gideon said.

Leaving his family was the beginning of a long and complicated series of identity problems, the "real battle" of his life, as he characterized it. In the process of assimilation, he lost his black identity, then slowly reclaimed it. When he was younger, he was unable to come to grips with his homosexual feelings and had believed he was a transsexual. Like Linda in Soweto, the gay man who faced similar confusions, Gideon had started taking female hormones. Eventually, he landed in a psychiatric hospital. "First I was ashamed of being black, then I was ashamed of being gay," he said. "The reason why I wound up in the hospital is because I was black and gay. That's all!"

For a while, Gideon worked as an actor. But he was constantly cast in stereotypical roles—the black servant or the obsequious Koori. He was never able to surmount "type." For someone who had identity and self-image problems, the narrow range of roles he could play was personally destructive. "I was very limited in what I could do onstage," he said. "Society does that to you. It limits your capabilities because of your race."

Of his fellow Kooris, he said, "We lost our land and so now we only have each other. We look in each other's eyes and see the land we lost."

We talked some more, and then it was time for the promised lunch. But as the hour drew nearer, Gideon became increasingly tense about arriving at the restaurant with a white (and gay) man. Finally, he proposed we bring along an Aboriginal woman, a colleague at the agency where he worked. "She knows all about me," he said, reassuringly.

The restaurant was cafeteria-style. We sat with other social-service workers, all Kooris, except for the tattooed boyfriend of one of the women. "You're the only bloke who works in the office," the white man said to Gideon. Gideon laughed uneasily; in his own family, after all, he was not viewed as a "bloke." He asked me not to mention what I was writing about.

Nonetheless, in the restaurant Gideon seemed happy and relaxed in a way he hadn't been in the white world of Brunswick Street. He would greet various Koori men as they came in for lunch, rushing over to shake their hands; he bantered with the waitress. He and his colleagues chatted about office politics and people they knew in common. It was standard lunchtime conversation.

After the meal, Gideon and I left together. He asked to borrow twenty dollars. He seemed upset, perhaps because he was embarrassed about asking me for money, perhaps because he felt he had to act in a such a closeted manner in the restaurant. He pleaded with me to come visit him the following evening. "I'm not inviting you for personal reasons," he said reassuringly. But I was leaving Melbourne. I felt I was letting him down.

As we parted, he ripped a sheet of paper out of his notebook. "It's a poem I wrote," Gideon said, "a poem about being dispossessed." It began

> Am I Fijian?
> Am I Indian?
> Who am I? . . .

The poem didn't offer any answers.

Wellington, New Zealand

The Maori, the native people of New Zealand, were better off. When I arrived in New Zealand, it was the hundred and fiftieth anniversary of the Treaty of Waitangi. The queen of England was visiting. The treaty, signed by the British and by Maori tribal leaders on February 6, 1840, gave the British political control of the country. It also granted the Maori chiefs "full, exclusive, and undisputed possession of their lands and estates." That part of the agreement had rarely been honored.

It wasn't clear what had brought the queen to New Zealand—the anniversary of the Treaty of Waitangi or the Commonwealth Games, being played in Auckland at the same time. At a ceremony marking the treaty, the queen dressed in a *korowai,* a Maori feather cloak, and began and ended her speech in the Maori language. A few in the crowd shouted, "Go home, Go home."

Unlike the Australian Aboriginals, the Maori were warriors. They were a Polynesian people who had come to New Zealand by canoe in the Great Migration of the fourteenth century. They called the country Aotearoa. In the 1860s and 1870s, they had fought the

British in a series of bloody wars; earlier in the century, tribe had fought against tribe in wars that were even bloodier, thanks to British muskets. In modern-day New Zealand, the Maori were more economically advanced and more educated, with fewer social problems, than the Aboriginals across the Tasman Sea. They were "probably the most thoroughly assimilated of all the old Empire's indigenous subjects," as James Morris wrote in *Heaven's Command,* his book on nineteenth-century British imperialism.

When I looked up "Maori" in my 1958 edition of the *Encyclopaedia Britannica,* it stated, "The native population is currently 54,000, but the percentage of white blood is rapidly increasing, so that ultimately miscegenation may be expected to absorb the Maori into *our* New Zealand population." (Italics mine.) The *Britannica* reflected out-of-date statistics; today, the number of New Zealanders of Maori origin is estimated at four hundred thousand. It also reflected out-of-date attitudes.

Over the past fifteen years, there had been a revival of Maori pride in New Zealand. Deracinated urban Maoris began learning their own language once again, rediscovering their culture and spirituality. Maori separatism became influential among the younger generation. Terms like "Maori sovereignty" and "land rights"—Maori claims to their ancestral lands, which covered much of the country—gained widespread currency. White New Zealanders sprinkled their conversation with Maori terminology such as "*whanau*" ("extended family"), and "*hui*" ("conference" or "meeting"). "Pakeha," the Maori term for whites, had long been in use.

At the same time, New Zealand was becoming increasingly multicultural. Estimates were that by the year 2000, people of Pacific Island descent would make up a third of the population of Auckland, the nation's largest city. The re-"Polynesiazation" of New Zealand was under way.

In the decade of the 1980s, New Zealand's gay and lesbian community began to stir as well. In 1985 and 1986, the country was absorbed by a rancorous effort to repeal the sodomy laws. Parliamentary maneuverings and debate continued for sixteen months; fundamentalist ministers from the United States flew in to lobby against repeal. In the end, law reform was narrowly approved, forty-nine to forty-four. In the process, a conservative society, often compared to postwar Britain's, openly confronted the subject of homosexuality for the first time. The campaign "was more useful than the change in the law itself," Wellington law-reform leader Bill Logan told me. New Zealand was a small country, a country where people trusted one another and listened to one another, where small groups of people could make an impact.

These social movements had a significant impact on homosexual Maori. They still faced many of the same issues that Gideon faced in Melbourne and that preoccupied black and other Third World gays and lesbians in South Africa and in the United States: Who am I? Whom do I identify with? Is being gay or lesbian just a "white man's ideology"? Is my homosexual identity as integral to me as my black identity or my tribal identity? Where do I fit in? In New Zealand, combining Maori cultural awareness with gay pride, many lesbian and gay Maori seemed to be figuring it out.

I had initially come to New Zealand to examine the effect of the law reform on the lesbian and gay community. One evening, sitting in an Auckland bar with Paul Kinder, the head of safe-sex education programs for the New Zealand AIDS Foundation, the subject of the Maori came up. Paul, a Pakeha, was a great admirer of Maori culture. He chastised me. "Don't pronounce it 'May-ori,' " he said. "It's 'Mao-ri.' Like in 'Mao Tse-tung.' " It was through Paul that I became increasingly interested in gay Maoris and their efforts to assert themselves.

The Commonwealth Games were plunging Auckland into a nightmare of traffic and confusion. I headed for Wellington, the country's capital, at the southwest tip of North Island. If Auckland is New Zealand's Sydney, money-minded and trendy, Wellington is its Melbourne—artsy, political, intellectual. Wellington activist Bill Logan put it differently. In his view, Auckland was Tinseltown, while Wellington was Petrograd—the name of St. Petersburg during the period of political ferment just before the Russian Revolution.

In Wellington, restored Victorian houses hug the hills surrounding a magnificent harbor. The parliament building is a funny-looking, modern structure in the shape of a beehive. Despite its status as the nation's capital, Wellington retains many of the characteristics of a provincial British seaside town—a harbor parade, a cricket field, a splendid botanical garden. Like a provincial British town, too, by seven in the evening on weeknights it is quite dead.

The pattern of gay migration in New Zealand was generally north to Auckland, and then overseas, usually to Sydney. Nonetheless, for many years Wellington had had a rich and varied gay life. In a novel called *That Other Realm of Freedom,* about a young gay man who migrates from Glasgow to New Zealand, Barry Nonweiler described a 1970s Wellington gay bar, "with its towering heavy-weight Maori drag-queens, its carefree Pacific Islanders, its Japanese sailors, rubbing shoulders with the most conventional and conservative of white gay men, whose clothes and camp style seemed to belong to a distant decade, yet who were equally rubbing shoulders with the city's handful of aggressive young activists. There was the strong sense of community here, in what was virtually the one gay pub in the area, which could never be reproduced in some larger, more cosmopolitan city, gay mecca though it might be."

During the law-reform campaign, it had been a Member of Parliament from Wellington who had introduced the bill to overturn the sodomy laws. The city's gay and lesbian community took a high profile. Now, with the battle won, things were quiet. "Nothing political has happened since law reform," Bill Logan said. Wellington certainly didn't *feel* like Petrograd.

I was staying at a gay bed-and-breakfast called the Cottage. It was an old Victorian wreck that had only three guest rooms as far as I could ascertain and was presided over by a white-haired Pakeha ex-lawyer who knew everyone in town. Twice a week, he cooked lunch for a distinguished group of elderly clergymen. A Maori teenager, who seemed to be the host's houseboy, was staying there. He would go off to school in the mornings. One day, I ran into him on a bus. He was going to meet his mother, he told me. There was another Pakeha man, rather withdrawn, who was a permanent resident. Assorted Pacific Islanders wandered in and out of his room at odd hours. In the morning, I would find remnants of breadfruit and other Samoan dishes on the kitchen counter.

When he wasn't cooking for the clergy, my host was winning money at the horse races—seven hundred New Zealand dollars in one day, after correctly picking the first- and second-place finishers.

He hadn't had any more cash to bet on a third-place winner. He would have correctly picked the winner in that one, too, he assured me. "The third-place winner was a female jockey I have been following closely for a while now," my host said. The prize for correctly choosing all three was $32,500.

The afternoon I arrived, a rather large Maori man was sitting on the living room couch and watching the Commonwealth Games on TV, wearing only a blue-and-red towel. All his clothes had been stolen from his car while he, too, was at the races. He had only one other outfit: tennis whites. They were being washed. He was a psychologist in charge of Maori health programs at a town north of Wellington. A man in his thirties with a gentle, thoughtful manner, he stayed at the Cottage whenever he came in to town.

As soon as I sat down, he told me a love story. It seems that when he was seven years old, he started writing to an American pen pal; the correspondence continued for many years. When he was twenty-three he visited the United States to study and stayed with the same pen pal and his family. Neither knew the other was gay, but there was an immediate attraction. "We knew each other's souls," he said.

So began a relationship that had lasted ever since. Now, they lived on different continents and only saw each other six weeks a year. The psychologist couldn't emigrate to the United States, and his lover worked in the family business in Southern California and couldn't relocate. Besides, the New Zealander feared that if his American lover came to live in New Zealand, somehow it wouldn't work out. Both had other relationships during their months apart, but it was difficult to make a commitment to someone else with this connection hovering in the background.

The psychologist had grown up in a large extended family—eleven siblings, plus three adopted ones. He had been raised speaking the Maori language, unlike many young urban Maori of today, who knew only English. "I admire the Maori radicals," he told me. "The changes in this country are due to them."

The following day I went to see one of those Maori radicals, a man named Lee Smith. He was a researcher at the Wellington office of Te Roopu Taukoko Trust ("The Support Group"), an agency funded by the New Zealand government to deal with AIDS among the Maori population. On the wall of Lee's office were various posters; "Like Maui, we can control our destiny," said one, referring to the figure of Polynesian mythology who was said to have fished New Zealand out of the Pacific. Another poster, composed largely of black faces, went, "We don't have AIDS but if we did, we would look like this."

Because the Maori were viewed as vulnerable to the epidemic (fifteen percent of the one hundred and fifty or so AIDS cases in the country were among Maori, according to Lee), the New Zealand government was spending a substantial amount on Maori AIDS education. It wasn't enough, of course. "Under the Treaty of Waitangi, we are supposed to get fifty percent of all resources," said Lee. "In fact, we get five percent." His office had a staff of three, and another six full-time staffers worked in various regional branches around the country. Although the trust's programs were aimed at educating all segments of the Maori population, it was gay Maori men, many of whom went off to live in Sydney and returned infected with HIV, who were most at risk.

Like all the Maori I met, Lee immediately told me his tribal affiliation, Ngati Kahungunu. Lee was eager to prove that the Maori had long been a tolerant people, in stark contrast to whites. Unlike the Samoans, he admitted, the Maori had no tradition of *fa'afafine,* men raised as women. But transvestites were part of the *marae,* the traditional Maori community. No word for "homosexual" existed in the Maori language, he said. For this reason, one anthropologist had tried to argue that homosexuality was unknown in pre-European New Zealand. But the lack of a need to designate or label didn't prove anything, Lee maintained. "The Maori have a holistic kind of sexuality," he said. "There is a lot of touching. When you use the word gay, often Maori will say, 'Ah, stop using that word! We're all Maori.' "

Similarly, it was generally easier for gay and lesbian Maori to come out than for Pakehas to do so he noted. Maori families were less apt to reject their children. "I have heard so many tragic Pakeha stories!" he said dismissively.

"We Maori are lucky," he went on. "There is more variety in the Maori gay world than in the Pakeha gay world. We are less ghettoized. We are interacting all the time with other Maori, with our families."

I mentioned to Lee that all the gay Maori I met seemed to have sexual relations with Pakehas, not with other Maori. He admitted this was true. "Basically, interracial gay relationships are more controversial than gay relationships themselves," Lee said. But in the current Maori cultural revival, he believed an increasing number of Maori gay men were starting to become involved with other Maori. In the new atmosphere, "finding other Maoris attractive has been positivized," he said.

With his nationalistic point of view, Lee tended to minimize the effects of the 1985–1986 law-reform campaign on homosexual Maori. At one point, a delegation of lesbian and gay Maori had gone to persuade Maori MPs to support the bill. But their arguments he said, were halfhearted, at best. "We already felt so disadvantaged as a people," he said. "This almost seemed minor. It was just another white law." A follow-up meeting was sparsely attended.

The close-knit nature of the Maori community—and the fact that most gay Maori men knew someone who was HIV-positive—made AIDS education easier. "At first we were worried about inner-city street kids being forced into having unsafe sex," Lee said. "We have cleaned that up now. Now, that group is aware of safe sex and condoms." At the same time, for many Maori, AIDS was a low priority compared to basic survival issues. Lee's challenge as an AIDS educator was to make the disease relevant to his people, to prove it wasn't a "minor issue." So Te Roopu Tautoko emphasized the connection between AIDS education and Maori survival—and between Maori pride and gay pride. "Live safe, live long, for your race, your family," went one of its slogans. Another was "Know your language, know your *marae,* be proud about being gay."

As much as Lee and other gay Maori tried to paint a picture of traditional Maori culture as relatively accepting of homosexuality, the situation was complex. The older generation was often less than tolerant; so were those Maori strongly influenced by Christianity. (The two groups often overlapped.) There were also differences between tribes. "Up north, I've heard that gay people were traditionally killed," one gay Maori told me. "But in other tribes, they were revered as priests. In my own tribe, gay men hold positions of respect. They are caretakers of knowledge and of the family." This man had a gay uncle, aged fifty-five, who made decorative baskets from flax and looked after the family treasures. The uncle was the young man's role model.

In some respects, the issue of acceptance or nonacceptance of homosexuality was beside the point. The keys to the Maori culture are a series of ties and allegiances—to the tribe (*iwi*), to the subtribe or clan (*hapu*), and to the extended family (the *whanau,* pronounced "fano"). As among the Australian Aboriginals, these loyalties overrode everything, including what people might think about sexuality or sexual orientation. Kinship ties provided gay and lesbian Maori a sense of security that many white gays and lesbians didn't have. Your kin were always there when you needed them.

That was the experience of a Maori lesbian named Rawhiti (pronounced "Rafiti") Searancke. In the Maori language, "Rawhiti" means "Sunrise" or "To the East." Before Rawhiti took that name, she had been known simply as Sandra Anne. She worked as the curator of Maori film at the New Zealand Film Archive in Wellington.

One afternoon, as we sat in the far recesses of the archive, amidst film canisters and editing machines, Rawhiti dug out a Maori-English dictionary and leafed through the pages. "There *is* a word for homosexuality in the Maori language," Rawhiti declared. "I just don't know what it is!" The Maori had no written language until the British came, she explained. It was the missionaries who had preserved it in written form, which didn't bode well for preserving cultural references to homosexuality. "Here it is!" Rawhiti said triumphantly. " '*Takatapui:* intimate companion of the same sex.' That word was lost for many years."

Rawhiti, who was thirty-five, was dressed in a white T-shirt and pleated slacks and had a long, thin braid down to her waist. She was poised and graceful, almost aristocratic in her bearing; when she started to speak, she would put her hands behind her neck, as if to help concentrate her thoughts.

The first incident in which her family stood up for her, her lesbianism notwithstanding, occurred when she was eighteen and involved in her first relationship, with a another young Maori woman. One afternoon, the young woman jumped into bed with Rawhiti's brother. Rawhiti was devastated. She felt she had to tell her mother what was going on. Her mother and four sisters rallied around her, and virtually drove the offending woman out of town. "It was at that point, I recognized the power of *whanau*," Rawhiti said.

Her mother's attitude, she said, was always "I don't care who you sleep with. But I'll question that relationship if you come home with a black eye."

In her early twenties, Rawhiti had lived and traveled in Europe, where she had a number of relationships with men. Eventually she returned home and came to terms with her sexuality. That was a struggle she had had to fight alone. Then, years later, the *whanau* came to her assistance again. It was in 1987, when Rawhiti was politically active, and openly lesbian. She was part of a delegation of Maori women invited to an international women's health conference in Costa Rica. Rawhiti announced to the other women that she intended to make contact with other lesbians at the conference. "It went down like a dead fly," she recalled. Seven out of nine delegates—all women in their fifties—withdrew from the delegation. But Rawhiti wouldn't back down.

She returned to her own people and asked if she should go to Costa Rica. They were supportive. "The women who opposed me were all from another tribe," Rawhiti said. "So, it was a little bit of a tribal war." In the end, nineteen people in her subtribe, her *hapu,* signed a letter supporting Rawhiti, and Rawhiti went off to the conference.

It was at this time that she changed her name from Sandra Anne to Rawhiti.

Living in Auckland in the early 1980s, Rawhiti was caught up in the ferment of the Maori revival. Maori separatism was on the rise, and separatists were challenging Maori women whose partners—male or female—were white. Rawhiti was in the midst of her first adult lesbian relationship. Her lover was a Pakeha woman, as all her lovers had been since, and she wasn't about to give her up in the name of racial and ideological purity. "Separatism didn't match how I was brought up," she said. "It didn't match the free-spirited existence that I had." As a result, she was ostracized by the militant political group in which she had been active. At one point some two hundred women weren't on speaking terms with her—"and the Maori are always greeting one another," Rawhiti noted. But she held her ground, refusing to leave the group *or* her lover. "My mother always said, no one could take your Maori away," she said. "And sexuality is on a par with all things that make me Maori. So I stayed and fought. I come from warrior stock!"

Like Lee Smith, Rawhiti contended that Maori families tended to be less rejecting of their homosexual offspring than Pakehas. "We haven't had the need to divorce ourselves from our families," she said. "I have a lesbian sister who has a child. I think my father is happy not to lose his lesbian daughters. He is happy not to have to spend all that time with sons-in-law."

It was was easier for gay and lesbian Maori to become involved in child-rearing than their white counterparts, she thought. In the Maori tradition, it was the extended family that raised the child. Being the foster parent of a relative's child was commonplace. "I was held in the arms of my lesbian aunts," said Rawhiti. But the idea of having a child through artificial insemination—much discussed among Wellington lesbians, these days—made Rawhiti uncomfortable. There was a great stress on genealogy among the Maori, and they traced their descent through both the father's and the mother's lines. "We have seen our kids, Maori kids, fostered in white families where they lose their Maori roots," she said. For a people rediscovering their culture, the idea of not knowing where you came from was unthinkable.

Rawhiti introduced me to a gay Maori friend of hers who was crazy about Marilyn Monroe. His name was Keri DeCarlo and he was in the process of writing a one-person show about Monroe. Keri had already written and performed pieces called *The Death of Billie Holiday* and *Seven Songs for Marlene Dietrich*. He had a large collection of photographs of American movie stars and claimed to have owned two signed photos of Marilyn Monroe herself. One, appraised at five thousand dollars, had been stolen.

It was Saturday morning, and everyone in New Zealand was glued to the Commonwealth Games on TV, watching bowls (lawn bowling). The saga of a bowls player called Millie Khan had captured the country. Khan's baby grandchild had died suddenly, but the news was being kept from her for an entire week so she could compete. New Zealand wasn't doing well in the Commonwealth Games, and bowls was one of its best hopes. Millie Khan won the silver medal.

Keri wasn't particularly interested in sports. He was a classical pianist and singer. He lived in Auckland and was visiting friends in Wellington for a few days. We sat in the backyard of the Cottage, battling the fearsome Wellington wind that roared through the city even on the balmiest midsummer days.

Keri had recently rediscovered his Maori heritage. He took a book from his backpack, by way of example. "See this spine," he said. "This is Maori culture—language, the *marae*. Under it is Maori spirituality. I have always had that, the spirituality. But only in the past few years have I found the cultural part. That is my true self."

He had trouble being *too* earnest, though. "I know it sounds so New Age," he said. "I have to confess I've been been reading Shirley MacLaine!"

Keri, who had grown up speaking only English, was now learning Maori for the first time. For the first time, he was taking a stand on political issues—specifically, the issue of land rights, the Maori claim to large chunks of the country. His Pakeha friends were dismayed.

He hadn't turned into a Maori separatist, he assured me. "I used to think I had to choose between my Maori identity and my Pakeha and gay identity," he went on. "Now, I don't think I have to make a choice." These days he was "celebrating" his Pakeha cultural background, as well. "I consider that I have refined taste," he said. "For a while I thought I had to throw that all overboard. I don't feel that way now."

Unlike others I spoke to, he didn't view Maori culture as necessarily affirming of homosexuality. Traditionally, the Maori man was a warrior and a producer of children, he noted. "We don't have any tradition of *fafa,* of men raised as women, like the Samoans," he said. "I don't consider that gay anyway." He had heard of transvestites and gay men being denied traditional Maori funerals.

He himself had taken his boyfriend to the *marae* and felt strong hostility from other Maori men. In some ways Keri was the typical urban Maori, cut off from his roots: Both his parents were dead and he had little contact with the *whanau,* except for his maternal grandmother.

Nor did he have any illusions about the place of the Maori in the Pakeha gay community. There were numerous instances of "the uptight, repressed European ripping off the sensuality of the Maori, exploiting young boys," he said. White gay men often just wanted to "take, take, take" from the Maori. "The message," he said, "is that they want to fuck you but they don't care about you. So you are left feeling bereft and ripped off. Whites respond to Maori sensuality but give nothing. This replicates the entire colonial experience."

Reconciling the political and the personal was not necessarily easy. Keri himself had relationships only with Pakeha men.

There were other contradictions, too. Drag was popular among gay Maoris, and Keri had performed in some drag shows in the past. Now he viewed female impersonation as demeaning to women. Instead of putting you in touch with your feminine side, he said, drag just brought out the oppressive view of women with which we had all been indoctrinated. "As a people, the Maori are extroverted and outgoing," he said. "Maybe that is why drag has appealed to us so much." But, as with a preference for Pakeha men, today he saw female impersonation as another manifestation of the "colonized mind."

Keri proposed that we go downtown. I was happy to do so, considering the dubious relations between Pakehas and Maori and Pacific Islanders that I feared might be going on in the upper rooms of the Cottage at that very moment. Keri was looking for a particular book on Marilyn Monroe that he hadn't been able to find in Auckland. The streets were crowded with weekend shoppers; after one o'clock, downtown Wellington would become a virtual ghost town until Monday morning. We wandered in and out of bookshops without any luck. Then we stopped by the box office of the Wellington Arts Festival for Keri to buy a ticket to a concert by the American singer Blossom Dearie, another of his favorites. But she was only performing on a weeknight, when Keri couldn't make it down to Wellington.

Keri was undaunted. He kept barraging me with questions. Why did Monroe become *the* cultural icon? he asked. Why not Mamie Van Doren? Why not Jayne Mansfield? Had I seen Mansfield in *The Girl Can't Help It*? And had I ever seen *Pink Flamingos*?

"Never underestimate the impact of American culture on this society," Keri told me. "It was held up for us as Nirvana. We have been polluted by it. Talking and writing about it serves as a laxative."

In Melbourne, Gideon, the Aboriginal man, wondered in a poem who he was. In Wellington, Keri, the classical pianist and chronicler of Marilyn and Marlene and Billie Holiday, asked some of the same questions: Was he culturally Maori, Pakeha, American, gay? All those things? "My goal is to be authentic as a Maori and a gay man," he said. In the heart of at least one gay Maori, the road back to the tribal *marae* passed through Hollywood.

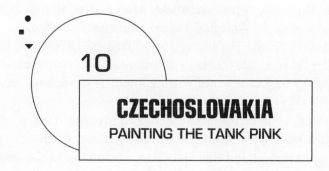

10

CZECHOSLOVAKIA
PAINTING THE TANK PINK

Prague

Šárka tugged at her hair, peered into her muddy coffee, leaned back in her chair, and informed me, in the most blasé and sophisticated tones an eighteen-year-old could muster, "I'm going to take the bus to Paris tomorrow. There is an exhibition by a sculptor that I must see. Monday is the last day."

Have you been to Paris before? I asked.

"Oh, yes, of course," she replied, mildly offended. "And to Amsterdam, too. Are you going to Amsterdam? I can give you the address of a lesbian friend in Amsterdam!"

The Velvet Revolution, which toppled one of the harshest Communist regimes in Eastern Europe, was a year and a half old. Travel to the West was the ultimate status symbol for people whose dreams, for years, had extended only as far as the Black Sea beaches of Bulgaria. I was a hemisphere away from Australia and New Zealand now: The sense of buoyancy and freedom and optimism, of vast open space and limitless possibilities, was gone. Or was it? For, despite a tragic history, here the doors to the world had suddenly been thrown wide open. It was on to Paris and Amsterdam! There was skepticism, to be sure, but also that same sense of hope, of starting afresh, that one found Down Under. For Šárka, and for Czechoslovakia, life was just beginning.

We were sitting in a vegetarian restaurant—more accurately, a restaurant that had recently added a vegetarian menu—on a side street off Wenceslas Square. In other respects, the restaurant was left over from the "old," pre-revolutionary Prague. All the characteristic features of state ownership were in evidence: plain metal chairs, faded checkerboard tablecloth, dreary decor, and waitresses who scowled and grabbed your plate from under you before you finished. It was lunchtime and the place was packed: Everyone was sharing tables. I had just devoured a piece of soy that looked like steak, and a vast portion of mashed potatoes cooked in chicken fat that was right out of my Eastern European Jewish grandmother's kitchen. Šárka had finished most of a meal of cornmeal mush and blueberries. Like virtually every young lesbian I met in Eastern Europe, Šárka was a vegetarian. Eastern European lesbians were learning how to be lesbian in the Western sense, and vegetarianism was a sign of that new "political correctness."

"What do you call this in English?" Šárka asked, nodding toward what remained of her lunch.

"Mush," I said.

"Mush?" she repeated skeptically.

Šárka was serious about improving her English vocabulary. She spoke English when she visited her lesbian friends in Paris and Amsterdam.

It was June in Prague, city of bookstores and butcher shops. The lilacs were in bloom. The portrait painters and postcard vendors had set up shop on the Charles Bridge, with its statues of sad-eyed saints. The Staré Město, the old section of the city, had been restored to its baroque and Gothic splendor, its churches, palaces, and public buildings transformed into what the writer Paul Fussell calls a "pseudo place," a tourist bubble. It was crowded with boutiques and galleries and hordes of German vacationers. I realized I had come to Prague five years too late.

There was an atmosphere of cautious gaiety—and self-assertion. Although the last Soviet troops were leaving Czechoslovakia, years of Soviet domination had not been forgotten or forgiven. Across a pedestrian mall downtown, Russian military uniforms were strung on wires like scarecrows. On the other side of the Moldau, a Soviet tank, a monument to that nation's role in the liberation of the city from the Nazis, had been spray-painted pink a couple of months before by a defiant art student. The authorities, worried about offending the Soviets, restored the tank to its original military green. Then fifteen members of Parliament painted it pink again, and so it remained. People came and gawked, immensely pleased. (Later, the tank was moved to a museum.)

The transition to a market economy was on. The government was selling off state-run enterprises to foreign capital; Volkswagen had just bought seventy percent of Skoda, the automobile manufacturer. Prices for transport, gas, and electricity were going up. For the first time in years, you could see prostitutes on the streets of Prague. There was a shortage of restaurants open in the evening; when you did find one, there was rarely anyone to seat you and getting the check took nearly as long as eating the meal itself— usually a few pieces of overcooked beef swimming in gravy. "Service," that nasty symbol of capitalist exploitation, was slow to put down roots in Prague.

Still, Prague's charm lay no longer in those spruced-up baroque and Gothic splendors but in the vanishing traces of the ancien Communist régime: the store windows decorated with stacks of canned mushrooms from China and canned pineapple from Vietnam and giant, sweating bottles of Pepsi-Cola; the shops without names that said simply MASO ("Meat") in crude block letters; and "family-style" restaurants like the one where Šárka and I were having lunch—uncomfortable, unadorned places where you could eat for pennies.

I had come to Prague to see what happens to lesbians and gays after the revolution, when the heavy hand of repression is lifted. I was also curious to hear how they had survived previously—in the case of Czechoslovakia, under an ideology that pronounced homosexuality a symptom of "bourgeois decadence" that would most assuredly vanish with the emergence of the New Socialist Man (and Woman). Šárka didn't know very much about the past, of course. She was a blank slate.

Šárka was short and just a little squarish in her build; her brown hair, cut smartly, was tinted red—"for the summer," she explained. Under her houndstooth wool jacket, she was all in black: black blouse, short black skirt, black stockings, black shoes. You would have thought she was twenty-two, not eighteen; that was exactly the impression she was trying to create.

She was carrying around a novel by the Yiddish writer Isaac Bashevis Singer. Šárka, whose family, like most Czechs and Slovaks, was nominally Catholic, was planning to convert to Judaism. When I told her I was Jewish, she was thrilled. Prague had a renovated Jewish quarter and a functioning synagogue, but few members of its Jewish community had survived the Nazi occupation. To Šárka, the absence and suffering of Jews gave Judaism an appealing exoticism and a lack of connection to the ideologies—communism, Catholicism, even bourgeois liberalism—that had dominated twentieth-century Czechoslovakia. "The Jews are such a brave nation," she said. And then brightly: "My mother thinks we might have had some Jewish relatives."

It was her last day of high school. She had had her final exam, in Spanish, the day before. Šárka lived alone, or so she said (I suspected that she rented a room in someone's house) and made puppets and marionettes, which she sold to earn some extra money. She was full of plans, breathtaking in their scope, the kind of plans that just two years before would have been impossible for Czechoslovak lesbians and gays, for almost anyone in Czechoslavakia. A few of her plans were:

1. live in Paris and Amsterdam
2. study art and sculpture
3. make a film
4. become a performance artist (preferably in San Francisco)
5. open a women's café in Prague
6. write for *Soho Revue* [the lesbian and gay monthly magazine recently started up in Prague]
7. study Hebrew
8. read, read, read

I was reminded of some famous lines by Wordsworth about the French Revolution. I looked them up when I got home:

> Bliss was it in that dawn to be alive,
> But to be young was very heaven!

That was Šárka.

• • •

Šárka had grown up in a town of sixty thousand near the Polish border. Her parents were divorced; her father was a physician and her mother worked in a medical laboratory. Šárka had come to Prague at fourteen to go to school. "That is when I realized how bad the system was," she said. "At school, there were pictures of Lenin on the walls. My teachers told me I was too individualistic." Šárka realized she was gay during the time of the revolution, but insisted one thing had nothing to do with the next. A boy had fallen in love with her at the time—writing poems and letters to her, swearing undying love. Perhaps this forced Šárka to acknowledge her sexual orientation. "When I told him, he said he didn't care," Šárka recalled. "He said he would love me forever, even if I was a lesbian." Until then, Šárka's emotional life had mostly consisted of crushes on female teachers.

Telling her mother she was attracted to other girls was easy. Her mother had always said, "The nicest body is a girl's body."

I was intrigued. "Is your mother a lesbian?"

"Something like that," she said.

All of Šárka's lesbian and gay friends had had a difficult time when they told their parents. As for Šárka, shortly after she announced to her mother that she was a lesbian, her mother started a relationship with another woman. "We both had girlfriends at the same time!" she laughed.

Šárka had actually met her first girlfriend shortly after the revolution, through a classified ad. It was the easiest way to meet people, she said. A month before I met her, she had advertised again, in a popular newspaper devoted to classified advertising; the newspaper had a section called "On hledá jeho, ona hledá ji," which meant "He is looking for him, she is looking for her." This time, she had been disappointed with the results. She had found some new friends through the ad, but no girlfriend.

After lunch, we went to Šárka's high school to pick up her school-leaving papers. (She had no interest in going to something as conventional as a graduation ceremony.) She had studied economics and foreign trade; in Czechoslovakia you studied a very specific program in high school. Depositing me in a classroom crowded with eighteen-year-old girls downing celebratory bubbly water and cheesecake and chatting animatedly about their exams,

Šárka went off to contend with the bureaucracy. "Don't be nervous," she admonished me. She seemed at ease with her fellow students, but claimed she wasn't really close to them. "I hate my school," she confided. "The only good thing about this school is the math teacher. I wish you could meet her."

Once we were outside, Šárka asked, "Will you go to the synagogue with me tomorrow night?"

"Sure," I said. "But what about Paris?"

"Paris? Oh, Paris can wait till Saturday!" Šárka said.

I had first met Šárka the evening before at a meeting of a lesbian group at a gay disco called U Petra Voka, located in a basement in Smíkov, a section of Prague just across the Moldau from downtown. In Prague, there were no lesbian bars, discos, or cafés. The U Petra Voka gathering, which took place every Wednesday at six P.M.—the women had to be out by eight, sharp—was all there was.

It was the first lesbian group ever in Prague and had been going for a year and a half now. Before the revolution there had been a few bars catering to gay men, and a largely male organization called the Lambda Union (established in 1987, although never officially recognized under the Communist regime). Homosexual relations between consenting adults had been legal since 1961. But there had been no gay or lesbian publications—and nothing, absolutely *nothing,* in the way of social activities for women.

Šárka claimed she and her friends didn't like the group very much. After childhoods of Communist regimentation, they were averse to being part of anything that smacked of an organizational structure. "Maybe I'm some kind of anarchist," she suggested.

Still, for the other twenty-five or so women in attendance (and I suspected, really, for Šárka, too), it was Wednesday evening lesbian heaven—a dark, smoky lesbian heaven, to be sure, with red lamps hanging from the ceiling and signs for Cinzano and Martini plastered over the bar, but it was heaven nonetheless. "There are two new women here tonight!" one of the group leaders told me, enthusiastically. There was still that sense of novelty and excitement. No one seemed to mind that a man was present.

I was introduced to a woman named Marzela. If Šárka exemplified the younger generation of Prague lesbians, full of plans and ideas, Marzela, forty-five, was the product of a less hopeful time. Tall, trim, stylishly dressed in a simple white blouse and black trousers, her hair piled up on her head, Marzela took things seriously. She didn't smile very much. She worked in the customer-relations department of the state-run gas company. The Soviet Union had stopped selling cheap, subsidized fuel to Czechoslovakia, and the price of gas was going up. That day, three pensioners had come in to complain about rising prices. Marzela's role was to play the diplomat. "It is not easy to stay calm and explain things to people," she said.

Like most of the women in the room, Marzela didn't speak any English. "We were discouraged from learning foreign languages," she said apologetically. "Besides, we couldn't travel, so we didn't have any incentive to learn them anyway." A woman named Karla translated. Šárka listened in.

Before the revolution, Marzela told me, when there had been no social outlets for lesbians, "I just lived for my partner and she lived for me." The two had met through a personal advertisement twelve years previously, during a brief period when it was permissible to put a gay or lesbian classified in the newspaper. The authorities revoked the policy soon after. "We never associated with other lesbians," she said. "We didn't know any. Just the former partner of my partner. That was all." Long before that, Marzela had known that she was lesbian but felt there was no possibility of living as one. At twenty-seven she married, a marriage that lasted six years.

Karla, the translator, who was about the same age as Marzela and worked as a computer programmer, had lived a similar life. "We were all isolated, so isolated," she said. Gay men could meet one another at bars and cruising spots; lesbians had no such meeting places. Travel to the West was virtually impossible; they knew nothing of lesbian and gay movements in Western Europe.

A year before my visit, after the Communist regime fell, the Lambda Union had held a party on a boat on the Moldau. Prague Castle was lit up on the hill above, and there was dance music on deck. Karla recalled how Marzela had turned to her and said, "This is the first time I have ever been dancing with my partner. And we have been together for more than ten years!"

The years of isolation ended with the formation of the Wednesday night group. "I always knew I wasn't the only lesbian in the world," Marzela said. "But it was wonderful to actually see with my own eyes that there were so many of us."

Today, Marzela was less closeted than in the past. "I am not consistent, but I am a little more open," she said. Her lover worked as a nurse and while the other nurses knew the two were "friends for life," the nature of the relationship was never stated explicitly. At Marzela's job, no one had known she was a lesbian until last year; now there was one colleague who knew. She hadn't told her mother, who was very religious and believed Marzela could do no wrong. "We both have trouble telling our mothers," said Karla. "The younger women don't have this problem."

Karla said that many of the political and social changes in Czechoslovakia affected gays and lesbians indirectly. After the Soviet invasion of 1968 put an end to the brief period of liberalization known as the Prague Spring, everyone and everything was "normalized," she said. "The mentally and physically handicapped were settled far away, near the East German border. I was shocked when I discovered this. Gays and lesbians were out of the norm, too. We didn't exist. We were tolerated because we didn't come out."

Today, there wasn't really a change in social attitudes toward lesbians and gays, she thought. It was true that there had been an increase in newspaper articles on the subject, but "publicity doesn't necessarily create friendliness," Karla said. "We have to educate people about sex. Abortion is the method of contraception in this country. So many young people get married because they are pregnant. The divorce rate is astronomical. People have a complete misunderstanding of homosexuality. They think of it as group sex."

Marzela, in particular, was cautious, unsure that much could be changed. She was very much the product of her time and place. "I have no illusions about our group achieving something socially and politically," she said. "The majority of women are here just happy to have a meeting place. They have no other ambitions."

As for Czechoslovakia itself, Marzela was skeptical. "I know the history of our nation," she said. "Since the eleventh century, there was always some possible hope which lasted for two or three weeks."

• • •

The day we had lunch, Šárka took me to the office of *Soho Revue*, the Czechoslovak monthly magazine for lesbians and gays, which was now in its fourth issue. The magazine featured a glossy cover, and articles that ranged from profiles of gay celebrities like Andy Warhol and Allen Ginsberg to articles on travel and gay history. There were personal ads, and pictures of scantily clad men and women on virtually every page. The pictures of women were, unexpectedly, as erotic as any I had ever seen in a lesbian and gay publication, East or West.

Perhaps the most interesting feature was an ongoing mini-dictionary that explained a variety of gay terminology, much of it in English: "A" for "ACT UP," "Adonis," "amyl nitrate," and "androgyny"; "B" for "butch" and "blue denim"; "C" for "Christopher Street," "coitus," and "coming out." The idea was to give previously isolated Czechoslovak lesbians and gays a crash course in Western homosexual culture. As an education, it was rather remote, however—Christopher Street was beyond the financial means of most Czech gays, amyl nitrate was unavailable, and *Blue Denim* was merely the name of a movie you might see on late-night TV. (ACT UP seemed more relevant, however. Although by the spring of 1991, there had been only twenty-five reported cases of AIDS and one hundred ninety-seven of HIV infection in Czechoslovakia, draconian laws left over from the old regime punishing the "intended or unintended" spread of AIDS discouraged HIV testing; activists feared the official numbers were just the "tip of the iceberg.")

At the magazine's office, staff members were huddled over a contact sheet of photos of a male model. When the model had found out that his photographs, in some of which he wore just briefs, would be used in a gay magazine, he balked. "It's the same old story," Šárka said, knowingly.

The magazine was having economic problems. A local publishing company had provided the start-up financing for six issues, but then *Soho* had to make it on its own. It was printing fifteen thousand copies an issue but selling only half of them. Many vendors wouldn't stock the magazine. As a result of the small number of private enterprises in Czechoslovakia, *Soho* had no display advertisements at all. The gay bars didn't bother to advertise; they had a captive audience. And because *Soho* was a monthly, its personal ads couldn't compete with those in the more frequently published classifieds newspaper, *Annonce,* where Šárka had placed her ad for a girlfriend. "I don't know what will happen to us," the editor told me. "We can survive for six issues. But then we will need a sponsor. And who will that be?"

Magazines such as *Soho Revue*—if they could survive—were examples of the new possibilities opening up for Eastern European homosexuals. They were "one of the most positive changes that have occurred in Eastern Europe since the fall of communism," according to Andrzej Selerowicz, a Polish émigré who lived in Vienna and organized lesbians and gays throughout Eastern Europe for the International Lesbian and Gay Association (ILGA). In the days when the Communist party was in power in Eastern Europe and had a monopoly on all sources of information, a gay and lesbian press was not permitted to exist, at least not legally. Now, slick, professional-looking gay publications were emerging. "In Poland, one gay paper has a circulation of twenty thousand," Selerowicz told me. "That is a bigger circulation than *Gai Pied* in Paris."

The fall of communism also meant that groups like Prague's Lambda Union could receive legal status. Previously, only state-run and state-initiated organizations and institutions had been officially recognized. Now, amidst the new entrepreneurship, gay bars and discos were opening as well. Although Prague had had gay bars during the Communist period, that hadn't been true in Bratislava, the capital of the Slovak republic. Today, Bratislava had a popular lesbian and gay disco that Selerowicz said had transformed the gay community there.

Yet, virtually all the Czechs I spoke with were reluctant to attribute the growth in gay community institutions solely to the overall political changes. Marzela, for instance, argued that "it would have happened anyway." Perhaps Marzela and people like her didn't want to make it appear that lesbian and gay freedom had been handed to them on a platter in November 1989; they wanted some recognition of their struggles in the years before the revolution.

Jan Lány, who founded the Lambda Union when the Communists were still in power, was particularly incensed at Western gay assumptions that "during the Communist regime, everything was impossible and now it is possible." To him, that view was "complete nonsense." For one thing, he noted, the first really long article about homosexuality appeared in the Communist daily, *Rudé právo,* before the revolution. "I'm sorry," he told me, "I must say that the Communist newspaper people helped us very much. They discussed things with us and were together with us at our parties. In these so-called socialist countries, the evil system had some very good people. There are homosexuals even among Communists! I cannot put as opposites homosexuality and communism. A lot of people would. They would say, 'Now we have got the organization!' But we have had the organization since 1987. That was two years before the revolution."

In its early days, Lambda didn't have a political agenda. Its activities largely consisted of conversation and companionship, weekend trips to the countryside, and preparations for the balls. "You know, the gay balls have been held for ten years," said Lány. "Even drag balls, yes. When I studied here in Prague, in the early seventies, it was not very common to dance with another man. Even the gay people didn't want to. But in that decade, you began to see it more and more. Today it is quite normal.

"It is the fashion for everyone to say, 'I couldn't do anything because there was the Communist regime,' " Lány went on. "But it was not this. It was the laziness. It was the being afraid. I would say that seventy percent of the objections to the Communist regime were personal objections and thirty percent were objective objections—those that really had to do with the political situation."

Lány, the headmaster of a prestigious school that specialized in foreign languages, was no apologist for the Communist regime. Founding a gay organization in Prague in 1987 took a degree of courage—and risk. A slightly fussy man in his forties, who puttered around the house in slippers, looked after his cats, and answered calls to the gay hotline (mostly from foreign tourists asking for accommodation or the location of the bars), he admitted he couldn't have been hired at his current job under the Communist government. When I arrived at his apartment, he pulled out a color photo of himself posing with Barbara Bush. She had visited his school a few months before, when her husband was in Prague to mark the anniversary of the revolution. Lány was amused by this, and also rather pleased.

Yet, I couldn't help but think of Marzela, dancing for the first time with her lover on the boat on the Moldau. Surely, I suggested, the change in regime had some impact on the lives of lesbians and gays. "For lesbians, it is different," Lány admitted. "For lesbians it is quite fantastic today! For lesbians it was impossible to make contact before. For gay men, it was common to walk in the streets and try to meet one another. Lesbians don't do this. Outside cruising is just for gay men. The women must have really felt isolated. About lesbians, there were virtually no articles in the press. About gay men, there were articles from time to time, but not about lesbians."

There had been other gains since the revolution, as well. In June 1990, the age of consent for homosexual sex had been lowered to fifteen, the same as for heterosexuals. Although an attempt in Parliament to insert language forbidding discrimination on the basis of sexual orientation into the nation's human-rights charter had failed, gay activists like Lány had established a working relationship with centrist and liberal politicians. Czechoslovakia was the best-organized country in Eastern Europe, with lesbian and gay groups in every major city. "It is a question of playing chess with the society," Lány said. "If the game is very long, you know there are a lot of little details you must prepare. You must know the strategy—what you will do now, and what you will do in the future. You've got the aim, and society doesn't have an aim, really. You've got the aim to get homosexuals on the same level of any other citizens, on the level of equality, and you must use the small steps."

Communists, capitalists—in Lány's view, it was all a game of chess. You just played more cautiously under communism. Far more cautiously. Meanwhile, Václav Havel, the Czechoslovak playwright-president, hadn't answered Lány's letters (even though Lány had a picture of himself with Mrs. Havel, too).

"Sure, it's easier to organize today," he said. "But we haven't got money, so it's practically the same."

Czechoslovak lesbians and gays were anxious about the future. Czechoslovakia was a predominantly Roman Catholic country, and the Christian Democratic party, allied to the Catholic church, was gaining support. "The Christian Democrats haven't made any antigay statements yet," Lány said. "But it is hidden. The Catholic church always takes homosexuality as an enemy, in this country and in Poland. This is the danger for the future."

ILGA organizer Andrzej Selerowicz was also concerned about rising nationalistic, even neo-fascist, trends in the region. "Eastern European societies are becoming awake to their own political power," he noted. "But these societies have had little democratic political experience. In Poland, for example, where there is strong church influence, the minister of health recently called AIDS 'the province of perverts.' So these countries may not be as democratic as they want to be." Lesbians and gays could easily be scapegoats, he felt.

In contrast to the Communist period, when the demands of political ideology had determined social and political life, today everything was contingent on the economic situation. The emergence of gay magazines like Prague's *Soho Revue* was a hopeful sign. But if gay entrepreneurship could create community, it was also dependent on the vagaries of the market. Fragile lesbian and gay institutions could come crashing down if the economies of Eastern European countries were unable to revive. If the economic situation worsened significantly, the forces that Communist repression had kept in check—antigay hooliganism and right-wing Christian nationalism—could become a major threat. "Before the change," Selerowicz said, "people thought the whole of the new life would be positive. Now, they see it as another style of living, but not a better one entirely. Gays are now facing the same situation as in the West: If we want to achieve something, we have to fight."

Still, there was optimism in Prague. Šárka was going to Paris to a sculpture exhibit. Marzela had danced with her lover, at long last. Jan Lány was immersed in his game of political chess. They had painted the Soviet tank pink. The lilacs were in bloom.

But in East Berlin, the hopes of revolution had already given way to the disillusion of summer's dog days.

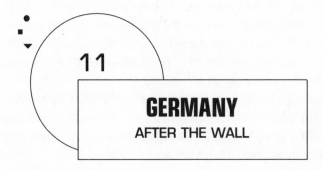

11

GERMANY

AFTER THE WALL

East Berlin

It was the pathos of the East that got to me. Take the case of Herr M., for example. He had been teaching economics at an academic institute in East Berlin. When East Germany was absorbed by the West and ceased to exist as an independent state, his institute closed. At age forty-five, he was suddenly out of a job. No one in the West would hire him to teach the East Bloc's discredited brand of economics: A lifetime's knowledge was worthless. So he opened a little gay bar on a shabby street in the Prenzlauer Berg section of East Berlin. Entrepreneurship was the way to get on in the new Germany, he thought. The bar, which had been open for two months now, was all spit and polish and good taste: shiny wood floors and fine old windows, wallpaper in the William Morris style. But business was bad. The economy of the East was in tatters; almost everyone you met was either unemployed or working at a menial job or immersed in some sort of retraining program.

Herr M.'s swift descent from respected academic to struggling small businessman had eroded his self-esteem. He had lost his social position, his identity. The past—his academic work; the book he had written; his country, whatever you might have thought of it—was "mostly memories," he said. He was physically and emotionally exhausted: he had done most of the renovation work on the bar himself. The financial insecurity was frightening; despite the drawbacks of the Communist system, one never worried about the future. "The people at the banks, the insurance company, they all seemed so friendly!" said Herr M. "What did I know?"

He was still a handsome man, with deep-set blue eyes, a fine head of gray hair, and a gentle and thoughtful manner. But he had lost twenty-four pounds in two months. He wasn't eating. By his own admission, he was smoking and drinking too much.

We sat at a table and drank beer. An Edith Piaf record was on the stereo, and later, the Andrews Sisters. A few customers wandered in. I told Herr M. that I had seen a translation of his book at a bookshop in Boston. He didn't seem to care.

He looked around the bar and then down at his beer. "I worry," he said, "that I'm not going to make it."

These days, it takes about fifteen minutes on the S-Bahn to get from the center of former West Berlin to Alexanderplatz, in the eastern section of the city. You board the elevated train at Zoo, the grimy Western railway station where Poles sell VCRs on the street and kids with rucksacks line up for a reserved seat to Copenhagen or Amsterdam. The train passes through the Tiergarten, the leafy park where gay sex takes place at twilight. A few minutes later, the landscape begins to resemble no-man's-land, all ditches and dumping grounds. The still-charred hulk of the Reichstag, burned by the Nazis in 1933 and soon to become the seat of the German parliament, is off to the right. Behind it, hidden by trees, is the Brandenburg Gate. Somewhere along here—it's hard to make out where exactly—stood the Wall that for twenty-eight years divided Communist East Berlin from the capitalist West, until it was demolished in the popular uprising in the autumn of 1989. You feel the history of the twentieth century passing by your window in a rush.

It is easy to ride the train for free. Although you are supposed to buy your *Fahrkarte* (ticket) from a machine, there are no turnstiles and rarely does a conductor venture by to check on you. It is an honor system; the old joke is that if Germans wanted to storm a railway station, they would line up to buy tickets first. At first I paid my fare dutifully, but once I realized there was no enforcement at all, I grew lax. I joined the ranks of the "black riders," as Berliners call them.

After a few more stops, you pull into Friedrichstrasse station, with its vaulted ceiling and banks of dirty windows. The crowds waiting for the train begin to look shabbier: their jackets imitation leather, their suits ill-fitting. In the old days, Friedrichstrasse was the frontier; passengers had to show their passports to East German border guards, surrender Western books and newspapers, and pay the five deutsche marks that the hard currency–strapped East extorted from every visitor.

But today, the doors open and close quickly, and the train continues, without even the briefest bow to the past. The next stop is Marx-Engels-Platz, still Marx-Engels-Platz eight months after unification. (There were also still a Leninallee, a Ho-Chi-Minh-Strasse, and another street named after Jacques Duclos, the French Communist party leader. But these were changed shortly after my visit.)

And then Alexanderplatz—vast, windy, empty, with its high-rises of cheap-looking glass and steel. The East German television tower still dominates the square, and lovers meet at the clock that tells the time in Moscow and Beijing, Havana and Hanoi. This is the heart of East Berlin, capital of a country that is no longer—the Deutsche Demokratische Republik, the German Democratic Republic, the DDR, the GDR. These days they call it by other names—"the former DDR," "the ex-GDR," "the new provinces," "eastern Germany." Even East Berlin has become, somewhat clumsily, eastern Berlin.

But the new names never sound quite right. To me, it is still East Germany, a very different world from the Federal Republic of Germany, with which it officially merged on October 3, 1990, one year after the Wall fell. Once the euphoria of unification faded, it became clear how extraordinarily different the East was—a ruin of a country, with a devastated infrastructure, archaic industries, dilapidated housing stock. Unable to compete in the greater German (and global) economy, its industries were bought out by West German capital or simply shut down. Eastern products, suddenly unavailable and widely scorned, became the subjects of museum exhibits in the West. Unemployment was widespread in a country that had only known full employment. For many, the psychological fallout was the most difficult: feelings of inferiority to the West; loss of identity; a rejection of the material deprivation and the state repression of the old GDR, on the one hand, and a longing for its comforting familiarity and security, on the other.

Two populations became one in an uneasy fit, breeding mutual suspicion and stereotypes. The "Wessies," as West Germans were called, were convinced that their Eastern cousins were lazy, clumsy, lacking in initiative, couldn't drive properly, and didn't know how to dress. To the "Ossies," on the other hand, the West Germans were superficial, selfish, arrogant—conquerors.

In the city of Berlin itself, the clash of cultures was at its most stark. For East Berliners, it was as if they had gone to sleep sometime around 1950 and awakened forty years later to find themselves grafted onto one of the most sophisticated cities in Europe: a city of minimalist chic; of boutiques, cafés, and sex shops, and a gay scene as open and freewheeling as any in Western Europe; of Kreuzberg, punk capital of the world. As Herr M. put it, "In spirit, East Germans are like Middle Americans. For us, becoming part of the West is like a small-town boy who suddenly finds himself in the big city and doesn't know his way around." It was a shotgun wedding of Oshkosh and the East Village, of Peoria and Paris.

Eight months after unification, I came to East Berlin to see how gays and lesbians of the old GDR were faring in the new Germany. For gay people, as for everyone else, the initial euphoria had passed. Life was far more complicated than anyone could have imagined in those heady days when an entire populace took sledgehammers and chisels to the Wall. But if unification was a raw deal for the East—and I was convinced that it was a raw deal, that it should have been accomplished more slowly, with less economic and psychological pain—it did enable me to see the West through the eyes of Eastern lesbians and gays, and for that I was grateful.

My first journey to the East was not by train, but by Trabi. The Trabant is the noisy, polluting, two-stroke East German–made automobile that came to symbolize all the quaint inefficiency of the GDR. One West German compared the Trabi to a "cardboard box on wheels"; another maintained that its small size made passengers look like "bears on tricycles." One day, I saw a Trabi trying to pull out of a parking space on the Fasanenstrasse, amidst the most stylish boutiques in West Berlin. It took several minutes to start up, and slowly coughed its way down the street until it reached the intersection; then it gave one last gasp and died completely. Trabis were like toy cars; they might have never met emissions standards in most U.S. states, but they were also sweet, endearing. There was a movie called *Go, Trabi, Go,* about an East German family's holiday journey by Trabi to the south of Italy. The Trabi was the film's unlikely hero. A sequel followed: *Trabi Goes to Hollywood.* In the spring of 1991, production of Trabis was discontinued. No one, least of all ex-GDR citizens, wanted ex-GDR goods. Six thousand workers lost their jobs.

The Trabi that took me to the East that first evening belonged to Jörg, a gay man who had dreamed of becoming an East German Frank Sinatra. I met Jörg at a "men's art gallery" in West Berlin, where he was working as a clerk, selling postcards. He spent most of his days sitting under framed photographs of Calvin Klein models, absorbed in crossword puzzles. Jörg, who was twenty-seven, had formerly made his living singing with a ten-piece swing band at the Grand Hotel in East Berlin, and later with a twenty-piece "big band" that performed at government functions and conventions. When the East German government collapsed, the band had no work. Jörg was an unassuming person, good-natured, with thinning hair and a smile that lit up his face. He considered himself fortunate to have a job.

We were going to a gay bar in East Berlin. Jörg was behind the wheel, accompanied by Thomas, another East Berliner who had come down in the world. Thomas was dressed in full leather. He was a little older than Jörg, theatrical, always demanding the center of attention, a "type." You would mention something—New York, for instance—and he would burst into a chorus of "New York, New York." Thomas had made his living as a performer in a drag show at East Berlin's Hotel Metropol. The show, which the GDR authorities had viewed with suspicion when it first opened, eventually ran for four and a half years and was a smashing success. (The audiences were primarily straight.) Once the Wall came down, though, and the West's multitude of entertainments beckoned, no one wanted to watch men dressed as women on the stage of the Hotel Metropol. The show closed. Now Thomas was working as a clerk in a West Berlin shop that sold leather goods.

Thomas was full of disdain for the West. Gay men in West Berlin were spoiled and superficial, he thought. He had been stunned the first time he met someone at a gay bar in the West who handed him his card and said, "Give me a call sometime." In the East, no one would do that. For one thing, hardly anyone had telephones, to say nothing of calling cards. So friends were constantly dropping by, creating an atmosphere of intimacy and informality. Thomas wanted to have a card printed up with his name and telephone number that read "0000." He was convinced that no one ever looked at a calling card; a week later the recipient might discover it under a pile of papers and notice that funny telephone number. The joke would be on him—and on the impersonal, self-satisfied Wessie way of doing things.

Gay men Thomas met in West Berlin were always complaining about some imperfection, like hair loss or acne. They would say, "But I can live with *this!*" Thomas thought the expression was hilarious. He kept repeating it: "But I can live with *this!*" The phrase was an indication of the pampered life most Westerners led, especially when contrasted with the travails of existence in the East.

For his part, Jörg had been shocked to find people in the West who had been friends for ten years but had never seen the inside of each other's apartments. As for the gay bars in West Berlin, he found them primarily concerned with sexual pickups. "In the East, gay life has always been warm and friendly," he said. "The focus has been on friendship and communication. You could meet a long-term lover in a bar. Many of my friends are afraid of the West. They come for a look and then go back."

Of course, the GDR was politically repressive, Jörg conceded. "But maybe it was because of that that people gravitated to one another, that they talked intimately," he suggested. "In the East, they told all."

The Trabi sputtered bravely ahead. It was a little cramped, but otherwise seemed to run perfectly well. In the GDR, a Trabi cost a year's salary, and you had to wait, sometimes as long as fifteen years, to get one. Jörg had bought his car on the black market—it was three days old when he purchased it—so he didn't have to wait. But it had cost almost twice as much as if he had bought it through legal channels.

"Look over there," Jörg said, pointing to an ominous line of mercury vapor lights, spaced about ten feet apart. "That was where the Wall was." Even now, a year and a half after it had come down, you could never cross the old frontier between the two Germanies without someone pointing out where the Wall had been.

We were in the East now—the lights dimmed, large apartment blocks pressed from all sides, the tiny Trabi began to toss us to and fro as it navigated the rutted, cobblestoned streets. Orange-and-cream-colored trams plied the avenues; in West Berlin, the tram lines had been ripped out long ago. The gay bars were in Prenzlauer Berg, an older part of the city with five- and six-story apartment buildings that were once imposing and ornate, but looked as if they hadn't been taken care of for years. We continued down wide, seemingly depopulated avenues, until we reached a smaller street, where newly renovated façades alternated with hopelessly crumbling ones. On the corner was a postunification establishment that announced itself as CAFÉ NORD—OPEN AIR MIT FLAIR. Otherwise the street was typical of East Berlin, with few lighted shops or pedestrians. A few doors down was the Burg Frieden, the East's most popular gay bar.

Beer was cheap at the Burg Frieden—a mark and a half, as opposed to four marks at most West Berlin bars. "When the Wall came down, they immediately raised the prices," said Jörg. "Then the regular customers stopped coming. So they lowered the prices back to where they had been." The bar was dark and a little rundown, with abstract collages on the walls and yellowing blow-ups of James Dean and Humphrey Bogart, obligatory decor even in the East. It had a neighborhoody feel, the kind of place you went to meet your friends and didn't have to worry about impressing anyone. Two older women worked behind the counter; they seemed to know all the customers.

We sat at a table off to the side, and Thomas placed his leather jacket neatly on the back of his chair and began to talk. (He had never really stopped talking.) He was involved in a relationship with a Stockholm makeup artist who worked in the Swedish film industry. The two had met in Budapest right before the Wall came down. After a week together, Thomas flew home "in tears," he said, only to awake the next morning to discover that the Wall had fallen. "I called my friend in Budapest," he recalled. "He was still asleep. He hadn't heard the news. And I said, 'You won't believe where I am—in a telephone booth in *West* Berlin!' It was so romantic!" Now, they saw each other every month and talked on the phone daily. Thomas was tempted to move to Stockholm. "Gays have a very good situation there," he said. "But I want to see what happens *here.*"

A friend of Jörg and Thomas joined us. He was a fashion designer who worked in the West and seemed to be the only person in the bar wearing the de rigueur West Berlin black. Like everyone else, he had his story of where he had been when the Wall came down. "That night was the premiere of *Coming Out,* the first gay film ever made in the GDR," he explained. "There were two showings and then a party here at the Burg Frieden. But when I got here, the place was empty. Everyone was at the Wall. I went to work the next day and there was no one there, either. I even missed my dentist appointment. When I called to apologize, they told me, 'Don't worry. No one else showed up. You're the only one who bothered to call!' "

The fashion designer was luckier than Jörg or Thomas. Unification had not resulted in a loss of social status; he could still work in his profession. But he shared many of their attitudes. "Before the Wall fell, for us in the East, there weren't thousands of discos, there weren't thousands of bars," he said. "People didn't get caught up in a gay *strudel.* You had time to concentrate on your life. I could draw. I could read. I could paint. I could meet with my friends. My life wasn't just my sexuality. I just lived like everyone else did. I can't say that it's bad that there are more things to do today. But it's this whirl, this *strudel.*"

In the GDR, he said, because there had been few options for entertainment and relatively few social differences, gays were integrated into society. In the West, by contrast, different groups tended to isolate themselves; economics, class, and sexual orientation pulled people away from one another. As a result, Western gays were forced to make a more conscious effort to be a part of society. "It is easy to get pulled into an isolationist kind of existence," he said. "I don't like closing things off, like 'gay life.' I would find it totally boring just to go to gay bars and to be only with gay people."

He thought that in trying so hard to fit into the new Germany, many East Germans were rejecting who they were. Before unification, he recalled, he and a friend would argue about whether there was a specific GDR identity or an all-German identity. He would always contend there was no such thing as a GDR identity. "I was wrong," he said. "You can see that now. The problem is that people are ashamed of that identity. They are hiding it. They are covering it up with West shine and not dealing with it. The West just gobbled up the East. There wasn't any new way of thinking developed. It will take a while before some of the old is brought up again, the idea of the East having something from its past."

Still, he was encouraged that many of the new lesbian and gay establishments opening up in East Berlin were maintaining some of the flavor of the GDR. Even if they added a touch of "West shine," as he put it, they were free of glitz and pretension. "They are GDR bars and cafés," he said. "There really is a difference. Maybe, not everything is getting swallowed up."

A couple of nights later, Jörg took me to one of those postunification, GDR-style bars that his friend had been referring to. The bar was called Da Capo and was owned by two lesbians. Da Capo was newly renovated and immaculate—the paint was still fresh; there were plants everywhere, and a large bowl of red tulips on the bar. The front door was kept locked for reasons of security; customers had to ring the doorbell to be admitted. It was Saturday night but the place was relatively quiet. A group of what appeared to be straight couples sat at one table. They left early. At another table, four lesbians chatted animatedly. The remaining customers were gay men—conservative, on the older side. "On Friday and Saturday nights, people will go to bars in the West, but during the week, it's crowded," Moni, one of the owners, reassured us. This particular night, there was a complicating factor. It was Hitler's birthday. "People are afraid to go out," Moni said. "They are afraid there might be trouble."

The bar had been open for a year and a half in the waning days of the Communist regime, then shut down for another year and a half. In the GDR days, Moni and her lover, Duscha, ran Da Capo on a commissary basis. They owned the furniture and the equipment, but the beverages were owned by a state monopoly. The state took two-thirds of the profits. Then, it was a mixed gay-and-straight bar. "Bars have always been mixed in the East," said Moni. "Our heterosexual customers always knew about the owners and about some of the patrons. And the authorities knew it attracted a gay-lesbian clientele."

Now, Moni and her lover owned the business outright. A bank loan enabled them to be independent of the large breweries that controlled many bars in Germany. Their clientele these days was ninety percent lesbian and gay. "And ninety percent of that ninety percent are gay men," Moni explained, adding that Da Capo was the only bar in the East that drew any lesbian crowd at all. Moni feared that competition between bars in the West and East was beginning. "I have heard that bar owners in the West are saying that bars in the East are demanding an entry fee," Moni noted. "And that is just not true."

Moni, blond and buxom, looked like a classic barmaid from Central Casting. She wore a paisley vest, a white blouse, and jeans. She and Duscha had met five years before, when they were working together in a cafeteria. Moni had been married, which was not unusual in the East for lesbians of her generation. She had a twenty-year-old son. "My life was rather average for GDR homosexuals," Moni said. "I've never had a problem. I didn't carry a sign, but I didn't pretend I was heterosexual. If a man started flirting and I liked him, I would tell him I was gay. If I didn't like him, I would tell him to get lost." One day, someone in the cafeteria where she worked made an antigay comment. Moni gave him a lecture. The next day the offender came back with chocolate and flowers. "People understood in the GDR," she said. "Of course, it depended. And it depended on the gay person and his or her personality, too."

Moni and Duscha were Da Capo's only staff. They both worked the bar and the tables. So, even though it was a quiet night, Moni could only chat with us intermittently. Duscha, tall, dark-haired, and less sociable, stayed aloof.

While Moni busied herself with customers, I chatted with Jörg and a West German friend of his named Hubertus, who worked for an American company. Hubertus—he asked me to call him Burt, as his American colleagues did—told me his age was "twenty-nine C."

I was mystified.

"I have decided always to stay twenty-nine," he explained. "When I became thirty, my age became twenty-nine A, you see. The year after, I was twenty-nine B. And so it goes."

Burt, who was pro-unification, and Jörg, who would have preferred a more gradual approach, engaged in some political sparring. Jörg said that he had had "everything" in the East. "I never thought of leaving," he said. "I traveled everywhere in Eastern Europe. Toward the end, I could even apply to go to performances in the West."

"Privileges," growled Burt. Jörg was offended.

When Jörg claimed that homosexuals had held high positions in the East and hadn't suffered discrimination, Burt informed him he was dreaming.

Still, Burt was not completely unsympathetic to the problems of ex-GDR lesbians and gays. Once the Wall came down, he said, there were numerous cases of West German gay men taking advantage of Ossies. "It was like a meat market with a new delivery of meat," said Burt. "People were telling East Germans, 'I will support you for life,' and then they dropped them. Before the Wall came down, there were Westerners who worked in Woolworth's and came over here and pretended to be kings.

"We in the West are cool," Burt continued. "We know our way around. The Easterners don't. The majority of them feel they are being raped by the government and politicians and Westerners."

One area where Easterners were particularly naïve was that of safe sex. Burt had had "intimate relationships," as he delicately put it, with five ex-GDR gays, none of whom had known anything about condoms. Burt had strong feelings on the subject. He had thirty acquaintances who had died of AIDS, including six close friends. Two had died in his arms. "I lived the same life they did, but look at me, I'm all right," he said, with disbelief. "I lived the same life!"

Today, as a result of this experience, Burt valued different things than he did before. "AIDS enriched my life," he said. "I know that is strange to say, but it did. I discovered there are more important things than sex. My life was unreal. I was playing with people and they were playing with me. I learned through AIDS, and I am proud to say I learned it on my own."

Jörg remained silent. AIDS remained something totally outside his experience. Burt knew more people with AIDS than the total number of reported cases in the GDR.

As the evening came to a close, Moni had more time to chat with us. For her part, the solitary Duscha seemed to be investing most of her share of the evening's profits in Da Capo's slot machine.

Have you been making more money since unification? I asked Moni.

"Yes and no," she said. "But I am buying better things with my money. Now I can buy fresh fruit. You know, we didn't see a real pineapple in twenty years. Canned pineapple cost fourteen marks in the GDR. Today, it costs one mark. We could never get canned goods."

As she detailed the deprivations of life under the old regime, Moni grew more animated than she had been all evening. "In the GDR, it took fifteen years to get a new car," she said. "It took two to four years to get a driver's license. It took twenty years to get a telephone—unless you were a Stasi [secret police] agent or a sick person at home. Then it only took eight or ten years. People are forgetting about the negative things in the past. They are only concentrating on the negative things in the present!"

At about three A.M., it was time to leave. The last stragglers had long since departed. Duscha was drawing the blinds and wiping down the bar. "Please don't write anything about Hitler in your book," Moni said to me as we headed out the door. "It wouldn't be good for business."

East Berlin was plastered with signs featuring a pink triangle and a dove of peace. LESBEN UND SCHWULE GEGEN FASCHISTISCHE GE-WALT, the posters proclaimed: "Lesbians and gays against fascist violence." You found them amid the Stalinist monumentalism of the Alexanderplatz and under the elevated tram line along Schön-hauser-Allee, the closest East Berlin came to a gay boulevard. Neo-Nazi and skinhead violence against lesbians and gay men was becoming a serious problem, particularly in the East: A gay coffee shop in the Alexanderplatz had been attacked; neo-Nazis had in-vaded a garden party in Mahlsdorf, just outside East Berlin, spray-ing the crowd with Mace; and in West Berlin a hotline at a gay men's center was receiving thirty reports of antigay violence a month. Alarmed lesbians and gays were organizing a march through working-class neighborhoods of East Berlin, where support for neo-Nazis, previously suppressed by the heavy hand of the East German security apparatus, was growing.

Not everyone thought the protest was a good idea. One East Berlin lesbian told me that parading through neo-Nazi strongholds was a provocation that would just worsen the situation. In fact, the march itself went off without incident, helped along by a visible police presence. The organizers estimated that eight thousand people marched; the newspapers put the number at thirty-five hundred. It was a spirited display. The demonstrators blew whistles and banged drums. Loudspeakers blared antifascist slogans. From the window of an apartment building someone had unfurled a sign that said, SKINHEADS AGAINST FACISM AND RACISM. Anti-Nazi graffiti was scrawled along Warshauerstrasse, where the march began, and onlookers crowded on street corners and apartment balconies along the narrow residential streets. From their dress and general appearance, many of the marchers appeared to be West Berliners—punks and students, predominantly. There were few women: West German gays and lesbians were badly split along gender lines. Still, I doubted East Berlin had ever seen anything quite like it.

Until the neo-Nazis started making trouble, there hadn't been much cooperation between gay groups in East and West Berlin. The same suspicions and stereotypes that divided the new Germany into two societies were at work in the homosexual world as well. With East Berlin lesbians and gays preoccupied with economic hard times, and West Berliners coping with AIDS, there seemed to be few shared issues. Now, violence was giving East and West common cause.

Gay sex had been legal in the GDR since 1968; the age of consent for both homosexuals and heterosexuals was sixteen, whereas in West Germany gays had to wait until eighteen to have sex legally. (In the West, the age of consent for heterosexuals was fourteen.) The GDR, too, had been the first country in the Soviet bloc to have a lesbian and gay movement of any significance. Homosexual groups began in the early 1980s, under the protection of the Protestant church—and under the watchful eye of the Stasi, the ubiquitous secret police. Soon after, some gay clubs, not church-affiliated, began to form. Creation of a movement involved some risk and some difficulty: No organizations were supposed to exist independent of state control. The SED, as the ruling Communist party was known, monopolized all sources of information. Receiving permission to do anything required torturous dealings with the government and with party bureaucrats. "These groups were a resistance," said Jürgen Lemke, author of one of the few books about homosexuals published in the GDR. "They were another way of opposition to the government."

In 1988, as state control diminished, a lesbian and gay political organization called Courage was established. Courage built channels of communication with the national youth movement—the Free German Youth—and in 1989 even had its own information booth and café at the youth movement's massive annual fair in Berlin. The first glimmers of gay culture began to appear: the film *Coming Out,* which told the story of a young man's acceptance of his homosexuality; Jürgen Lemke's book *Ganz Normal Anders* ("Normal but Different"), a compilation of interviews with gay men, published in East and West Germany in March 1989.

The GDR, said Courage leader Uvd Zobel, "had good preconditions for the integration of gay people into society."

The fact that *Coming Out* had its premiere, by mere coincidence, the night the Wall fell was a harbinger of things to come. During the year-long transition period between the fall of the Communist party from power and the merger of the two Germanys, the homosexual movement began to flower in the East. Courage, able to organize openly, started chapters in a number of cities. With the relaxation of state control of the media, a lesbian and gay newspaper, *Die Andere Welt,* appeared for the first time. Gay-rights provisions found their way into the platforms of the newly formed political parties—with the notable exception of the right-of-center Christian Democratic Union, which won the only free election ever held in the GDR. Even the restructured Communist party became a born-again supporter of homosexual rights. In its last days, the GDR parliament debated a proposal to legalize lesbian and gay partnership.

But with the advent of unification and the ensuing economic problems, gay organizing in the East began to suffer. Gays and lesbians, like other East Germans, moved West in search of jobs; the Western gay commercial scene attracted others; questions of economic survival absorbed those who remained, especially women, the group hardest hit by rising unemployment. Newly formed chapters of Courage folded or struggled on with a handful of members. "It is a reflection in the gay world of general social developments," said Uvd Zobel. Meanwhile, *Die Andere Welt,* a serious-minded monthly that took a left-wing political line, was suffering financial difficulties; its survival was very much in doubt.

One chilly evening, I went to visit Julia Ritter, a member of the *Die Andere Welt* editorial board, at her flat in the eastern section of the city. "I'm the one who writes all those long, analytical articles," she informed me. Julia possessed a fierce intelligence; she was the kind of intellectual one frequently met in the East, nurtured by isolation, repression, and the analytical rigor of the close study of Marxist-Leninist texts. She lived near Rosa-Luxemburg-Platz, on a crumbling block the authorities hadn't bothered to maintain in forty years. To get to Julia's flat, you walked through an asphalt courtyard strewn with garbage bins, and then climbed six flights. Her apartment consisted of a small main room, a kitchen, and a bathroom. The lighting was dim, in the East German manner; the walls were painted the grayish–brownish–off-white noncolor characteristic of the East; the place was pervaded by the acrid smell of brown coal mixed with disinfectant. The apartment was full of papers, files, books (I noted a copy of Bernard Malamud's novel *The Fixer,* in German)—and a layer of dust.

Julia, a stern-looking woman with short hair and wire-rimmed glasses, was feverishly cleaning when I arrived. "I thought you'd be late," she said, apologetically. She spent half the week at the apartment of her girlfriend, a printer, and never quite found the time to tidy things up.

Julia and I had something in common. In 1982, when she was a student at Rostock University in the north of the GDR, she had spent a semester at Brown University, from which I had graduated some years before. She had begun acknowledging her sexual feelings and, before leaving for the States, confided to a presumably sympathetic professor at her university that she was a lesbian. "Do you think you should go under these circumstances?" he asked disapprovingly. Julia did go, but she opted for caution. The closest she came to the lesbians and gays on the Brown campus was to look up "lesbian" in the card catalog at the Rockefeller Library. Julia was studying about Latin America, so she didn't have to go beyond the letter "L." Even in Providence, Rhode Island, she must have imagined that Stasi agents were looking over her shoulder.

When I mentioned to West Berlin friends that Julia had studied in the United States, they all concluded that her family undoubtedly had close Party connections. Otherwise, they said, she never would have been allowed to go to the West. Julia insisted her U.S. study had more to do with the intricacies of the Rostock-Brown student-exchange program than anything else, but she didn't deny having been a Communist party member.

After finishing university, she had started work at an East German government ministry, spending most of her days reading Western newspapers. When the government dissolved, she lost her job. Now, she had begun an eighteen-month training course in banking, sponsored by a West German firm.

"Can you imagine that! The GDR social scientist now studying banking and enterprise economy!" she said, as baffled as anyone at the turn her life had taken. Still, she was convinced that, despite her training course, she would never get a decent job. "We will finish this program and wind up doing the work the Turks do," she said. "Menial work." She believed, as did many other East Berliners, that there was "a collective sanction" in the united Germany against anyone over thirty who hadn't attempted to flee to the West before the Wall fell. (Julia was thirty-two.) "There is such a strong anti-GDR prejudice," she said. "I worry about this far more than antigay prejudice."

To Julia, the short year of post-Communist East Germany, before it was absorbed by the West, was a kind of "golden age" for gays and lesbians. During that period, she joined the staff of *Die Andere Welt,* her first foray into lesbian and gay activism. She began to be open about her sexuality at her work—"On Mondays, the other people I worked with would talk about what they and their family had done over the weekend, and I talked about what my lover and I had done." It was true that lesbians and gays had been viewed as "exotic animals" in the GDR. But, she added, echoing what was by now sounding to me like the gay party line in the East, "there were very great possibilities for the integration of gays and lesbians in our society."

Now the golden age was over. Lesbians and gays, like everyone else, found their lives dominated by economic pressures. People were hiding their sexual orientation in order to get a job or keep one they already had. "From month to month, it is more horrible," she said. "People have to keep their eyes on earning money. There is a lot of resignation in the former GDR. People had such big illusions. Now, there is this resignation among lesbians and gays, too."

Since the Wall came down, Julia had had some contact with West Berlin lesbians but preferred to do her political work in the East. "Unconsciously the Westerners feel as victors," she maintained. "They express this somehow. Easterners feel it." Another major difference between West and East Berlin lesbians involved attitudes toward men. Recently, for example, Julia had been selling copies of *Die Andere Welt* at a café in the West that was frequented by lesbians. A prospective customer told her, "I would never buy a newspaper that men worked on!" It was the first time that Julia had encountered such an attitude.

Julia served tea. She then unwrapped a chocolate Easter bunny that someone had left her as a gift and began to consume it ravenously. With all her tidying up, she had apparently neglected to eat dinner.

"In the GDR," she went on, "gays and lesbians worked together. The lesbian movement didn't exist as a separate movement. Both gay men and lesbians saw themselves in the same situation. They felt themselves to be homosexuals, not gays and lesbians. Only later on did lesbians realize that what men need and what women need don't always overlap."

Julia suspected that separatist attitudes would become increasingly pronounced among ex-GDR lesbians. This was partly due to Western influence. But it was also partly because of what she called "the process of differentiation" in the homosexual movement in the East, as women began to focus on issues specific to them and became more aware of discrimination within the gay movement. That wasn't necessarily bad, she thought. "It may be an important thing for lesbians to find their own identity," she said. "Only when you know who you are can you come back together and decide what to do jointly."

Like others I spoke with in the ex-GDR, Julia maintained that being homosexual was not the most important facet of her life. "Maybe this is a characteristic of ex-GDR lesbians and gays," she said. "We didn't see ourselves first as homosexuals. We understood ourselves as normal human beings, not just lesbians and gays."

I suggested that in part this might have to do with the fact that, at least until the very end of the Communist regime, lesbian and gay culture had been suppressed in the GDR.

Julia didn't deny this. "The restrictions made it difficult for us to develop as lesbians and gays," she said. "But at the same time, there was another side—we could be part of society."

In Julia's attitudes there was a certain degree of apologia for the old regime. She still believed—not in the repressive system of the former East Germany, but in a more abstract idea of socialism. If she was nostalgic, her yearning was for the brief, shining moment in which the GDR was free of Communist domination and not yet under West German political and economic control.

"How can you, once a good Party member, become a banker?" I wanted to know.

She couldn't give me an answer.

Julia, like so many in the East, seemed to subsist in a state of cultural schizophrenia. The familiar externals of the old GDR remained: the cozy, rundown East Berlin street on which she had lived for years; the harsh but somehow soothing smell of brown coal; the dimly lit, paper-strewn room; the utter quiet (no ringing of telephones to disturb). But a "new province" of the capitalist West? How could it have happened?

I took the S-bahn back to West Berlin, where I was staying. The Kurfürstendamm, the West's major shopping avenue, was ablaze with lights. The bright colors—the blues of the buses, the yellows of the telephones—seemed garish after the dimness of the East. The cafés were full of noisy tourists, and the streets were crowded, even though it was late. A sidewalk display case offered men's ties, painted in the style of Van Gogh, Toulouse-Lautrec, and Henri Rousseau, at prices that would have paid Julia's rent for two months. I stopped at Häagen-Dazs for an ice cream: maple walnut, with M&Ms on top. Two scoops.

12

DENMARK
HOW LOVELY
TO BE TOGETHER

Copenhagen

The Bryllupsalon, or "wedding chamber," located on the second
floor of the heap of turn-of-the-century brick that is Copenhagen's
town hall, is a particularly beautiful room—all low vaulted ceilings
and graceful Romanesque arches. The walls are covered with murals, primitive in style, that depict various Danish folktales and
ballads. The murals depict a world where forests are deep green and
skies a deeper blue, where the women are golden-haired and wear
long dresses and the men are clad in tunics with swords on their
belts. The erotic is suggested only obliquely. In one mural, the
groom combs the locks of the bride's hair; in another, a family
group surrounds a canopied wedding bed; in still another, a young
woman is transformed into a bird of fabulous plumage. The decor
would be trite—a Scandinavian version of a New Age greeting
card—if it didn't have such a mysterious quality, if the colors
weren't so vivid, the mood so consistent.

Vibeka Nissen was married in the Bryllupsalon—twice. On the
first occasion, twenty years ago, she married a man. The second
time, four months before my visit to Copenhagen, she pledged
herself to Inge-Lise Paulsen, her partner of seven years.

As of October 1989, Denmark became the first country in the world
to give legal recognition to same-sex partnerships. Since then, more
than eight hundred lesbian and gay couples have married in Copenhagen's Rådhus and in other town halls throughout the country.

In Copenhagen, where many people don't get married in church these days, civil marriages take place in the Bryllupsalon. On Tuesday and Thursday mornings, heterosexual marriages are scheduled at ten o'clock; gay and lesbian partnerships follow promptly at eleven. Straight and gay couples fill out the same forms. The same phraseology is used when they take their vows: solemn words about the importance of "mutual affection and tolerance" and of "living together in a harmonious way." After the ceremony, the newlyweds and their friends and relatives gather on the outdoor steps that front on the Town Hall Square, amidst confetti and the popping of champagne corks and the clinking of glasses.

In Denmark, the equivalence between heterosexual marriage and same-sex partnership goes beyond the ceremonial. Registered gay and lesbian couples have the same legal rights as married couples with respect to taxes, inheritance, insurance, and pension benefits. They have the same responsibilities, as well—to support the other economically, if need be, for instance. To receive a divorce, homosexual partners have to go through the same process as heterosexual couples do: They must either claim their spouse was unfaithful, in which case a divorce can be obtained immediately, or they must wait six months. (As of January 1, 1991, only seven lesbian and gay couples out of 718 registered at the time had applied for divorce.) Even the bigamy laws apply equally to married heterosexuals and to same-sex partners: Straight or gay, the penalty is three to six years in prison.

In most of the world, all this might sound like the fulfillment of everything for which lesbians and gays have been struggling. But, instead of rejoicing about their recent marriage, Vibeka and Inge-Lise couldn't stop apologizing.

Vibeka blamed their banker. "We have this socialist bank—" Vibeka explained.

"Anarchist bank," interjected Inge-Lise.

"Anarchist bank, okay," continued Vibeka. "Whenever we'd ask anything about our finances, the banker would say, 'It's not possible what you ask. Why don't you two marry?' And we'd just scream, 'We don't like marriage!' "

Inge-Lise elaborated, "It happened several times. He would say,

'It would be much easier if you married.' And then the idea grew. It became something possible to do. I don't know what happened. I still don't know why we did it. In philosophical or political terms, I don't believe marriage is a very good idea."

Inge-Lise and Vibeka had bought an apartment together. That was the problem.

The apartment, which was located in a pleasant surburban neighborhood of red brick houses with peaked roofs, was spacious and airy. There were polished floors, jade and rubber trees, a violin on a stand with sheet music open to "Ragtime Annie," and a FREE TIBET sign on a door. It was tasteful, comfortable—worth marrying for, one might say.

On the June evening when I stopped by for a visit, Vibeka was outdoors trimming hedges. Inge-Lise was at her computer. She was translating the latest Don DeLillo novel for a Danish publisher. "I like the book," she said, with enthusiasm. "It is so full of ideas!"

For many years, Inge-Lise and Vibeka had been active in the Danish women's movement, which had viewed marriage as the enemy. They couldn't help but feel they had compromised their principles by registering their partnership. They weren't the only women reluctant to sign on. In 1990, for example, gay male couples made up about seventy-five percent of all same-sex partnerships registered. Partly, this was due to economics. Women in Denmark, as in most other nations, make far less money than men, so they don't have as much need of the tax and inheritance advantages afforded by partnership. But the ideological aspect was important, too.

"The thing that helps me to overcome the political point is that getting married is still like being gay on the front page of the newspaper," said Vibeka, who had come in from her gardening. "It is something! They really get crazy, those people out there! For me to marry another woman, they just can't stand it. And I love it!"

I was sitting in a comfortable chair in the living room, opposite Inge-Lise, who was curled up on the coach. Vibeka was sprawled on the floor. "I work at a women's crisis center where everyone knows that I'm a lesbian," Vibeka went on. "After we married, we decided to have a little party and I gave one of my co-workers an invitation. She put it on her desk and everyone saw it. Some people went completely crazy. One woman came up to me, and said, 'But *who* are you marrying?' That was when I discovered how provoking this really was. Because they reacted so much more than I thought they would.

"And the other thing is that I love Inge-Lise, and everyone is allowed to know that. And they now understand it in a new way."

When Vibeka married the first time, twenty years before, she also did so in order to get an apartment. In those days, the government controlled large blocks of flats, and it was much easier for couples to obtain housing than for single individuals.

I suggested to Vibeka that she always seemed to marry for material reasons. She laughed.

"The reasons you seem to give," I continued, "are one, an apartment; two, to get people mad at you; and three, love."

"Oh, yes, by the way, love!" she said and laughed again.

Sometimes, Vibeka reminded me of a rebellious teenager, even though she was forty-four and had a son from her first marriage who was about to enter university. She told me how she had just returned from her twenty-fifth high school reunion, at which everyone informed her she hadn't changed a bit—she was still provocative, impossible, alive!

"Isn't it nice, you haven't lost that certain something!" I suggested.

"That certain something! She certainly hasn't lost that!" said Inge-Lise.

Inge-Lise had a certain something, too, but it was something different. She was more calm—white-haired and thoughtful.

Inge-Lise and Vibeka enjoyed a full life. They had traveled together in China and Tibet, and Inge-Lise had lived in Boulder, Colorado, for a year and worked as a travel guide in Yugoslavia and Bulgaria. They both had taught at the Free University for Women in Copenhagen. Inge-Lise was the editor of the monthly newspaper of the LBL, the Danish national lesbian and gay organization; that very month, she was going to the International Gay and Lesbian Association conference (ILGA) in Guadalajara, Mexico, as a Danish delegate. She had translated books by a number of major American novelists into Danish. Vibeka was a therapist, whose specialty was working with the terminally ill. Besides her son and Inge-Lise, Vibeka had an additional familial responsibility.

Her former husband and his wife had adopted a Korean girl, now twelve, and Vibeka was that child's "unofficial mother," as well.

They prided themselves on being flexible and being independent, and now they had bought this apartment together and gotten married.

"You see, if I die," Vibeka explained, "Inge-Lise couldn't stay in this apartment if we weren't married. Because she doesn't own my part. My family would come and take everything, and the law would come here and take everything." Denmark had some of the highest inheritance taxes in the world, as high as eighty percent in cases where you wanted to leave property or money to someone who wasn't a blood relative or legal spouse. Ironically, a law had been passed in 1986—before same-sex marriage had been approved—that exempted gay and lesbian cohabiting couples from these taxes. But now, with the legalization of partnerships and the equality of gay and straight relationships in the eyes of the law, that special exemption had been abolished. If you didn't register your partnership, your lover risked losing your share of the property. The effect of the new legal situation was to make it almost impossible for gay couples *not* to marry.

Another incentive was the matter of pensions. Vibeka had a private pension from the time when she worked as a government employee; but, as long as she remained unmarried and had living relatives, she wasn't allowed to sign it over to anyone else. Now, with the legalization of gay and lesbian partnerships, Inge-Lise could have the pension should Vibeka die.

"One of the reasons behind my decision to marry is my age," said Vibeka. "I never used to think about saving for my old age. But I am forty-four. Now I can imagine that I can get sick and things like that." The demographics of lesbian and gay partnerships indicated this was a factor for many people. Most of the couples who registered under the new law were in their forties and fifties.

Still, there were those political and philosophical objections. "If you study the philosophy behind the law and its consequences," Inge-Lise noted, "it is difficult to say if it makes things more or less conservative, if it makes things more difficult for people who aren't registered to exist, or if it changes the minds of people in some other ways and is a good thing."

Inge-Lise noted that because of the law, some things had actually gotten worse for unmarried Danish lesbians and gays, beyond the abolition of the exemption from the inheritance tax. A woman who had a child and lived with a female lover used to receive child support from the state because she was officially single. Now, because of the partnership law, the state tended to view the two as a couple (even if they hadn't registered their partnership) and often wouldn't give her the money. If the two women married, the mother would completely lose benefits.

But what Inge-Lise and Vibeka—and many Danish lesbians and gays—most disliked about the new law was that it stated categorically that registered same-sex partners could not adopt children—not even the biological child of the other partner. That was a compromise agreed to by the lesbian and gay organization, LBL, Landsforeningen for Bøsser og Lesbiske, to ensure passage of the law. Other concessions included a statement that the law did not authorize church weddings for same-sex partners and that one member of a registered couple had to be a Danish citizen. "It was a typical Danish compromise," said Vibeka disparagingly. "Society says it is okay to be a lesbian but we are too dirty to be around kids. So we're still not okay."

Despite the law's imperfections, despite their soul-searching and ideological doubts, and despite Vibeka and Inge-Lise's noisy claims that getting married had made no difference whatsoever to their relationship, still there was *something*. When they finally agreed to marry, they were determined not to do so just for financial reasons. So they went around for some time "trying to be romantic," as they put it. "I don't know how we did it," said Inge-Lise. "Talking about it, I suppose. But it worked to some extent. You know how you build up like an athlete. Then we had this wonderful party."

A wonderful party they did have: fourteen friends at home, plus Vibeka's son. The invitation stated that guests were requested to put on theatrical pieces about Inge-Lise and Vibeka. "The party was when we concentrated on the love part, not the marriage," said Vibeka. "I wanted people to tell me why Inge-Lise was so wonderful. And I wanted them to give me advice about things that weren't so good about Inge-Lise. About her bad side!"

"It was very entertaining," Inge-Lise noted dryly.

"You see," said Vibeka, "we are very positive about each other and very, very negative about the idea of marriage." On the other hand, they couldn't forgo the traditional Danish wedding cake: round, filled with ice cream, delicious.

Although Vibeka's son was at the wedding celebration, conspicuously absent were both sets of parents. When Vibeka and Inge-Lise told their parents they planned to marry, the response, on both sides, was virtual silence. "That is a very sad thing," said Vibeka. "I told my parents I was a lesbian at twenty-seven, and they said all the stupid things then. And now they are reasonable about it. But my mother, she didn't know what to say about the marriage—only, 'Is that possible?' and later, 'How do you do that?' She didn't say congratulations. Or 'I hope you are happy.' And that is not nice."

Inge-Lise's experience was similar. "My parents didn't say anything," she recalled. "They are nicer people than Vibeka's parents in many ways but they didn't say anything!"

There were humorous moments—as when Vibeka and Inge-Lise filled out their marriage papers at the Rådhus. The documents are the same for heterosexuals and homosexuals, including blanks for "first partner" and "second partner." Vibeka, without paying much attention, signed as "first partner." They discovered that was the place where the groom signed. "Now we know who is the man!" they roared at the marriage office. The officials didn't seem to get the joke.

One of the odd things about same-sex partnerships in Denmark is that, because no other country recognizes such arrangements, once you leave the country you are in effect no longer married. At Easter, shortly after their marriage, Vibeka and Inge-Lise went on a trip to England. As they were walking down a London street holding hands, they began to worry about antigay laws recently enacted by the Tory government. Did these laws apply to public displays of affection? "I said to Inge-Lise, 'They can't arrest us, because we're married,' " recalled Vibeka. "And Inge-Lise answered, 'No, we're not married. We're in England. We're not married.' "

"There are funny problems," said Inge-Lise. "What happens if you move to another country? When they get older, Danish heterosexual couples sometimes move to southern Spain. What happens to gay couples in that case? Suppose you work for Danish Railways? Does your spouse get free tickets? And what happens if the train crosses the border?"

By now, Vibeka and Inge-Lise were warming to their subject. They had to admit how remarkable it was that little Denmark had actually come up with this trailblazing law. At the time the partnership bill was being debated, a Gallup poll showed that sixty-four percent of the Danish public supported it. Increasingly, Inge-Lise noted, lesbians and gays from other countries wanted to come to Denmark to marry. "Gay men from the Soviet Union write to LBL all the time," she said. "They want to use Denmark as a refuge by marrying. They think it is easy. But if you are not a Danish citizen, you have to live with the person you marry for two years. The government actually comes and checks you out. To many people from abroad, that is what Denmark is like—you find someone and you get married and your problems are solved."

The phone rang and Inge-Lise disappeared for a while. She came back looking slightly stricken. The ILGA conference scheduled for Guadalajara later that month—the first annual meeting the organization had planned to hold outside Europe—had suddenly been canceled. Local opposition had been brewing for months; conference organizers had received death threats. Finally, the Guadalajara police announced they would refuse to provide security for the gathering. Hotels that had agreed to put up guests and hold conference sessions were supposedly told by city officials that they would lose their licenses and be closed down. It all sounded too dangerous, so ILGA headquarters in Stockholm decided to call it off. And Inge-Lise already had her ticket!

When you looked at other countries, even other countries in Western Europe, Denmark really was remarkable. The legal situation of homosexuals, while not perfect, was probably the best in the world—an age of consent of fifteen for both homosexual and heterosexual sexual relations, an antidiscrimination law, and, now, the legalization of lesbian and gay partnerships.

But why Denmark? I posed the question to the LBL's Dorthe Jacobsen over Sunday afternoon coffee at the organization's Pan Café. "You see, the worst that a person can be in Denmark is intolerant," she said. "We have a long tradition of trying to treat minority groups reasonably well. Sometimes, we are surprised by our own bravery. I think the only reason we get away with it is because we are such a small country. Denmark is not really a threat. So we can get away with a lot of things—small, good-hearted things. I don't think the Danes are that much better than other people. But sometimes it gets the better of us."

Dorthe knew as much as anyone in Denmark about the lesbian and gay partnership law. As the LBL's sole employee for the two-year period leading up to the law's passage, she had been in the thick of the political maneuvering. Now, as the organization's legal adviser, she kept a watchful eye on the implementation of the law.

The LBL was Denmark's only nationwide lesbian and gay organization, and Dorthe was proud of that fact. Other countries might have several groups competing and squabbling, but Denmark was united. It was a sign of maturity, she believed. The LBL funded itself through the ownership of six café-restaurant-discos in various cities throughout the country. Since 1981, the organization had hired out the management of the Copenhagen Pan café and Pan disco, instead of trying to run the establishment on its own. According to Dorthe, LBL's political progress dated from that year. "Once we got out of the restaurant business, we started to have some success," she said.

Enactment of a partnership law had been one of LBL's major priorities—if not *the* major priority—since the beginning of the 1980s. In part, this had to do with the peculiarities of Danish inheritance laws, which particularly affected lesbian and gay couples. When the Folketing, the Danish parliament, enacted the 1986 law exempting lesbian and gay couples from the high inheritance tax, it was the initial step toward partnership. "That law marked the first time the politicians acknowledged our existence, our different way of living," said Dorthe. "They recognized that we were in long-term relationships and that we had problems that they could help us solve."

Still, there were a number of issues affecting lesbian and gay couples that weren't addressed in the 1986 law: pensions and life insurance; the right of lesbian and gay partners to be considered next of kin for decisions regarding medical procedures; and the like. Rising numbers of AIDS cases in Denmark—which had one of the highest AIDS rates in Europe—made such issues particularly crucial to gay men. The advent of AIDS also brought about a close working relationship between gay activists and government officials. "The politicians began to look at us not as queers or perverts or funny people," Dorthe said. "They found out that we were serious people with good minds."

A year later, opposition deputies introduced a proposal into the Folketing legalizing lesbian and gay partnerships. At the time, Denmark was governed by a center-right coalition government that lacked a parliamentary majority. The opposition was constantly attempting to embarrass the government by introducing relatively popular legislation that the governing parties opposed, but whose passage they didn't have the votes to stop. The same-sex partnership bill was one such piece of legislation.

If the governing coalition was unhappy with the proposed law, so was Copenhagen's lesbian community. Lesbians had strong reservations about the restrictions on second-parent adoptions that were included in the proposal. A divided LBL held a general meeting to decide whether to press for the bill under those circumstances. Tensions ran high. By a slim two-vote majority, the LBL voted to continue to fight for partnership, even with the restrictions on adoption. Dorthe was among those who voted no. "At the time," she said, "I believed that if the ban on adoption remained in the law, then it wouldn't represent a real acceptance of us and our relationships, that we wouldn't be viewed as equals. But today, I think it was the correct tactical and strategic thing to do. The men were right."

On May 26, 1989, the Folketing approved the partnership proposal by a vote of seventy-one to forty-seven, with five absentions. The law came into force on October 1 of that year, when eleven gay and lesbian couples were married at Copenhagen's Rådhus. For Denmark, Dorthe said, "It was the final acknowledgment that 'You can have the same shit we have—marriage. You are *so* okay that you can have the same shit.' You see, most people in Denmark think marriage is kind of a drag. But it is the way to secure children, family life, and money."

Since the passage of the law, the LBL had been working hard to amend it to legalize stepchild adoption by gay and lesbian partners.

Negotiations with politicians on the issue were "going a little better," Dorthe said, adding: "Luckily, there are some stupid politicians, saying the most horrifying things. This makes it easy to argue with them."

Although the adoption changes might take time, more likely to be approved soon was a proposal extending public financing of artificial insemination to lesbians and single mothers. (Currently, the government health service paid only for married heterosexual women to be inseminated in public hospitals.) Much to Dorthe's surprise, a Member of Parliament had told her that this proposal was likely to pass in the autumn. She was convinced that once the Folketing voted to pay for lesbians to have babies through artificial insemination, approval of second-parent adoptions would logically follow.

All this was important because Copenhagen lesbians, like their counterparts in large American cities, were experiencing a baby boom. In each monthly edition of the LBL newspaper, there were three or four announcements by women looking for gay men to be sperm donors. "Lesbians as a community today are having children like nothing," Dorthe said.

I asked if lesbian opposition to the partnership law was ebbing. "The fact that you can see Inge-Lise and Vibeka getting registered now is significant," Dorthe said. "They are very much representative of the women who belonged to the women's movement in Denmark and who were opposed to anything that had to do with marriage. Now, the women have assessed the problem and considered the good and the bad about it. They now say, 'It was probably an okay decision because it looks like we can get the thing solved about the children.' "

Gay men continued to make up the majority of same-sex partnerships, a fact that Dorthe attributed partly to lingering lesbian resistance and partly to AIDS. "People die horribly young but they might still have accumulated some money or have their pensions," Dorthe said. "They don't want them to go to their family. A lot of men sick with AIDS will marry their best friend. That is a good thing, I think."

A young lesbian I met in Copenhagen told me she and her lover married "because we wanted to shout our love from the rooftops."

That was exactly the sort of thing that annoyed Dorthe, who frequently counseled couples considering partnership registration. If a couple who were in their twenties came in to see her and one had AIDS or one was a foreigner seeking a Danish "green card," she was usually supportive. Otherwise, she believed it unwise to get married when you were in your twenties. If, on the other hand, a couple was in their forties and had accumulated money and property, then marriage made more sense. "If people come in saying that they met last Sunday and want to get married, I would kick them out of my office," she said. "Luckily, I haven't had people like that, yet. The thought of us being as stupid as straight people, saying, 'If you love me, let's get married.' Oh, I would *hate* that! But it is probably going to happen in our society like any other society."

Did she plan to get married herself? I inquired. I thought that Dorthe, who was in her mid-thirties, would be a good catch. "If I am going to marry," she said, "it will be with one of my oldest friends in order to share pensions and things like that. But I'd never marry a lover. That is the advantage of being married to a close friend. Then, you never have to marry a lover!"

I had my own theory about homosexual partnerships in Denmark, at least about why lesbians and gays had fought so long and hard for the right to marry. It was a theory that evolved as I wandered around Copenhagen, usually on drizzly June evenings when the sun, if you could find it, didn't set till ten or ten-thirty. There just wasn't much to do in Copenhagen, I concluded—except settle down into domestic coziness. That explained it.

For, despite its reputation as "salty old girl of the sea," Copenhagen was a family town; couples pushed strollers and baby carriages along the shopping streets of the pedestrian zone downtown, and everybody, not just lesbians, seemed to be having babies. With its blocks of working-class housing, the city resembled an Eastern European capital. Except for the sleazy and overwhelmingly heterosexual district of prostitution and sex shops and topless bars on the other side of the train station, Copenhagen, on those long summer evenings, seemed utterly sedate.

Gay life reflected this. In contrast to Berlin, for example, there wasn't much of an overt lesbian and gay presence on the streets. I

wasn't sure whether it was Danish decorum or just plain closeted-
ness. A lesbian and gay pride march held a few years back fizzled
and there hadn't been one since. The gay bars and the most popular
gay sauna were unobtrusive and located primarily in the older,
quieter part of town.

In the area of sex shops and topless bars near the railway station,
I did discover a sauna called the Copenhagen Gay Center. The
place aggressively advertised itself from its large second floor windows as HOMO BIO SAUNA; at street level was a window display of sex
toys and videos featuring American porn star Jeff Stryker. But that
was the only gay-oriented place in the area. Next door, and down
the block, were heterosexual sex shops, one after another—such as
"Topluse Piger Fraek Sex Bar," featuring "Non Stop Sex" and a
window display of dildos and vibrators. Compared to heterosexual
bars and prostitution, Copenhagen's gay scene, by and large, was
the epitome of respectability.

An exception to the low-key gay presence was the headquarters
of the LBL. The organization owned a rather distinguished-looking
three-story stone building half a block down from the city's main
shopping street. There were hundreds of square meters of office
space and meeting rooms, an art gallery, a bookstore, the headquarters of the lesbian and gay radio station ("Radio Rosa,"
broadcasting forty-five hours a week). All the gay and lesbian
groups had offices there; the most popular groups, I was told, were
one for lesbians over forty and one for young gays and lesbians. An
entire floor was devoted to AIDS-prevention activities, including
the AIDS hotline, funded by the Danish government. Inside a
courtyard was the Pan coffeehouse, where I had met Dorthe, and
the LBL's Pan disco. On weekends, the disco was one of Copenhagen's trendiest nightspots, with high-tech decor and a stylish young
crowd that was increasingly mixed gay and straight.

"I won't ever get married," a young man told me there, on the
edge of the dance floor, one rainy Saturday evening. He was tall and
blond and twenty-four and looked like a brush-cut Norse god; his
muscles bulged under his white T-shirt. He lived about thirty miles
north of Copenhagen, in an industrial town where he worked in a
steel mill, the only one in Denmark. He didn't do anything quite as
glamorous as forging steel; he was employed in the office. His sister

was a flight attendant. The following week, he was going with her to Los Angeles and San Francisco. She had already taken him to Moscow—the worst week of his life, he assured me. He didn't like Copenhagen much, either. "How can you stand to breathe the air in this city?" he asked.

We wandered downstairs to the café, away from the music. He had been at another disco a few weeks before—not a gay one—and as he was coming out of the men's room had almost collided with a member of the Danish royal family, accompanied by two body-guards. This person, it was rumored, was "a little gay."

As for my friend, he wasn't quite convinced about his own sexuality. "I'm not sure if I'm gay or not," he said. "I'm trying to find out." No one in his hometown knew anything about his sexual questioning—not his friends, not his sister. "I haven't told a soul," he said. The gay people at the Pan disco were "normal," he thought; at the other gay bars, people were "outside," by which I assumed he meant weird. Sometimes he went to the sauna.

"I had sex with a girl a couple of months ago, but it was *nothing*," he said. There had been a few relationships with other men, but they never lasted more than three weeks. "After that I can't stand them," he said.

I asked him what he thought about gay marriage. A frown settled over his perfect features. "I don't agree with it," he said. "It makes fun of the church."

"But if you met some nice guy you really liked, wouldn't you consider settling down with him?" I pressed, thinking of those Russians who wrote letters to the LBL in search of a Danish dream spouse.

"I won't ever get married," he replied solemnly. "I'll just stay by myself, in my town, and go into Copenhagen whenever I want."

We chatted some more and he shook my hand and headed back to the dance floor. The conversation provided a dose of reality. Legal changes were just a first step; changes in psychological and social attitudes took a great deal longer. Denmark wasn't perfect. It was still hard to come out, especially in a steel town, and not everyone wanted to settle down with a dog and a Volvo station wagon.

• • •

It was easy to lose sight of how much had changed in Denmark. When the LBL was started back in 1948 in the northern city of Ålborg, its founder, Axel Axgil, had been practically run out of town. He lost his job and apartment. One afternoon in Copenhagen, I went to visit Axel and his spouse, Eigil Axgil. They had had the honor of being the first couple to be married under the new partnership law.

Axel and Eigil had been a couple for forty-one years. "We've been engaged for forty years and married for one and a half," they joked. They had taken the same surname—a combination of their first names—way back in 1958. The day after they married, on October 1, 1989, a Swiss newspaper printed a picture of them sitting in a carriage in front of Copenhagen Town Hall, giving one another a kiss. In the photo, Axel and Eigil were both wearing suits, with carnations in their buttonholes. The headline said, ROMEO AND JULIO.

They remembered the good times and the bad: the first LBL meeting in Copenhagen in 1948, attended by some two hundred people, after Axel had fled Ålborg; how they first met, at a party, two years later; serving time in prison in 1957 in a pornography scandal; the passage of what gays called the "ugly law" in the early 1960s, which banned homosexual prostitution and could land you in jail if you so much as gave another man a cigarette or bus fare home following a sexual encounter. And after all that, many years later, the passage of the antidiscrimination law, the partnership law, their own marriage.

For lesbians and gays, Denmark today was a very different country than it had been in 1948 or 1968—or even 1988—and much of that had to do with the efforts of Axel and Eigil. "So many things have happened," they said. "The young people just have no idea."

We sat around their dining room table and drank coffee and ate strudel. Axel and Eigil's apartment was filled with memorabilia. On the walls were framed pictures of four dogs they had had over the years (all looking interchangeable) and three country houses (including a mansion they had run as a gay hotel in the 1960s and 1970s). There was a recent photograph of them in front of the Great Pyramid on an Egyptian holiday, and another taken in 1950, the year they met. In that photo, in formal dress, with their hair combed back at the temples, they looked a little like a piano duo, Ferrante and Teicher or Gold and Fizdale.

Today, they both still combed their hair back at the temples, although after forty-one years it was a bit thinner. Axel, seventy-five, was relaxed, good-natured, placid even. There was something a bit countrified about him—he might have been a successful retired dairy farmer. Eigil, sixty-six, seemed more sophisticated. In dark glasses, smoking a cigarette from a cigarette holder, he might have just dropped in from 1920s Berlin.

When they met at that LBL party back in 1950, it was love at first sight. Eigil was twenty-seven then, and Axel thirty-five. They moved in together almost immediately, living in a variety of condemned buildings around Copenhagen. Axel was the chairman of the LBL from 1948 to 1952. Within two years of its founding, the organization had three thousand members. But differences soon surfaced. Axel wanted to work for political changes, such as lowering the age of consent. Most of the other members were interested only in social activities. So Axel resigned.

The pornography scandal in which they were jailed five years later ushered in a very difficult period, both for them personally and for the organization. The LBL had been selling pictures of naked men, apparently in an effort to raise funds. According to Axel, the district attorney at the time had told them it was legal. Then, in 1955, a new district attorney took office. He had a different opinion. Some eighty men, many associated with LBL, were jailed. Axel served a year in prison, Eigil a year and a half. The LBL's membership dwindled to little more than one hundred.

"At first we were in the same prison but on different floors," recalled Axel. "Then the guards found out we were waving to one another. We were moved. We couldn't see one another, but we could write letters. They censored any reference to our case. But we could still write, 'I love you.' "

It was in 1958, immediately after they were released from jail, that Axel and Eigil took the same surname. They wanted to demonstrate that they belonged to one another.

Shortly after, they left Copenhagen. It was the period of the "ugly law." Blackmail of gay men was commonplace. The age of consent for homosexual sex was raised from eighteen to twenty-one. The LBL was weak. The Axgils bought a twenty-two-room mansion thirty-five miles from Copenhagen, and turned it into an international gay hotel called Axel House. Although they hosted a few gay conferences there, they mostly stayed aloof from politics. They kept the hotel until 1980. By then, they were getting older, and there were the usual problems with the tax law—if one of them died, the other would have to raise eight hundred thousand kroner (about a hundred and thirty thousand dollars) to pay the inheritance tax. So they sold the hotel for a substantial amount. "If the parntership law had been enacted then, we would have kept the hotel," Eigil said.

Of the two, Eigil, the nonpolitical one, was the more cautious. "We were poor sometimes and Axel wanted to spend money but I would say no," he told me. "It was Axel who had the ideas, though. He wanted to see things through *right now.*" Over the years, there had been occasional disagreements, Eigil admitted, but they weren't serious. "Axel would drop a word, and after a while, I would come around, and realize it was a good idea," he said. "It was never boring."

What made their relationship last so long? "We have the same interests," said Eigil. "And we always felt it was very important to give the other person in the relationship freedom, instead of tying him down." In his view, honesty was more important than monogamy. "If one of you gets a good offer, why say no?" Eigil insisted. "There is nothing taken from the other partner. But if you meet a sweet guy and don't tell your partner, the day will come when he discovers it. Then everything breaks down. It is better to tell, to be honest. Lies and saying nothing break up many partnerships. To be open and able to give freedom to the other partner, that makes it last."

By the 1980s, the controversies of the past had been forgotten. Pornography was as Danish as herring for breakfast or the Tivoli Gardens on a Saturday afternoon in summer. And so, increasingly, was homosexuality. The Axgils became tireless campaigners for the partnership law. Today, they were heroes, role models for young lesbians and gays. When Axel turned seventy, the LBL held a month-long tribute to him, with lectures, parties, and other events. The organization wanted the Danish government to give the Axgils a medal. Axel and Eigil showed me a letter they received shortly after their wedding, from two gay German medical students. The letter was addressed simply "Axel and Eigil Axgil, Copenhagen, Denmark." Even the post office knew who they were.

Ironically, the partnership law had hurt the Axgils financially. Unlike Inge-Lise and Vibeka, they were actually losing money as a consequence—some twenty thousand kroner (a little more than three thousand dollars) a year. A married couple received less money in government old-age benefits than two single people did. But the Axgils still had savings from the sale of their hotel and could absorb the financial loss. "It's no problem," said Eigil.

The enactment of the law after all those years had been "fantastic, proof that we weren't discriminated against any longer," according to Axel. "Danish society has changed very much. But people worked very hard to make it happen." Yet today they were a little disillusioned with Danish gay politics. The LBL no longer had a vision, they felt. Now that the organization had achieved its goal, it didn't know what to do next. "Nothing much has happened since the passage of the partnership law," Axel said. "We are saying to each other that we should fight for adoption rights—but next year. We should do it now!"

Whatever one thought about lesbian and gay marriage as a thing in itself, it had played a major role in the transformation of Denmark's gay community. Eventually, the inequalities that Danish gays had had to accept to achieve passage of the partnership law would be overturned. As Inge-Lise had put it, "The people who have fought for this, have fought for it not because they necessarily believe in marriage. They believe in equality. Even if they felt marriage was a bad thing, they would fight for it anyway because the others should have this right. That is the main point. The equality point."

The week before, Axel had given a speech about issues facing gays and lesbians to a Copenhagen Rotary Club luncheon. Eigil accompanied him. Rotary Club members, a group of businessmen not exactly known for progressive social views, open each meeting with a song. The week Axel and Eigil were their guests, the members got up and sang a Danish hymn that is traditionally performed at church weddings. Its name was "Det Er Så Yndigt At Følges Ad": "How Lovely It Is to Be Together." Axel and Eigil stood at the front, facing the audience and glowing. They had triumphed.

Afterword

▲

What did they have in common: ancient Danish activists serenaded by the Rotary Club of Copenhagen; farm boys shooting kangaroos in the Australian outback; barboys in Bangkok; eighteen-year-old Šárka in Prague, out to discover the world? Was there any way of bringing such disparate people together, any conclusions that one could draw about lesbian and gay life around the globe, any general statements one could make? Were we all traveling in similar directions, perhaps toward Denmark—the quiet life, the suburban apartment, marriage?

In Buenos Aires, Rafael Freda had maintained that what homosexuals had in common was the experience of discrimination. But could one even go that far? There were those Japanese gays and lesbians who didn't feel persecuted at all, merely ignored. And what did homophobia mean to an Egyptian man who liked to have sex with other men—in a country where there was no such thing as a homosexual?

Any attempt at a worldwide perspective had to take into account the cultural divide between two very different approaches to sexuality and homosexuality. There was the contemporary, Western model—that of a world divided into heterosexuals and homosexuals and perhaps bisexuals, of lesbian and gay identity, of discrimination and homophobia. Out of this emerged the political movement to improve the status of homosexuals; in the process, gay and lesbian identity was given impetus, a sense of community based on sexual orientation was created. Situations varied from place to place: In Denmark, gays and lesbians had achieved a significant degree of legal and social progress; in Czechoslovakia, they were only starting out; in Argentina, social and state hostility held the upper hand. But in all these societies, the self-identification and worldview of gay people were similar, by and large.

In the non-Western countries I visited, the situation was more complicated. Historically, in the Arab world and in much of Asia, few distinctions had existed on the basis of homosexuality or heterosexuality. Categories were based on age, gender, and social status, not sexual orientation, as David F. Greenberg points out in his book *The Construction of Homosexuality.* In Egypt, China, Japan, Thailand, a counterpart of the ancient Greek model had been the norm: Men could have sex with other men, and no one minded, as long as you didn't jeopardize the family system. In such societies, the terms "gay" and "homosexual," if they existed at all, had referred to transvestites or extremely overt "queens," sometimes to male prostitutes; there was virtually no such thing as a lesbian. I found this was all still largely true, today.

The existence of these varying models of sexuality lent credence to theories that sexual behavior and identity are socially and culturally formed. In particular, the relaxed mores of non-Western cultures cast doubt on biological "explanations" of the basis of homosexuality. The protean sexual patterns of Egypt or Thailand seemed to open up vistas unexplored (and unexplained) by theories about the biological origins of homosexuality or by studies that suggested that homosexual men had smaller hypothalamuses than did heterosexual men.

Within the past two centuries, attitudes toward sexuality in Asia and Africa had been strongly influenced by the West. The colonial powers, particularly the British, were the great exporters of homophobia, upsetting cultural and social arrangements that had long tolerated same-sex behavior. The sodomy laws that gay activists from Hong Kong to Hobart to Cape Town were battling to this day were manifestations of this. Revealingly, the two countries I visited that seemed most tolerant of gay male sexuality—Japan and Thailand—had never been colonized by Western powers.

By the late twentieth century, the role of the West had changed. Europe and North America were now the world's leading exporters of the ideas of gay liberation and feminism. The gay and lesbian teachers who came to work in Japan were nurturing gay identity and pride, a very different stance from that of the missionaries and teachers a century before. In the West African nation of Liberia—before the civil war that has devastated the country—an American Peace Corps volunteer established the country's first gay group. The European-based International Lesbian and Gay Association was attempting to spread the gay gospel in the Third World, as its attempt to hold its international conference in Mexico showed. International AIDS activism played a role, as well. The British man I met in Bangkok, who was trying to set up an AIDS hotline for gay and bisexual men, was an example; after he finished his job in Thailand, he was off to Chile. Meanwhile, gays and lesbians from Asia, like Natee and Kai in Bangkok, traveled West and returned home with new ideas. The countries most antagonistic to the Western powers—Iran, China, Cuba—were among those where homosexuality met with the greatest degree of hostility. Today, the relatively accepting traditional attitudes were being undercut, not by Western colonialism, but by other ideologies and influences: communism, nationalism, religious fundamentalism.

Japan and Thailand were two non-Western nations where the construction of a Western-style gay identity was making some headway. Yet the question remained whether Western models were appropriate for those societies—or even desirable. In countries like Thailand, Japan, and perhaps Egypt, why not leave well enough alone? If there wasn't any real opposition or hostility to same-sex relationships, why not keep the old ideas and ways of doing things? Why create sexual orientation as a social category, an identity, at all? Didn't these societies come closer to an ideal of universal bisexuality than anything in the "advanced" West?

Still, if one believes, as I do, in values that stress the integration of the sexual and the emotional and the importance of mutuality in relationships, then the emergence of a strong gay identity and community was desirable. It was certainly desirable, if only as a form of self-defense, for gays and lesbians in countries like mainland China, where a previously tolerant culture had turned hostile. And clearly, women attracted to other women hadn't benefited from the traditional mores, with their patriarchal character.

Conflicting conceptions of sexuality made the creation of a universal gay and lesbian identity, culture, and movement difficult at best. But whatever reservations one might have, the spread of Western notions of sexuality and relationships appeared inevitable. Communication and travel were creating a new world in which Western ideas, including those regarding sexuality, were reaching every corner of the globe. Even the mainland Chinese were watching *Dynasty* on Hong Kong TV.

Interestingly, videocassettes played an important role. It was after watching a porn video that Karima, the Egyptian woman I met, concluded that having sex with another woman was something she might like to do; Thai men learned from watching gay pornography that you could be both "king" and "queen" (and have egalitarian relationships). The VCR provided other kinds of images, as well: In Tokyo, Hiroshi Niimi of the gay youth group OCCUR was earnestly studying videotapes of gay and lesbian Town Meetings in New York and San Francisco.

A danger was that North American and Western European hegemony would make it difficult for various societies, East and West, to develop their own particular gay and lesbian cultures. Hence the Prague newspaper with its glossary of gay terminology—most of it emanating from San Francisco and New York. Another example was the gay bookshop in Sydney, where there were exactly two books about gay and lesbian life from an Australian perspective. I met any number of gay men in Australia, New Zealand, and South Africa who had come out after reading gay American novelists like Edmund White and David Leavitt, but had virtually no one to chronicle their own experiences. Whatever one might think of the drag pajama parties of Soweto or the handsome-boy contests of Bangkok, they were at least cultural expressions of an indigenous community.

In my estimation, there were four preconditions necessary for a modern-style gay and lesbian identity and community to emerge in a given society: a modicum of personal freedom and social tolerance; a level of economic development that offered some degree of independence and social mobility; a relatively high status for women; and a decline of the power of the family and religious institutions in defining and determining every aspect of an individual's life.

Most of the countries I visited did offer a substantial degree of political tolerance. Before the revolution of 1989, that hadn't been the case in Czechoslovakia and the former East Germany; gay communities there had been largely underground. Before the waning of apartheid, black South African gays had been in a similar situation, reduced to living at the margins of white society. In those countries, only after political changes could gay and lesbian movements emerge with any degree of visibility. As of this writing, Argentina, despite its nominally democratic institutions, was a particularly problematic place for gays and lesbians. During my visit, police raids on gay bars created an atmosphere of fear. In late 1991, the Argentine Supreme Court refused to recognize the right of homosexuals in that country to organize, stating that "the defense of homosexuality injures nature and the dignity of the human person." Finally, after strong pressure from international gay groups, President Carlos Saúl Menem personally intervened and granted legal status to the CHA, the national gay organization.

Argentina was also a country where it was difficult for gays and lesbians to live by themselves. To lead an openly gay life, one needed the financial means to live away from one's family, to have, at the very least, "a room of one's own." A flat was freedom. In places where this was a problem—Argentina, Egypt, and Hong Kong, to name three—gay movements were weak. Where it was increasingly possible, such as Japan, the gay and lesbian community was becoming stronger.

For women, economic independence was the sine qua non of being able to live as a lesbian. Even in the non-Western cultures where male-male sexual behavior was tolerated, women attracted to other women appeared to have little opportunity to avail themselves of homosexual relationships. They were constrained partly by traditional mores, but equally by a lack of economic independence. That is why, in Egypt, I was told that the only lesbians in Cairo were "very rich," and why the only lesbian relationship I found there was taking place within the family circle.

As the result of its affluent society and the increasing role of women in the economy, Japan was one place in the non-Western World where an openly lesbian community, albeit a small one, was becoming visible. The emergence of a Japanese women's movement was important as well. Until the status of women in a particular society rose, there was little chance that lesbian relationships or community could flourish.

In Japan, the issue was not homosexuality per se, but settling the question of marriage with family and bosses. In Argentina, if a young man or woman moved outside the family home, it was considered an insult to his or her parents. In Chinese culture, ancestor worship put a value on carrying on the family line that young people flouted at their peril. Even with a degree of economic independence, the power of family, culture, and tradition was formidable.

In the West, the more power that religious institutions held, the more difficult the situation for lesbians and gay men. In most Australian states, in New Zealand, and in Denmark, the influence of the church on public policy was limited, and the situation of gays and lesbians correspondingly good. In Argentina, where the church was powerful, the situation was reversed. In Islamic countries, the situation was more complex, although the rise of fundamentalism from Tehran to Algiers posed a threat to the cultural blind eye customarily turned same-sex relations. Buddhist societies, given that religion's tradition of tolerance, tended to be the exception to this pattern.

In few of the countries I visited had AIDS created the same degree of crisis for the gay population as it had in many large cities of the United States and Western Europe. Nonetheless, the epidemic was playing an important international role in forging gay community. Even in Japan, with few gay cases of AIDS, the disease had focused attention on the gay population and helped in the formation of the first gay and lesbian organizations. In Malaysia, Pink Triangle seemed to be evolving from an AIDS organization into a gay-rights organization. In Egypt, the lack of AIDS activism of any sort may have been a factor in the failure of a gay movement to develop there—and vice versa. East and West, AIDS education meant education about sexuality and, at the very least, brought the issue of homosexuality into the open.

Often, in places with few AIDS cases, the emphasis on the AIDS epidemic tended to skew the gay community, making it difficult to address more immediately pressing needs. One young activist in Christchurch, New Zealand, complained, "Here, suicide is a much greater killer of young gay men than AIDS. I know of one case of HIV in Christchurch. But I know six or seven gay kids who have committed suicide since I've been out. Yet all the attention in this country seems to be on AIDS." On the other hand, in New Zealand as in Australia, the existence of government-funded AIDS organizations made it possible to establish gay youth groups as part of fighting the epidemic.

AIDS was clearly one issue that could unite homosexuals across cultures and stages of economic development. Interestingly, lesbian and gay marriage was another. That issue seemed to capture the imagination of gay people from the black townships of South Africa, where gay community was just emerging, to countries such as Denmark, where there had been a strong gay movement for years. I was particularly struck by the interest in the subject in the Third World. If the development of gay community, particularly outside the West, depended on the formation of long-term relationships that could offer an alternative to pressures for heterosexual marriage, a focus on gay and lesbian marriage rights made sense. Often, the option of gay marriage and the creation of gay or lesbian identity seemed intertwined. "Gay people can marry in Denmark?" asked Hani in Cairo. "Let's go there!" Hani, it should be recalled, was a man who wouldn't define himself as gay.

Generally, the gays and lesbians I met tended to reflect their societies: Thailand was relaxed about sexual matters, and so were Thai gays; Argentine gays and lesbians mirrored the fearful nature of that country's historical experience, always expecting the worst; in the former East Germany, the economic situation was the over-riding issue for everyone, whatever their sexual orientation.

Yet in many of the places I went, East and West, North and South, I found gay and lesbian communities emerging and gay identity beginning to solidify. For lesbians, this was often a more cautious and difficult process, but one could see the first steps. The Arab world tended to be an exception to this trend, especially in view of the rise of Islamic fundamentalism: for example, the program of Algeria's powerful Islamic Salvation Front called for the execution of homosexuals. In some Latin American countries, the twin factors of machismo and Catholicism made the situation of gays and lesbians very difficult as well. Still, they were marching in

Johannesburg, lining up for women's dances in Tokyo, educating Bangkok barboys in safe sex, heading for the altar in Copenhagen. A gay *Pravda,* published in Western Europe, appeared in the last days of the Soviet Union; *The Advocate,* the U.S. gay newsmagazine, named a Russian gay activist as its 1991 "Man of the Year." In Nigeria, an organization called the Gentlemen's Alliance became the first gay group on the African continent, outside of South Africa, to apply for membership in the International Lesbian and Gay Association.

International organizations were becoming aware of the issue. In 1991, after many years of internal debate, Amnesty International agreed to take up the situation of gay prisoners of conscience. In January 1992, an Argentine gay man who claimed he had been raped and tortured by the country's federal police was granted refugee status in Canada, marking the first time on the North American continent that another country's antigay policies were recognized as a basis for political asylum. There was a gradual movement toward taking the problems of gays and lesbians worldwide seriously, toward the recognition of an international lesbian and gay community.

While I was in South Africa, I attended a Hawaiian-dress party in a suburban backyard in Cape Town. The event was sponsored by the local gay Christian organization. The night was warm and there were heaps of pineapples and bananas and mangoes, and a decor that consisted primarily of palm leaves. Two young white men dressed in iridescent grass skirts lip-synched to Elvis Presley's "Blue Hawaii."

The partygoers were a varied lot. A man of Indian descent was engaged to marry a girl in Durban, up the coast, an arranged marriage; he was taking refuge in Cape Town. A dimpled, half-Afrikaner, half-Coloured man from Namibia, dressed in running shorts and a white T-shirt, explained why he had left home: "There is nothing to do in small towns in Namibia," he said. "Just church." A student at an Afrikaner university, troubled by Biblical injunctions against homosexuality, confided that he had made a "deal" with God—he would only have sex in the context of a relationship. Surely, God wouldn't object to *that.* A white woman who had lived in Zimbabwe in the days when it was Rhodesia inquired if I had been questioning people as to "why" they had become gay. She had her own theory: Effeminate men and mannish women were "born that way"; everyone else became homosexual because they had been molested as children.

Toward the end of the evening, someone got up and told jokes, the punchline of which always seemed to be "The real McCoy." Then, two white men, a white woman, and a black man, all wearing leis around their necks, sang "Amazing Grace."

The party stays in my mind, in part because of the mix of people. Indians, blacks, mixed-race Namibians, Afrikaners, an expatriate from the days of Rhodesian colonial rule, there they all were, wearing Hawaiian leis and singing an American song. Many of the partygoers had ideas that I considered slightly wacky—deals with God, theories about the origins of being gay. They were trapped by their various cultures, too—the Indian man and his fiancée, for instance, and almost everyone else attempting the daunting task of bringing together antigay religious teachings and a positive sense of being gay and lesbian. At the very tip of Africa, they were trying to sort it all out, to the tunes of "Blue Hawaii" and "Amazing Grace." They, too, were out in the world.

About the Author

NEIL MILLER's book *In Search of Gay America* won the 1990 American Library Association Prize for lesbian and gay nonfiction, as well as a Lambda Literary Award. He lives in Somerville, Massachusetts.